A RECORD OF THE BUDDHIST RELIGION AS PRACTISED IN INDIA AND THE MALAY ARCHIPELAGO (A. D. 671-695)

A RECORD OF THE BUDDHIST RELIGION AS PRACTISED IN INDIA AND THE MALAY ARCHIPELAGO (A. D. 671-695)

BY I-TSING

TRANSLATED BY J. TAKAKUSU, B.A., PH. D.

WITH A LETTER FROM THE RIGHT HON, PROFESSOR F. MAX MULLER

WITH A MAP

GYAN

Published by

GYAN

Gyan Publishing House
5, Ansari Road
Daryaganj, New Delhi-110002
Phone: 011-47034999, 9811692060
E-mail: books@gyanbooks.com

Distribution Network
gyanbooks.com
India, USA, Canada, UK, Australia, France

ISBN : 978-81-212-3945-5 (PB)
First Published, Oxford, 1896

2nd Impression 2020

Printed at: Gyan Press, Delhi.

A Record of
The Buddhist Religion as Practised in India
and The Malay Archipelago
(A. D. 671-695)
Author: I-Tsing

I-TSING'S ROUTE TO INDIA AND BACK, WITH SOME GEOGRAPHICAL NAMES MENTIONED IN HIS RECORD (A.D. 671-695).

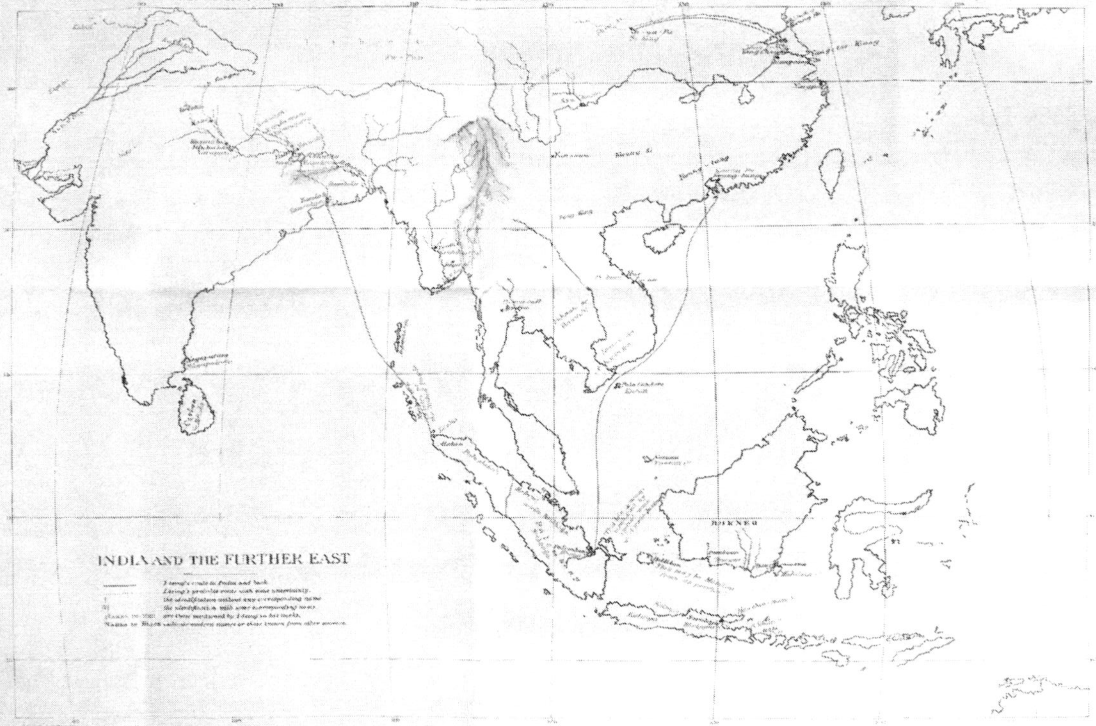

NOTES

A.D. 671. I-tsing was at Yang-fu, and made an agreement with a few friends to go to India together.

A.D. 671, he passed the summer in Yang-fu. He departed from Kwang-fu in the eleventh month of the same year.

After twenty days' sail, he reached Bhoga, where he stayed six months, learning Sabdavidya.

A.D. 672, in the seventh month, he started on a ship by the king's help for Malayu, which has now become a part of Bhoga, and reached there after fifteen days, and stayed two months.

He started again for Kacha, and reached there after fifteen days. He remained till the twelfth month in Kacha, when he started for India on a king's ship. After ten days' sail towards the [illegible]

[illegible] forty yojanas from Nâlandâ.

A.D. 673, he stayed in Tâmralipti till the fifth month, when he started for Central India [illegible]

[illegible]

in the Nâlandâ monastery.

[illegible] of Nâlandâ.

He collected the Buddhist [illegible]

[illegible]

passed Kacha and returned to Bhoga.

[illegible]

CONTENTS.

ABBREVIATIONS.

Chavannes = Mémoire composé à l'époque de la grande dynastie T'ang sur les religieux éminents qui allèrent chercher la loi dans les pays d'occident, par I-tsing. Traduit en Français par Édouard Chavannes. Paris, 1894.

Childers = A Dictionary of the Pâli Language, by R. C. Childers. London, 1875.

Dharmasaṅgraha = An Ancient Collection of Buddhist Technical Terms, prepared for publication by Kenjiu Kasawara. Edited by F. Max Müller and H. Wenzel. Oxford, 1885.

J. = The New Japanese Edition of the Chinese Buddhist Books in the Bodleian Library, Jap. 65.

Julien = Méthode pour déchiffrer et transcrire les Noms Sanscrits qui se rencontrent dans les Livres Chinois. Par Stanislas Julien. Paris, 1861.

Kâsyapa = A Commentary in MS. on I-tsing's Record, written in 1758. By Ji-un Kâsyapa (On-kō),—the Nan-kai-kai-ran-shō.

Nanjio = A Catalogue of the Chinese Translation of the Buddhist Tripiṭaka, the Sacred Canon of the Buddhists in China and Japan. Compiled by Order of the Secretary of State for India, by Bunyiu Nanjio. Oxford, 1883.

S. B. E. = The Sacred Books of the East, translated by various Oriental Scholars, and edited by F. Max Müller. Clarendon Press, Oxford.

Yule = Travels of Marco Polo. By Colonel Yule. 2nd edition. London, 1875.

N.B.—When a word or passage is marked with an asterisk *, it has an additional note at the end.

LETTER FROM THE RIGHT HONOURABLE PROFESSOR F. MAX MÜLLER

TO

MR. J. TAKAKUSU.

OXFORD:
January, 1896.

MY DEAR FRIEND,

Ever since I made the acquaintance of Stanislas Julien at Paris, in 1846, being constantly with him while he translated Hiuen Thsang's Travels in India, I felt convinced that the most important help for settling the chronology of mediaeval Sanskrit literature would be found in Chinese writers. I was particularly anxious for a translation of I-tsing's work; and as far back as 1880[1] I expressed a hope that the Record of that great Chinese traveller's stay in India would soon be rendered accessible to us in an English translation. Some of the contents of his book became known to me through one of my Japanese Buddhist pupils, Kasawara; but he unfortunately died before he could finish his translation of the whole Record. From the fragments of his translation, however, I gathered some important facts, which were published first in the Academy, October 2, 1880, then in the Indian Antiquary[2], and in the

[1] See the Academy, October 2, 1880.

[2] See further on, p. xviii, 2.

appendix to my 'India, what can it teach us?' under the title of *Renaissance of Sanskrit Literature.*

From I-tsing or from any of the Chinese travellers in India we must not expect any trustworthy information on the ancient literature of India. What they tell us, for instance, on the date of the birth of Buddha, is mere tradition, and cannot claim any independent value. It is interesting to know that the name of Pâ*n*ini and his great Grammar were known to them, but what they say about his age and circumstances does not help us much. All that is of importance on this subject has been collected and published by me in my edition of the Prâti*s*âkhya, 1856, Nachträge, pp. 12–15.

The date of Pâ*n*ini can be fixed hypothetically only. It has been pointed out that Pata*ñg*ali in his Mahâbhâshya speaks of Pushpamitra, and according to some MSS. of *K*andragupta also. *K*andragupta was the founder of the Maurya dynasty, Pushpamitra was the first of the dynasty which succeeded the Mauryas. As it seems that Pata*ñg*ali in one place implies the fall of the Mauryas, which happened in 178 B.C., it has been supposed that he must have lived about that time. And this date seemed to agree with the statement, contained in the Râ*g*atarangi*n*î (1148 A.D.), that his work, the Mahâbhâshya, was known in Kashmir under king Abhimanyu, that is, in the middle of the first century B.C. As there is a series of grammarians succeeding each other between Pata*ñg*ali and Pâ*n*ini, it was argued with some degree of plausibility that Pâ*n*ini cannot have lived later than the fourth century B.C.

But all this is constructive chronology only, and would have to yield as soon as anything more certain could be produced. It was quite right, therefore, that Professor Weber, of Berlin, should point out and lay stress on the fact that Pâ*n*ini quotes an alphabet called *Yavanânî* which he (Weber) takes to mean Ionian or Greek. This alphabet, he argues, could not have been known before the invasion of Alexander, and Pâ*n*ini could therefore not have written before 320 B.C.

Although Professor Boehtlingk maintains that writing, at least for monumental purposes, was known in India before the third century, he has produced no dated inscription to support his assertion, still less has he proved that this non-existent alphabet was called *Yavanânî*. We cannot deny the possibility that a knowledge of alphabetic writing may have reached India before the time of Alexander; nor need *Yavanânî* have meant Ionian or Greek. No one has ever held that any one of the Indian alphabets was derived direct from the Greek letters such as they were at the time of Alexander. No writer of any authority has derived these Indian alphabets from any but a Semitic or Aramaic source. Even Semitic (Phenician) inscriptions before that of Eshmunezar at the end of the fifth century B.C. (fourth century, according to Maspero) are very scarce. I only know of that of Siloam about 700 B.C., and that of Mesha about 900 B.C. Professor Weber's argument cannot therefore be brushed away by a mere assertion.

Still less could any scholar say that the existence of the ancient Vedic literature was impossible or inconceivable without a knowledge of alphabetic writing. Where the art of alphabetic writing is known and practised for literary purposes, no person on earth could conceal the fact, and I still challenge any scholar to produce any mention of writing in Indian literature before the supposed age of Pâ*n*ini. To say that literature is impossible without alphabetic writing shows a want of acquaintance with Greek, Hebrew, Finnish, Estonian, Mordvinian, nay with Mexican literature. Why should all names for writing, paper, ink, stylus, letters, or books have been so carefully avoided if they had been in daily use? Besides, it is well known that the interval between the use of alphabetic writing for official or monumental purposes and its use for literature is very wide. Demand only creates supply, and a written literature would presuppose a reading public such as no one has yet claimed for the time of Homer, of Moses, of the authors of the Kalevala, of Kalevipoeg or of the popular and religious songs of Ugro-Finnish or even Mexican races. To say that the art of writing was kept secret, that the Brâhmans probably kept one copy only of each work for themselves, learnt it by heart and taught it to their pupils, shows what imagination can do in order to escape from facts. The facts on which I base my negative vote are these:—

The inscriptions of Asoka are still the earliest inscriptions in India which can be dated, and the tentative character of the local alphabets in which they are written forms in my eyes a proof of the recent introduction of alphabetic writing in different parts of India. I see no reason to doubt the possibility that the Brâhmans were acquainted with alphabetic writing at an earlier time, and I should hail any discovery like that of Major Deane (if indeed they are Indian inscriptions) as an important addition to the history of the migrations of the Hieratic or so-called Phenician alphabet. But that is very different from asserting that writing was known, or must have been known, whether for monumental or literary purposes, before say 400 B.C. I have still to confess my ignorance of any book having been written on palm leaves or paper before the time of Vattagâmani (88–76 B.C.), or of any datable inscription before the time of Asoka.

But though the works of Chinese pilgrims throw little light on the ancient literature, or even on what I called the Renaissance period up to 400 A.D., they have proved of great help to us in fixing the dates of Sanskrit writers whom they either knew personally or who had died not long before their times. I pointed this out in a paper on the Kâsikâ-vritti[1] published in the Academy, October 2, 1880.

Professor von Boehtlingk, in the introduction to his edition of Pânini's Grammar (p. iv), referred the Kâsikâ-vritti to about the eighth century A.D., on the supposition that Vâmana, the author of the Kâsikâ,

---

[1] Kâsikâ, a commentary on Pânini's Grammatical Aphorisms, by Pandit Vâmana and Gayâditya. Edited by Pandit Bâlasâstrî (Benares, 1876, 1878).

was the same as the Vâmana mentioned in the Chronicle of Kashmir (iv, 496). Kalha*n*a Pa*nd*ita, the author of that chronicle, after mentioning the restoration of grammatical studies in Ka*s*mîra under *G*ayapî*d*a, and the introduction of Pata*ñg*ali's Mahâbhâshya, passes on to give a list of the names of other learned men at the king's court, and he mentions more particularly Kshîra (author of Avyaya-v*ri*tti and the Dhâtutaraṅgi*n*î), Dâmodaragupta, Manoratha, *S*aṅkhadatta, *K*ataka, Sandhimat, and Vâmana. This Vâmana was supposed to have been the author of the Kâ*s*ikâ. There was nothing to support this conjecture, and Professor von Boehtlingk has himself surrendered it.

Another conjecture was stated by Professor H. H. Wilson that the Vâmana at the court of *G*ayapî*d*a was the same as Vâma*n*a, the author of the Kâvyâlaṅkâra-v*ri*tti. But this Vâmana quotes among other authors Kavirâ*g*a, the author of the Râghavapâ*nd*avîya [1], who lived after 1000 A.D. [2], while *G*ayapî*d*a died in 776 (or 786) A.D.

Lastly Dr. Cappeller, the editor of the Kâvyâlaṅkâra-v*ri*tti, after ascribing its author Vâmana to the twelfth century, tried to identify him with Vâmana, the author of the Kâ*s*ikâ-v*ri*tti.

Professor Goldstücker referred the grammarian Vâmana to a period more recent than the thirteenth century.

Among later scholars Dr. Bühler placed Vâmana in the tenth, Burnell in the twelfth century, while Schönberg [3] showed that he was quoted by Kshemendra in the eleventh century.

This will show the uncertainty of chronology even in the later history of Indian literature. And it will show at the same time the value of Chinese travellers such as I-tsing. I-tsing studied Sanskrit in India

---

[1] Pâthak in Indian Antiquary, 1883, p. 20, tries to ascribe the poem to Ârya *S*rutakîrti, Sâka 1045.

[2] Mr. Rice in his Karnata Authors (Journ. R. A. S., 1883, p. 298) fixes his date at 1170 A.D.

[3] Schönberg, Kshemendra's Kavika*nth*âbhara*n*a, p. 15, note.

before the end of the seventh century, and he knew the Kâsikâ-vritti. This book, which is a commentary on Pânini's Sûtras, was really the work of two authors, Vâmana and Gayâditya. It is sometimes ascribed to one, sometimes to the other; nay the two names have also been assigned to one and the same person. There was, however, a tradition which assigned certain portions of the Grammar to Vâmana, and others to Gayâditya[1]. I-tsing quotes the Vritti-sûtra as the work of Gayâditya. The name Vritti-sûtra is strange. We expect Sûtra-vritti. But Bhartrihari uses the same name[2]. I-tsing states that Gayâditya died not later than 661–662 A.D., that is, about ten years before his own arrival in India.

It can thus be shown that what I-tsing calls a commentary on this work, or a Kûrni[3], was meant for Patañgali's Mahâbhâshya, as taught in I-tsing's time, as a commentary on the Kâsikâ arrangement of the Sûtras of Pânini. Patañgali is actually called Kûrnikâra by Bhartrihari, who himself commented on Patañgali's Mahâbhâshya. This Bhartrihari also, a Buddhist of the Vidyâmâtra sect, died, as I-tsing tells us, in about 651–652 A.D. Among his contemporaries is mentioned Dharmapâla, and this Dharmapâla would seem to have been the teacher of Sîlạbhadra, the same who received Hiuen Thsang at Nâlanda in 635 A.D. Other works of Bhartrihari mentioned by I-tsing are the Vâkya-discourse and Pei-na. The former contains 700 slokas, and its commentary 7,000 slokas. As it is a grammatical work, we can hardly be wrong in taking it to be Bhartrihari's Vâkyapadîya[4]. As to the Pei-na, Professor Bühler has proposed a very ingenious conjecture that it may stand for Bedâ, a boat, i.e. a commentary[5]. Such a name, however, never occurs with reference to any work of Bhartrihari.

---

[1] Below, p. 176, note 3.

[2] Mahâbhâshya, ed. Kielhorn, vol. ii, p. iii, p. 21.

[3] Below, p. 178, note 2.

[4] Cp. Kielhorn, Indian Antiquary, xii, p. 226.

[5] Below, p. 225, additional note to p. 180.

I need not repeat what I have written in my 'India, what can it teach us[1]?' about the remaining grammatical works, the book on the so-called Three Khilas, the Dhâtupâ*th*a, and the Si-t'an-chang, mentioned by I-tsing. Some difficulty still remains as to the nature of some of these works, but this, I hope, will be cleared up in time.

All those who know how few certain dates there are in the history of Indian literature will welcome a text, such as I-tsing's, as a new sheet-anchor in the chronology of Sanskrit literature. We have as yet only three such anchors, as I have pointed out in my Introduction to the Amitâyur-dhyâna-sûtra[2]:—

1. The date of *K*andragupta (Sandrokyptos) as fixed by Greek historians, and serving to determine the dates of A*s*oka and his inscriptions in the third, and indirectly of the Buddha in the fifth century, before our era.
2. The dates of several literary men as supplied by Hiuen Thsang's travels in India (A.D. 629–645).
3. The dates supplied by I-tsing in the latter half of the seventh century (A.D. 671–695).

The most important of all the dates given by I-tsing are those of Bhart*ri*hari, *G*ayâditya, and their contemporaries. They serve as a rallying-point for a number of literary men belonging to what I called the 'Renaissance period of Sanskrit literature.'

Let me now congratulate you on the completion of your translation, which realises a wish long entertained by me. Your work will be a lasting memorial of my dear departed pupil Kasawara, who began it, though he was not allowed to finish it. It will show what excellent and useful work may be expected from Japanese scholars. If I have gladly

---

[1] The 1st edition, 1883, pp. 343–345.

[2] S. B. E., vol. xlix, translated by Takakusu. See my Introduction, p. xxi.

given my time and help to you as formerly to Kasawara and Bunyiu Nanjio, it was not only for the sake of our University, to which you had come to study Sanskrit and Pâli, but in the hope that a truly scholarlike study of Buddhism may be revived in Japan, and that your countrymen may in time be enabled to form a more intelligent and historical conception of the great reformer of the ancient religion of India. Religions, like everything else, require reform from time to time; and if Buddha were alive in our days he would probably be the first to reform the abuses that have crept into the Buddhism of Tibet, China, and Japan, as well as of Ceylon, Burma, and Siam. A reformed Buddhism, such as I look forward to, would very considerably reduce the interval which now separates you from other religions, and would help in the distant future to bring about a mutual understanding and kindly feeling between those great religions of the world in place of the antagonism and the fiendish hatred that have hitherto prevailed among the believers in Christ, in Buddha, and Mohammed—a disgrace to humanity, an insult to religion, and a lasting affront to those who came to preach peace on earth, and good will toward men.

Your sincere Friend,

F. MAX MÜLLER.

GENERAL INTRODUCTION.

PRELIMINARY REMARKS.

AFTER the introduction of Buddhism into China, A.D. 67[1], Fâ-hien was the first to make a pilgrimage in India, the holy land of the Buddhists. His journey, which lasted about sixteen years (A.D. 399–414), was detailed in his Fô-kue-ki[2]. Next followed the travels of Sun-yun and Hwui-seng, A.D. 518; unfortunately, however, their narrative[3] is very short, and not to be compared with that of the other travellers. Much later, in the T'ang dynasty, the Augustan age of Chinese Buddhist literature, we have first the famous Hiuen Thsang, of whom we know so much through his work, Si-yu-ki, the Record of the Western Kingdom[4]. His travels in India covered some seventeen years (A.D. 629–645), and anything that came under his notice was fully recorded in the said work, which is an indispensable text-book for Indian history and geography.

Soon after Hiuen Thsang's death, another, by no means less famous, Buddhist, I-tsing by name, started for India, A.D. 671, and arrived in Tâmralipti, at the mouth of the Hooghly, A.D. 673. He studied in Nâlanda, the centre of Buddhist learning, at the east end of the Râ*g*agr*i*ha valley, for a considerable time, and collected some 400 Sanskrit texts, amounting to 500,000 *s*lokas. On his way home he stayed

---

[1] This is the date of the arrival of the first Indian *S*rama*n*as, Kâ*s*yapa Mâtaṅga and Bhâra*n*a (or Dharmaraksha), who were invited by the Chinese Emperor Ming-ti (A.D. 58–75), and it is the historical beginning of Buddhism in China, though there are some traces of it in the earlier literature.

[2] Fâ-hien's Fô-kue-ki, by Rémusat, 1836; by Beal, 1869 and 1884; by H. A. Giles, 1877; a notice by T. Watters in the China Review, 1879 and 1880; lastly by Professor Legge, 1886 (Clarendon Press).

[3] A translation in Beal's Fâ-hien, pp. 174–208.

[4] Mémoires sur les Contrées Occidentales, by Stan. Julien, 1858; the Records of the Western Kingdoms, by Beal, 1884; Histoire de la Vie de Hiouen Thsang, by Julien, 1853; the Life of Hiuen Thsang, by Beal, 1888.

in *S*rîbhoga (Palembang, in Sumatra), where he further studied and translated Buddhist books, either Sanskrit or Pâli.

From *S*rîbhoga, I-tsing sent home his work, which is here translated, A.D. 692, through another Chinese priest, Ta-ts'in, who was then returning to China. The book is therefore called 'Nan-hai-chi-kuei-nai-fa-ch'uan,' a 'Record of the Inner Law sent home from the Southern Sea[1],' the islands which lie off the Malay peninsula being then known as the islands of the Southern Sea. Our author returned home A.D. 695, and was well received by the ruling empress, Wu-hou of Chou (as the period of her reign was called). Thus his stay abroad covers, roughly speaking, a period of twenty-five years (A.D. 671–695), though we must allow a few months' stay at home after his chance return to China, about which we shall have to speak presently. After 695 he was at home engaged in interpreting Buddhist texts with some nine Indian priests, *S*ikshânanda, Î*s*vara, and others. He completed fifty-six translations in 230 volumes, A.D. 700–712; besides, there exist five works of his compilation[2], among which the chief is our Record here given.

Now as to our knowledge of this book.

1. Mons. Stanislas Julien made use of our Record in collecting the specimens of the Chinese transcriptions of Sanskrit terms, as may be seen in his Méthode pour déchiffrer et transcrire les Noms Sanscrits qui se rencontrent dans les Livres Chinois (Paris, 1861).

2. Prof. Max Müller first recognised the importance of the contents of this work. His earliest notice about the grammatical works mentioned by I-tsing appeared in the Academy for September 25 and October 2, 1880; the next in the Indian Antiquary for December, 1880 (p. 305). A portion of the translation prepared by the late Kenjiu Kasawara, a Japanese Buddhist and pupil of the Professor, was published in 'India, what can it teach us?' 1883, pp. 210–213 and 343–349[3].

3. Mr. Samuel Beal's notice of I-tsing's work appeared in the Indian Antiquary, 1881, p. 197. Some matters contained in it were discussed by him in the Academy for September 9, 1883. He gave also a short abstract of the Record as well as the Memoirs in his Life of Hiuen Thsang, 1888, pp. xxxii–xxxvi.

4. Prof. W. Wassilief published a Russian translation of chapter ix of our Record in the Memoirs of the Historico-Philological Branch of the Academy,

---

[1] Nanjio's Catalogue of the Chinese Buddhist Books, No. 1492.

[2] Loc. cit., Nos. 1491, 1506, 1507, 1508.

[3] See pp. 183, 296 ff., in Prof. Cappeller's German translation, Indien in seiner weltgeschichtlichen Bedeutung, Leipzig, 1884.

St. Petersburg, for October 24, 1888. I have carefully compared his translation with mine, with the help of Dr. Grusdef of Moscow. Both agree on the whole, while there are many insignificant points in which we differ from each other; but I am glad to say that there was nothing to necessitate an alteration of my translation, which was already printed, when I received a copy of the Russian translation through the kindness of Prof. Serge d'Oldenbourg.

5. Mr. R. Fujishima, a Japanese priest, translated into French two chapters of the forty in the Journal Asiatique for November–December, 1888, entitled 'Deux Chapitres des Mémoires d'I-tsing,' pp. 411–439. The points of difference between his renderings and mine have been carefully noted in the present work, for these chapters (xxxii and xxxiv) are of special importance, inasmuch as they contain the names and dates of several literary men of India, the account of an eye-witness, which cannot be obtained from any other source.

Mr. Kasawara left his MS. with Prof. Max Müller when he went home from England in 1881. We see, in the Journal of the Pâli Text Society, 1883, p. 71, how the Professor was entertaining the hope of printing our Record. He says: 'I may add that I possess an English translation of I-tsing's "Nan-hai-chi-kuei-nai-fa-ch'uan," made by Kasawara during his stay at Oxford. It is not complete, and he hoped to finish it after his return to Japan, where a new edition of the Chinese text is now being published from an ancient Korean copy, collated with several Chinese editions. With the help, however, of Mr. Bunyiu Nanjio and some other scholars, I hope it will be possible before long to publish Kasawara's translation of that important work.' Mr. Nanjio once examined the MS., and noted: 'Kasawara leaves out more than a half of the original work in his translation. But I think the portion he has translated agrees with the original pretty well.' In reality his translation covered some seventy-two pages out of 206 in all, the obscure and uninteresting portion naturally being left out. With the exception of chapters xxxii and xxxiv, his MS. was either incomplete or an abstract only. It was his labour, however, that prepared the way for my present work, and the memory of his early death continually served to encourage me while handling his MS. or trying to make out the obscure passages of our Record.

The object of I-tsing's work was to correct the misrepresentations of the Vinaya rules, and to refute the erroneous opinions held by the schools of the Vinaya-dharas then existing in China. He therefore dwells chiefly on the monastic life and discipline of his time; but mingled with this we have also several important facts recorded in our work. As to the importance of I-tsing's contribution to the history of Indian literature (chaps. xxxii, xxxiv), the book will speak for itself. The other chapters also are indispensable for the study of the development of

Buddhism, especially of the Schools of the Chinese Vinaya, our knowledge of which is still very limited. The present work is an exclusive representation of the Mûlasarvâstivâda School, one of the four chief Nikâyas prevalent in India, and this will, I hope, lead some Chinese scholars to a study of the Vinaya, which is still almost an unbeaten track in Chinese literature. The Vinaya of this particular school is rich and by far the most complete of all, having also with it a complete commentary (Vibhâshâ) and several 'helps' to its study, almost all of which have been translated by I-tsing himself (below, p. xxxvii). We have, besides, two other Vinaya-pi*t*akas, which bear a close relation to the above, belonging to the Mahî*s*âsaka and Dharmagupta Schools—two subdivisions of the Mûlasarvâstivâda, according to I-tsing (p. 20)[1]. All these schools are known both to the Si*m*halese and to the Tibetans, and the Mahî*s*âsaka and Sarvâstivâda existed as early as A*s*oka's time; both of them are said to have developed out of the Sthavira-nikâya, which is identified by Prof. Oldenberg with the Vibha*gg*yavâdî[2] of the historical records of Ceylon (the name being also found in Tibetan and Chinese). We have now in existence the Vinaya-pi*t*aka in six recensions, represented in three languages. The complete text of the Theravâda is preserved in Pâli (1), which in substance closely corresponds with the Mahî*s*âsaka-vinaya in Chinese (2)[3]; that of the Mûla-sarvâstivâda in Tibetan (3) as well as in Chinese (4), along with these that of the Dharmagupta—a subdivision of the last (5). Moreover, of the school furthest removed from the orthodox, we have the Mahâsaṅghika-vinaya (6), in a complete state, brought home by Fâ-hien, A.D. 414, from Pâ*t*aliputra, and translated A.D. 416.

Seeing that we have such ample materials, a careful examination of them and a scientific comparison of all the results would much help us in ascertaining the stages of development of the traditional opinions of all the schools, for the Vinaya was held by them as the most important in determining the difference of traditions handed down by various authorities. When all these works have been examined, and the historical developments traced out, some chapters of our Record relating

---

[1] But it does not necessarily follow that the subdivisions are chronologically later than the school to which they belong, for it is possible that the schools which had been originally independent may later have come under a more flourishing school and made it the chief, seeing that there are not many material differences in their doctrines. In the Dîpava*m*sa the Sarvâstivâda is said to have separated itself from the Mahî*s*âsaka.

[2] Vinaya-pi*t*akam, p. xvii. In the Chinese translation of Buddhaghosa's Samantapâsâdikâ, the Vibha*gg*avâdî, under A*s*oka's Council, is rendered Fên-pieh-shuo, 'He who adheres to the doctrine of distinction.' Nanjio's Catal., No. 1125; book ii, fol. 9[a].

[3] Vinaya-pi*t*akam, p. xlvii.

to the Disciplinary Rules, though they may seem to some to be uninteresting at present, will, I hope, turn out a valuable manual showing how they modified and practised the original rules of the Buddha in the seventh century of our era.

The Mûlasarvâstivâda School.

In the course of 100–200 years after the Buddha's Nirvâ*n*a [1], that is to say, after the Council of Vai*s*âlî, the object of which was chiefly to refute the ten theses of the Vaggian Bhikshus, the Buddhist Church is said to have split into various schools. The Sarvâstivâda-nikâya, to which I-tsing himself belonged, as it is one of the earliest schools, must have developed itself in the same period. In the Dîpava*m*sa V, 47, it is said that the Mahi*m*sâsaka first separated itself from the Theravâda, and from the Mahi*m*sâsaka, the Sabbatthivâda, and Dhammagutta. The history of our school, however, begins with the Kathâvatthu of Moggaliputta Tissa (B.C. 240), the head of A*s*oka's Council. It does not seem to have played a very important part at that time, for Tissa's work directs only three questions against the Sabbatthivâdas:—1. Can an Arhat fall from Arahatship? (Parihâyati Arahâ Arahattâ ti); 2. *Does everything exist?* (Sabbam atthîti); 3. Is continuation of thought samâdhi? (*K*itta-santati samâdhîti) [2]. All these would be answered in the affirmative by the Sabbatthivâdas against the opinions of the orthodox school. This materialistic school appears later on as the Vaibhâshika, which is most likely identical with that of Sâya*n*a's Sarvadar*s*ana-saṅgraha,—the Presentationalist, as Prof. Cowell (p. 15) calls it. About 300 years after the Nirvâ*n*a, Kâtyâyanîputra compiled the *G*ñânaprasthâna-*s*âstra [3], which is the fundamental work of the Sarvâstivâdas. It is on this book Vasumitra and others composed, at the time of Kanishka, an elaborate commentary called the Mahâvibhâshâ-*s*âstra (No. 1263), belonging to this school, and they were consequently collectively called the Vaibhâshikas. About 400 years later, in the fifth century A.D., Vasubandhu wrote the Abhidharma-ko*s*a-*s*âstra (No. 1267), in which he, as an adherent of the Mahâyâna, refuted the views of the Vaibhâshikas. Thereupon, his contemporary and former teacher, Saṅghabhadra of the Sarvâstivâda-nikâya, refuted in turn the opinions expressed in the Ko*s*a in his Nyâyânusâra-*s*âstra (No. 1265). But it was before these two teachers that this school found a home in C. India. Fâ-hien (A.D. 399–414), who went to India to collect the Vinaya

---

[1] Dîpava*m*sa V, 16–18; Mahâva*m*sa V, 8. [2] J. R. A. S., 1892, p. 8 f., i, 2, 6; xi, 6.

[3] Compare Hiuen Thsang's Mémoires, iv, 200; Wassilief, Buddhismus, pp. 217, 218; Burnouf, Introduction, 399; Nanjio's Catal., No. 1275.

texts, says that this school was followed in Pâ*t*aliputra as well as in China, and that the Vinaya of it had not as yet been reduced to writing[1]. In Hiuen Thsang's time (A.D. 629–645), this school seems to have been widely followed. He mentions some thirteen places as belonging to it; Kashgar, Udyâna, and many other places on the northern frontier, Persia in the west, Matipura, Kanoj, and a place near Râ*g*ag*ri*ha in C. India. The Tibetan Vinaya, which was translated between the seventh and thirteenth centuries[2], is said to belong to this school[3], though the analysis of the Dulva (=Vinaya) in reality presents a closer resemblance to the Da*s*âdhyâya-vinaya, which is, according to I-tsing, not exactly the text of the Sarvâstivâdas (p. 20). I-tsing in our Record gives the geographical extension of this school (p. xxiv). It flourished in C. and N. India, and had some followers in E. and W. India, but it seems to have had very few adherents in S. India, and was entirely absent in Ceylon. In Sumatra, Java, and the neighbouring islands, almost all belonged to this school, and in China all the four subdivisions of it were flourishing. Even in Champa a trace of it was found. No other school, so far as we can ascertain, ever flourished so *widely* as the Sarvâstivâda, either before or after the seventh century; though its adherents in India alone, in Hiuen Thsang's time, were not so numerous as those of the other schools[4].

This school no doubt belongs to the Hînayâna, though our author does not expressly say so. He mentions the two Bauddha systems, Mâdhyamika (of Nâgâr*g*una) and Yogâ*k*ârya (of Asaṅga), found in Sâya*n*a's philosophical work, and says that only these two were the Mahâyâna then existing or that ever existed. I-tsing makes an attempt to harmonise the two extreme Yânas, pointing out some facts common to both, such as the adoption of the same Vinaya and the same Prohibitions (p. 14). What constitutes the difference between the two is, according to him, the worship of a Bodhisattva and the reading of a Mahâyâna-sûtra, which are peculiar to the Mahâyânists. But it seems to have been the case that some of the eighteen schools, after coming into contact with the Mahâyâna, adopted its custom, or at all events, studied its system along with their own[5]. I-tsing's statement (p. 14) seems to imply that one and the same

---

[1] Chap. xxxix; Legge, p. 99.

[2] As. Res. xx, p. 41 seq. The first Buddhist king, Sroṅ-tsan-gam-po, sent his minister, Thonmi Sambhota, to India for the scriptures in 632 A. D.

[3] Wassilief, Buddhismus, p. 96.

[4] J. R. A. S., 1891, p. 420.

[5] The Mahâbodhi-vihâra in Gayâ, for instance, adheres to the Sthavira School, yet belongs also to the Mahâyâna; the surrounding circumstances may have occasioned this. See below p. xxxii, note 2.

school adheres to the Hînayâna in one place and to the Mahâyâna in another; a school does not exclusively belong to the one or the other.

As to the difference of the opinions held by the eighteen schools, he does not say a word; but we can see, from the fact that he is very particular in stating that his Record is in accordance with his own school only and no other[1], that the opinions of the other schools were irreconcileable. He gives some trifling points of difference in their practices, such as the arrangement of lodging-places, the methods of accepting alms or wearing garments[2], though they are not sufficient to draw a line between the Mûlasarvâstivâda-nikâya and the other schools[3].

The Result of I-tsing's Description of the Buddhist Schools (A.D. 671–695).

(His Introduction, pp. 7–14.)

The eighteen schools[4] of Buddhism under the four principal heads:—

I. The Ârya-mahâsaṅghika-nikâya.

1. Seven subdivisions.
2. The Tripi*t*aka in 300,000 *s*lokas.
3. It is in practice in Magadha (C. India); a few in Lâ*t*a and Sindhu (W. India); a few in N. and S. India. Side by side with the other schools in E. India. Rejected in Ceylon. Lately introduced into the islands of the Southern Sea (Sumatra, Java, &c.). Some followers in Shen-si (W. China).

II. The Ârya-sthavira-nikâya.

1. Three subdivisions.
2. The Tripi*t*aka in 300,000 *s*lokas[5].
3. Almost all belong to it in S. India; it is in practice in Magadha (C. India). All belong to this in Ceylon. A few in Lâ*t*a and Sindhu (W. India). Side by side with the other schools in E. India. (Not in N. India.) Lately introduced into the islands of the Southern Sea. (Not in China.)

---

[1] Pages 20, 215.

[2] Pages 6-7, 66-67.

[3] I may add here that there is no trace of Brahmanic hostility in our Record; this is in harmony with the dates of Kumârila Bha*tt*a (about 750) and *S*aṅkarâ*k*ârya (about 788–820).

[4] Compare Burnouf, Lotus, 357; Csoma, As. Res. xx, 298; Dîpava*m*sa V, 39-48; Mahâva*m*sa V; Rhys Davids, J. R. A. S., 1891, p. 411; 1892, p. 5; Wassilief, Buddhismus, 223; Beal, Ind. Ant., 1880, 299.

[5] Compare Rhys Davids, Buddhism, p. 19.

III. The Ârya-mûlasarvâstivâda-nikâya.

1. Four subdivisions :—
   a. The Mûlasarvâstivâda School.
   b. The Dharmagupta School.
   c. The Mahîsâsaka School.
   d. The Kâsyapîya School.
2. The Tripi*t*aka in 300,000 *s*lokas.
3. Most flourishing in Magadha (C. India); almost all belong to this in N. India. A few in Lâ*t*a and Sindhu (W. India) and in S. India. Side by side with the other in E. India. Three subdivisions, *b*, *c*, *d*, are not found in India proper, but some followers in Udyâna, Khara*k*ar, and Kustana. (Not in Ceylon.) Almost all belong to this in the islands of the Southern Sea. A few in Champa (Cochin China). *b* is found in E. China and in Shen-si (W. China). *a*, *b*, *c*, *d*, flourishing in the south of the Yang-tse-kiang, in Kwang-tung and Kwang-si in S. China.

IV. The Ârya-sammitîya-nikâya[1].

1. Four subdivisions.
2. Tripi*t*aka in 200,000 *s*lokas; the Vinaya alone in 30,000 *s*lokas.
3. Most flourishing in Lâ*t*a and Sindhu (W. India). It is in practice in Magadha. A few in S. India. Side by side with the other in E. India. (Not in N. India.) (Not in Ceylon.) A few in the islands of the Southern Sea. Mostly followed in Champa (Cochin-China). (Not in China proper.)

The geographical distribution of the schools in India and in other places:—

India in general. Eighteen schools are in existence (p. 8, iv).

C. India. Magadha; all the four Nikâyas in practice, but III flourishes the most (except *b*, *c*, *d* of it).

W. India. Lâ*t*a and Sindhu; IV is most flourishing; a few of I, II, III.

N. India. Almost all belong to III; a few to I (II, IV not found).

S. India. [2]Almost all belong to II; a few to the other schools.

E. India. I, II, III, IV side by side.

Ceylon. All belong to II; I is rejected (III, IV not found).

Sumatra, Java, and the neighbouring islands. Almost all belong to III; a few to IV; lately a few to I, II.

Cochin-China. Champa; mostly IV; a few III (no I, II).

Siam. No Buddhism at present, owing to the recent persecution of Buddhists by a king.

---

[1] This seems to be most common; Sammiti in Dîpav. V, 46 (plural -tî), also in Wijesinha, Mahâv., p. 15, note.

[2] This fact is in harmony with Prof. Oldenberg's opinion expressed in his Vinaya-pi*t*akam, i, p. liii, that the Ceylonese Buddhism might have been introduced through the southern coasts which had commercial relations with Ceylon in early times.

E. China. *b* of III flourishing.
W. China. Shen-si: *b* of III, and also I followed.
S. China. South of Yang-tse-kiang, Kwang-tung, and Kwang-si: all III (*a*, *b*, *c*, *d*) flourishing.

The Mahâyâna and Hînayâna.

China in general belongs to the Mahâyâna.
Malayu (=*S*rîbhoga), a few Mahâyânists.
N. India and the ten or more islands of the Southern Sea (Sumatra, Java, &c.) generally belong to the Hînayâna.

All the remaining places in India. Both Yânas are found, i.e. some practise according to the one, some according to the other.

THE LIFE AND TRAVELS OF I-TSING.

I. His Boyhood, to his Departure from China.

I-tsing, one of the three great travellers in India, was born in the year 635 A.D. in Fan-yang[1], during the reign of T'ai-tsung[2]. When he was seven years old (641), he went to the teachers, Shan-yü and Hui-hsi, who both lived in a temple on the mountain T'ai in Shan-tung[3]. He was probably instructed by these teachers in the elements of general Chinese literature, with a view to his proceeding to the priesthood.

His Upâdhyâya Shan-yü died, to his great sorrow, when he was only twelve years old (646)[4]. He then, laying aside his study of secular literature, devoted himself to the Sacred Canon of the Buddha. He was admitted to the Order (Pravragyâ) when he was fourteen years of age. It was, he tells us, in his eighteenth year (652) that he formed the intention of travelling to India, which was not, however, carried out till his thirty-seventh year (671)[5]. During some nineteen years of the interval he seems to have applied all his youthful vigour to

---

[1] Modern Cho-chou (= Juju of Marco Polo, near Peking), a department in the province of Chi-li.

[2] Reigned A.D. 627-649; 635 is, in Chinese, the ninth year of the Chêng-kuan period.

[3] Below, pp. 199, 207.

[4] Page 204; Hiuen Thsang returned from India in this year.

[5] Page 204.

the study of religion, so as 'not to render his life useless by indulging himself in secular literature[1].'

He received his Full Ordination (Upasampadâ) at the required age of twenty (654), his Karmâkârya, Hui-hsi, then becoming his Upâdhyâya to take the place of the deceased Shan-yü. On the same day, pointing out to him the importance of holding firm to the Noble Precepts of the Buddha, and also the fact that the Buddha's teaching was becoming misinterpreted, the Upâdhyâya instructed him in earnest[2]. The words of his teacher must have guided him throughout the whole of his life, for what he did or wrote afterwards perfectly accords with them.

After that incident, he devoted himself exclusively to the study of the Vinaya text during the following five years (654–658). He made great progress in his pursuit, and his teacher ordered him to deliver a lecture on the subject; in fact he calls himself on one occasion 'One versed in the Vinaya,' so far as the Chinese study of it is concerned[3].

Next to the Vinaya he proceeded to learn the larger Sûtras, practising some of the thirteen Dhûtâṅgas[4] during his residence in the mountain Vihâra. Owing to the instigation of his Upâdhyâya he then went to Eastern Wei[5] to study Asaṅga's two Sâstras belonging to the Abhidharma-piṭaka; thence he moved to the Western Capital[6], where he further read the Abhidharma-kosa and Vidyâmâtra-siddhi of Vasubandhu and Dharmapâla respectively[7]. While he stayed at Ch'ang-an he may have witnessed the 'noble enthusiasm of Hiuen Thsang[8],' and probably also the grand ceremony of his funeral carried out under the special direction of the emperor, for his death occurred during I-tsing's stay in the capital (664).

Stirred up perhaps by the great personality of Hiuen Thsang and by the honour and glory that attended him, I-tsing seems to have made a great effort to carry out his long meditated enterprise of a journey to India, which was in his time the home of Buddhist literature. I-tsing indeed became a great admirer of Hiuen Thsang as well as of Fâ-hien, as his biographer tells us[9]. He stayed in the capital till A.D. 670, the year prior to his departure from home.

As to his travels, the reader will perhaps prefer to read them in I-tsing's own words, though the record is unfortunately short[10].

---

[1] Page 209; this was his teacher's instruction. [2] Page 209. [3] Page 65.
[4] Compare pp. 56, 57, note. [5] Or, Yeh, now Chang-teh Fu in Honan.
[6] Si-an Fu or Ch'ang-an (= Kenjanfu of Marco Polo) in Shen-si. [7] Page 210.
[8] Compare the Life of I-tsing (Nanjio's Catal., No. 1495); Chavannes, Memoirs, p. 193.
[9] See l. c.; for his own words about his two predecessors, see below, pp. 184, 207.
[10] It would have seemed superfluous to give a long account after Hiuen Thsang; I-tsing must have known the Si-yu-ki, see e.g. his sayings against 'Indu' (p. 118; cf. Hiuen Thsang, Mémoires, ii. 56) and about the six seasons (p. 102, notes 3, 4).

II. His Journey to India.

[1]I, I-tsing, was in the Western Capital (Ch'ang-an) in the first year of the Hsien-hêng period (670), studying and hearing lectures. At that time there were with me Ch'u-i, a teacher of the Law, of Ping-pu[2]; Hung-i, a teacher of the *S*âstra, of Lai-chou[3], and also two or three other Bhadantas; we all made an agreement together to visit the Vulture Peak (G*ri*dhrakû*t*a), and set our hearts on (seeing) the Tree of Knowledge (Bodhidruma) in India. Ch'u-i, however, was drawn back by his affection towards (his home in) Ping-ch'uan[4], for his mother was of an advanced age, whereas Hung-i turned his thought to Sukhâvatî[5] on meeting Hiuen-Chan in Kiang-ning[6]. Hiuen-k'uei (one of the party) came as far as Kwang-tung; he, however, as others did, changed his mind which he had formerly made up. So I had to start for India, only with a young priest, Shan-hing, of Tsin-chou[7].

The old friends of mine in the Divine Land (China) thus unfortunately parted with me and all went their ways, while not a single new acquaintance in India was yet found by me. Had I hesitated then, my wish would never have been fulfilled. I composed two stanzas imitating, though not in earnest, the poem on the fourfold Sorrow[8].

During my travel I passed several myriads of stages,
The fine threads of sorrow entangled my thought hundredfold.
Why was it, pray, you let the shadow of my body alone
Walk on the boundaries of Five Regions of India?

Again to console myself:

A good general can obstruct a *hostile* army,
But the resolution of a man is difficult to move[9].
If I be sorry for a short life and be ever
Speaking of it, how can I fill up the long Asańkhya age[10]?

---

[1] The Ta-t'ang-si-yu-ku-fa-kao-sêng-Ch'uan, vol. ii, fol. 4^b; Chavannes, § 46, p. 114.

[2] Ping-chou or T'ai-yuen in Shen-si.

[3] Lai-chou Fu, in the Shan-tung promontory, said to have been named after the Lai aborigines.

[4] A Japanese text has Ping-chou.

[5] To be born in the Land of Bliss it is necessary to repeat daily the name of Amitâbha according to the Old Pure Land School; An-yang = Sukhâvatî.

[6] In Kiang-su.

[7] A place in P'ing-yang in Shen-si. This priest was a pupil of I-tsing; he came as far as Sumatra and returned to China owing to illness, Chavannes, § 47, p. 126.

[8] An ancient poem composed by Chang-heng (A.D. 78–139), loc. cit., p. 115.

[9] Cf. the Analects, IX, 25.

[10] A Bodhisattva passes through three Asańkhya (immeasurable) ages, practising charity, &c.; I-tsing is here alluding to this.

[1]Previous to my departure from home I returned to my native place (Cho-chou) from the capital (Ch'ang-an). I sought advice from my teacher, Hui-hsi, saying: 'Venerable Sir, I am intending to take a long journey; for, if I witness that with which I have hitherto not been acquainted, there must accrue to me great advantage. But you are already advanced in age, so that I cannot carry out my intention without consulting you.' He answered: 'This is a great opportunity for you, which will not occur twice. (I assure you) I am much delighted to hear of your intention so wisely formed. If I live long enough (to see you return), it will be my joy to witness you transmitting the Light. Go without hesitation; do not look back upon things left behind. I certainly approve of your pilgrimage to the holy places. Moreover it is a most important duty to strive for the prosperity of Religion. Rest clear from doubt!'

[2]On the eve of my departure, I went to the tomb of my master (Shan-yü) to worship and to take leave. At that time, the trees around the tomb (though) injured by frost had already grown so much that each tree would take one hand to span it[3], and wild grasses had filled the graveyard. Though the spirit-world is hidden from us, I nevertheless paid him all honour just as if he had been present[4]. While turning round and glancing in every direction, I related my intention of travelling. I invoked his spiritual aid, and expressed my wish to requite the great benefits conferred on me by this benign personage.

[5]In the second year of the Hsien-hêng period (671) I kept the summer-retreat (varsha or vassa) in Yang-fu[6]. In the beginning of autumn (seventh moon) I met unexpectedly an imperial envoy, Fêng Hsiao-ch'üan of Kong-chou[7]; by the help of him I came to the town of Kwang-tung, where I fixed the date of meeting with the owner of a Persian ship[8] to embark for the south. Again accepting the

---

[1] Page 210. [2] Page 204. [3] This is an alternative translation, cf. l. c.

[4] Cf. the Analects, III, 12.

[5] The Si-yu-ku-fa-kao-sêng-ch'uan, vol. ii, fol. 5[a]; Chavannes, p. 116.

[6] Yang-chou (= Yangju of Marco Polo) in Kiang-su.

[7] Old name for the S.E. part of Kwang-si.

[8] In I-tsing's time there was regular navigation between Persia, India, the Malay islands, and China. I think this explains the route of the first Nestorian missionary, Olopuen or Alopen, who went to China A.D. 635. Dr. Legge supposed that he would have come to China overland through Central Asia (Christianity in China in the Seventh Century, p. 45). Dr. Edkins says that Sîlâditya received the Syrian Christians, Alopen and his companions, A.D. 639 (Athenaeum, July 3, 1880, p. 8). If so, it would seem that he went back to India. If, on the other hand, these were two different men, the fact would rather favour Yule's conjecture that Alopuen, which is supposed to be Syriac 'Alopano,' might be merely a Chinese form of the Syriac 'Rabban,' by which the Apostle had come to be generally known (Cathy, p. xciv). For Adam, the writer of the Syro-Chinese inscription, see p. 169 note, and also my additional note at the end (p. 223).

invitation of the envoy I went to Kang-chou[1], when he became my Dânapati (Benefactor) for a second time. His younger brothers, Hsiao-tan and Hsiao-chên, both imperial envoys, Ladies[2] Ning and P'ên, all the members of his family, favoured me with presents.

Things of superior quality and excellent eatables were given me by them; each striving to do the best. In doing so, they hoped that I might not be in any want during the sea voyage, yet they feared that there might be some troubles for me in the dangerous land. Their affection was as deep as that of my parents, readily granting whatever the orphan wished to have. They all became my refuge or resource, and together supplied the means of (visiting) the excellent region.

All I could have done regarding my pilgrimage (to the Holy Land) is due only to the power of the family of Fêng. Moreover the priests and laymen of the Lin-nan[3] experienced a bitter feeling at our parting; the brilliant scholars of the northern provinces were all distressed by our bidding farewell, as they thought never to see us again.

In the eleventh month of this year (A.D. 671)[4] *we started* looking towards the constellations Yi and Chên[5], and having P'an-yü (Kwang-tung) right behind us. I would sometimes direct my thoughts far away to the Deer Park (M*ri*gadâva at Benares); *at other times* I would repose in the hope of (reaching) the Cock Mountain (Kukku*t*apadagiri near Gayâ).

At this time the first monsoon began to blow, when *our ship* proceeded towards the Red South[6], with *the ropes* a hundred cubits long suspended from above, two by two[7]. In the beginning of the season in which we separate from the constellation Chi[8], the pair *of sails*, each in five *lengths*[9], flew away, leaving

---

[1] A place in Kwang-chou in the province of Kwang-tung.

[2] Chün-chün is a daughter of an imperial prince of the third degree, but often used as a title of honour of a noble lady, as here.

[3] South of the Plum Range, i. e. Kwang-tung and Kwang-si. [4] Page 211.

[5] Yi = serpent, twenty-two stars in Crater and Hydra; Chên = worm, $\beta, \gamma, \delta, \epsilon$ Corvus. Long. $170^\circ\ 56'\ 9'' - 187^\circ\ 56'\ 52''$, i. e. about the south.

[6] The colour assigned to the south is red, and that to the north is sombre, see below.

[7] I. e. 'the preparation of the spars having been duly made.' Prof. Chavannes' correction of 'Kuei' to 'Kua' is confirmed by Kâ*s*yapa's copy of the Record; Memoirs, p. 118, note 4.

[8] Chi stands for the constellation $\gamma, \delta, \epsilon, \beta$ Sagittarii = Leopard. Long. $268^\circ\ 28'\ 15''$. This constellation consists of the stars which are visible in heaven only when the sun is 16° or more below the horizon. Accordingly, the first heliacal rising (ortus heliacus) at dawn for Lat. 20° (Canton) is on about Feb. 8, and the last heliacal setting (occasus heliacus) in the evening dusk, for Lat. 20° is on about Dec. 11. The corresponding day in the lunar month to our Dec. 11 will be about the 1st of the eleventh month, being about the time when the Chi constellation disappears.

[9] For this note, see next page.

the sombre north behind. Cutting through the immense abyss, the great swells of water lie, like a mountain, on the sea. Joining sideways with a vast gulf-stream, the massive waves, like clouds, dash against the sky.

Before sailing twenty days the ship reached Bhoga[1], where I landed and stayed six months, gradually learning the *S*abdavidyâ (Sanskrit grammar). The king gave me some support and sent me to the country of Malayu, which is now called *S*rîbhoga[2], where I again stayed two months, and thence I went to Ka-cha[3]. Here I embarked in the twelfth month, and again on board the king's ship I sailed to Eastern India. Going towards the north from Ka-cha, after more than ten days' sail, we came to the country of the Naked People (Insulae Nudorum). Looking towards the east we saw the shore, for an extent of one or two Chinese miles, with nothing but cocoa-nut trees and betel-nut forest[4], luxuriant and pleasant (to be seen). When the natives saw our vessel coming, they eagerly embarked in little boats, their number being fully a hundred. They all brought cocoa-nuts, bananas, and things made of rattan-cane and bamboos, and wished to exchange them. [5]What they are anxious to get is iron only; for a piece of iron as large as two fingers, one gets from them five to ten cocoa-nuts. The men are entirely naked, while the women veil their person with some leaves. If the merchants in joke offer them their clothes, they wave their hands (to tell that) they do not use them.

By this time the wind begins to blow from N. E.; hence the common expression: 'Chi hao fêng, Pi hao yü,' 'the constellation Chi (Sagittarius) loves wind, and the Pi (Taurus) loves rain,' that is, the two draw wind and rain respectively towards themselves, and it means 'wind comes from the N.E., and the rain from the S.W.' The Chinese Æolus is therefore Chi-po, i.e. Lord Chi or Uncle Sagittarius.

[9] Lit. 'the pair of fives flew alone;' the sail may have consisted of five lengths of canvas. Chavannes: 'et la girouette de plumes flotta isolée.'

[1] See below.

[2] This is I-tsing's note. We must thus recognise Bhoga, *the Capital* and the country of *S*rîbhoga (= Malayu), though I-tsing uses both names indiscriminately. The notes in I-tsing's text have often been erroneously supposed to be by a later hand. As I have said elsewhere (pp. 8, 214, notes), we have no reason whatever to suppose this. He is wont to note any difficult passage throughout his works and translations. There are some such notes which no one but one who had been in India could add, e.g. see Memoirs, vol. ii, fol. 12ª; Record, vol. i, fol. 3ª; vol. iii, fols. 11ª, 11ᵇ; vol. iv, fol. 14ª. The commentator Kâ*s*yapa takes all the notes as by I-tsing. Besides, the note to the Mûlasarvâstivâda-eka*s*atakarman quoted below (pp. xxxiii, xxxiv) clears up all doubts, where he says that Malayu then became Bhoga.

[3] Ka-cha must be S. of the country of the Naked People, somewhere on the Atchin coast. This may represent Sanskrit ka*kkh*a, 'shore.' The Chinese characters are now pronounced Hsieh-ch'a or Chieh-ch'a (ch'a is often misprinted for t'u; if so here, then Chieh-t'u).

[4] Pin-lang, from the Malay pinang; Sanskrit pûga.

[5] These agree with an account given of the Nicobar Islands, see below, p. xxxviii, 1.

This country is, I heard, in the direction of the south-west limit Shu-ch'uan (Ssŭ-ch'uan, in China). This island does not produce iron at all; gold and silver also are rare. The natives live solely on cocoa-nuts (nâlikera) and tubers; there is not much rice. And therefore what they hold most precious and valuable is Loha[1], which is the name for iron in this country. These people are not black, and are of medium height. They are skilled in making round chests of rattan; no other country can equal them. If one refuses to barter with them, they discharge some poisoned arrows, one single shot of which proves fatal. In about half a month's sail from here in the north-west direction we reached Tâmralipti[2], which constitutes the southern limit of E. India. It is more than sixty *yoganas* from Mahâbodhi and Nâlanda (C. India).

[3]On the eighth day of the second month of the fourth year of the Hsien-hêng period (673) I arrived there. In the fifth month I resumed my journey westwards, finding companions here and there.

I met for the first time Ta-ch'êng-têng (Mahâyânapradîpa)[4] *in Tâmralipti*, and stayed with him a (part of the) year, while I learned the Brahma-language (Sanskrit) and practised the science of words (grammar, *S*abdavidyâ). Lastly, I started together with the master Têng (=Ta-ch'êng-têng), taking the road which goes straight to the west, and many hundreds of merchants came with us to C. India.

At a distance of ten days' journey from the Mahâbodhi Vihâra we passed a great mountain and bogs; the pass is dangerous and difficult to cross. It is important to go in a company of several men, and never to proceed alone. At that time I, I-tsing, was attacked by an illness of the season; my body was fatigued and without strength. I sought to follow the company of merchants, but tarrying and suffering, as I was, became unable to reach them. Although I exerted myself and wanted to proceed, yet I was obliged to stop a hundred times in going five Chinese miles. There were there about twenty priests of Nâlanda, and with them the venerable Têng, who had all gone on in advance. I alone remained behind, and walked in the dangerous defiles without a companion. Late in the day, when the sun was about to set, some mountain brigands made their appear-

---

[1] Lo-ho in the Japanese text, but Lo-a in the Chinese. They evidently used the Sanskrit name.

[2] Page 185, note. [3] Page 211.

[4] A pupil of Hiuen Thsang. He travelled in Dvâravatî (W. Siam), Ceylon, S. India, and came to Tâmralipti, where he stayed twelve years; skilled in Sanskrit. I-tsing goes with him to Nâlanda, Vais*â*lî, and Ku*s*inagara; died in the Parinirvâ*n*a Vihâra at the last-mentioned town (Memoirs, i, fols. 13, 14; Chavannes, § 32, p. 68).

ance; drawing a bow and shouting aloud, they came and glared at me, and one after another insulted me. First they stripped me of my upper robe, and then took off my under garment. All the straps and girdles that were with me they snatched away also. I thought at that time, indeed, that my last farewell to this world was at hand, and that I should not fulfil my wish of a pilgrimage to the holy places. Moreover, if my limbs were thus pierced by the points of their lances, I could never succeed in carrying out the original enterprise so long meditated. Besides, there was a rumour in the country of the West (India) that, when they took a white man, they killed him to offer a sacrifice to heaven (Devas). When I thought of this tale, my dismay grew twice as much. Thereupon I entered into a muddy hole, and besmeared all my body with mud. I covered myself with leaves, and supporting myself on a stick, I advanced slowly.

The evening of the day came, and the place of rest was as yet distant. At the second watch of night I reached my fellow-travellers. I heard the venerable Têng calling out for me with a loud voice from outside the village. When we met together, he kindly gave me a robe, and I washed my body in a pond and then came into the village. Proceeding northwards for a few days from that village, we arrived first at Nâlanda and worshipped the Root Temple (Mûla-gandhaku*t*i), and we ascended the G*ri*dhrakû*t*a (Vulture) mountain, where we saw the spot on which the garments were folded[1]. Afterwards we came to the Mahâbodhi Vihâra[2], and worshipped the image of the real face (of the Buddha). I took stuffs of thick and fine silk, which were presented by the priests and laymen of Shan-tung, made a kâshâya (yellow robe) of them of the size of the Tathâgata, and myself offered this robe to the Image. Many myriads of (small) canopies (also), which were entrusted to me by the Vinaya-master Hiuen of Pu[3], I presented on his behalf. The Dhyâna-master An-tao of Ts'ao[4] charged me to worship the image of Bodhi, and I discharged the duty in his name.

Then I prostrated myself entirely on the ground with an undivided mind, sincere and respectful. First I wished for China that the four kinds of benefits[5]

---

[1] Hiuen Thsang, tom. iii, p. 21: 'Au milieu d'un torrent, il y a une vaste pierre sur laquelle le Tathâgata fit sécher son vêtement le religieux. Les raies de l'étoffe détachent encore aussi nettement que si elles avaient été ciselées.'

[2] Near the Bodhi tree, built by a king of Ceylon (Memoirs, Chavannes, p. 84). This Vihâra belonged to the Theravâda, yet adhered to the Mahâyâna (Hiuen Thsang, iii, p. 487 seq.); this fact perhaps misled Hiuen Thsang, who mentions Ceylon as belonging to both. Bharuka*kkh*a and Surâsh*t*ra also belonged to both, according to Hiuen Thsang. Compare Oldenberg, Vinaya-pi*t*akam, p. liii, note.

[3] Pu-chou in Shan-tung.

[4] Ts'ao-chou in Shan-tung.

[5] Page 196, note 3.

should widely prevail among all sentient beings (Han-shih=sattva) in the region of the Law (Dharmadhâtu), and I expressed my desire for a general reunion under the Nâga-tree to meet the honoured (Buddha) Maitreya and to conform to the true doctrine[1], and then to obtain the knowledge that is not subject to births. I went round to worship all the holy places; I passed *a house which is known* (to the Chinese) as 'Fan-chang' (in Vaisâlî)[2] and came to Kusinagara, everywhere keeping myself devout and sincere. I entered into the Deer Park (Mrigadâva at Benares) and ascended the Cock Mountain (Kukkutapadagiri near Gayâ); and lived in the Nâlanda Vihâra for ten years (probably A.D. 675–685).

[3] In the first year of the Ch'ui-kung period (685) I parted with Wu-hing in India (in a place six yoganas east from Nâlanda)[4].

After having collected the scriptures, I began to retrace my steps to come back[5]. I then returned to Tâmralipti. Before I reached there, I met a great band of robbers again; it was with difficulty that I escaped the fate of being pierced by their swords, and I could thus preserve my life from morning to evening. Afterwards I took ship there and passed Ka-cha[6]. The Indian texts I brought formed more than 500,000 slokas, which, if translated into Chinese, would make a thousand volumes, and with these I am now staying at Bhoga.

[7] Roughly speaking, the distance from the middle country (Madhyamadesa) of India to the border lands (Pratyantaka) is more than 300 yoganas in the east and in the west. The border lands in the south and in the north are more than 400 yoganas distant. Although I myself did not see (all the limits) and ascertain (the distance), yet I know it by inquiry. Tâmralipti is forty yoganas south from the eastern limit of India. There are five or six monasteries; the people are

---

[1] Page 213, note 1. Tsung here = 'school,' 'tenet,' 'doctrine.'

[2] Fan-chang = 'ten cubits square.' In Vaisâlî there was a house which is said to be the room of Vimalakîrti, contemporary of the Buddha; Wan-hiuen-ts'ê, chief envoy to Sîlâditya, when in Vaisâlî, measured the house and found that this room was ten cubits each way (Kâsyapa). Hence it was afterwards known as Fan-chang; later any room where a head priest lived was called so. Now any abbot and also any monastery are called Fan-chang. Compare Julien, Mémoires, vii, p. 385; Beal, Life of Hiuen Thsang, p. 100; Chavannes, Memoirs, p. 72, where I-tsing passes Vaisâlî between the Diamond Seat and Kusinagara.

[3] Memoirs, vol. i, fol. 6a; Chavannes, p. 10.

[4] Loc. cit., vol. ii, fol. 11b; Chavannes, p. 147. See below, p. xlvi.

[5] Yen here is not a verb but a particle; for an analogous use, see the Nestorian Inscription (Legge, Christianity in China, &c., p. 25), and Memoirs, vol. ii, fol. 13b, line 9.

[6] He landed here and met a man from the north (Tukhâra or Sûli), who told him that there were two Chinese priests travelling in the north (whom I-tsing considered to be his own friends), Chavannes, p. 106.

[7] The Mûlasarvâstivâda-ekasatakarman (Nanjio's Catal., No. 1131), book v, p. 57.

rich. It belongs to E. India, and is about sixty *yoganas* from Mahâbodhi and *S*rî-Nâlanda. This is the place where we embark when returning to China. Sailing from here two months in the south-east direction we come to Ka-cha. By this time a ship from Bho*g*a will have arrived there. This is generally in the first or second month of the year. But those who go to the Si*m*hala Island (Ceylon) must sail in the south-west direction. They say that that island is 700 *yoganas* off. We stay in Ka-cha till winter, then start on board ship for the south, and we come after a month to the country of Malayu, which has now become Bho*g*a; there are many states (under it). The time of arrival is generally in the first or second month. We stay there till the middle of summer and we sail to the north; in about a month we reach Kwang-fu (Kwang-tung). The first half of the year will be passed by this time.

When we are helped by the power of our (former) good actions, the journey everywhere is as easy and enjoyable as if we went through a market, but, on the other hand, when we have not much influence of Karma, we are often exposed to danger as if (a young one) in a reclining nest [1]. I have thus shortly described the route and the way home, hoping that the wise may still expand their knowledge by hearing more.

Many kings and chieftains in the islands of the Southern Ocean admire and believe (Buddhism), and their hearts are set on accumulating good actions. In the fortified city of Bho*g*a Buddhist priests number more than 1,000, whose minds are bent on learning and good practices. They investigate and study all the subjects that exist just as in the Middle Kingdom (Madhya-de*s*a, India); the rules and ceremonies are not at all different. If a Chinese priest wishes to go to the West in order to hear (lectures) and read (the original), he had better stay here one or two years and practise the proper rules and then proceed to Central India.

[2] At the mouth of the river Bho*g*a I went on board the ship to send a letter [3] (through the merchant) as a credential to Kwang-chou (Kwang-tung), *in order* to meet (my friends) and ask for paper and cakes of ink, which are to be used in copying the Sûtras in the Brahma-language, and also for the means (cost) of hiring scribes. Just at that time the merchant found the wind favourable, and raised the sails to their utmost height. I was in this way conveyed back (although

---

[1] Or does this refer to a robbers' den?

[2] Memoirs, vol. ii, fol. 17[b]; Chavannes, p. 176.

[3] Fu-shu means 'to send a letter.' I-tsing does not intend to go home, therefore he says (below): 'Even if I asked to stop,' &c. This was a very puzzling point. Beal makes out that I-tsing was intending to return but was left behind, while Chavannes thinks that I-tsing intended to return in order to get paper and ink, and did so.

not myself intending to go home). Even if I asked to stop, there would have been no means of doing so. By this I see it is the influence of Karma that can fashion (our course), and it is not for us, men, to plan it. It was on the twentieth day of the seventh month in the first year of the Yung-ch'ang period (689) that we reached Kwang-fu. I met here again with all the priests and laymen. Then in the midst of the assembly in the temple of Chih-chih I sighed and said: 'I first went to the country of the West with the hope of transmitting and spreading (the Law)[1]; I came back and stayed in the island of the Southern Ocean. Some texts are still wanting, though what I brought (from India) and left at Bhoga amounts to 500,000 *s*lokas belonging to the Tripi*t*aka. It is necessary under this circumstance that I should go there once again. But I am already more than fifty years of age (fifty-five); while crossing the running waves once more, the horses that pass through cracks[2] may not stay, and the rampart of my body may be difficult to guard. If the time for the morning dew (for drying) comes on a sudden, to whom shall those books be entrusted?

'The Sacred Canon is indeed an important doctrine. Who is then able to come with me and take it over? To translate (the texts) as we receive (instructions in them) we want an able person.'

The assembly unanimously told me: 'Not far from here there is a priest, Chêng-ku (Sâlagupta), who has long been studying the Vinaya doctrine; from his earliest age he has preserved himself perfect and sincere. If you get that man, he will prove an excellent companion to you.' As soon as I heard these words, I thought that he would, in all probability, answer my want. Thereupon I sent a letter to him to the temple of the mountain, roughly describing the preparation for the journey. He then opened my letter; on seeing it he soon made up his mind to come with me. To make a comparison, a single sortie at the town of Liao-tung broke the courageous hearts of the three generals, or one little stanza from (or, about) the Himâlaya mountain drew the profound resolution of the great hermit[3]. He left with joy the quiet streams and pine forests *in which he lived*; he tucked up his sleeves before the hill of the Stone Gate (Shih-mên, N.W. of Kwang-tung), and he raised his skirts in the temple of the Edict (Chih-chih). We bent our parasol (and talked friendly as Confucius did) and united our feelings in rubbing away the worldly dust; as we both gave up (to Religion) our five limbs,

---

[1] Liu-t'ung = 'propagating' or 'transmitting.'

[2] A strange simile in Chinese: 'Human life passes away as quickly as a white colt runs through a crack.'

[3] Liao-tung and the Himâlaya are well known, but I cannot explain at present to what incidents he is alluding.

we concluded (our friendship) in openheartedness, as if from former days. Although I never saw him before in my life, yet he was, I found, just the man who answered unexpectedly my wish. On a fine night we both discussed seriously as to what had to be done. Chêng-ku then said to me: 'When Virtue wishes to meet Virtue, they unite themselves without any medium, and when the time is about ripe, no one can stay it even if they wanted.

'Shall I then sincerely *propose* to propagate our Tripi*t*aka together with you, and to help you in lighting a thousand lamps (for the future)?' Then we went again to the mountain Hsia[1] to bid farewell to the head of the temple, K'ien, and others. K'ien clearly saw what was to be done at the right moment and acted accordingly; he never intended to retain us any longer with him. When we saw him and laid before him what we had meditated, he helped us and approved of all. He was never anxious about what might be wanting to himself, whilst his mind was intent only on helping others. He made, together with us, the preparations for the journey, so as not to let us be in want of anything. Besides, all the priests and laymen of Kwang-tung provided us with necessary things.

Then on the first day of the eleventh month of the year (A.D. 689) we departed in a merchant ship. Starting from P'an-yü we set sail in the direction of Champa[2] with the view of reaching Bhoga after a long voyage, in order to become the ladders for all beings, or the boats, to carry them across the sea of passion. While we were glad to accomplish our resolutions as soon as possible, we hoped not to fall in the middle of our journey.

[Chêng-ku, Tao-hung, and two other priests followed I-tsing and studied Sûtras three years in Bhoga; Tao-hung was then (689) twenty years old, and, when I-tsing wrote the Memoirs, twenty-three years[3].]

[4]I, I-tsing, met Ta-ts'in in *S*rîbhoga (where he came A.D. 683). I requested him to return home to ask an imperial favour in building a temple in the West. When he saw that benefits would be great and large (had this petition been granted), Ta-ts'in disregarding his own life agreed to re-cross the vast ocean. It is on the fifteenth day of the fifth month in the third year of the T'ien-shou period (692) that he takes a merchant ship to return to Ch'ang-an (Si-an-fu). Now I send with him a new translation of various Sûtras and *S*âstras in ten volumes, the Nan-hai-chi-kuei-nai-fa-ch'uan (the Record) in four volumes, and the Ta-t'ang-si-yu-ku-fa-kao-sêng-ch'uan (the Memoirs) in two volumes.

---

[1] A hill situated near Kwang-tung, where Chêng-ku lived.

[2] Zampa of Odoric (about 1323 A.D.); Chamba of Marco Polo (1288 A.D.). Skt. *K*ampâ.

[3] Chavannes, pp. 185, 187.

[4] Loc. cit., p. 160, § 56.

III. His Return Home, to his Death.

The Biography[1] tells us that I-tsing was twenty-five years (671–695) abroad and travelled in more than thirty countries, and that he came back to China at Midsummer in the first year of the Chêng-shêng period (695) of T'ien-hou (the queen-usurper, 684–704); further that he brought home some four hundred different texts of Buddhist books, the *s*lokas numbering 500,000, and a real plan of the Diamond Seat (Va*g*râsana) of the Buddha.

In A.D. 700–712 I-tsing translated 56 works in 230 volumes, though some of them were of an earlier date. Among these works there are several important Sûtras and *S*âstras, but to know how he represented the Mûlasarvâstivâda School, with which our Record is particularly connected, it will suffice to give here only the Vinaya texts as below:—

A. The India Office Collection.

1. No. 1110. Mûlasarvâstivâda-vinaya-sûtra, 1 vol.
2. „ 1118. „ „ „ -vinaya, 50 vols.
3. „ 1121. „ „ „ -sa*m*yukta-vastu, 40 vols.
4. „ 1123. „ „ „ -saṅghabhedaka-vastu, 20 vols.
5. „ 1124. „ „ „ -bhikshu*n*î-vinaya, 20 vols.
6. „ 1127. „ „ „ -vinaya-saṅgraha, 14 vols.
7. „ 1131. „ „ „ -eka*s*atakarman, 10 vols.
8. „ 1133. „ „ „ -nidâna, 5 vols.
9. „ 1134. „ „ „ -mât*ri*kâ, 5 vols.
10. „ 1140. „ „ „ -vinaya-nidâna-mât*ri*kâ-gâthâ (15 leaves).
11. „ 1141. „ „ „ -sa*m*yukta-vastu-gâthâ (10 leaves).
12. „ 1143. „ „ „ -vinaya-gâthâ, 4 vols.
13. „ 1149. „ „ „ -bhikshu*n*î-vinaya-sûtra, 2 vols.

B. The Bodleian Library Collection (Jap. 65⁰) besides the above.

14. No. (1). Mûlasarvâstivâda-pravra*g*yâ(-upasa*m*padâ-)vastu, 4 vols. (Cf. Mahâvagga, Khandhaka I.)
15. „ (2). Mûlasarvâstivâda-varshâvâsa-vastu, 1 vol. (Cf. Mahâv., Khandh. III.)
16. „ (3). Mûlasarvâstivâda-pravâra*n*a-vastu, 1 vol. (Cf. Mahâv., Khandh. IV.)
17. „ (4). Mûlasarvâstivâda-*k*arma-vastu, 1 vol. (Cf. Mahâv., Khandh. V.)
18. „ (5). Mûlasarvâstivâda-bhaisha*g*ya-vastu, 18 vols. (Cf. Mahâv., Khandh. VI.)
19. „ (6). Mûlasarvâstivâda-ka*th*ina*k*îvara-vastu, 1 vol. (Cf. Mahâv., Khandh. VII.)

---

[1] The Sung-kao-sêng-ch'uan, chap. i (Nanjio's Catal., No. 1495); Chavannes, Memoirs, p. 193 seq.

He thus represented the whole texts of the Vinaya belonging to his own Nikâya, and founded a new school for the study of this branch of Buddhist literature in China. He died A.D. 713, in his seventy-ninth year. His life and works are greatly commended by the emperor Chung-tsung, his contemporary, in the preface to the Tripi/aka Catalogue.

NOTES ON SOME GEOGRAPHICAL NAMES.

I. The Country of the Naked People (裸人國).

I-tsing passed this island when he sailed for India. It is ten days distant in the north from Ka-cha, and it points to one of the smaller Nicobar Islands lying on the north side. The description given by I-tsing agrees with some of the later accounts of the islands, so much so, that we are fully justified in identifying his Lo-jên-kuo with the present Nicobar. The group is believed to be the Lanja-bálús or Lankhabálús of the Arab navigators in the ninth century, who recorded as follows: 'These islands support a numerous population. Both men and women go naked, only the women wear a girdle of the leaves of trees. When a ship passes near, the men come out in boats of various sizes and barter ambergris and cocoa-nuts for iron[1].' The description of Marco Polo in the thirteenth century does not agree so well as the above. He says: 'When you leave the island of Java (Java the less = Sumatra) and the kingdom of Lambri, you sail north about 150 miles, and then you come to two islands, one of which is called "Necuveran" (or Necouran)[2]. In this island they have no king nor chief, but live like beasts; and I tell you they all go naked, both men and women, and do not use the slightest covering of any kind. They are idolators; there are all sorts of fine and valuable trees, such as red sanders and Indian nuts and cloves and brazil and sundry other good spices[3].'

---

[1] Colonel Yule, Marco Polo, vol. ii, chap. xii, p. 289 seq.; Relation des Voyages faits par les Arabes et les Persans dans l'Inde et à la Chine, dans le ixe siècle de l'ère Chrétienne, by Reinaud, tom. i, p. 8.

[2] Rashiduddin uses the name of Nákváram (not Lákváram), which may be a less corrupted form of the name, perhaps allied with Nâga (Yule, Cathy, p. 96). This may be Hiuen Thsang's Nâlikera-dvîpa (Cocoa-nut Island), as Yule thinks.

[3] Yule, Marco Polo, vol. ii, chap. xii, p. 289; he says (p. 291): 'The natives now do not go quite naked; the men wear a narrow cloth, the women a grass girdle. Famous for the abundance of Indian nuts or cocoa, also betel and areca-nuts; and they grow yams, but only for barter.'

The above two accounts as well as I-tsing's certainly refer to one and the same island, though the latter does not mention any name for it. It seems to have passed under the name of 'Lo-jên-kuo,' just like 'Insulae Nudorum,' as marked in Prof. Lassen's map [1]. The group of the Nicobar Islands was called the 'Land of Râkshasas' in the history of T'ang (618–906) [2].

II. The Islands of the Southern Sea (南海諸洲).

One must not confound what I-tsing calls the Islands of the Southern Sea with what we know as the South Sea Islands. By the term 'Nan-hai' is meant the Southern China Sea or Malay Archipelago, and I-tsing includes in it Sumatra, Java, and the then known neighbouring islands. There are, he tells us [3], more than ten countries, and all are under the influence of Buddhism. The Islands of the Southern Sea are:—

1. P'o-lu-shi Island; Pulushih (婆魯師洲).
2. Mo-lo-yu Country; Malayu (末羅遊州)[4]: or, Shih-li-fo-shih Country; *Srîbhoga* (尸利佛逝國).
3. Mo-ho-hsin Island; Mahâsin (莫訶信洲).
4. Ho-ling Island, or Po-ling; Kaliṅga (訶陵洲).
5. Tan-tan Island; Natuna (呾呾洲).
6. P'ên-p'ên Island; Pem-pen (盆盆洲).
7. P'o-li Island; Bali (婆里洲).
8. K'u-lun Island; Pulo Condore (堀倫洲).
9. Fo-shih-pu-lo Island; Bho*g*apura (佛逝補羅洲).
10. A-shan Island, or O-shan (阿善洲).
11. Mo-chia-man Island; Maghaman (末迦漫洲).

There are many more islands, not mentioned here.

The above eleven islands are, according to the author, enumerated from the

---

[1] Karte von Alt-Indien zu Prof. Lassen's Indischer Alterthumskunde, Bonn, 1853.

[2] Book 222; see also the Essays on Indo-China, second series, vol. i, p. 207. Some Chinese accounts of the Andaman Islands (Chinese, Yen-t'o-mang; Japanese, An-da-ban) also agree with I-tsing's, e. g. nakedness, iron, &c.; they were, of course, the same race. Chao-ju-kua's description of it was given by Dr. Hirth, J. A. S. China, vol. xxii, Notes and Queries, p. 103.

[3] Page 10.

[4] Marco Polo, 'Malaiur' (chap. viii).

west, and following this order, we shall try to assign each its own place, as far as possible.

1. P'o-lu-shi (Pulushih).

P'o-lu-shi may at first seem to represent the Barussae Insulae, which are, in Lassen's map, a group of the Andaman Islands in the Indian Ocean. I-tsing, however, does not seem to be referring to an island so far away, when he says that two Korean priests went on board to the country of P'o-lu-shi, west of *S*rîbho*g*a, and there they fell ill and died [1]. Prof. Chavannes found in the History of T'ang (chap. ccxxii c) a country called 'Lang-po-lou-se,' which is said to be the western part of Shih-li-fo-shih, and identified with our P'o-lu-shi and Marco Polo's Ferlec (=Parlák), which is the present Diamond Point. His identification seems to be correct, as the country of *S*rîbho*g*a extended (see below) as far as the coast of Malacca during the T'ang dynasty (618–906).

2. Mo-lo-yu (Malayu), or Shih-li-fo-shih (*S*rîbho*g*a).

*S*rîbho*g*a seems to have been a very flourishing country in the time of our author, who went there twice and stayed some seven years (688–695), studying and translating the original texts, either Sanskrit or Pâli. In his works he uses the name 'Bho*g*a' or '*S*rîbho*g*a' indiscriminately [2]. It seems that the capital of this country was from the first called Bho*g*a, probably a colony of Java, and that, when the kingdom became great, and extended so far as Malayu, which seems to have been annexed or to have come spontaneously under the realm of the Bho*g*a prince, the whole country as well as the capital received the name of *S*rîbho*g*a. The change of the name Malayu to *S*rîbho*g*a must have happened just before I-tsing's time or during his stay there, for whenever he mentions Malayu by name he adds that 'it is now changed into *S*rîbho*g*a or Bho*g*a.'

As our author is the earliest writer who mentions these names, his account well deserves a careful examination. From his Record and Memoirs we gather the following facts:—

1. Bho*g*a the capital was on the river Bho*g*a, and it was the chief trading port with China, a regular navigation between it and Kwang-tung being conducted by a Persian merchant (p. xxviii, note 8).
2. The distance from Kwang-tung to Bho*g*a was about twenty days by a favourable wind, or sometimes a month (pp. xxx, xlvi).

---

[1] Chavannes, Memoirs, p. 36, §§ 8, 9, and note.

[2] About nine times *S*rîbho*g*a and twelve times Bho*g*a (the latter more often referring to the capital).

3. Malayu, which newly received the name of *S*rîbho*g*a, was fifteen days' sail from Bho*g*a the capital, and from Malayu to Ka-cha was also fifteen days,—so that Malayu lies just halfway between the two places (p. xlvi).
4. The *country* of *S*rîbho*g*a was east of Pulushih (p. xl).
5. The king of Bho*g*a possessed ships, probably for commerce, sailing between India and Bho*g*a (pp. xxx, xlvi).
6. The Bho*g*a king as well as the rulers of the neighbouring states favoured Buddhism (p. xxxiv).
7. The capital was a centre of Buddhist learning in the islands of the Southern Sea, and there were more than a thousand priests (p. xxxiv).
8. Buddhism was chiefly what is called the Hînayâna, represented for the most part by the Mûlasarvâstivâda School. There were two other schools newly introduced, besides the Sammitîya. A few Mahâyânists were in Malayu (=*S*rîbho*g*a the New) (pp. 10, 11).
9. Gold seems to have been abundant. I-tsing once calls *S*rîbho*g*a 'Chin-chou,' 'Gold Isle[1].' People used to offer the Buddha a lotus-flower of gold (p. 49). They used golden jars, and had images of gold (pp. 45, 46).
10. People wear Kan-man (a long cloth) (p. 12).
11. Other products were: pin-lang (Mal. pinang, Skt. pûga), nutmegs (*g*âtî), cloves (lavaṅga), and Baros-camphor (karpûra) (p. 48). They used fragrant oil (p. 45). People in these places make sugar-balls by boiling the juice of plants (or trees)[2], and the priests eat them at various hours, while the Indians make sugar from rice-grain, and in making 'stone-honey' they use milk and oil (Nanjio's Catal., No. 1131, book x, p. 72).
12. In the *country* of *S*rîbho*g*a, in the middle of the eighth month and in the middle of spring (second month), the dial casts no shadow, and a man standing has no shadow at noon. The sun passes just above the head twice a year (pp. 143, 144).
13. The language was known as 'Kun-lun' (Malay, not Pulo Condore) (p. l).

Shih-li-fo-shih, though not unknown[3], has not been satisfactorily described by the Chinese historians, while the name seems to have been very familiar to Buddhist writers subsequent to I-tsing. Fo-shih (=Bho*g*a) is mentioned in the History of T'ang (618–906) as being on the south shore of the Straits of Malacca,

---

[1] Chavannes, p. 181, note 2. Cf. Reinaud, Relation, tom. i, p. lxxv. Sumatra is famous for gold; Yule, Marco Polo, vol. ii, chap. ix, p. 268.

[2] Or, 'by boiling the wine (syrup) prepared from plants.'

[3] E.g. the History of T'ang, book 222 c.

and four or five days distant from Ho-ling (=Java)[1]. Next in the History of Sung (960–1279)[2] there is a country in the Southern Sea called San-bo-tsai (San-fo-ch'i), which is in all probability Shih-li-fo-shih (=*S*rîbhoga) of I-tsing, and its description runs as follows :—

'The kingdom of San-bo-tsai is that of the southern barbarians. It is situated between Cambodja (Chên-la) and Java (Shê-p'o), and rules over fifteen *different states*. Its products are rattan, red kino, lignum-aloes, areca-nuts (pin-lang), and cocoa-nuts. They use no copper cash, but their custom is to trade in all kinds of things *with gold* and silver. The weather is mostly hot, and in winter they have no frost or snow. The people rub their bodies *with fragrant oil*. This country does not produce barley, but they have rice, and yellow and green peas. They make wine from flowers, cocoa-nuts, pin-lang or honey[3]. They write with Sanskrit[4] characters, and the king uses his finger-ring as a seal; they know also Chinese characters; in sending tributes (to China) they write with them. With a favourable wind the distance from this country to Kwang-tung (Canton) is *twenty days*. Many family names there are "P'u." In 960, the king Shih-li-ku-ta-hia-li-tan[5] sent tribute to China. In 992, this country was invaded by Java. In 1003, two envoys from San-bo-tsai related that a Buddhist temple was erected in order to pray for the long life of the Chinese emperor, and the emperor gave to that temple a name and a bell specially cast for the purpose. In 1017, an envoy from thence brought bundles of Sanskrit books, folded between boards. In 1082, three envoys came to have an audience of the emperor, and presented *lotus-flowers of gold*[6] (Chin-lien-hua) containing pearls, *camphor-baros*, and sa-tien.'

The Descriptions of the Barbarians[7], compiled under the same dynasty (960–1279), gives a long account of San-bo-tsai (San-fo-ch'i), which agrees in the main with the above history of Sung. According to this book, San-bo-tsai lies right

---

[1] Book 436, p. 20, as quoted by Chavannes, p. 42.

[2] Book 489; some portion has been translated in the Notes on the Malay Archipelago, by W. P. Groeneveldt; see the Essays on Indo-China, second series, vol. i, p. 187.

[3] Cf. Crawfurd, Hist. of Ind. Arch., vol. i, p. 398.

[4] Fan (barbarian) may mean any foreign characters, but here it seems to mean Sanskrit; so also Mr. Groeneveldt, see loc. cit., p. 188.

[5] Something like *S*rî-kû*t*a-harit, or *S*rî-gupta-hârîta.

[6] In the History of Liang (502–556), Kandari, eastern coast of Sumatra, sent an envoy and presented a Fu-yan flower of gold, loc. cit., p. 187; Fu-yan is 'mallow,' but often used for 'lotus.'

[7] Chu-f'an-shih, by Chao-ju-kua. It is a rather rare book, and I am obliged to Dr. Rosthorn of Vienna for lending it to me. Dr. Hirth is going to translate it (J. R. A. S., Jan. 1896).

to the south of Ch'üan-chou [1]; the people put *a cotton cloth* (sarongs) round their bodies, and use a silk parasol. They wage war on water as well as on land, and their military organisation is excellent. When the king dies, the people shave their heads as a sign of mourning. Those who follow another in death burn themselves in the pile of fuel. This custom is called 'T'ung-shêng-ssŭ,' 'living and dying together [2].'

There is an image of the Buddha called the 'Mountain of Gold and Silver.' The king is commonly called the 'Essence of the Snake.' The crown *of gold* worn by him is very heavy, and the king alone can wear it. He who can wear it succeeds to the throne.

This country being on the sea contains the most important points for trade, and controls the incoming and outgoing ships of all the barbarians. Formerly they made use of iron chains to mark the boundary of the harbour.

Among *the fifteen states* which are mentioned in the same work as dependent on San-bo-tsai, Tan-ma-ling, Pa-lin-fêng, Sin-da, Lan-pi, and Lan-wu-li may be identified respectively with Tana-malayu (the next to Palembang in the list of Sumatran kingdoms in De Barros) [3], with Palembang, Sunda, Jambi, and Lambri [4], all indicating that they belonged to Sumatra.

We have another important and somewhat earlier account by the Arab travellers of the ninth century, who speak of the island of Sarbaza [5], which was then subject to the kingdom of Zábedj [6] (=Iabadiu of Ptolemy, about A.D. 150,

---

[1] Ch'üan-chou and its bay (=Zayton of Marco Polo), in Fu-kien, lie lat. 25° N., opposite to N. Formosa.

[2] Or, 'sharing the life and death of another.' In the island of Bali there are the customs of Satya and Bela, generally speaking, 'Burning one's body after another's death,' the origin of which will be no doubt Indian. Satya is the well-known Satee (Satî), and Bela is supposed by Mr. Friedrich to be the Sanskrit Velâ, 'sudden and easy death.'—Wilson. Bela in Balinese means 'dying with the man of higher rank' (a wife with her husband, a slave with his master, a subject with his prince). Our T'ung-shêng-ssŭ evidently represents the custom of Bela.

[3] Yule, Marco Polo, vol. ii, chap. viii, p. 263.

[4] Lamori, or Lambri, included Atchin, or was near it, where the Pole Star is not visible (Odoric); Yule, Cathy, p. 84; Marco Polo, vol. ii, chap. xi, p. 283, note; cf. p. 289, note.

[5] Reinaud, Relation des Voyages, tom. i, p. 93; ii, p. 48. Mr. Groeneveldt identified San-bo-tsai with Sarbaza (Essays, p. 187, note); the identification of these two names has since been fully discussed by Prof. P. A. van der Lith, Ajâib el Hind, pp. 247–253 (see Serboza, and Beal's communication about I-tsing's account of it).

[6] I do not think *Srîbhoga* is Zábedj, as in Chavannes, but Sarbaza, subject to Zábedj (= Java). Palembang was a Javanese colony, Yule, Marco Polo, vol. ii, p. 263. Zábedj of the Arabs represents some great monarchy then existing in the Malay Islands, probably in Java, the king of which was known to the Arabs by the Hindu title Mahârâja (Relation, tom. i, p. 93). Dabag, one of the islands of the seas, where the Syrian bishops, Thomas and others, were sent by the

Yavadi (Ya-p'o-t'i) of Fâ-hien, A.D. 414, and Yavada (Ya-p'o-ta) of the History of the First Sung, A.D. 420–478), which seems to be a corruption of Yavadvîpa.

Now, as to the position of San-bo-tsai (San-fo-ch'i), it is generally understood to be the present Palembang[1] in the southern part of Sumatra, and we have nothing to say against this general belief, while there are on the other hand many points which indicate the correctness of this identification. In all accounts, this great kingdom of the Southern Sea is about *twenty days distant*, or sometimes a month, from Kwang-tung. The capital is an *important trading port*, and the people seem to have embraced *Buddhism* for some time; and there are several points which show that they were *of Hindoo origin*. The country is, according to all accounts, rich *in gold*, and the gift of *golden lotus-flowers* is peculiar to the people. The accounts as to the use of *fragrant oil*, *kan-man* (sarongs), &c., and the *products* also, though common to the other islands, are in general agreement. Above all, the names, Shih-li-fo-shih (= *S*rîbho*g*a) of I-tsing, Sarbaza of the Arabs, and San-bo-tsai (= San-fo-ch'i) of the Chinese historians, are the weightiest proof, especially when we see that none of the accounts given under these three names contradict each other.

The constant hostility with Java mentioned in the Chinese history may account for the Arabs making Sarbaza dependent on Zábedj (=Java).

Now we are in a position to see that the capital and trading-port of San-bo-tsai, which went under the name of Chiu-chiang ('Old Port' or 'Old River') after 1397, was what I-tsing called the river Bho*g*a where he went on board ship to send a message to Kwang-tung, and it is therefore the river Palembang of our time; and what he calls the 'fortified city of Bho*g*a' (p. xxxiv) is the modern Palembang, while the whole *country* of *S*rîbho*g*a is much larger than the present province of Palembang. There were many *dependent states*.

The Yin-yai-shêng-lan, compiled A.D. 1416, makes these points perfectly clear. It says: 'Chiu-chiang is the same country which was formerly called San-bo-tsai; it is also called Palembang (P'o-lin-pang), and is under the supremacy of Java.

'From whatever place ships come, they enter the strait of Banka (P'êng-chia) at the Freshwater River (Tan-chiang, the Chinese name for the river Palembang),

---

patriarch Elias (Assemanni, iii, part i, p. 592), is probably a relic of the form Zábedj of the early narratives, used also by Al-Biruni. Ibn Khurdadbah and Adrisi use Jaba for Zábedj; Yule, Cathy, p. civ.

[1] The History of Ming (1368–1643), book 324: 'In 1397, San-bo-tsai was for the last time conquered by Java, and the name was changed into Chiu-chiang' ('Old Port' or 'Old River,' which is the name for Palembang up to the present day). See Essays, &c., p. 195.

and near a place with many pagodas built with bricks, after which the merchants go up the river in smaller craft, and so arrive at the capital.'

As to the name 'Malayu,' it seems to have existed for a long time. The Tan-ma-ling (Tana-malayu) of the Descriptions of the Barbarians (960–1279), and Malaiur of Marco Polo in the thirteenth century, are in all probability the remnants of the name Malayu, which was used before our author's time.

Unfortunately, however, *the city of Malaiur* of Marco Polo has not been satisfactorily traced. Colonel Yule says[1]: 'Probabilities seem to me to be divided between Palembang and its colony Singhapura (Palembang itself is a Javanese colony). Palembang, according to the commentary of Alboquerque, was called by the Javanese Malayo. The list of Sumatran kingdoms in De Barros makes Tana-malayu[2] the next to Palembang. On the whole I incline to this interpretation.'

This point, I think, becomes clear from the notice I have given above that the country Bhoga, i.e. Malayu, lay on the southern shore of Malacca; if Malaiur be Singapore, it must lie on the northern shore where, according to the same history, the country was called Lo-yüeh[3]. Further for the determination of the position of Śrîbhoga-Malayu, I-tsing furnishes us with important data (pp. 143, 144): 'In the Śrîbhoga *country* (not the capital), we see the shadow of the dial-plate become neither long nor short (i.e. "remain unchanged" or "no shadow") in the middle of the eighth month (=autumnal equinox), and at midday no shadow falls from a man who is standing on that day. So it is in the middle of spring (=vernal equinox)[4].' From this we can see that the *country* of Śrîbhoga covered

---

[1] Marco Polo, vol. ii, book iii, chap. viii, p. 263.

[2] The Descriptions of the Barbarians says that this country uses trays of gold and silver for barter.

[3] This is the place where Shinnio Taka-oka, an imperial prince of Japan, died, A. D. 881, on his way to India to search for the Law. He was twenty years in China learning Buddhism, whence he started for the West. The place of his death is supposed to be near Saigon in Champa or in Siam. If, however, our identification be right, it must have been in or near Singapore.

[4] We are perfectly justified in taking these two dates as the two equinoxes. A year is divided into four seasons, each of three months (1st, 2nd, and 3rd, Spring; 7th, 8th, and 9th, Autumn). Therefore, the 'Middle of Spring' is the middle of the second month. The Chinese names for the two equinoxes are accordingly Ch'un-fên[a] and Chiu-fên[b], 'Division of Spring' and 'Division of Autumn.' I-tsing uses Ch'un-chung[c], 'Middle of Spring,' which conveys the same idea as the above, and Pa-yüeh-chung[d], 'Middle of the eighth month' (when the calendar is exact, this will be the 'Middle of Autumn'). In the Japanese calendar, the autumnal equinox is marked

---

[a] 春分. [b] 秋分. [c] 春中. [d] 八月中.

the places lying on the Equator; and the whole country therefore must have covered the N.E. side of Sumatra from the southern shore of Malacca to the city of Palembang, extending at least five degrees, having the equatorial line at about the centre of the kingdom.

With the last conquest of 1379, the name San-bo-tsai, *S*rîbho*g*a, once a great monarchy, wellnigh disappears from the history, the new conquerors establishing themselves at the 'Old Port.' By this time Sumatra was perhaps thoroughly converted to Islam, though we find no traces of it in Marco Polo's travels at the close of the thirteenth century[1].

To better understand I-tsing's route viâ Bho*g*a and Malayu, the following extract from his work may be useful. He says[2]:—

'Wu-hing came to *S*rîbho*g*a after a month's sail. The king received him very favourably, and respected him as the guest from the Land of the Son of Heaven of the Great T'ang. He went on board the king's ship to the country of Malayu, and arrived there after fifteen days' sail. Thence he came to Ka-cha again after fifteen days. At the end of winter he changed ship and sailed to the west. After thirty days he reached Nâgapatana (now Negapatam, 10° 8′ N., 79° 9′ E.). From here he started again on board for the Si*m*hala Island; he arrived there after twenty days. He worshipped the Buddha's tooth there, and again sailed for the north-east. He came to Harikela, which is the eastern limit of E. India, and is a part of *G*ambudvîpa. He stayed there one year and went to Mahâbodhi, Nâlanda, and Tila*dh*a[3]. Near Tila*dh*a lived a teacher of logic, from whom Wu-hing learned the logical systems of *G*ina and Dharmakîrti, &c. He wanted to come back by the northern route. When I, I-tsing, was in India, I saw him off six *y*o*g*anas east of Nâlanda, and we said goodbye, each hoping to see the other once again in this world.'

Chiu-pa-yüeh-chung[a] (=middle of the eighth month of the old calendar). That I-tsing meant the equinoxes by those terms is certain from the following passage (p. 144), in which he clearly recognises the equinoxes by saying: 'the sun passes just above the head twice a year.' When we take *S*rîbho*g*a here as the capital, the result is as I have noted, p. 144, but our author expressly says the *country* of *S*rîbho*g*a, and we must not limit it to the capital, which he very often, if not always, calls simply Bho*g*a.

[1] The first Mohammedan king in Atchin began to reign A. D. 1205, probably the time of the introduction of Islam (Marco Polo, vol. ii, p. 269); the stimulus of conversion to Islam had not taken effect on the Sumatran States at the time of Polo, but it did so soon afterwards, and, low as they have now fallen, their power at one time was no delusion (loc. cit., p. 270).

[2] Cf. Chavannes, Memoirs, p. 144.

[3] See below, p. 184, note 2.

---

[a] 舊八月中.

3. Mo-ho-hsin (Mahâsin).

The only name which comes near to this is Masin of the Syrians. The bishops, Thomas, Taballaha, Jacob, and Denha, were ordained by the Syrian patriarch Elias, A.D. 1503, 'to go to the lands of the Indians and the islands of the seas which are between Dabag (Java, cf. Zábedj) and Sin (China) and Masin [1].' Mahâsin and Masin may be the present Bandjermasin on the southern coast of Borneo.

4. Ho-ling (Po-ling, Kaliṅga).

This name is no doubt Indian, probably taken from Kaliṅga on the coast of Coromandel [2]. According to the Chinese history [3], this is another name for Java, or a part of it [4], which had the earliest intercourse with Ceylon and perhaps also with the southern coasts of India. But the following statement of the Chinese historians, if correct, points to a place in the Malay Peninsula (6° 8′ N.):—

'In Ho-ling, when at the summer solstice a gnomon is erected 8 feet high, the shadow (at noon) falls on the south side and 2 feet 4 inches ($=2\frac{2}{5}$ feet) long [5].'

Thus—North latitude of the place of observation $=\phi$
Zenith distance of the sun . . . $=z$
North declination of the sun . . . $=\delta$

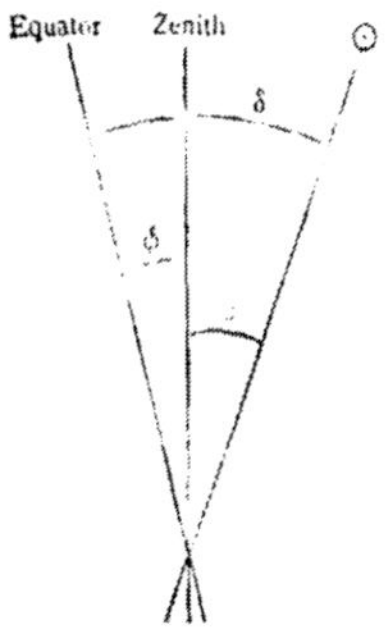

We have—

$$\tan z = \frac{2\frac{2}{5}}{8} = \frac{2\cdot4}{8}$$

$$\log \tan z = 9\cdot477$$

$$z = 16^\circ\ 7'$$

$$\delta = 23^\circ\ 5'$$

$$\phi = \delta - z = 23^\circ\ 5' - 16^\circ\ 7' = 6^\circ\ 8'\ \text{N.}$$

[There is clearly a confusion in the statement, if a place in Java (6° 8′ S.) be meant. I must leave the point unsettled, until I have examined all the parallel passages in the Chinese books.]

---

[1] Assemanni, iii, part i, p. 592; Yule, Cathy, p. ciii.

[2] See Lassen, Indische Alterthumskunde, ii, p. 1076; iv, p. 711.

[3] The New History of T'ang (618–906), book 222, part ii: 'Kaliṅga is also called Java;' book 197: 'Kaliṅga lies to the east of Sumatra.'

[4] Mr. Groeneveldt places it on the north coast (long. 111° E.), while Prof. Chavannes on the western part of Java (Memoirs, p. 42, note).

[5] The New History of T'ang (618–906), book 222, part ii; see also Essays on Indo-China, second series, vol. i, p. 139.

As to the names of Java, the oldest Iabadiu of Ptolemy (circa A.D. 150), Javadi of Fâ-hien (414), and Yavada of the history of the first Sung (420–478) probably represent Yavadvîpa [1], the 'country of millet.' The same name appears in some later accounts as Zábedj (the Arabs) or Dabag (the Syrians). Neither of them, however, seems to have been used in I-tsing's time, though the name 'Java' occurs later in the History of Sung (960–1279) [2] and in Marco Polo's travels [2] at the close of the thirteenth century; and till the present day. Now a word about the Javanese civilisation will not be out of place. Java in Fâ-hien's time (414) was already settled by the Hindus; he says: 'Heretic Brahmans flourish there, and the Buddha-dharma hardly deserves mentioning.' One of the old inscriptions from Pagaroyang in Sumatra, dated A.D. 656, calls the king Âdityadharma, the ruler of the 'first Java' (or Yava). Moreover some of the Sanskrit inscriptions found in Java seem to date from the fifth century and they are Vaishnava [3]. Buddhism was, according to I-tsing, chiefly the Hînayâna, but it is remarkable indeed that the ancient ruins of the temple of Kalasam (Kâlasa) and the Vihâra of Chandi Sari (dating from 779) indicate that the Buddhism here prevalent was a later form of the so-called Mahâyâna, as proved by the discovery of the images of Dhyâni Buddhas, Akshobhya, Ratnasambhava, Amitâbha or Amoghasiddha [4]. The Buddhist faith, whether the Hînayâna or Mahâyâna, possibly lasted till the propagation of Islam, as was the case with Sumatra.

5. Tan-tan (Natuna).
6. P'ên-p'ên (Pempen).
7. P'o-li (Bali).

According to Mr. Bretschneider [5], the islands of Natuna were called Tan-tan, which is probably I-tsing's Tan-tan. Tan-tan (Don-din) of the History of Sui (518–617) [6], which is supposed to be in Southern Siam or Northern Malacca, if correct, is not the island here mentioned, for our author knows that Siam

[1] Lassen, vol. iv, p. 482. Not the 'country of barley,' for Java and Sumatra never produce barley, but millet is there called Java (Essays, second series, vol. i, pp. 132, 137).

[2] Loc. cit., p. 141; the Descriptions of the Barbarians, of the same date, mentions Java, at one place Mahâ-Java; Yule, Marco Polo, vol. ii, chap. ix, p. 266; Sumatra is also 'Java the less.' Sumatra, perhaps Skt. Samudra, the 'sea.' Cf. Ch. Nan-hai.

[3] Prof. Kern, Over den invlow der Indische, Arab. en Europ. beschaving op de Volken van den Ind. Archipel., p. 7; Yule, Marco Polo, vol. ii, chap. ix, p. 267.

[4] Minutes of the Batavian Society, April, 1886; Essays, pp. 140, 141.

[5] The Knowledge possessed by the Ancient Chinese of the Arabs, &c., p. 19; see also Julien, Hiuen Thsang, tom. i, p. 451.

[6] Book 82; Essays, p. 205.

(Dvâravatî) is not one of the islands of the sea, and mentions no continental place among them. Besides, the identification of Dondin is by no means conclusive Colonel Yule marks Andaman Islands 'Dondin?'

P'ên-p'ên, I think, represents modern Pembuan on the southern coast of Borneo. This seems to be right, for I-tsing says that P'u-p'ên (=P'ên-p'ên) was situated in the north of Kaliṅga (N.E. Java)[1]. There is, however, a place named P'an-p'an[2] in the southern part of Siam, which may be the present P'un-p'in or Bandon. But this identification is again very doubtful.

P'o-li, probably the present Bali Island, E. of Java, was called P'ang-li by the Chinese[3], but the accounts given of this island are very scanty. Owing to the interesting discovery of the Kavi literature there, the name is now well known to us. I should refer my readers to Mr. R. Friedrich's Account of the Island of Bali (Essays on Indo-China, second series, vol. ii).

8. K'u-lun (K'un-lun, Pulo Condore).

K'u-lun is identical with K'un-lun, the Chinese name for Pulo Condore. The native name is Kon-non, Condore being a corruption of it. The Arab travellers of the ninth century call this group of islands by the name of Sundar[4] Fúlát, while Marco Polo names the same Sundur and Condur. It consists of one isle of twelve miles long, two of two or three miles, and some six other smaller isles, the largest being specially called Pulo Condore. According to I-tsing, the people of these isles alone are woolly-haired with black complexion (p. 12).

We often hear from Chinese writers of the 'slaves from K'un-lun[5],' later signifying slaves in general, without any reference to the land where they came from. The inhabitants in I-tsing's time appear to have been negroes; the commentator Kâsyapa also, quoting an early authority, describes them as if of a different race: 'K'u-lun, Ku-lun, and K'un-lun are one and the same country. In this country no ceremony or courtesy is observed. The people live by robbing and pirating. They are fond of man's flesh, like Râkshasas or some wicked demons.

'Their language is not correct. They differ from the other barbarians. They are skilled in diving in the water, and if they will, can stay all day long in the

---

[1] Chavannes, Memoirs, p. 77.
[2] The New History of T'ang (618–906), book 222[b]; Essays, p. 241.
[3] The Hsing-ch'a-shêng-lan (1436).
[4] Or, Sondor; Yule, perhaps Sanskrit Sundara, 'beautiful.'
[5] See, e.g. Essays, p. 257, note.

water without any suffering.' This peculiar people, however, seems to have embraced Buddhism to some degree, for I-tsing mentions a monastery with a peculiar clepsydra given by the king of the island (p. 145), and further says, though accidentally, that they praise Sanskrit Sûtras (p. 169). Two kinds of cloves grow there (p. 129).

One may well wonder why the K'un-lun language was prevalent in Sumatra or *S*rîbho*g*a in I-tsing's time[1]. One must not, however, be misled by the word K'un-lun, when used as the name of a language, for it has been for some time a general name for all the Southern Sea (cf. p. 11), and therefore the 'K'un-lun-yü' must mean the Malay language. The islands of Pulo Condore had nothing to do with it, though the inhabitants might have shared in speaking a dialect of the K'un-lun language.

9. Fo-shih-pu-lo (Bho*g*a-pura).

Fo-shih-pu-lo is no doubt Bho*g*a-pura in its original form, but it is not Bho*g*a, the capital of *S*rîbho*g*a, the modern Palembang. Mr. C. Baumgarten, writing to Prof. Max Müller (Feb. 20, 1883), says that Surabaja is the second city in Java, and that we still have a place there called Boja-nagara and the whole province Boja; and he adds that the seventh century seems to have been the golden age of Buddhism in Java[2]. This is probably I-tsing's Bho*g*apura, and further we have here perhaps the origin of the name *S*rî-Bho*g*a, for Palembang was certainly a colony of Java.

10. A-shan or O-shan.

11. Mo-chia-man (Maghaman).

A-shan may at first seem to represent Atchin in Sumatra. But this is not likely, for the original and correct form of Atchin seems to have been Atjeh or Ach'i, which was afterwards corrupted by Europeans into Atchin or Acheen.

As it comes after Bho*g*apura, it seems to be somewhere in the eastern part of Java near Bali; it may be the present Ajang[3].

As to Mo-chia-man, I have nothing to say about it, except that it may phonetically represent Maghaman or Maghavan. Ma-shê-wêng or Ma-yeh-wêng[4],

---

[1] Chavannes, Memoirs, p. 159; Koen-luen there.

[2] This is well founded; the temple of Kâlasa and the adjoining monumental Vihâra date from 779, as attested by a Sanskrit inscription in Old Nâgarî; besides, I-tsing's Record indicates the same.

[3] As to such names as Ajang, Bandjermasin, or Kota, I am not able to judge whether they are of ancient or modern origin.

[4] Essays, p. 202.

the position of which is not certain, may be the same island. It may have been meant for Madura.

III. Further India or Indo-China.

1. *S*rî-kshatra or -kshetra (Thare Khettara).
2. Lañkasu (Kâmalañkâ).
3. Dvâravatî (=Ayuthya) } in Siam.
4. Poh-nan (=Fu-nan) } in Siam.
5. Champa (originally *K*a*m*pâ).
6. Pi-king, in Annam.
7. Kwan-chou (probably near Tong-king).

The position of *S*rî-kshatra can be settled pretty satisfactorily. According to the Burmese, the king Mahâsambhava built a city called Thare Khettara in the sixtieth year of the Buddha [1], and established the Prome dynasty, which flourished 578 years. Some remains of the city are still to be seen a few miles to the east of the present town of Prome [2]. This account alone is enough to determine its position, and it is not to be placed in Upper Burma as in Vivien de Saint-Martin's map to Julien's Si-yu-ki. The identification with Silhat is therefore quite inadmissible. I-tsing's description roughly corresponds with the position of Thare Khettara; besides, we have the account of Hiuen Thsang, which we shall consider presently. According to I-tsing, Lañkasu is S.E. of *S*rî-kshatra, and Dvâravatî is E. of Lañkasu. Thus we have to give up the supposition that I-tsing's Dvâravatî may be that Dwârawati of the Burmese, which latter is, if Captain St. John is correct (p. 10 below), Old Tangu and Sandoway, for these lie in quite an opposite direction and cannot be S.E. of Prome. Hiuen Thsang's Dârapati or Dvârapati as well as our Dvâravatî no doubt represents Ayuthya (or Ayudhya), the ancient capital of Siam; this becomes clear from the fact that I-tsing's description of the positions of the countries counted from China's side actually ends with Poh-nan, E. Siam (p. 9). Hiuen Thsang [3] mentions Kar*n*a-suvar*n*a, Samata*t*a, and *S*rî-kshatra, and says: 'Going S.E. from *S*rîkshatra there is in the bay of the sea Kâmalañkâ; to E. of this, Dvârapati (or Dârapati). Further to E., there is Îsânapura [4]; to E. of this, Mahâ*k*a*m*pâ, and to S.W. of Mahâ*k*a*m*pâ, Yen-mo-lo-

[1] The Burmese calendar places the Buddha's death in 544 B.C.; A.B. 60 is therefore B.C. 484, if corrected, about B.C. 424.

[2] Asiatic Researches, vol. xx, p. 171.

[3] Julien, Mémoires, liv. x, pp. 82, 83; Beal, Life, p. 132.

[4] Îsânapura was very successfully identified with Cambodja by Prof. Chavannes (p. 58); in

chou' (probably 'Yavanadvîpa,' meaning Sumatra). The reader will see that I-tsing's Laṅkasu is here Kâmalaṅkâ, Poh-nan, Îsânapura, and Champa (p. 12), Mahâ*k*am*p*â; and we know from our Record that Pi-king (Turan or Hue) is N. of Champa, and that still further north one reaches Kwan-chou (near Tong-king) after a month's journey on foot, or five or six tides, if aboard ship. Thus all these statements are pretty clear, and in harmony with one another[1].

IV. India and Ceylon.

I-tsing calls India in general the West (Si-fang), the Five *Countries* of India (Wu-t'ien), Âryade*s*a (A-li-ya-t'i-sha), Madhyade*s*a (Mo-t'i-t'i-sha), Brahmarâsh*t*ra (Po-lo-mên-kuo), or *G*ambudvîpa (Chan-pu-chou). 'Hindu (Hsin-tu)[2],' he says, 'is the name used only by the northern tribes (p. 118), and the people of India themselves do not know it. Indu (Yin-tu) is by some derived from the name of the moon, Indu (Hiuen Thsang, Mém. ii, 56), but it is not a proper name.' Hindu in Persian and Indo in Greek were perhaps corrupted from Sindhu, but it is curious that the Chinese should have known both forms of the name. Indu (Yin-tu) as the name of India came to be generally used in China from Hiuen Thsang's time, while T'ien-chu and Chüan-tu (both from Sindhu) are probably as old as the introduction of Buddhism into China (A.D. 67). The name for Ceylon is, in the Record, Si*m*hala (Sêng-ho-lo) Island (or Shih-tzŭ-chou, Lion Island), or occasionally Ratnadvîpa (Pao-chu, Jewel Isle).

As to his travels in India, he may have visited many a place, more than thirty countries in all, according to the Biography (p. xxxvii, note), but nothing certain

---

626 A.D. the king of Cambodja was Î*s*ânavarman, according to M. Aymonier, and in perfect conformity with this, the History of T'ang states that the king of Cambodja, Î*s*âna, a Kshatriya, in the beginning of the Chêng-kuan period (627–649) conquered Fu-nan (E. Siam) and took the territory. I-tsing may be referring to this king when he says that a wicked king destroyed Buddhism in Fu-nan (p. 12). See, however, Crawfurd, Journal of the Embassy to the Court of Siam, p. 615; Siam first received Buddhism in 638.

[1] Mr. Beal's identifications widely differ from ours, and they are not, according to our opinion, tenable when we compare them with the original. Fu-nan, for instance, is transcribed 'Annam' (Life, p. xxxiv), Lin-i (= Champa) is Siam (Life, p. 133), and Pi-king, owing to a misprint, is read by him Shang-king, and identified with Saigon. According to Beal, I-tsing speaks of himself as interpreting the language of Pulo Condore (Life, pp. xv, note, xxxi); it is not I-tsing, but Ta-ts'in, who is said to have been skilled in the K'un-lun language (Malay), Chavannes, p. 159, § 56. I-tsing was thirty-seven years of age, but, according to Beal, he started with thirty-seven priests (Life, p. xv).

[2] The text has 'Hsi,' but I-tsing directs that it should be pronounced by taking the first and last parts of *Hs*ü-l*in*, i.e. 'Hsin.' 呬 = 哂 used for 'hin' of Ma*hin*da.

can be gathered from his own writings. The places which he says definitely he visited are very few[1], i.e. Kapilavastu, Buddhagayâ (in Magadha), Varâ*n*asî (Benares), *S*râvastî (N. Ko*s*ala), Kânyakub*g*a (Kanoj), Râ*g*agr*i*ha (ten years in Nâlanda), Vai*s*âlî, Ku*s*inagara, and Tâmralipti (Tamluk). I doubt whether he visited Ceylon; although he often mentions it, his description does not appear to be that of an eye-witness. So it is in the case of Lâ*t*a[2], Sindhu, Valabhî, Udyâna, Khara-*k*ar, Kustana (Khoten), Ka*s*mîra, and Nepâla. Besides the above, he mentions Tibet (T'u-fan), Persia (Po-la-ssŭ), the Tajiks (Ta-shih and To-shih)[3], Tukhâra (T'u-ho-lo), Sûli (Su-li), the Turks (Tü-chüeh), and accidentally Korea (Kau-li, Kukkute*s*vara).

The Date of I-tsing's Work.

If I-tsing had expressly stated when he came back to *S*rîbho*g*a, we should have had no difficulty at all in fixing the date of his work. That point, however, is left entirely blank. We shall try to find out a date which may come nearest the mark, if not quite correct, chiefly resting on the foregoing data of his life and travels.

First of all the place where he compiled his work must be in *S*rîbho*g*a (Palembang in Sumatra)[4] as he says towards the end of chap. xxxiv. His return from India to this place must be later than A.D. 685[5], when he was still near Nâlanda, and, as he says that he already passed four years in *S*rîbho*g*a before he wrote chap. xxxiv, his Record cannot be in any case earlier than A.D. 689 (685 + 4 = 689), even if we suppose that he returned there immediately after his parting with Wu-hing near Nâlanda. Further, he uses throughout the new dynastic name[6] adopted A.D. 690 by the Usurper Queen (reigned A.D. 684–704); this shows clearly that

---

[1] The Mûlasarvâstivâda-sa*m*yuktavastu (Nanjio's Catal., No. 1121), chap. xxxviii, p. 85 (J.), and chap. xxxvi, p. 76[b].

[2] See p. 137, note 1, and p. 217.

[3] This is generally the name for the Mohammedan Arabs in Chinese. I-tsing says that the Tajiks occupied the way to Kapi*s*a; Memoirs, vol. i, fol. 4[b]; Chavannes, p. 25.

[4] Not 'in Ceylon' as Messrs. Shimaji and Ikuta suppose in their Short History of Buddhism in the Three Kingdoms (India, China, and Japan), 1890, Tokio. Evidence, if any, is too weak to prove that I-tsing visited Ceylon.

[5] This date is in the Chinese text 'the first year of the Chui-kung period,' being the second year of the Usurper Queen, though she still used the dynastic name T'ang, which she changed in A.D. 690 into Chou, Chavannes, p. 10.

[6] Chou, p. 214 below; Chou-yun and Chou-i, p. 7; the Great Chou, p. 118; Chou-yü, p. 148; lastly, in his text, not in his notes, the Great Chou, p. 214 (note 3). See the Chinese text, respectively, vol. i, fol. 3[a]; vol. iii, fol. 12[a]; vol. iv, fols. 2[b], 27[a].

our Record cannot be earlier than A.D. 690. It will be remembered that he sent this Record on the fifteenth day of the fifth month of A.D. 692, and we must therefore find the date of his whole composition within the period A.D. 690–692. Let us now examine the chapters which we can make use of for our purpose.

1. I-tsing's *Introduction*, as is usual with us, must be the latest, i.e. when all the chapters were ready, for he says in it that he sends home this very Record in forty chapters[1].

2. Chap. xviii. He accidentally says that he toiled during two decades of years[2]. This chapter must therefore have been written in about 691 (671–691=20; A.D. 671, having only one month left).

3. Chap. xxviii. He was 'more than twenty years abroad.' This brings us again to A.D. 691. To be quite safe, we will put down A.D. 691–692, because it is '*more*' than twenty years[3].

4. His Memoirs must be later than the contents of our Record (except the *Introduction*), for the former quotes the latter twice by name[4]. But the *conclusion* of the Memoirs must be at about the same time as the *Introduction* of the Record, for both mention the Memoirs in two vols. and the Record in four vols. (forty chapters)[5], one by the other. In other words, the finishing up of the two works must be at about the same time.

Now it will not be very difficult to see that about seven folios of a *Supplement*[6] to the Memoirs have been written about the same time, for it is not likely that he would write a *Supplement* before the text. May it be an addition at a later date? According to my opinion, it cannot be later than A.D. 692, because he must have sent it with the texts. We see in the *Supplement* that a priest, Tao-hung, who was ordained in his twentieth year, soon after met I-tsing in Kwang-tung, and followed the party to Srîbhoga, A.D. 689, was twenty-three years of age[7] (A.D. 689–692=3) when our author wrote the supplementary portion.

From this it is clear that he wrote it[8], or at any rate, he sent it at the same

[1] Page 18 below.

[2] Page 95 below; for the impossibility of taking it as 'two dozen,' see note at the end, p. 220.

[3] Page 135 below. Compare p. 176, note 4.

[4] Chavannes, p. 88, note 1; p. 92, note 1, chap. 30 of our Record is quoted.

[5] Page 18 below; Chavannes, p. 160.

[6] Chavannes, p. 161; about twenty-four pages in French.

[7] Chavannes, pp. 185, 187. See p. xxxvi above.

[8] It is true that there is a portion which I-tsing might have added afterwards, but this part can be clearly seen in the text, as it is a general remark, not coming under any name; see Chavannes, p. 189, six lines from the bottom, beginning with 'Ces quatre hommes.'

time with the other texts. Thus the *Introduction* to the Record, the Memoirs and its *Supplement* will have to be referred to about the same time, the last mentioned being the last composed. Observe that I-tsing reckons three years from the latter half of A.D. 689 till the fifth month of A.D. 692.

5. Now, towards the end of chap. xxxiv—the most important of all chapters—he says that he remained over four years in *S*rîbhoga, since his return from India, the date of which we do not know. Only one year added to the period which I-tsing reckons as three years (A.D. 689–692) will give us the year of his second visit to *S*rîbhoga, i.e. A.D. 688[1] (he was in Bhoga A.D. 689 as we have seen). Thus the date of chap. xxxiv must fall in 691 or 692; the safest limit will be A.D. 691–692, the result being the same as that of chap. xxviii, &c.

All the evidence that can be adduced from the text points thus to the correctness of the date A.D. 691–692, strictly speaking A.D. 691 to the fifth month of A.D. 692, as the time when I-tsing wrote his Record. Resting on this result we can place with certainty the death of *G*ayâditya[2], joint author with Vâmana of the Kâ*s*ikâv*ri*tti, in A.D. 661–662, and that of Bhart*ri*hari[3], contemporary of Dharmapâla, in A.D. 651–652.

TABLES OF SEVERAL LITERARY MEN AND BUDDHIST TEACHERS OF INDIA, WITH THEIR DATES AND SUCCESSIONS, MADE FROM THE RECORD OF BUDDHIST PRACTICES (A.D. 691–692) OF I-TSING (A.D. 671–695 ABROAD; 673–687 IN INDIA).

(*Those in Italics are not given in I-tsing's text.*)

I. (Chap. xxxii, pp. 156–157.)

The Sârdha*s*ataka-Buddhastotra (150 verses, Nanjio's Catal., No. 1456).

1. Composed by Mât*riketa*. *In Târanâtha's Geschichte des Buddhismus, p. 89, Mât*riketa *is said to have lived about the time of Bindusâra, son of* K*andragupta.*
2. Admired by Asaṅga } *Brothers and contemporaries.*
3. and by Vasubandhu, }
4. Some verses were added by *G*ina. *Two of his works have been translated by Paramârtha, who worked in China* A.D. 557–569 (*Nanjio's Catal., Nos.* 1172, 1255).

---

[1] The time of the arrival of the ship was the first or second month of the year, see above, p. xxxiv. We shall not here speak of three months' stay in China after his chance return, for we are not sure as to whether he reckoned the period; it will not, I think, make any difference in the year.

[2] Page 176 below. [3] Page 180 below.

5. A further addition by *S*âkyadeva of the Deer Park (at Benares).
6. Translated by I-tsing *while in the Nâlanda College* (*Nanjio*), about A. D. 675–685. Sent home A. D. 692 (p. 166).

II. (I-tsing's Introductory Chapter, p. 14.)

The following names are to be taken each as independent, not one after another.

α. (I-tsing's Introductory Chapter, p. 14.)

a. Asoka, 100 or more years after the Buddha's Nirvâ*n*a. (*This mistake arises either from confounding Dharmâsoka with Kâlâsoka or from taking the period* (118) *between the Second Council and Asoka as that between the Nirvâna and Asoka.*)

β. (Chap. xxxii, pp. 163–166.)

b. A*s*vaghosha.
1. His poetical songs.
2. Sûtrâlaṅkâra*s*âstra (*translated into Chinese* A. D. 405, *Nanjio's Catal.*, *No.* 1182).
3. Buddha*k*aritakâvya (*translated* A. D. 414–421, *Nanjio's Catal.*, *No.* 1351).
4. *His Life was translated by Kumâragîva* A. D. 401–409, *Nanjio's Catal.*, *No.* 1460.

c. Nâgâr*g*una. His Suh*ri*llekha.
1. Addressed to a king of S. India (Ko*s*ala), *S*âtavâhana (or Sadvâhana), whose private name was *G*etaka.
2. *Translated into Chinese* A. D. 431 *and* 434 (*Nanjio's Catal.*, *Nos.* 1464 and 1440), and by I-tsing, while abroad. Sent home A. D. 692 (p. 166).
3. *His Life was translated by Kumâragîva* A. D. 401–409, *Nanjio's Catal.*, *No.* 1461.

d. *S*îlâditya.
1. *G*âtakamâlâ, by literary men living under him. (*Ârya Sûra's may be one of them.*)
2. *G*îmûtavâhana-nâ*t*aka (= Nâgânanda), composed and popularised by himself.
3. *Patron of Hiuen Thsang* (A. D. 629–645). *Death of Sîlâditya in about* 655 A. D. (*my note, p.* 163, *and Chavannes, Memoirs, p.* 19, *note*).

γ. (Chap. xxvii, pp. 127–128; cf. p. 131, note; pp. 222–223.)

e. An epitomiser of the Eight Books of Medicine (Âyur-veda), at about I-tsing's time.

III. (Chap. xxiv, pp. 170–180.)

Grammatical Works.

1. The Si-t'an-chang (or Siddha-composition), for beginners.
2. The Sûtra of Pâ*n*ini.
3. The Book on Dhâtu (*a Dhâtupâ*tha).
4. The Book on the Three Khilas (Ash*t*adhâtu, Wen-ch'a, U*n*âdi-sûtra).

5. The Vritti-sûtra (Kâsikâ-vritti).
   By *Gayâditya*, died nearly thirty years before the date of I-tsing's Record (A. D. 691-692) = A. D. 661-662.
   Contemporary of Vâmana, who was joint author of the Kâsikâ.
6. The *Kûrni* (*Mahâbhâshya*), [Commentary on the above Vritti, *sic!*]
   By Patañgali.
7. The Bhartrihari-sâstra, Commentary on the *Kûrni*.
   By Bhartrihari, died forty years before the date of I-tsing's Record = A. D. 651-652.
   Contemporary of Dharmapâla.
8. The Vâkya-discourse (*Vâkyapadîya*).
   By Bhartrihari.
9. The Pei-na (a Bedâ-vritti).
   The Commentary in prose by Bhartrihari, } contemporaries.
   The Sloka portion by Dharmapâla, }
   The latter was teacher of Sîlabhadra, who was too old to teach Hiuen Thsang (about A. D. 635), *and appointed Gayasena to instruct him.*
   The translations of four works attributed to Dharmapâla all date A. D. 650-710, *see Nanjio's Catal., Appendix* i, 16.

The Result.

a. *The above makes all the four authors contemporaries, who must all have lived about* A. D. 600-660:—(1) *Gayâditya*, (2) *Vâmana*, (3) *Bhartrihari*, (4) *Dharmapâla*.

b. *Dharmapâla, head of the Nâlanda College, must have died earlier than Gayâditya and Bhartrihari, because he does not seem to have been alive when Hiuen Thsang went to Nâlanda*, A. D. 635, *Sîlabhadra having succeeded Dharmapâla*.

N. B.—As to a discussion about all these grammatical works, I should refer my readers to Prof. Max Müller's 'India, what can it teach us?' pp. 338-349, and the corresponding pages in the German translation by Prof. Cappeller (above, p. xviii, note 3).

IV. (Chap. xxxiv, pp. 181-184.)

Famous Buddhist Nâgas of India and Srîbhoga.

a. Of an early age (before A. D. 400)[1].

1. Nâgârguna.
2. Deva, *Ârya Deva* or *Kâna Deva*.
3. Asvaghosha.

   These three are generally made to be contemporaries of Kanishka, who is said to have lived in the first century.

---

[1] I do not mean by putting down these limits that every individual under *a, b, c, d* lived at these dates, but I wish to show the fair limits we can put from the present state of our knowledge to the terms, 'early age,' 'middle ages,' and 'late years.'

b. In the middle ages (about A. D. 450–550)[1].

1. Vasubandhu, } *Brothers.* } *Contemporaries* (*Hiuen Thsang, Mémoires*, iv, 223).
2. Asaṅga,
3. Saṅghabhadra.
4. Bhavaviveka. *Contemporary of Dharmapâla* (*Hiuen Thsang, Mémoires*, x, 111–113).

c. Of late years (about A. D. 550–670).

1. *G*ina (in Logic). *Composed a work on Logic in Andhra* (*Hiuen Thsang, Mémoires*, x, 106). (*He seems to have lived earlier than* 550; *cf.* I, 4 *above.*)
2. Dharmapâla. Contemporary of Bhart*ri*hari, who died A. D. 651–652. *Must have died before* A. D. 635; *see above*, III.
3. Dharmakîrti (in Logic). *Referred to in the Vâsavadattâ* (*p.* 235), *and in the Sarvadarsana-saṅgraha* (*p.* 24, *Cowell*). *Contemporary of King Sroṅ-tsan-gam-po* (A. D. 629–698), *Wassilief, p.* 54.
4. *S*îlabhadra. *Pupil of Dharmapâla* (*Hiuen Thsang, Mémoires*, viii, 452).
5. Si*m*ha*k*andra. *A fellow-student of Hiuen Thsang* (*Vie*, v, 219, 261; 218), Life, v, 190.
6. Sthiramati. *Referred to in a Valabhî grant* (*Ind. Ant.*, 1877, *p.* 91; 1878, *p.* 80), *and Hiuen Thsang, Mémoires*, xi, 164, *in Valabhî*. *Pupil of Vasubandhu* (*Wassilief, p.* 78).
7. Gu*n*amati (in Dhyâna). *In Valabhî together with Sthiramati* (*Mémoires*, xi, 164), *and in Nâlanda* (*Mémoires*, ix, 46).
8. Pra*gñ*âgupta (in refutation). *Teacher of the Sammitîya and contemporary of Hiuen Thsang* (*Hiuen Thsang, Vie*, iv, 220; *Life*, iv, 159).
9. Gu*n*aprabha (in Vinaya). *His pupil, Mitrasena, was ninety years old, and taught Hiuen Thsang* Sâstras (*Vie*, ii, 109; *Life*, ii, 81). *Guru of Srîharsha, and pupil of Vasubandhu* (*Wassilief, p.* 78).
10. *G*inaprabha. Teacher of Hiuen Chao, who was in Nâlanda about A. D. 649, Chavannes, Memoirs, p. 17.

d. Those mentioned as I-tsing's contemporaries or personal acquaintances (all were alive A. D. 670–700).

I-tsing's teachers {
1. *Gñ*âna*k*andra (in the Tila*dh*a Vihâra, *near Râgagriha*). *Mentioned as a priest in Nâlanda* (*Hiuen Thsang, Mémoires*, ix, 47).
2. Ratnasi*m*ha (in the Nâlanda Vihâra, *near Râgagriha*). Teacher of Hiuen Chao, who was in Nâlanda about A. D. 649, Chavannes, Memoirs, p. 18.
3. Divâkaramitra (in E. India).
4. Tathâgatagarbha (in S. India).
5. *S*âkyakîrti (in *S*rîbhoga, *in Sumatra*).

6. Râhulamitra (chief of the priests in E. India; thirty years old in I-tsing's time, p. 63). *He is mentioned in Târanâtha's Buddhisms, p.* 63; *his favourite Ratnakûta-sûtra also belongs to the same period.*
7. *K*andra (in E. India; author of a dramatic poem on Vessantara [Visvantara = Sudâna], p. 164; he was still alive when I-tsing was in India (A. D. 673–687), p. 183).

[1] See note on preceding page.

Notes.

a. We have not made any progress in fixing the dates of 1, 2, and 3. But that these three lived at about the same time and before A.D. 400 seems to be quite certain. Hiuen Thsang (645) places them at one and the same period (Mémoires, xii, 214). Deva was a pupil of Nâgârguna (Life, ii, 76; so also the Tibetan), and both contemporaries of Kanishka (Schiefner, Ratnadharmarâga's Work, Mém. Acad. St. Pét., 1848). Asvaghosha and Pârsva lived in Kanishka's time (Wassilief, Buddhismus, p. 52, note). The Chinese Samyukta-ratna-pitaka-sûtra (No. 1329, vol. vi, dated A. D. 472) makes Asvaghosha Bodhisattva, the physician Karaka, and Mâthara, a great minister, the contemporaries of Kan-dana-kanita (= Kanishka), king of the country of Yueh-chi; and again, in the Record of the Twenty-three Patriarchs, Fu-fa-tsang-yin-yuen-king (No. 1340, vol. v, p. 13ª, dated 472), Karaka, Asvaghosha, and Mâthara appear under Kanishka. The dates of the translations alone show us that the three (Karaka, Asvaghosha, Mâthara) must have lived before A. D. 400; besides, the lives of Asvaghosha, Nâgârguna, and Deva were translated A. D. 405 by Kumâragîva, who left India A. D. 383. Cf. the date of the translations of Asvaghosha's Buddhakarita and Sûtrâlankâra, and Nâgârguna's Works (II. *b.* above). Further the 1, 2, 3 are said to have lived after 400 years of the Nirvâna, and Kanishka is believed to have reigned in the first century of our era, and his second successor Vâsudeva about A. D. 178. So far as our knowledge goes, nothing is against making them contemporaries of Kanishka. Nâgârguna was a contemporary of Sâtavâhana or Sâlivâhana (p. 159, note). Cf. Prof. Cowell, Buddhakarita (text), p. v. According to Prof. Kielhorn, Karaka must be placed before the middle of the seventh century (Ind. Ant., vol. xii, p. 227). Asvaghosha is perhaps the oldest, then Nâgârguna and Deva. The last is Ârya Deva (Schiefner, Lebensbeschreib., 331), called Kâna Deva because he was one-eyed (Record of the Twenty-three Patriarchs, vol. vi); or Nîlanetra, because he had two spots like eyes on his cheeks; but his real name was Kandrakîrti (J. A. S., Bengal, 1882, p. 94; also Nanjio, App. i, 4).

b, c. *b* and *c* cannot be separated by a long period, for b^1 is a contemporary of c^2; c^7, c^9 are pupils of b^1, while c^3, c^6 are pupils of b^2 (according to the Tibetan). c^4, c^5, c^8 are all contemporaries of Hiuen Thsang, and c^3 is said to have lived at the time of Sron-tsan-gam-po, who sent envoys to India A.D. 632. c^1, c^2 are perhaps older than the others; Hiuen Thsang styles them 'Bodhisattvas,' and they lived probably early in the seventh century. Some of the others may have lived to the time of I-tsing's arrival, A. D. 673. As to the name Sthiramati, see my note to p. 181 at the end; for Dharmakîrti (Fa-chan), see Nanjio's Catal., App. i, 19, p. 374 (not Dharmayasas; cf. Vimalakîrti, Wu-keu-chan). Burnouf tried to identify Gunamati with Gunaprabha, but, according to our Record, the one is a teacher in Dhyâna, the other in Vinaya, and they seem to be quite different persons. For the dates of the translated works of those under *b, c,* see Nanjio's Catal., App. i. We cannot place Vasubandhu and Asanga much later than 500, for the translations of their works date from 509 and 531 respectively. In *c, G*ina must be much earlier than the rest, see above, I. 4.

d. Gñânakandra must have lived from a period earlier than 650, for he was known by Hiuen Thsang; the same is the case with Ratnasimha. It is difficult to draw a line between *c* and *d*; many of them must have been contemporaries. I-tsing seems to distinguish those dead (*c*) from those still living (*d*). For Sâkyakîrti, see Nanjio's Catal., App. i, 54, p. 378 (not Sâkyayasas; I-tsing has translated his teacher's work).

THE TEXT.

The text of our Record is very corrupt, as Mr. Kasawara told us in 1882[1], but we must remember that since then the new edition of the Chinese Buddhist books has been completed, and a copy of it was sent to the Bodleian Library for the use of European scholars. This Japanese edition is excellent, being based on a careful collation of the five different editions brought out in China, Korea, and Japan. Its arrangement is more convenient for the reader than that of the older; the print is clear, as it was executed by the modern movable type.

Above all, the sentences are accurately punctuated, and the various readings are found in the notes. It may safely be regarded as the standard edition of the Chinese Pi*t*aka, and Japanese Buddhists may be proud of the service they have rendered in this field of Chinese literature[2]. Our Record, in particular, gives evidence of a careful study and collation, shedding light on several passages hitherto unintelligible. I-tsing's works as well as the whole canon were preserved in MS. only, and not printed till A. D. 972[3]. Thus we may safely say that our Record, which is now found with the Pi*t*aka, existed in MS. for about 280 years before it came down to us as a printed text. This fact may account for several minor points of difference in the existing editions. But there are some passages missing which we cannot well ascribe to the copyist's mistakes. They may have been struck out by I-tsing himself after his return home; it is certain, however, that the original copy which was sent home from abroad contained them all.

Among others, there is a passage relating to the Sanskrit alphabet quoted in some early works. In the Siddha-tzŭ-chi, 'Record of the Siddha-letters,' compiled by a Chinese priest, Chi-kwang (A. D. 800), the author says: 'I-tsing said that among the twelve finals (a â, i î, u û; e ai, o au, a*m* a*h*) the first three of the former three pairs (a, i, u) are short, while the second three of the same (â, î, û) are long, and that, of the latter three pairs (e ai, o au, a*m* a*h*), the first three (e, o, a*m*) are long (sic), while the second three (ai, au, a*h*) are short (sic).'

A Japanese book called 'Sittan-zô,' or 'Siddha-ko*s*a' (A. D. 880), gives the above quotation in its full form, and shows that it once formed a part of I-tsing's Record. (See Bodl. Jap. 15, vol. v, fol. 6.)

義淨寄歸傳云. अ 惡, आ 痾, इ 益, ई 伊, उ 屋, ऊ 烏,

---

[1] Max Müller, 'India, what can it teach us?' 1883, p. 349.

[2] It is to be hoped that an accurate comparative catalogue will be drawn up; the arrangement is very different from that of the India Office copy, and several books found in the new are wanting in the old.

[3] See Nanjio's Catalogue, p. xxii.

ऋ頡里,(是一字), ॠ蹊梨,(是一字), ऌ里, ॡ離, ए翳, ऐ藹, ओ汙, औ奧; अं菴, अः阿. क脚, ख佉, ग伽, घ嚧, ङ我; च者, छ捙, ज社, झ縒, ञ喏; ट吒, ठ詑, ड荼, ढ椗, ण拏; त哆, थ他, द挖, ध但, न娜; प跛, फ叵, ब婆, भ嘙, म麽. य野, र囉, ल攞, व婆, श捨, ष灑, स娑, ह訶; ळ藍, क्ष乞叉. (末後二字不入其數.) 惡等十六皆是聲韵, 向餘字之上配之. 凡一一之字便有十六之別, 猶若四聲於一字上有平上去入四番之異. 脚等之二十五字, 並下八字, 總有三十三字, 名初章. 皆須上聲讀之不可看其字而爲平去入也. 又云十二聲者謂是क脚, का迦(上短下長); कि枳, की雞(姜移反; 上短下長); कु矩, कू俱(上短下長); के雞, कै計(上長下短); को孤, कौ告(上長下短); कं甘, कः箇(兩聲俱短; 箇字用力出聲). 呼佉等十二聲並效此.

此十二字皆可兩兩相隨呼之, 仍須二字之中看字註而取短長也(抄).

‘ It is said in the Record sent home by I-tsing: a, â, i, î, u, û, *ri*, *rî*, *lri*, *lrî*, e, ai, o, au; a*m*, a*h*. Ka, kha, ga, gha, *n*a; *k*a, *kh*a, *g*a, *gh*a, *ñ*a; *t*a, *th*a, *d*a, *dh*a, *n*a; ta, tha, da, dha, na; pa, pha, ba, bha, ma. Ya, ra, la, va, *s*a, sha, sa, ha; lla*m*, ksha. (The last two are not included in the number of *the alphabet*.) The first sixteen, a to a*h*, are final sounds [meaning vowels], and these are to be distributed among the other letters [consonants]. Each letter *of the alphabet* [consonant], therefore, produces sixteen different *sounds* when combined, just as in Chinese a character has four different tones, even (p‘ing), rising (shang), sinking (ch‘ü), and entering (ju).

'The twenty-five letters, ka to ma, and the last eight, ya to ha, thirty-three in all, are called the "first composition;" all these must be pronounced according to the Chinese "rising" (shang) tone, in spite of the Chinese equivalents being other tones, such as "even," "sinking," or "entering." Further, what are called the "twelve sounds" [probably "Dvâdasa-aksharâni"] are ka, kâ (the first short, the second long); ki, kî (the first short, the second long); ku, kû (the first short, the second long); ke, kai (the first long, the second short); ko, kau (the first long, the second short); ka*m*, ka*h* (both are short); ka*h* is obtained by pronouncing the Chinese ka emphatically. The "twelve sounds" of kha, &c., are pronounced after the above manner. These twelve letters [meaning syllables] are to be pronounced two by two in succession [ka, kâ; ki, kî; &c.], and of these pairs one should distinguish a short from a long, guiding oneself by the note I have given under each pair (quoted).'

The Chinese characters here given well accord with those used in the Record, with the exception of a very few, and the quotation contains nothing whatever contrary to the passages in the existing Record. In chap. xxxiv, under the Si-t'an-chang, he says (p. 171): 'There are forty-nine letters[1] (of the alphabet), which are combined together and arranged into eighteen sections.' After this, very likely he added the above by way of notes, as he generally did in other cases, to explain what the forty-nine were and how they were to be pronounced, and at the same time to show his friends at home a correct transliteration of the Sanskrit alphabet. That the above quotation once formed a part of our author's Record is confirmed by a much later work, a commentary on the Siddha-tzŭ-chi (published A.D. 1669)[2]. The commentator, Yû-kwai, says that whether I-tsing's pronunciation was that of C. India or of S. India is a question discussed from olden times. 'But why is it,' he asks, 'that the citation of the text of the Siddha-tzŭ-chi[3] is somewhat different from the actual words of I-tsing found in the Record, according to which a*m*, a*h* are both short?' He himself answers this question, attributing the difference to the careless citation on the part of the author of the Siddha-tzŭ-chi. From this we see that the original Record with the above quotation existed as late as 1669. Another commentator (A.D. 1696)[4] of the same work seems to have still

---

[1] Kâsyapa adds: 'The number of the letters of the alphabet is severally recorded in Buddhist books, e.g. as fifty in the Mahâvairo*k*anâbhisambodhi (No. 530), Mañgusrîpari*prikkh*â (No. 442), Vagrasekhara-sûtra (Nos. 1033, 1036), and Mahâparinirvâ*n*a-sûtra; as forty-six in the Lalitavistara (Chinese, No. 159; forty-four in the Sanskrit text (Calcutta), p. 146); as forty-seven in the Siddha-tzŭ-chi (Bodl. Jap. 10); and now by I-tsing, as forty-nine.'

[2] Bodl. Jap. 11; it may have been written earlier, though published so late.

[3] Above, p. lx.

[4] Bodl. Jap. 12, 13.

possessed a text different from ours; for he quotes a passage from our Record, which we have not in the existing text. While discussing the Nirvâ*n*a aspiration [Visarga], he says: 'Among the twelve mata[1] (=mât*ri*kâ), given in I-tsing's Record, a*h* is transcribed by "a-han[2]" in Chinese, which is against the pronunciation in C. India, where a*h* is read by the Chinese "entering" tone. He may have introduced the pronunciation of S. India. He was, however, in Nâlanda for years, and it is but natural that he should represent C. India in reading. Thus we see in his translations that whenever a Nirvâ*n*a aspiration comes, he notes it as an "entering" tone. There are some in C. India, it may be noticed, who read a*h* like the Chinese a or o (in an "even" tone)[3].' This quotation again shows us that the Record had once contained something more about the alphabet. Later in the year 1758 Kâ*s*yapa Ji-un wrote a commentary on the very Record of I-tsing. He had the same text as we have now. As this priest was one of the best Siddha scholars in Japan, well versed in the canon, and very curious about any book relating to Sanskrit, and yet did not come across any text but ours, the original text which contained all the quotations above referred to seems to have wellnigh disappeared in Japan as well as in China. He says: 'There seem to have been several texts of the Record. Many quotations found in the works of Tsang-ning (A. D. 988) of the Sung dynasty, Shou-kwang of the Ming dynasty (A. D. 1368–1628), and Annen of Japan (A. D. 880), are not found in the existing text. I request the learned antiquaries of later times to seek and discover the original text in a stone depository of some famous temples of China and Japan. My commentary has been written only on the current edition, and awaits correction or addition by a later hand.'

In my present translation I have used the India Office copy (A. D. 1681), Prof. Legge's (A. D. 1714), Mr. Nanjio's (text with commentary in MS., A. D. 1758), and the new Japanese edition in the Bodleian Library (1883), all based on one and the same older text without the quotations in question. There is, besides these, another elaborate commentary on our Record, written by a Japanese. I am sorry to say that I failed to get it copied in time to be used for our translation.

I must now fulfil the pleasant duty of acknowledging the kind help severally rendered. First of all I thank the Delegates of the University Press for under-

---

[1] Here we have mata, but not mota. For mât*ri*kâ, see Prof. Bühler's note in the 'Ancient Palm Leaves,' Anecd. Oxon., Aryan Series, vol. i, pt. iii, 1884, p. 67.

[2] 阿漢.

[3] 阿; so in the quotation above, see p. lxi, line 2.

taking the publication on the recommendation of Prof. Max Müller, who has taken an unceasing interest in this work from the beginning to the end. Without his instruction, advice, and help I should never have been able to introduce I-tsing's work to students of Sanskrit Literature and Buddhism. For his patience and attention in the revision of the whole of my MS., the settlement of the meaning of a number of passages, &c., and for several other valuable suggestions, I here express my sincere gratitude. For some matters I am obliged to Profs. Bühler and Oldenberg, and also to Profs. Kern, Kielhorn, and Legge, Dr. Winternitz, and Mrs. H. Smith. Prof. Nagaoka of Tokyo, now in Berlin, kindly looked through the points relating to astronomy. Thanks are due also to Prof. Windisch, who pointed out some matters of importance, just before my Introduction was ready for Press. The printing reflects great credit on the University Press of Oxford, and has been carefully superintended by Mr. J. C. Pembrey, the Oriental Reader.

J. Takakusu.

Berlin, *January* 6, 1896.

ADDITIONAL NOTES TO THE MAP.

1. The degree of longitude from Ferro is given on the map. To know that from Greenwich, reduce about 18° (exactly, 17° 39′ 46″) from the given numbers.
2. The position of Lâ*t*a on the map is not right; see my note at the end (p. 217, note to p. 9).

A RECORD OF BUDDHIST PRACTICES

SENT HOME FROM THE SOUTHERN SEA

BY I-TSING.

INTRODUCTION.

IN the beginning, as the three thousand worlds were being produced, there appeared a sign of their coming into existence. When all things were created, there was as yet no distinction between animate and inanimate things. The universe was an empty waste, without either sun or moon revolving. While misery and happiness were in an undistinguished state, there was no difference between positive and negative principles. When the Brahman gods (lit. 'pure heaven') came down to the earth, their bodily light naturally followed them. As they derived their nourishment from the fatness of the earth, there sprang up a greedy and grasping nature, and they began to consume one after another the creeping plants of the forest and fragrant grains of rice. When their bodily light gradually faded away, the sun and moon became manifest. The state of marriage and agriculture arose, and the principles relating to sovereign and subject, father and son, were established. Then *the inhabitants* looked up to the azure firmament above, and saw its heavenly bodies high and majestically floating in their splendour. Looking down they saw the yellow earth with the water ever moved by the wind, and *the earth* becoming more and more solid. The statements that the two principles, positive and negative, converted themselves into heaven and earth, and men came into being in the space between them[1]; that, influenced by impure and pure air, the dualisation of nature came into existence of its own accord[2]; and that the fashioning power of the two divisions of nature may be compared to the art of casting with its large furnace[3], and that the production of all things can be likened to the making of clay images[4],—all these are only absurd statements resulting from narrow learning. Thereupon the mountains stood firm, the stars were scattered above, and the inanimate beings spread and multiplied. At last their views became different, and they were classed under ninety-six heads; the principles (tattva) were divided into twenty-five classes. The Sâṅkhya system of philosophy teaches that all things came into existence from One[5]. But the Vai*s*eshika system declares that the five forms of existence arose from the six categories (padârtha). Some think it necessary, in order to get rid of rebirth, to have their body naked (Digambara) and the hair plucked out; others insist, as the means of securing heaven, on anointing their body with ashes[6] or tying up their locks of hair. Some say life is self-existent, while others believe that the soul becomes extinct on death. There are many who think that existence is a perfect mystery, dark and obscure, and its reality is not to be explored, and it is too minute and complicated for us to know whence we have come into being.

Others say that man always regains human form by recurring births, or that after death men become spirits. 'I do not know,' one says[7],

---

[1] See the I-king (Sacred Books of the East, vol. xvi, p. 373).

[2] See the Lieh-tze, book i, p. 3 a (Faber's Licius, p. 4) *.

[3] See the *K*wang-tze (Tâ-sung-shi), S. B. E., vol. xxxix, p. 250.

[4] See the Lao-tze, S. B. E., vol. xxxix, p. 55.

[5] For the tenets of Indian Philosophy, see Prof. Cowell's Sarvadar*s*ana Saṅgraha under each system, and Colebrooke's Miscellaneous Essays, vol. i.

[6] These are the Bhûtas according to Hiuen Thsang, probably *S*aivas.

[7] See the Writings of *K*wang-tze, S. B. E., vol. xxxix, book ii, sect. 11, p. 197.

'whether a butterfly became myself or whether I became a butterfly.' Once, when gathered together men imagined that they saw wasps in the place, and again coming together they were perplexed on finding caterpillars there[1]. One compares Chaos with a bird's egg (*anda*), or Darkness with the state of an embryo (or infancy).

These people do not as yet realise that birth is in consequence of the grasping condition of mind and heart (T*r*ish*n*â. 'thirst'), and that our present existence is due to our former actions (Karma). Are they not thus plunged and floating in the sea of suffering, borne to and fro, as it were, by the stream of error?

It is only our Great Teacher, the highest of the world (Loka*g*yesh*th*a), the *S*âkya, who has himself pointed out an easy path, teaching an admirable principle, he who has explained the twelve chains of causation (Nidâna)[2] and acquired the eighteen matchless qualities (Dharma)[3], who has called himself the teacher of gods and men (*S*âstâ Devamanushyâ*n*âm), or the Omniscient One (Sarva*g*ña); he alone has led the four classes of living beings[4] out of the House of Fire (the world), and delivered the three stages[5] of existence from abiding in Darkness. He has crossed over the stream of Kle*s*a (passion), and ascended to the shore of Nirvâ*n*a.

When our Sage first attained to Buddhahood on the Dragon River

---

[1] This is a famous simile in China. When caterpillars have young ones, wasps come and carry them off, and this has given rise to the belief that caterpillars are changed into wasps. 小補韻會 gives this story.

[2] For the twelve Nidânas, see Prof. Oldenberg's Buddha, &c., chap. ii.

[3] These are: perfect deed, speech, and thought; knowledge of past, present, and future; Pra*g*ñâ, Moksha, calm mind, and the like.

[4] I.e. Those born of the womb (1), of eggs (2), from moisture (3), or miraculously (4). The fourth 'miraculously born' is aupapâduka in the Northern Buddhist texts; this is a misrepresentation of the Pâli Opapâtiko. See Childers, s. v., and Burnouf, Lotus, p. 394. Cf. Va*g*ra*kkh*edikâ III, S. B. E., vol. xlix, p. 113. The fourth is generally udbhi*gg*a, i.e. 'produced from sprouts,' but not so with the Buddhists.

[5] The three stages of existence: (1) the world of passion (kâma); (2) the world of form (rûpa); (3) the world without form (arûpa). See bhavo, Childers.

(Nâganadî, i.e. Nairañganâ)[1], the nine classes of beings[2] began to entertain hopes of emancipation. Then the removal of Light to the Deer Park (mrigadâva at Benarcs) brought satisfaction to the religious cravings of the six paths[3] of existence.

As soon as he had begun to set in motion the Wheel of the Law, five persons[4] first enjoyed the benefit of his teaching. Next, he taught the typical virtue (lit. 'the footsteps of Sîla') of discipline, and thousands of people bowed their heads before him. Thereupon His Brahma-voice was heard in the city of Râgagriha, bringing salvation (fruit) to numberless souls.

Returning home to requite parental love in the Palace of Kapilavastu, he found numerous disciples who inclined their hearts to his teaching. He began his teaching with (the conversion of) Âgñâta Kaundinya[5], whose first prayer he accepted in order to reveal the truth.

He concluded his career with *the ordination of* Subhadra[5], so that the last period of his life should accord with his original wish (lit. 'tied-up mind, resolution').

Eight decades he lived, founding and protecting *the Brotherhood;* he preached his doctrine of salvation in the nine assemblages[6]. Any doctrine, however hidden, he expounded in teaching. Even a man of little ability he received without reserve.

When he preached to the lay followers he expressed himself in a concise form, and taught the five prohibitive precepts (pañkasîla) only.

---

[1] Here the Nâganadî must mean Nairañganâ (Nilajan), as it is the place where Sâkyamuni attained Buddhahood. Cf. Nâganadî, Lalita-vistara, p. 336.

[2] The nine classes of beings are the subdivisions of the above three stages; each of those three are divided into three.

[3] The six paths of existence are as follows: human beings, Devas, Pretas (spirits), the brute creation (Tiryagyoni), Asuras (demons), and hells.

[4] Âgñâta Kaundinya and his friends first received the teaching of the Buddha. Rhys Davids, Buddhist Suttas, p. 155; Oldenberg, Buddha, p. 130.

[5] Âgñâta and Subhadra are here translated 了教 and 妙賢 respectively. The last convert of the Buddha was Subhadra, Rhys Davids, Buddhism, p. 81; Buddhist Suttas, pp. 103–111. For Âgñâta Kaundinya, see the last note.

[6] The commentator Kâsyapa understands this to mean the nine classes of beings above referred to.

But in instructing the priests exclusively, he fully explained the purport of the seven skandhas (i.e. groups)[1] *of offences*. He considered that even the great sins of those who dwell in the existing world would disappear at the advance of morality (*s*îla), and the faults, however small they might be, would be done away with, when his law of discipline (Vinaya) had been clearly taught. Since anger expressed against a small branch of a tree brought, as a punishment, a birth among the snakes[2], and mercy shown towards the life of a small insect raised one to the heavenly abode[3], the efficacious power of good or bad actions is indeed evident and indisputable. Therefore the Sûtras and *S*âstras were both given to us, and meditation (dhyâna) and wisdom (pra*gñ*â) were established by the Buddha; is not the Tripi*t*aka the net *par excellence* for catching people? Thus, whenever one came in person to the Great Master, His teaching was of one kind; and when the Master desired to teach and save people according to their abilities, he would lay aside those arguments which were most adapted to another. When we see that the Prince of Mâra bewitched the mind of Ânanda[4] when the latter received the first words of the Buddha at Vai*s*âlî, and that by the last declaration on the Hira*n*yavatî (i.e. the

---

[1] See the Pâtimokkha, S. B. E., vol. xiii, pp. 1–67; *K*ullavagga IX, 3, 3, S. B. E., vol. xx, p. 309.

[2] This story is told in the Sa*m*yuktavastu, book xxi (Nanjio's Catal., No. 1121). A priest named Elapatra was engaged in meditation under a former Buddha Kâ*s*yapa. When he ceased from his meditation, a bough of the ela tree under which he was sitting touched and hurt his head as he moved. He lost his temper and broke off the bough and threw it away. In consequence of this action he was born as a snake.

[3] See below, chap. vii, p. 32, note 3.

[4] Ânanda is translated into Chinese by the 'Delight.' The 'first word of the Buddha at Vai*s*âlî' refers to the following story. The Buddha spoke to Ânanda concerning the length of his life, at Vai*s*âlî (Hiuen Thsang, Mémoires, Julien, livre vii, p. 390), and further said to him: 'Those who have obtained the four supernatural powers can live one kalpa or even more if they like.' He repeated this three times, but Ânanda could not understand it as his mind was perplexed by the influence of Mâra the tempter. This is told in the Sa*m*yuktavastu, book xxxvi (Nanjio's Catal., No. 1121). Cf. Mahâparinibbâna-sutta III, 4, 5 and 56.

river A*g*iravatî), Aniruddha[1] (a disciple of the Buddha) proved the indisputable truth *set forth* by the Buddha, we can say that His teaching career on earth had come to an end, and His work was crowned with success. His footsteps were no more on the banks of the two rivers (Hira*n*yavatî and Naira*ñg*anâ); men and gods were therefore in despair, and His shadow faded away in the avenue (or 'two rows') of the Sâla-trees, when even snakes and spirits became broken-hearted.

They all mourned and wept so much that their tears made the path under the Sâla-trees wet and muddy, and those who grieved the most shed tears of blood all over their bodies which then looked like flowering trees.

After our Great Master had entered Nirvâ*n*a the whole world seemed empty and deserted. Afterwards, there appeared able teachers of the Law, who collected the Sacred Books of the Buddha, *assembling* at one time to the number of 500 (at the cave of Vihâra) and at another of 700 (at Vai*s*âlî). Among the great guardians of the Vinaya, there arose eighteen different divisions[2]. In accordance with several views and traditions, the Tripi*t*akas of various sects differ from one another. *There are small points of difference such as where* the skirt of the lower garments is cut straight in one, and irregular in another, and the folds of the upper robe are, in size, narrow in one and wide in another.

When Bhikshus lodge together, there is a question whether they are to be in separate rooms or to be separated by partitions made by ropes, though both are permitted in the Law. There are other cases: when receiving food, one will take it in his hand, while another will mark the ground where the giver should place food, and both are in the right. Each school has traditions handed down from teacher to

---

[1] Aniruddha is here translated into Chinese by the 'Non-prevention.' This refers to the following incident. The Buddha was about to die, and said to the disciples: 'If you have doubt about the Four Noble Truths, you must ask me at once. Do not let it remain unsettled.' He repeated this three times, but no one spoke out. Aniruddha, who was possessed of a Divine-eye, said to the Buddha as he saw the minds of all Bhikshus: 'The sun may become cold, the moon hot, yet the Four Noble Truths set forth by the Buddha cannot be disproved.' This is told in the Sûtra of Buddha's Last Instruction * (Nanjio's Catal., No. 122).

[2] See the note on eighteen schools above.

pupil, each perfectly defined and distinct from the other (lit. 'the affairs are not confounded or mixed').

(Note by I-tsing)[1]: 1. The Âryamûlasarvâstivâdanikâya (school) cuts the skirt of the lower garment straight, while the other three schools (see below) cut it of irregular shape. 2. The same school ordains separate rooms in lodgings, while the Âryasammitinikâya school allows separate beds in an enclosure made by ropes. 3. The Âryamûlasarvâstivâdanikâya (school) receives food directly into the hand, but the Âryamahâsaṅghikanikâya (school) marks a space on which to place the food.

There exist in the West (India) numerous subdivisions of the schools which have different origins, but there are only four principal schools of continuous tradition. These are as follows:—

I.

The Âryamahâsaṅghikanikâya (school), translated in Chinese by Shêng-tâ-sêng-pu, meaning 'the Noble School of the Great Brotherhood.' This school is subdivided into seven. The three Piṭakas (canonical books) belonging to it contain 100,000 stanzas (ślokas) each, or 300,000 stanzas[2] altogether; which, if translated into Chinese, would amount to 1,000 volumes (each volume representing 300 ślokas).

II.

The Âryasthaviranikâya, translated in Chinese by Shêng-shang-tso-pu, or 'the Noble School of the Elders.' This school is subdivided into

---

[1] Notes in I-tsing's text are often supposed to be by another hand; but when we carefully examine the whole of the annotations in I-tsing's works and translations, we cannot attribute the notes to any but the same author. The 'Chou-yun' in the commentary does not mean the Chou dynasty (951–960), but the reign of the Queen usurper, which was also called 'Chou' (690–704). So this by no means proves that the commentary or notes in I-tsing's text are by a later hand.

[2] Hardy's Eastern Monachism (p. 168 sq.) gives the number of letters in the Piṭakas and commentaries as follows:—

1. The Vinaya,	69,250	stanzas (32 syllables a stanza).
2. The Sutta,	396,500	"
3. The Abhidhamma,	126,250	"
Total,	592,000	stanzas.

three. The number of stanzas in the three Pi*t*akas belonging to it is the same as in the preceding school.

III.

The Âryamûlasarvâstivâdanikâya, translated in Chinese by Shêng-kên-pên-shuo-yi-chieh-yu-pu, or 'the Noble Fundamental School which affirms the Existence of All Things.' This school is subdivided into four. The number of stanzas (*s*lokas) in the three Pi*t*akas belonging to it is the same as in the above.

IV.

The Âryasammitinikâya, translated in Chinese by Shêng-chêng-liang-pu, or 'the Noble School of the Right Measure' (or inference). This school is subdivided into four. The three Pi*t*akas of this school contain 200,000[1] stanzas, the Vinaya texts alone amounting to 30,000 stanzas; it is to be noticed, however, that certain traditions handed down by some of these schools differ much with regard to this view of division, and that I have mentioned here these eighteen schools as they at present exist. I have never heard, in the West (India), of the division into five principal schools (Nikâya), of which some Chinese make use.

As to their separation from one another, their rise and decline, and sectarian names, there is much difference of opinion. As this subject, however, has been treated elsewhere[2], I shall not take the trouble to describe them here.

Throughout the five divisions of India, as well as in the islands of the Southern Sea, people speak of the four Nikâyas. But the number of the votaries in each school is unequal in different places.

In Magadha (Central India) the doctrines of the four Nikâyas are generally in practice, yet the Sarvâstivâdanikâya flourishes the most.

---

[1] J. has 300,000 instead of 200,000; the latter seems to be the right number, for if it were 300,000, I-tsing would say that it is the same as in the above school.

[2] Not by I-tsing himself. For books treating of the eighteen schools, see Nanjio's Catalogue, Nos. 1284, 1285, 1286. See also Rhys Davids' note on the eighteen schools, J. R. A. S., 1891 and 1892.

In Lâ*t*a[1] and Sindhu—the names of the countries in Western India—the Sammitinikâya has the greater number of followers, and there are some few members of the other three schools. In the northern region (N. India) all belong to the Sarvâstivâdanikâya, though we sometimes meet the followers of the Mahâsaṅghikanikâya. Towards the South (S. India), all follow the Sthaviranikâya, though there exist a few adherents of the other Nikâyas. In the eastern frontier countries (E. India), the four Nikâyas are found side by side (lit. 'The eastern frontier countries practise mixedly the four Nikâyas').

(Note by I-tsing): Going east from the Nâlanda monastery 500 *yog*anas, all the country is called the Eastern Frontier.

At the (eastern) extremity there is the so-called 'Great Black[2]' Mountain, which is, I think, on the southern boundary of Tu-fan[3] (Tibet). This mountain is said to be on the south-west of Shu-Chuan (Śsu-Chuan), from which one can reach this mountain[4] after a journey of a month or so. Southward from this, and close to the sea-coast there is a country called *S*rîkshatra[5] (Prome); on the south-east of this is Laṅkasu (probably Kâmalaṅkâ)[6]; on the east of this

---

[1] Lâ*t*a* cannot be identified with certainty, perhaps it is a place in Rajputana or Delhi; Lâ*t*a represents Râsh*t*ra, according to Lassen. Cf. Böhtlingk-Roth, s.v.

[2] This may be Mahâkâla, or some word of the like meaning.

[3] Tibet is Bod in Tibetan, pronounced like French 'peu;' the Chinese for 'Bod' is Fan (番), the Sanskrit Bho*t*a. Upper Tibet is Teu-peu, hence another name for Tibet in Chinese is Tú-fan, as we have here in I-tsing's text. Istakhri (circa A.D. 590) speaks of 'Tobbat,' see Yule, Glossary of Anglo-Indian Words, s.v. India, p. 332. See Mr. Rockhill, 'Tibet,' J. R. A. S., 1891, p. 5.

[4] Beal thought 'this mountain' was a name, and he calls it Sz'ling, see Ind. Ant., July, 1881, p. 197.

[5] For *S*rîkshatra, see Hiuen Thsang (Julien), tom. iii, pp. 82–83, and Beal, Si-yu-ki, vol. ii, p. 200.

[6] Laṅkasu is, in all probability, Kâmalaṅkâ of Hiuen Thsang, i.e. Pegu and the Delta of the Irawadi, see Beal, Si-yu-ki, vol. ii, p. 200. There is a country called Laṅkasu in a Chinese history (see History of the Liang Dynasty (502–557), book 54) which Mr. Groeneveldt doubtfully identified with a part of Java (see Essays on Indo-China, 2nd series, vol. ii, p. 135).

is Dvâ(ra)pati (Dvâravatî, Ayudhya)[1]; at the extreme east, Lin-i (Champa)[2]. The inhabitants of all these countries greatly reverence the Three Jewels (Ratnatraya)[3]. There are many who hold firmly to the precepts and perform the begging dhûta[4] which constitutes a custom in these countries. Such (persons) exist in the West (India) as I have witnessed, who are indeed different from men of ordinary character.

In the Si*m*hala island (Ceylon) all belong to the Âryasthaviranikâya, and the Âryamahâsaṅghikanikâya is rejected.

In the islands of the Southern Sea—consisting of more than ten countries—the Mûlasarvâstivâdanikâya has been almost universally adopted (lit. 'there is almost only one'), though occasionally some have devoted themselves to the Sammitinikâya; and recently a few followers of the other two schools have also been found. Counting from the West there is first of all P'o-lu-shi (Pulushih) island, and then the Mo-lo-yu (Malayu) country which is now the country of *S*rîbho*g*a (in Sumatra), Mo-ho-sin (Mahâsin) island, Ho-ling (Kaliṅga) island (in Java), Tan-tan island (Natuna island), Pem-pen island, P'o-li (Bali) island, K'u-lun island (Pulo Condore), Fo-shih-pu-lo (Bho*g*apura) island, O-shan island, and Mo-chia-man island[5].

There are some more small islands which cannot be all mentioned here. Buddhism is embraced in all these countries, and mostly the

---

[1] Dvâ(ra)pati was identified with Old Tangu and Sandoway in Burma by Capt. St. John (see Phoenix, May, 1872), lat. 18° 20′ N., long. 94° 20′ E. Cf. History of Burma (Trübner's Oriental Series), see Index, Dwârawati. But this position does not at all agree with I-tsing's description. Professor Chavannes notes in his Memoirs of I-tsing (p. 203) that Dvâravatî was the Sanskrit name of Ayuthya or Ayudhya, the ancient capital of Siam. This agrees very well with I-tsing's description, though I do not know the authority for Chavannes' note.

[2] Champa was a Buddhist country, Buddhism having been introduced from Ceylon, and generally connected with the name of Buddhaghosa according to Dr. Bastian (see Colonel Yule, Marco Polo, chap. v, book ii, p. 250). But this country was afterwards converted to Islam.

[3] Buddha, Dharma, and Saṅgha.

[4] The begging dhûta, one of the thirteen or twelve dhûtas, see note below, p. 56, and Childers, s.v.

[5] For all these countries, see my geographical notes above.

system of the Hînayâna (the Smaller Vehicle) is adopted except in Malayu (= *S*rîbho*g*a), where there are a few who belong to the Mahâyâna (the Larger Vehicle).

Some of these countries (or islands) are about a hundred Chinese miles round, some many hundred in circuit, or some measure about a hundred yo*g*anas. Though it is difficult to calculate distance on the great ocean, yet those who are accustomed to travel in merchant ships will know the approximate size of these islands. They were generally known (to Chinese) by the general name of the 'Country of Kun-lun,' since (*the people of*) K'u-lun first visited Kochin and Kwang-tung[1].

---

[1] This sentence is not very clear; more literally, 'Because, indeed, the K'u-lun first came to Chiao-kwang (Kochin and Kwang-tung) all were afterwards called the "Country of Kun-lun."' The vagueness of the Chinese sentences puzzles us much. Professor Chavannes' rendering may be seen from the following extract: 'Voici, d'après I-tsing lui-même (Nan-haï..., chap. 1, p. 3 et 4) quelle est l'origine de ce nom: ce furent des gens du pays de Kiue-loen (掘倫) qui vinrent les premiers dans le Tonkin et le Koang-tong; c'est pourquoi on prit l'habitude d'appliquer le nom de Kiue-loen ou de Koen-loen (崑崙) à toutes les contrées des mers du sud qui étaient alors fort peu connues. Cependant, remarque I-tsing, ce nom a pris ainsi une extension que rien ne justifie; en effet, les gens du pays de Kiue-loen sont noirs et ont les cheveux crépus, tandis que les habitants des grandes-îles des mers du sud (les Malais) ne diffèrent guère des Chinois.' Professor Chavannes further remarks: 'If we compare the text of the history of the T'ang (chap. ccxxii c) with this passage, we see that in the Fou-nan (Siam) the people are black and go naked, and that the sovereign has the family name of Kou-long 古龍 likewise, in the state P'an-p'an (in the peninsula of Malacca) the sovereign has the title of emperor Koen-loen or Kou-long. Thus the country that I-tsing calls Kiue-loen must be Siam and the states of the peninsula of Malacca, where the sovereign calls himself by a name that one can transcribe Koen-loen, Kou-long, or Kiue-loen; the people of this country are black. When their name had been applied by the Chinese to all the people of the southern seas, it happened that the greater part of these people were of the Malay race, not black, and very different from the inhabitants of Siam; it is there that the name of the Kiue-loen tribes came improperly to designate the Malay race.' See Chavannes' Memoirs of I-tsing, p. 63, note. Cf. my note to Kun-lun above.

Except in the case of Kun-lun (Pulo Condore) where the people are woolly-haired (lit. curly-headed) and of black skin, the inhabitants of the (other) islands are similar in appearance to the Chinese; it is their habit to have their legs bare and to wear the Kan-man (a cloth)[1]. These things will be more fully discussed elsewhere in the Description of the Southern Sea[2]. Setting out from Kwan-chou (a district in Annam)[3], right to the south, one will reach Pi-king[4] after a journey of rather more than half a month on foot, or after only five or six tides if aboard ship; and proceeding still southwards one arrives at Champa[5], i.e. Lin-i.

In this country Buddhists generally belong to the Âryasammiti-nikâya, and there are also a few followers of the Sarvâstivâdanikâya.

Setting out south-westwards, one reaches (on foot) within a month, Poh-nan (Kuo[6]), formerly called Fu-nan. Of old it was a country, the inhabitants of which lived naked; the people were mostly worshippers of heaven (the gods or devas), and later on, Buddhism flourished there, but a wicked king has now expelled and exterminated them all, and there are no members of the Buddhist Brotherhood at all, while adherents of other religions (or heretics) live intermingled. This region is the

---

[1] Kan-man is said to be a Sanskrit word; the Chinese is sometimes 合曼 'Ho-man.' I think Kan-man here represents the Sanskrit Kambala. This, no doubt, refers to the Malayan 'Sarongs,' the native name of a piece of cotton or silk which is fastened round the middle and hangs down to the feet. In the History of the Lian Dynasty (502–557), book 54, it is said as follows: 'Men and women (in Siam) all use a broad and long piece of cotton, which they wrap round their body below the loins and called Kan-man (干縵) or Tu-man (都縵).' See Essays on Indo-China, 2nd series, vol. i, p. 260.

[2] See below, chap. xi.

[3] 驩州, somewhere near Tongking.

[4] 匕景 according to J., and 'Shang-king' is, no doubt, a misprint; Pi-king is in the north of Champa, and lies in the province of Jih-nan, which is, according to Chinese writers, a kind of colony on the spot or neighbourhood of Hue (see Essays on Indo-China, 2nd series, vol. i, p. 128 note, and Chavannes, Memoirs, p. 108 note). Thus Pi-king may be Turan or somewhere near it.

[5] See above, note 2, p. 10.

[6] Poh-nan is Siam, but also includes a part of Cambodja.

south corner of *G*ambudvîpa (India), and is not one of the islands of the sea. In the Eastern Hsia (i.e. China) Buddhists practise mostly according to the Dharmagupta school, but in many places in Kwan Chung (Shen-si) some belong, from olden times, to the Mahâsaṅghikanikâya as well as to the above. In olden times in Kiang-nan (south of the Yang Tze-kiang) and Ling-piao (south of the Range, i.e. Kwang-tung and Kwang-si) the Sarvâstivâdanikâya has flourished. When we speak of the Vinaya as being divided into the Daśâdhyâya ('Ten Readings') or into the *K*aturvarga ('Four Classes'), these names are chiefly taken from the divisions or bundles of the texts *adopted by* (those) schools. On examining carefully the distinctions between these schools and the differences of their discipline, we see that they present very many points of disagreement; that which is important in one school is not so in another, and that which is allowed by one is prohibited by another. But priests should follow the customs of their respective schools, and not interchange the strict rules of their doctrine for the more lenient teaching of another. At the same time they should not despise others' prohibitions, because they themselves are unrestricted in their own schools; otherwise the differences between the schools will be indistinct, and the regulations as to permission and prohibition will become obscure. How can a single person practise *the precepts* of the four schools together?

The parable of a torn garment and a gold stick shows how we (*who practise according to the different schools*) may equally gain the goal of Nirvâ*n*a [1]. Therefore those who practise in accordance with the Laws should follow *the customs* of their own schools.

(Note by I-tsing): King Bi*m*bisâra once saw in a dream that a piece of cloth was torn, and a gold stick broken, both into eighteen fragments. Being frightened, he asked the Buddha the reason. In reply the

---

[1] This idea is well expressed by Hiuen Thsang (Julien, Mémoires, I, 77); I borrow here Prof. Rhys Davids' wording of Hiuen Thsang's expression. (Man. of Buddhism, p. 218.)

'The schools of philosophy are always in conflict, and the noise of their passionate discussions rises like the waves of the sea. Heretics of the different sects attach themselves to particular teachers, and by different routes walk to the same goal.'

Buddha said: 'More than a hundred years[1] after my attainment of Nirvâ*n*a, there will arise a king, named A*s*oka, who will rule over the whole of *G*ambudvîpa. At that time, my teaching *handed down* by several Bhikshus will be split into eighteen schools, all agreeing, however, in the end, that is to say, all attaining the goal of Final Liberation (Moksha). The dream foretells this, O king, you need not be afraid!'

Which of the four schools should be grouped with the Mahâyâna or with the Hînayâna is not determined.

In Northern India and in the islands of the Southern Sea, they generally belong to the Hînayâna, while those in China[2] devote themselves to the Mahâyâna; in other places, some practise in accordance with one, some with the other. Now let us examine what they pursue. Both adopt one and the same discipline (Vinaya), and they have in common the prohibitions of the five skandhas ('groups of offences')[3], and also the practice of the Four Noble Truths.

Those who worship the Bodhisattvas and read the Mahâyâna Sûtras

---

[1] The following four dates of A*s*oka are found in the Chinese Tripi*t*aka:—

1. 116 years after the Buddha's Nirvâ*n*a.
2. 118 years " " "
3. 130 years " " "
4. 218 years " " "

This last is more interesting, for it agrees with the date obtained from the Pâli or Si*m*halese sources. This is found in a Vinaya book called the Sudar*s*ana-vibhâshâ Vinaya, which was translated into Chinese A. D. 489. This book contains many dates, which all agree with the Si*m*halese chronicle. The accounts of the Buddhist councils, names of the Indian and Ceylonese kings, A*s*oka's mission, and Mahendra's work in Ceylon, present much resemblance to the Ceylonese historical accounts. This again shows that we have to pay more attention to the Vinaya texts, which are the most trustworthy among the Chinese Buddhist works. As this book was preserved among the Vinaya works, no scholars have noticed as far as I know that this date '218 years P. B. N.' was found in this special work. (See Nanjio's Catal., No. 1125.) See my note at the end.

[2] The text has the 'Divine Land,' and the 'Red Province,' meaning 'China,' i.e. 神州, 赤縣.

[3] See *K*ullavagga IX, 3, 3 (S. B. E., vol. xx, p. 308).

are called the Mahâyânists (the Great), while those who do not perform these are called the Hînayânists (the Small). There are but two kinds of the so-called Mahâyâna. First, the Mâdhyamika; second, the Yoga. The former profess that what is commonly called existence is in reality non-existence, and every object is but an empty show, like an illusion, whereas the latter affirm that there exist no outer things *in reality*, but only inward thoughts, and all things exist only in the mind (lit. 'all things are but our mind').

These two systems are perfectly in accordance with the noble doctrine. Can we then say which of the two [1] is right? Both equally conform to truth and lead us to Nirvâ*n*a. Nor can we find out which is true or false? Both aim at the destruction of passion (kle*s*a) and the salvation of all beings. We must not, in trying to settle the comparative merits of these two, create great confusion and fall further into perplexity.

For, if we act conformably with any of these doctrines, we are enabled to attain the Other Shore (Nirvâ*n*a), and if we turn away from them, we remain drowned, as it were, in the ocean of transmigration. The two systems are, in like manner, taught in India, for in essential points they do not differ from each other.

We have as yet no 'eye of wisdom.' How can we discern right or wrong in them?

We must act just as our predecessors have done, and not trouble ourselves to form our judgement about them. In China, the schools of all Vinayadharas are also prejudiced; and lecturers and commentators have produced too many remarks on the subject. These have rendered difficult many hitherto easy passages of the five skandhas (groups of offences) and the seven skandhas (another enumeration of the five skandhas), and made obscure the helps to religion (Upâya) and the observance of the rules, and made offences which were obvious difficult to be recognised.

Consequently one's aspiration (*after the knowledge of the Vinaya*) is baffled at the beginning (lit. 'at one basketful of earth in making a mountain'), and one's attention flags after attending to but one lecture. Even men of the highest talent can only succeed in the study

---

[1] I-tsing seems to mean the Mahâyâna and Hînayâna.

after becoming grey-haired, while men of medium or little ability cannot accomplish their work even when their hair has turned perfectly white.

Books on the Vinaya were gradually enlarged, but became obscure, so that their perusal is the task of a whole life.

A peculiar method has been adopted by teachers and pupils. They discourse on paragraphs, separating them into smaller and smaller sections; they treat of the articles concerning the offences by dividing them sentence by sentence.

For the labour expended in this method an effort is required as great as that of forming a mountain; and the gain is as difficult to acquire as the procuring of pearls from the vast ocean.

Those who write books should seek to enable their readers to understand easily what they treat of, and should not use enigmatic language, which will require explanation afterwards, if ridiculed by others.

As, when a river has overflowed, and its water has been swept into a deep well, a thirsty man wishing to drink of the pure water of the well could only procure it by endangering his life, *so it is difficult to gain a knowledge of the Vinaya after it has been handled by many men.* Such is not the case when we simply examine the Vinaya texts themselves.

In deciding cases of grave or slight offences, a few lines suffice. In explaining the expedients for settling cases, one does not require even half a day. Such is the general object of study among the priests in India and in the islands of the Southern Sea. In the Divine Land (China) the teaching of duty to others (propriety) prevails everywhere; the people respect and serve their sovereign and their parents; they honour and submit to their elders. They are simple in manner of life, and meek and agreeable in character. They take what they honestly may take.

Filial children and faithful subjects act with caution and economise their expenditure. The emperor governs beneficially millions of his subjects, pitying the unfortunate people[1] with great care (lit. 'taxing his thought') from dawn; while his ministers, whose minds are awake to State affairs even the whole night, execute their duties with respect

[1] Lit. 'as though they had fallen into ditches.'

(lit. clasping the hands) and attention [1]. Sometimes an emperor greatly opens the way to the Triyâna [2] and invites the teachers, preparing hundreds of seats; sometimes he constructs *K*aityas (sepulchres) throughout his dominion, so that all the wise incline their hearts to Buddhism; or he builds temples (Saṅghârâma) here and there throughout his realm in order that all the ignorant may go and worship there to mature their merit. Farmers sing merrily in their fields, and merchants joyfully chant on board ship, or in their carts. In fact, the people who honour cocks (i.e. Korea. see below) and those who respect elephants (India), as well as the inhabitants of the regions of Chin-lin (lit. gold-neighbours) and Yü-lin (lit. Gem-hill) [3], come and pay homage at the Imperial Court. Our people manage their affairs peacefully in a peaceful state (or better, 'peace and tranquillity are our objects'), and everything is so perfect that there can be nothing to be added.

(Note by I-tsing): Those who respect the cocks are the people of Kau-li (Korea) which is called in India Kuku*t*e*s*vara, Kuku*t*a meaning 'cock,' î*s*vara, 'honourable.' People in India say that that country honours cocks as gods, and therefore people wear wings on their heads as an ornamental sign [4]. Those who honour elephants are Indians to whose kings the elephant is most *sacred;* this is so throughout the five parts of India.

As to the *Chinese* priests who have become homeless, they observe the rules and give lectures, while the students study seriously, and understand the deepest principles taught by their teachers. There are those who, having freed themselves from the bonds of worldly affairs,

---

[1] Lit. 'as if treading on thin ice.'

[2] *S*râvakayâna, Pratyekabuddhayâna, and Mahâyâna, according to the Dharma-saṅgraha II.

[3] Chin-lin (lit. Golden Neighbours) is, according to Kâ*s*yapa, the same as 'Chin Chou' (lit. Golden Island), which corresponds to Skt. Suvar*n*a-dvîpa. The 'Golden Island' is the name once applied, by I-tsing, to Sumatra or at any rate to *S*rîbho*g*a, where gold is said to have been abundant.

Yü-lin (lit. Gem-hill) is, Kâ*s*yapa says, Yü-mên-kwan (lit. Gem-gate-pass), which was constructed near the Ko-ko River (probably Ko-ko-nor).

[4] We do not know the origin of this story; but Korea is sometimes called Ki-lin, 'cock-forest.'

have retired to a deep valley, where they wash their mouths with the water of the stony stream or sit in woody thickets tranquillising their thoughts.

Walking and worshipping six times a day, they strive to requite the benefits conferred by those of pure faith; engaged in deep meditation twice a night, they become worthy of the respect of gods and men. These actions are authorised by the Sûtras and the Vinaya. How can there be a fault here? But on account of some misinterpretations handed down, the disciplinary rules have suffered, and errors constantly repeated have become customs which are contrary to the original principles. Therefore, according to the noble teaching and the principal customs actually carried on in India, I have carefully written the following articles which are forty in number, and have divided them into four books. This is called 'Nan-hai-chi-kuei-nai-fa-ch'uan,' i.e. 'The Record of the Sacred Law, sent home from the Southern Sea.' I am sending you with this another work of mine, 'Ta-t'ang-si-yu-ku-fa-kao-sêng-ch'uan,' i.e. 'Memoirs of Eminent Priests who visited India and Neighbouring Countries to search for the Law under the Great T'ang Dynasty' (A.D. 618–907), and several Sûtras and *S*âstras, in all, ten books[1]. I hope that the venerable priests with mind intent on the promulgation of their religion, without having any prejudice, will act with discrimination and in accordance with the teaching and practice of the Buddha, and that they will not disregard the weighty laws described in this work because they deem the author of no note.

Further, the principles and purports of the Sûtras and *S*âstras handed down by the ancients minutely correspond with the Dhyâna (meditation) doctrine (of India), but the secrets of calm meditation are difficult to describe to you in my message. I have, therefore, only roughly sketched the practices of the Law which accord with the Vinaya doctrine, in order to send home in advance, and lay before you the words which rest on the authority of my teachers. My life may sink with the setting sun this day, still I work to do something worthy of the promotion of the Law; the burning Light may go out at the early dawn, yet I hope

---

[1] Among these, there were Nâgârguna's Suh*ri*llekha, Mât*r*i*k*e*t*a's hymn in 150 verses, the Anitya-sûtra and others.

that hundreds of lamps may continue to burn for the future. If you read this Record of mine, you may, without moving one step, travel in all the five countries of India, and before you spend a minute you may become a mirror of the dark path for a thousand ages to come. Will you, I pray, read and examine carefully the Tripi*t*aka, and beat the Ocean of the Law, as it were, to stir up the four waves[1]; and resting on the authority of the five skandhas, launch the ship of compassion to carry across the beings who are plunged into the six desires. Although I have received the personal direction from my teachers, and have fully examined the deep purport of our doctrine, I must, nevertheless, further deepen and expand my knowledge; for if I do not, I am afraid I shall be an object of ridicule in the 'eye of wisdom.'

The following are the contents of the work:—

1. The non-observance of the Varsha does not entail degradation.
2. Behaviour towards the honoured ones.
3. Sitting on a small chair at dinner.
4. Distinction between pure and impure food.
5. Cleansing after meals.
6. Two jugs for keeping water.
7. The morning inspection of the water with regard to insects.
8. Use of a tooth-wood in the morning.
9. Rules of the Upavasatha ceremony.
10. Special requirements as to raiment and food.
11. Method of vestments.
12. Garments of a nun.—Rules of burial ceremonies.
13. Rules as to sacred enclosures.
14. The Varsha of the Parishads.
15. The period of Pravâra*n*a (relaxation after the Varsha).
16. The mode of using spoons and chopsticks.
17. Proper times for religious worship.
18. On evacuation.
19. Regulations for ordination.
20. The proper occasions for ablutions.

---

[1] I. e. 'all the people.'

21. Concerning the mat to sit on.
22. Rules of sleeping and resting.
23. On the advantage of proper exercise to health.
24. Worship not mutually dependent.
25. Behaviour between teacher and pupil.
26. Conduct towards strangers or friends.
27. On symptoms of bodily illness.
28. Rules on giving medicine.
29. Hurtful medical treatment must not be practised.
30. On turning to the right in worship.
31. Rules of decorum in cleansing the sacred objects of worship.
32. The ceremony of chanting.
33. The unlawful reverence to the sacred objects.
34. Rules for learning in India.
35. On the propriety of long hair.
36. On disposing of the property of a deceased priest.
37. Use of the property of the Brotherhood.
38. The burning of the body is unlawful.
39. The bystanders become guilty.
40. Such hurtful actions were not practised by the virtuous of old.

All the things mentioned in this work are in accordance with the Âryamûlasarvâstivâdanikâya, and should not be confounded with the teaching of other schools. The matters contained in this work resemble generally the Vinaya of the Dasâdhyâya (Ten Readings).

There are three subdivisions[1] of the Âryamûlasarvâstivâdanikâya: 1. The Dharmagupta; 2. the Mahîsâsaka; 3. the Kâsyapîya.

These three do not prevail in India, except in the following places: Udyâna, Kharakar, and Kustana, where there are some who practise the rules laid down in these schools.

The Vinaya of the so-called Dasâdhyâya (Ten Readings), (though not unlike), does not belong to the Âryamûlasarvâstivâda school.

---

[1] Cf. p. 8, iii; there we have four subdivisions and here only three. That is, one school is called Mûlasarvâstivâda, and as it is the same name as that of the original school, I-tsing does not name it separately here.

CHAPTER I.

REGARDING THE NON-OBSERVANCE OF THE VARSHA (OR VASSA, SUMMER RETREAT).

THE Bhikshus who did not observe the Varsha[1] fail, of course, to obtain the ten benefits[2] derived from it, but there is no reason why they should be degraded from their original position in the Order to a lower place. Nor is it seemly for a priest to be obliged to suddenly alter his action and pay respect to an inferior, one day, from whom but the day before he received due honour. Such degradation in rank was customary, however, (in China), though without any authority or proof in its support. For if, when observing the Varsha, one accept an invitation outside, it is as great a fault as theft. One should, therefore, carefully examine the principles *on which the custom rests*, and should never disregard them. The rank of a Bhikshu ought to be determined by the date of his ordination.

Even if he have not observed the Varsha, let him not be degraded. If we read and examine the teaching of the Buddha, there is no authority in it (*for this custom*).

Then who at some former date introduced this practice (among the Chinese)?

CHAPTER II.

BEHAVIOUR TOWARDS THE HONOURED.

ACCORDING to the teaching of the Buddha, when a priest is in presence of the holy image, and approaches the honoured teachers, it is right for

---

[1] Varsha is originally 'rainy season,' including four months from the middle of June to the middle of October. These four months are a period of retreat for the Buddhist priests, who are forbidden to travel, but live in some place away from their monasteries. This summer retreat is called the Varsha (Vassa in Pâli), and kept up as the most important period in the Buddhist life. For further particulars see Childers' Pâli Dictionary, s. v., and Mahâvagga III, S. B. E., vol. xviii.

[2] Ten benefits are possession of garments, freedom in sojourning, &c.; the five privileges are given in Mahâvagga VII, 1, 3, and the Vinaya-saṅgraha (Nanjio's Catal., No. 1127).

him, except in case of illness, to have his feet bare; he is never allowed to put on sandals *before teachers or images*, and must always have his right shoulder bare and the left covered with his cloak, wearing no cap. He may walk about (*with sandals, &c.*), in other places without blame, if he have (his superior's) permission. In a cold region, a priest is allowed to wear small sandals or any kind of shoes suitable to the climate. Countries lying in different latitudes (lit. directions) have widely different climates.

In following the teaching of the Buddha, some rules must admit of slight modification.

It may reasonably be allowed that we should temporarily wear more clothes in the months of severe winter in order to protect the body, but during the warm spring and summer, one ought strictly to live in accordance with the Vinaya rules[1]. That one should not walk round the holy stûpa with sandals on was taught expressly from the beginning.

And it has long been proclaimed that a priest must never approach the temple (lit. gandhaku*t*î) with his slippers[2] on. But there are some who perpetually disobey the rules; and it is indeed a grave insult to the golden rule of our Buddha.

CHAPTER III.

ON SITTING ON A SMALL CHAIR AT DINNER.

In India the priests wash their hands and feet before meals, and sit on separate small chairs. The chair is about seven inches high by a foot square, and the seat of it is wicker-work made of rattan cane. The legs are rounded, and, on the whole, the chair is not heavy. But for junior members of the Order blocks of wood may be used instead. They place their feet on the ground, and trays, (*on which food is served*),

---

[1] 'Vinaya' is the discipline laid down by the Buddha. The whole is called 'Vinaya pi*t*akam;' the Pâli text was published by Prof. Oldenberg, 1879.

[2] The text has 'pu-ra,' which is, according to Kâ*s*yapa, a kind of shoes in Sanskrit, but I cannot find a Sanskrit word corresponding to the sound *.

are placed before them. The ground is strewn with cow-dung, and fresh leaves are scattered over. The chairs are ranged at intervals of one cubit, so that the persons sitting on them do not touch one another. I have never seen one sitting at a meal cross-legged on a large couch. The measurement of a couch according to the rule laid down by the Buddha ought to be the width of the Buddha's eight fingers; as the Buddha's finger is said to have been three times larger than that of an ordinary individual, the width of his eight fingers is equal to that of our twenty-four fingers. This is one and a half feet in Chinese measurement. In the temples of China (lit. the Eastern Hsia) the height of a couch exceeds two feet; this of course is not to be used for sitting upon. For he who sits on it incurs the blame of using a high couch (one of the Buddha's eight *s*ilas). Many Bhikshus of the present time break this rule; but how do they mean to exonerate themselves? All those who are guilty of this breach of rule should consult the code of measurement.

But couches used in the temples of the Holy Rock and the Four Dhyânas (i. e. *K*aturdhyâna)[1] are one foot high; this height was laid down by the virtuous men of old and is indeed authoritative.

To sit cross-legged side by side, and to have meals with knees stretched out, is not a proper way—pray notice this. I have heard that after the introduction of Buddhism into China, the Bhikshus were accustomed to sit on chairs (not cross-legged) at meals. At the time of the Tsin dynasty (A. D. 265–419) the error was introduced, and they began to sit cross-legged at meals. It is nearly 700 years (B.C. 8; 700–692 = 8)[2] ago that the noble doctrine of the Buddha first passed into the East (China); the period of ten dynasties has gone by, each having its able representative. Indian Bhikshus came to China one after another, and the Chinese priests, of the time being, crowded together before them, and received instruction from them. There were some who went to India themselves and witnessed the proper practice there. On their return home they pointed out wrong customs, but who of them has ever been followed?

---

[1] These are two Chinese temples, being Ling-yen (靈巖) and Ssŭ-shan (四禪) respectively. There seem to have been several so-named temples in China; Kâ*s*yapa mentions two as examples.

[2] This date must not be taken too literally.

It is often said in the Sûtras[1], 'Wash your feet after a meal;' from this it is clear that they did not sit cross-legged on a couch (*for there would be no use in washing feet, if they had not touched the ground*).

And also it is said: 'Food is thrown down near to the feet;' from this we can see that the priests used to sit with their feet straight on the ground. The disciples of the Buddha ought to have the Buddha's methods. Even if it be not possible to follow out his rules, it is wrong to ridicule them.

If one sit cross-legged, and with his garment folded round the knees, it is difficult to keep clean and not to spill food (lit. to 'protect one's purity'), and spilled food and stains easily cling to the garment.

To preserve what has been left from the meal, as is done in China, is not at all in accordance with Indian rules. By being gathered from the table the food pollutes the trays, and those who serve touch the clean utensils. Thus making the preservation of purity vain, no good result has as yet been obtained. Pray carefully notice these points, and see the comparative merit of each practice.

CHAPTER IV.

DISTINCTION BETWEEN PURE AND IMPURE FOOD.

AMONG the priests and laymen in India, it is customary to distinguish between clean and unclean food. If but a mouthful of the food have been eaten, it becomes unclean (lit. 'touched'); and the utensils in which food was put are not to be used again. As soon as the meal is finished, the utensils used are removed and piled up in one corner. All the remaining food is given to those who may legally eat such (i. e. the departed spirits, birds, and the like); for it is very improper to keep the food for further use.

This is the custom among both rich and poor, and is not only a custom observed by us, but even by the Brâhmans (Devas, gods). It is said in several *S*âstras: 'It is considered to be mean not to use a tooth-wood, and not to wash the hands after evacuation, and not to

[1] See the Vagra*kkh*edikâ, translated by Prof. Max Müller (i), p. 112, vol. xlix, S. B. E.

distinguish between clean and unclean food.' How can we consider it seemly to use again the utensils that have already been touched, to preserve food remaining over in the kitchen, to keep in a jar the rice that has been left from a meal, or to put back the remainder of the soup in a pot? Nor is it right to eat next morning the soup and vegetables that have been left, or to partake later of the remaining cake or fruits. Those who observe the Vinaya rules may know something of this distinction, but those who are idle and negligent combine to pursue the wrong course. At a reception or any ordinary meals, no one ought to touch another or taste any fresh food until he has rinsed his mouth with pure water, and after each course, a mouthful of which would defile him, he must repeat the rinsing. If he touch another person before rinsing his mouth, the person touched is defiled and must rinse his mouth. When a man has touched a dog he has to purify himself. Those who have partaken of a meal must remain together on one side of the hall, and should wash their hands and rinse their mouths, and also wash the things used during the meal and the soiled pots.

If they neglect these points, any prayers or charms that they may have offered will have no efficacy, and any offerings they may make will not be accepted by the Spirits. Therefore, I say, everything must be clean and pure, if you prepare either food or drink, intending to offer it to the Three Jewels, or to the Spirits, or mean it for an ordinary meal for yourselves. Until the person is purified after a meal or after evacuation, he is unfit to sit at table again. Even the world speaks of a fast for the purpose of purification. When people are sacrificing to Confucius in his temple, they ought first to clip their nails, and keep their body under control and free from defilement. Purification is required thus even in the matters concerning Confucius, his disciple Yen Hui, and others, and people do not offer the leavings from a meal. In preparing food for a reception or for an ordinary meal of the Bhikshus, there must be a superintendent in the matter. If there be a delay in preparing food at a reception, and if the guests fear that they should be behind the prescribed meal-time in waiting, the invited, be he priest or layman, can partake of a meal separately out of what has been provided, though not yet served. This is allowed by the Buddha, and does not cause guilt.

I have heard that of late meals are often delayed till the afternoon (noon being the prescribed meal-time), while the preparation is being superintended by priests or nuns. This is not right, as one commits a fault in doing good. Now the first and chief difference between India of the five regions and other nations is the peculiar distinction between purity and impurity.

Once upon a time when the Mongolians of the North sent men to India, the messengers were despised and ridiculed, as they did not wash themselves after evacuation, and preserved their food in a tray. This was not all; they were scorned and spoken ill of, as they sat together (*on the floor*) at a meal, with their feet straight out, and touching one another's, and they did not keep out of the neighbourhood of pigs and dogs, and did not use a tooth-brush. Therefore those who are practising the Law of the Buddha ought to be very careful on these points. But in China the distinction of pure and impure food has never been recognised from ancient time.

Although they hear my admonition on this point, they will not adhere to the rules, and will not be awakened until I shall see them and speak to them in person.

CHAPTER V.

CLEANSING AFTER MEALS.

WHEN a meal is finished, do not fail to cleanse the hands. In getting the water, fetch a water-jar yourself or order others to do so. The cleansing may be done with water taken (from a spring) out of a basin; or it may be done in some secluded place (where water is always at hand) or on a conduit (Pra*n*âlî) or on the steps leading down. Chew tooth-wood in the mouth; let the tongue as well as the teeth be carefully cleansed and purified. If the (unclean) spittle be yet remaining in the mouth, the religious fast may not be observed, while the lips should be washed either with pea-flour or with mud made by mixing earth with water, so as not to leave any taint of grease.

Afterwards the water must be poured (for rinsing) out of the clean jar into a conch-shell cup, which is to be held over fresh leaves or in the hands. If the cup touches the hand, it is necessary to rub it with the three kinds of cleansing material, i. e. pea-flour, dry earth, and cow-dung[1], and to wash it with water to take off the taint. In a secluded place water may be poured right into the mouth from a clean jar, but this is forbidden in a public spot. After rinsing the mouth two or three times it will generally be cleansed. Before doing this it is not allowed to swallow the mouth-water or spittle. Any one breaking this rule and so lowering his dignity will be considered faulty. The saliva must be spit out before the mouth has been rinsed with pure water; if noontide be passed *without cleansing*, the offender will be guilty of failing to observe the prescribed time. Men know little of this point. Even if they know it, it is not easy to observe it rightly. Judging from this *strict* point of view, it is difficult indeed to keep entirely free from fault even if pea-flour or ash-water be used, for there may be a taint of food in the teeth or grease on the tongue. The wise should see this and be careful in the matter. It is surely not seemly for any one to spend his time after meals chaffing and chattering, nor is it right to remain impure and guilty all day and night, without preparing *water* in a clean jar or without chewing a tooth-wood. If such laziness be indulged in during one's lifetime, no end of trouble is to be found. It is, be it added, also lawful to let one's pupils fetch and pour out the clean water from a jar.

CHAPTER VI.

TWO JUGS FOR KEEPING WATER.

THE clean water is kept separately from water for cleansing purposes (lit. 'touched' water)*, and there are two kinds of jars (i. e. ku*n*d*î* and kala*s*a) for each. Earthenware or porcelain is used for the clean jar, and the jar for water for cleansing purposes (lit. 'touched' water) is made of copper or iron. The clean water is ready for drinking at any time, and the 'touched' water for cleansing purposes after having been to the urinal. The clean jar must be carried in a clean hand, and be

---

[1] Kâ*s*yapa remarks that the Skt. for the cow-dung is 'Gomaya' or 'Gomayî,' and that Chinese cow-dung is unfit for the purifying purpose, being so dirty.

placed in a clean place, while the jar for the 'touched' water should be grasped by the 'touched' (or 'unclean') hand and be put in an unclean (or 'touched') place. The water in a pure and fresh jar can be drunk at any time; the water in any other jar is called 'special water' (more lit. 'seasonable water,' i. e. water to be used at certain prescribed times, probably kâlodaka).

To drink from a jar holding it upright in front is no fault; but drinking in the afternoon is not permissible. A jar must be made to fit one's mouth; the top of the cover should be two fingers[1] high; in it a hole as small as a copper chopstick is made.

Fresh water for drinking must be kept in such a jar. At the side of the jar there is another round hole as large as a small coin, two fingers higher than the drinking-mouth. This hole is used for pouring in water; two or three gallons may be put in it. A small jar is never used.

If one fear that insects or dust may enter in, both the mouth and the hole may be covered by means of bamboo, wood, linen, or leaves. There are some Indian priests who make jars according to this style. In taking water, the inside of the jar must be first washed in order to get off any dirt or dust, and then fresh water must be poured in. Is it seemly to take water without distinction between the clean and the unclean, or to keep only one small jar made of copper, or even to pour out the remaining water while the attached lid is held in the mouth? Such a jar is not fit to be used, for in it pure water cannot be distinguished from impure. Within such a jar there may be dirt or stain; it is unfit to keep fresh water in, and being small, the water is little in quantity, wanting about one gallon or two kilograms every time.

As to the construction of a jar-bag, it is made of cotton cloth about two feet long and one foot wide, which is doubled by putting both ends together, and the edges which meet are sewed together. To its two corners cords about seven and a half inches[2] long are attached; the bag

---

[1] Two finger-widths (aṅgulas), not 'two finger-joints;' Kâsyapa says 'it would be about one Chinese inch.'

[2] The text has 一 磔 'a span' (vitasti), i. e. 'the length of thumb and middle finger stretched;' this is twelve aṅgulas long, or seven and a half inches, according to Kâsyapa. For 'Sugata-vitasti,' see Pâtimokkha, p. 8, note 2, S. B. E., vol. xiii.

containing a jar is carried in travelling hung from the shoulder. The shape of the bag of a begging-bowl is similar to the above. It covers the mouth of the bowl in it sufficiently for dust to be kept off. The bottom is made pointed, so that the bowl does not move about. But the bag for the bowl is different from that for the jar, as is explained elsewhere [1].

A priest who travels carries his jar, bowl, necessary clothes, by hanging them from his shoulders over his cloak, taking an umbrella in his hand. This is the manner of the Buddhist priest in travelling.

He takes also, if his hand be not much occupied, a jar for unclean water, leather shoes in a bag, at the same time holding a metal staff obliquely, and going about at ease . . . [2]

At the season of pilgrimage to the *K*aityas of Râ*g*ag*ri*ha, the Bo-tree, the Vulture-peak, the Deer-park, *the holy place where* the Sâla-trees turned white [3] like *the wings of* a crane (in Ku*s*inagara), and the lonely grove that has been dedicated to a squirrel [4].

---

[1] The Mûlasarvâstivâda-sa*m*yuktavastu, chap. xxxiii (Nanjio's Catal., No. 1121).

[2] Here there is a sentence, the meaning of which is not clear to me. The Chinese 烏喩月經雅當其況 seems to mean something like this: 'The manner exactly corresponds to what is in the Parable of the Crow—the Sûtra on the moon.' The commentator says nothing but that the parable of the Bird—the Sûtra on the Moon is the name of one Sûtra, i. e. Sûtra on the Parable of the Crow and the Moon, which is, according to him, 23, vol. ii of the Catalogue of the Tripi*t*aka, published in the Ming Dynasty (Nanjio's Catal., No. 948, the *K*andropamâna-sûtra). But this Sûtra has nothing corresponding to our sentences.

The meaning of the context will not have to be altered even if we make out that particular sentence.

[3] 'This refers to the story that at the time of the Buddha's Nirvâ*n*a the trees blossomed at once, though not in season (Mahâparinibbâna-sutta V, 4, S. B. E., vol. xi, p. 86).

[4] 'The grove of the squirrel' is the Kalantaka-nivâpa, otherwise called the 'Ve*n*u-vana.' Kalantaka or Kalandaka is a bird which resembles the Chinese magpie (Kâ*s*yapa, so also I-tsing), but this must be a mistake *.

The Saṅghabhedakavastu, chap. viii (Nanjio's Catal., No. 1123), gives an account of the grove as follows:—

'This bamboo grove belonged to a rich man at one time. When Bi*m*bisâra

In these seasons travelling priests assemble by thousands in every one of the above places day after day from every quarter, and all travel in the same manner (as described above). Venerable and learned priests of the Nâlanda monastery ride in sedan-chairs, but never on horseback, and those of the Mahârâ*g*a monastery do the same. In this case necessary baggage is carried by other persons or taken by boys;—such are the customs among the Bhikshus in the West (India).

CHAPTER VII.

THE MORNING INSPECTION OF WATER AS TO INSECTS.

WATER must be examined every morning. According as it is found in different places, i. e. in jars, in a well, in a pond, or in a river.

The means also of examining it differ. Early in the morning jar-water is first to be examined. After pouring about a handful of it, by inclining the jar, into a pure bronze cup, a ladle made of bronze, a conch-shell, or a plate of lacquer-work, pour it slowly on a brick. Or, by means of a wooden instrument made for this purpose, observe the water for some moments, shutting the mouth with the hand. It is likewise well to examine it in a basin or in a pot. Insects even as small as a hair-point must be protected. If any insects are found, return the water again into the jar, and wash the vessel with other water twice until no insects

---

was yet prince he used to take pleasure in the grove and wanted the owner to give it to him. This was declined. When the prince succeeded to the throne he took possession of this grove by force. The owner was vexed and died of heart-disease. After death he became a snake to take vengeance on the king. In spring the flowers were beautiful; the king went out to the garden together with many female attendants. He fell asleep after having enjoyed the garden walk. All maids went away from the king, charmed by the flowers; there was only one maid who was guarding the king with a sword. There appeared a poisonous snake ready to attack the sleeping king. At this very moment the Kalandaka shrieked noisily, and the maid on guard noticed the snake and cut it asunder. As a reward for the good service to the king, His Majesty dedicated this grove to the memory of the birds and named it "Kalandaka-ve*n*u-vana."'

For Kalandaka *, see Mahâvagga (S. B. E.) III, 1, 1 note; and for the eight *K*aityas in the holy spots, see below, chap. xx, p. 108.

are left in it. If there is a river or a pond in the neighbourhood, take the jar there and throw away the water containing insects; then put in fresh filtered water. If there is a well, use its water, after filtering it, according to the usual manner. In examining well-water, after some has been drawn, observe it in a water-vessel, taking about a handful of it in a bronze cup, as stated above. If there is no insect, then the water can be used through the night, and if any be found it must be filtered according to the process mentioned above. As to the examining of the water of a river or pond, details are found in the Vinaya [1].

The Indians use fine white cloth for straining water; and in China fine silk may be used, after having slightly boiled it with rice-cream; for small insects easily pass through the meshes of raw silk. Taking a piece of softened silk about four feet of the Hu-ch'ih [2] (name of a common measure), lay it lengthwise by taking its edges, then double it by taking both ends, and sew them together so as to form them into the shape of a net. Then attach cords to its two corners, and loops to both sides; and put across it a stick about one foot and six inches long, in order to stretch it wide. Now fasten its two ends to posts, while placing a basin under it. When you pour water into it from a pot, its bottom must be inside the strainer, lest some insects drop off together with the drops of water, and should hardly escape destruction by falling on the ground or into the basin. When water comes out through the strainer, scoop and examine it, and, if it contains some insects, then return *the water*, and, if it is clean enough, use it. As soon as enough water has been obtained, turn up the strainer, which is to be held at both ends by two persons, put it into the 'life-preserving vessel,' rinse it with water three times, and again pour water over it outside. Pour in water once more in order to see, by means of straining it, whether some insects still remain in it. If no insects be found, remove the strainer in any manner. Even after being thus filtered, the water, when a night has passed, is liable to need examining again; for one who neglects to examine the water that has stood through a night, whether it contains insects or not, is said, in the Vinaya, to be guilty.

---

[1] See the Vinaya-saṅgraha (Nanjio's Catal., No. 1127).

[2] 笏尺 in Chinese.

There are many ways of protecting life while drawing water. The strainer just described is suitable in case of drawing water from a well. In a river or a pond you may filter the water by a double jar[1] within the willow vessel safely placed in the water. During the sixth or the seventh month the insects are so minute, and different from what they are in the other seasons, that they can pass even through ten folds of raw silk.

Those who wish to protect life should try to set the insect free by some means or other. A plate-like tray may be used for the purpose, but the silk strainer is also very useful. The tray is generally made of copper, in India, in accordance with the rules laid down by the Buddha: one must not neglect these points. The life-preserving vessel is a small water-pot with an open mouth as wide as the vessel itself. It has two knobs on the sides of the bottom-part, to which cords are fastened. When it is let down into water, it is turned upside down, and, after having been plunged into water twice or thrice, it is drawn up.

The high priests must not touch the filters used in the temple, nor the water kept in a room for filtering purposes. The lower priests who have not yet received full ordination, can take and drink any water; but if they drink at an improper time they ought to use a clean strainer, clean jar, and pure vessels, such as are fit to be used. As regards living creatures, an injury to them is a sin, and is prohibited by the Buddha.

It is this prohibition that is the most weighty of all, and an act of injury is placed at the head of the ten sins. One must not be neglectful of this. The filter is one of the six possessions[2] necessary to the priests, and one cannot do without it. One should not go on a journey three or five Chinese miles without a filter. If a priest be aware of the fact that the residents in the temple where he is staying do not strain their water, he must not partake of food there. Even if the traveller die on his way from thirst[3] or hunger, such a deed is sufficient to be looked upon as a splendid example. The daily use of water necessitates inspection.

---

[1] This may be the Da*nd*a-parissâvana*m* (a double strainer) of *K*ullavagga V, 13, 3, though the way of straining seems very different.

[2] For the six possessions, see chap. x, p. 54, i.e. the six Requisites.

[3] This story is told in the Sa*m*yuktavastu, book vi (Nanjio's Catal., No. 1121). Two Bhikshus from the south started for *S*râvastî to see the Buddha. They were

There are some who use the strainer, but let the insects die within it. Some are desirous of preserving life, but few know how to do it. Some shake (or 'upset') the strainer at the mouth of a well, and do not know the use of the life-preserving vessel. The insects will, no doubt, be killed when they reach the water of a deep well. Others make a small round strainer which only contains one quart or two pints. The silk of which it is made is raw, rough, and thin; and in using it one does not look for the insects at all, but after hanging it at the side of the jar, others are ordered to do the actual inspection.

Thus one pays no attention to the protection of life, and commits sins from day to day. Handing down such error from teacher to pupil, they yet think they are handing down the Law of the Buddha. It is indeed a grievous and regretful matter! It is proper for every person to keep a vessel for examining water, and every place must be furnished with a life-preserving vessel.

CHAPTER VIII.

USE OF TOOTH-WOODS.

EVERY morning one must chew tooth-woods, and clean the teeth with them, and rub off *the dirt of* the tongue as carefully as possible. Only after the hands have been washed and the mouth cleansed is a man fit to make a salutation; if not, both the saluter and the saluted are at fault. Tooth-wood is Dantakâsh*th*a[1] in Sanskrit—danta, tooth, and kâsh*th*a, a piece of wood. It is made about twelve finger-breadths in length, and even the shortest is not less than eight finger-breadths long[2]. Its size is like the little finger. Chew softly one of its ends, and clean the teeth with it. If one unavoidably come near a superior, *while chewing the wood*, one should cover the mouth with the left hand.

---

thirsty, but the water around them was full of insects. The elder did not drink, and died: he was born in heaven. The younger drank and was censured by the Buddha. Much the same story is told in the *G*âtaka Commentary (Rhys Davids' Buddhist Birth Stories, vol. i, p. 278); and in *K*ullavagga V, 13, 2.

[1] These passages are quoted in Julien's Hiuen Thsang, liv. i, p. 55 note.

[2] I.e. 'aṅgula' = one twenty-fourth hasta. In *K*ullavagga V, 31, 2, the length of a tooth-stick is limited to eight finger-breadths.

Then, breaking the wood, and bending it, rub the tongue. In addition to the tooth-wood, some toothpicks made of iron or copper may be used, or a small stick of bamboo or wood, flat as the *surface* of the little finger and sharpened at one end, may be used for cleaning the teeth and tongue; one must be careful not to hurt the mouth. When used, the wood must be washed and thrown away.

Whenever a tooth-wood is destroyed or water or saliva is spit out, it should be done after having made three fillips with the fingers, or after having coughed more than twice [1]; if not, one is faulty in throwing it away. A stick taken out of a large piece of wood, or from a small stem of a tree, or a branch of an elm, or a creeper, if in the forest; if in a field, of the paper mulberry, a peach, a sophora japonica ('Huai'), willow-tree, or anything at disposal, must be prepared sufficiently beforehand [2]. The freshly-cut sticks (lit. wet ones) must be offered to others, while the dry ones are retained for one's own use.

The younger priest can chew as he likes, but the elders must have the stick hammered at one end *and made soft;* the best is one which is bitter astringent or pungent in taste, or one which becomes like cotton when chewed. The rough root of the Northern Burr-weed (Hu Tai) is the most excellent; this is otherwise called Tsăng-urh or Tsae-urh, and strikes the root about two inches in the ground. It hardens the teeth, scents the mouth, helps to digest food, or relieves heart-burning. If this kind of tooth-cleaner be used, the smell of the mouth will go off after a fortnight. A disease in the canine teeth or tooth-ache will be cured after a month. Be careful to chew fully and polish the teeth cleanly, and to let all the mouth-water come out; and then to rinse abundantly with water. That is the way. Take in the water from the nose once. This is the means of securing a long life

---

[1] Kâ*s*yapa, quoting the Sa*m*yuktavastu, chap. xiii, says that the Buddha did not allow a tooth-wood or anything to be thrown away without making some noise beforehand for a warning.

[2] The Dantakâsh*th*as were bits of sweet-smelling wood or root, or creeper (*G*âtaka I, 80; Mahâva*ms*a, p. 23), the ends of which were to be masticated as a dentifrice, not rubbed on the teeth, and not 'tooth-brushes' as Childers translates. See *K*ullavagga V, 31, 1 (S. B. E.), note; B*ri*hat-sa*m*hitâ LXXXV; Su*s*ruta II, 135.

adopted by Bodhisattva Nâgârguna. If this be too hard to put in practice, to drink water is also good. When a man gets used to these practices he is less attacked by sickness. The dirt at the roots of the teeth hardened by time must all be cleaned away. Washed with warm water, the teeth will be freed from the dirt for the whole of life. Toothache is very rare in India owing to their chewing the tooth-wood.

It is wrong to identify the tooth-wood with a willow-branch. Willow-trees are very scarce in India. Though translators have generally used this name, yet, in fact, the Buddha's tooth-wood-tree (for instance) which I have personally seen in the Nâlanda monastery, is not the willow. Now I require no more trustworthy proof from others *than this*, and my readers need not doubt it. Moreover, we read in the Sanskrit text of the Nirvâ*n*a-sûtra thus: 'The time when they were chewing tooth-woods.'

Some in China use small sticks of willow which they chew completely in their mouth without knowing how to rinse the mouth and remove the juice. Sometimes it is held that one can cure a sickness by drinking the juice of the tooth-wood. They become impure, in so doing, contrary to their desire for purification. Though desirous of being released from a disease, they fall into a greater sickness. Are they not already aware of this fact? Any argument would be in vain! It is quite common among the people of the five parts of India to chew the tooth-wood. Even infants of three years old are taught how to do it.

The teaching of the Buddha and the custom of the people correspond on this point, and help each other. I have thus far explained the comparative merit of the use of the tooth-wood in China and India. Each must judge for himself as to whether he will adopt or reject the custom.

CHAPTER IX.

RULES ABOUT THE RECEPTION AT THE UPAVASATHA-DAY[1].

I SHALL briefly describe the ceremony of inviting priests, in India as well as in the islands of the Southern Sea. In India the host comes

[1] I. e. the fast-day; it is a day of religious observance and celebration for laymen and priests, and is a weekly festival when laymen see a priest and take upon themselves the Upavasatha-vows, i.e. to keep the eight *S*ilas during the day.

previously to the priests, and, after a salutation, invites them to the festival. On the Upavasatha-day he informs them, saying, 'It is the time.'

The preparation of the utensils and seats for the priests is made according to circumstances. Necessaries may be carried (from the monastery) by some of the monastic servants; or provided by the host. Only copper utensils as a rule are used, which are cleansed by being rubbed with fine ashes. Each priest sits on a small chair placed at such a distance that one person may not touch another. The shape of the chair has been already described in chap. iii. It is not wrong, however, to use earthenware utensils once, if they have not been used before. When they have been already used, they should be thrown away into a ditch, for used vessels (lit. 'touched') should not be preserved at all. Consequently in India, at almsgiving places at the side of the road, there are heaps of discarded utensils which are never used again. Earthenware (of superior quality) such as is manufactured at Siang-yang (in China) may be kept after having been employed, and after having been thrown away may be cleansed properly. In India there were not originally porcelain and lacquer works. Porcelain, if enamelled, is, no doubt, clean. Lacquered articles are sometimes brought to India by traders; people of the islands of the Southern Sea do not use them as eating utensils, because food placed in them receives an oily smell. But they occasionally make use of them when new, after washing the oily smell away with pure ashes. Wooden articles are scarcely ever employed as eating utensils yet, if new, they may be used once, but never twice, this being prohibited in the Vinaya.

The ground of the dining-hall at the host's house is strewn over with cow-dung, and small chairs are placed at regular intervals; and a large quantity of water is prepared in a clean jar. When the priests arrive they untie the fastenings of their cloaks. All have clean jars placed before them: they examine the water, and if there are no insects in it, they wash their feet with it, then they sit down on the small chairs. When they have rested awhile, the host, having observed the time and finding that the sun is nearly at the zenith, makes this announcement: 'It is the time.' Then each priest, folding his cloak by its two corners, ties them in front, and taking up the right corner of his skirt, holds it by the girdle at his left side. The priests cleanse their hands with powder made *of peas* or earth-dust; and either the host pours water, or the priests themselves use water out of the Ku*nd*î (i.e. jars); this is done according as they find one way or the other more convenient. Then they return to their seats. Next eating-utensils are distributed *to the guests*, which they wash slightly so that water does not flow over them. It is never customary to say a prayer before meals. The host, having cleansed his hands and feet (by this time), makes an offering to saints (images of arhats) at the upper end of the row of seats; then he distributes food to the priests. At the lowest end of the row an offering of food is made to the mother, Hâritî.

At the former birth of this mother, she from some cause or other, made a vow to devour all babes at Râ*g*ag*ri*ha. In consequence of this wicked vow, she forfeited her life, and was reborn as a Yakshî; and gave birth to five hundred children. Every day she ate some babes at Râ*g*ag*ri*ha, and the people informed the Buddha of this fact. He took and concealed one of her own children, which she called Her Beloved Child. She sought for it from place to place, and at last happened to find it near the Buddha. 'Art thou so sorry,' said the World-honoured One to her, 'for thy lost child, thy beloved? Thou lamentest for only one lost out of five hundred; how much more grieved are those who have lost their only one or two children on account of thy cruel vow?' Soon converted by the Buddha, she received the five precepts and became an Upâsikâ[1]. 'How shall my five hundred children subsist hereafter?' the new convert asked the Buddha. 'In every monastery,' replied the Buddha, 'where Bhikshus dwell, thy family shall partake of sufficient food, offered by them every day.' For this reason, the image of Hâritî is found either in the porch or in a corner of the dining-hall of all Indian monasteries depicting her as holding a babe in her arms, and round her knees three or five children. Every day an abundant offering of food is made before this image. Hâritî is one of the subjects of the four heavenly kings[2]. She has a power of giving wealth. If those who are childless on account of their bodily weakness (pray to her for children), making offerings of food, their wish is always fulfilled. A full account of her is given in the

---

[1] The conversion of the mythical monster is said to have occurred in the sixteenth year of the Buddha's ministry; see Rhys Davids, Buddhism, p. 73.

[2] *K*atûrmahârâ*g*adevâs (*K*âtummahârâ*g*ikâ devâ), Mahâvagga I, 6, 30.

Vinaya[1]; so I have only given it in brief. The portrait of 'the demon mother of the children' (Kuei-tze-mu) has already been found in China.

There is likewise in great monasteries in India, at the side of a pillar in the kitchen, or before the porch, a figure of a deity carved in wood, two or three feet high, holding a golden bag, and seated on a small chair, with one foot hanging down towards the ground. Being always wiped with oil its countenance is blackened, and the deity is called Mahâkâla or the great black deity. The ancient tradition asserts that he belonged to the beings (in the heaven) of the Great god (or Mahe*s*vara). He naturally loves the Three Jewels, and protects the five assemblies[2] from misfortune. Those who offer prayers to him have their desires fulfilled. At meal-times those who serve in the kitchen offer light and incense, and arrange all kinds of prepared food before the deity. I once visited the Pan-da-na monastery (Bandhana)[3], a spot where the great Nirvâ*n*a was preached (by the Buddha). There, usually more than a hundred monks dine. In spring and autumn, the best seasons for pilgrimages, the monastery is sometimes unexpectedly visited by a multitude (of travellers). Once five hundred priests suddenly arrived there, about midday. There was no time to prepare food for them exactly before noon. The managing priest said to the cooks: 'How shall we provide for this sudden increase?' An old woman, the mother of a monastic servant, replied: 'Be not perplexed, it is quite a usual occurrence.' Immediately she burnt abundant incense, and offered food before the black deity; and invoked him, saying: 'Though the Great Sage has gone to Nirvâ*n*a, yet beings like thyself still exist. Now (a multitude of) priests from every quarter has arrived here to worship the holy spot. Let not our food be deficient for supplying them; for this is within thy power. May thou observe the time.'

---

[1] The Sa*m*yuktavastu, chap. xxxi; Sa*m*yuktaratna-sûtra VII, 106.

[2] The five Parishads are: (1) Bhikshus, (2) Bhikshu*n*îs, (3) *S*ikshamâ*n*âs, (4) *S*rama*n*eras, (5) *S*rama*n*erîs. For four Parishads see Childers, s. v. parisâ (f), where *S*ikshamâ*n*âs, i. e. the women who are under instruction with the view of becoming *S*rama*n*erîs, are included in the *S*rama*n*erîs.

[3] This is no doubt a monastery in Maku*t*a-bandhana in Ku*s*inagara, see Mahâparinibbâna-sutta VI, 45, S. B. E., vol. xi, p. 129.

Then all the priests were asked to take seats. The food, provided for only the priests in residence at the monastery, when supplied was sufficient for that great multitude of priests, and there was as much remaining over as usual. All shouted 'Good!' and applauded the power of that deity. I myself went there to worship the spot; consequently I saw the image of that black deity before which abundant offerings of food were made. I asked the reason, and the above account was related to me. In China the image of that deity has often been found in the districts of Kiang-nan, though not in Huai-poh. Those who ask him (for a boon) find their wishes fulfilled. The efficacy of that deity is undeniable. The Nâga (snake) Mahâmu*k*ilinda[1] of the Mahâbodhi monastery (near Gayâ) has also a similar miraculous power.

The following is the manner of serving food. First, one or two pieces of ginger about the size of the thumb are served (to every guest), as well as a spoonful or half of salt on a leaf. He who serves the salt, stretching forth his folded hands and kneeling before the head priest, mutters 'Sa*m*prâgatam' (well come!). This is translated by 'good arrival.' The old rendering of it is Sam-ba[2] which is erroneous. Now the head priest says: 'Serve food equally.'

This word (Sa*m*prâgatam) conveys the idea that the entertainment is well provided, and that the time of the meal has just arrived. This is what is understood according to the sense of the word. But when the Buddha with his disciples once received poisoned food from some one, he taught them to mutter 'Sa*m*prâgatam;' then they all ate it. As much poison as was in the food was changed into nourishment. Considering the word from this point of view, we see that not only does it mean 'well-arrived,' but that it is also a mystic formula. In either language, whether of the East or of the West (i.e. in Chinese or in Sanskrit), one may utter this word as one likes. In the Ping and Fan[3] districts (in China) some pronounce Shi-chi, or 'the time has arrived,' which has a great deal of the original character.

He who serves food, standing before the guests, whose feet are in a

---

[1] Mu*k*ilinda, in Mahâvagga I, 3, comes to protect the Buddha, and even to hear the sermon; see S. B. E., vol. xiii, p. 80.

[2] 僧跋.

[3] 并汾.

line, bows respectfully, while holding plates, cakes, and fruits in his hands, serves them about one span away from (or above) the priest's hands; every other utensil or food must be offered one or two inches above the guest's hands. If anything be served otherwise, the guests should not receive it. The guests begin to eat as soon as the food is served; they should not trouble themselves to wait till the food has been served all round.

That they should wait till the food has been served equally all round is not a correct interpretation. Nor is it according to the Buddha's instruction that one should do as one likes after a meal.

Next some gruel made of dried rice and bean soup is served with hot butter sauce as flavouring, which is to be mixed with the other food with the fingers. They (the guests) eat with the right hand, which they do not raise up higher than the middle part of the belly. Now cakes and fruits are served; ghee and also some sugar. If any guest feels thirsty, he drinks cold water, whether in winter or summer. The above is a brief account of the eating of the priests in daily life as well as at a reception.

The ceremony of the Upavasatha-day is observed on a scale so grand that all the trays and plates are full of the cakes and rice remaining over; and melted butter and cream can be partaken of to any extent.

In the Buddha's time king Prasena*g*it[1] invited the members of the Buddha's Order, in order to offer them a feast, when drink, food, ghee, cream, &c., were served to such an extent that they overflowed profusely on the ground. There is some reference to this in the Vinaya texts. When I first arrived in Tâmralipti, in Eastern India, I wished to invite the priests on a small scale one fast-day. But people hindered me, saying: 'It is not impossible to prepare just enough food for the guests, but according to the traditional custom of olden times it is necessary to have an abundant supply. It is feared that men may smile, if the food supplied be only just sufficient to satisfy the stomach. We hear that you come from a great country in which every place is rich and prosperous; if you cannot prepare food in abundance you had better give up the idea.' Therefore I followed their custom, which is not at all unreasonable, for if the intention of giving food be generous the reward obtained *for the good work* will be correspondingly abundant.

[1] Or Pasenadi, king of Kosala.

He who is poor makes gifts, after a meal, of such trifles as he can afford. When the meal is finished the mouth is washed with a little water, which should be drunk. Some water must be poured out in a basin in order to wash slightly one's right hand; and that done, one can leave the table, when one should take a handful of food in the right hand and bring it out in order to give to others; this is allowed by the Buddha, whether the food belongs to the Buddha or to the Brotherhood. But to give away food before one eats is not taught in the Vinaya. Further a trayful of food is offered to the dead and other spirits who are worthy of offerings. The origin of this custom is traced to the Vulture Peak, as is found fully explained in the Sûtras[1].

One should bring that handful of food before the elder (i.e. Sthavira) and kneel down; the elder should sprinkle a few drops of water and say the following prayer:

'By virtue of the good works which we are about to accomplish, may we generously benefit the world of spirits who, having eaten the food, may be reborn in a pleasant state after death.

'The happiness of a Bodhisattva resulting from his good actions is limitless as the sky.

'He who benefits others can obtain such results as this (the happiness of a Bodhisattva); one should continue such actions evermore.'

After this, the food is to be brought out and to be placed in a hidden spot, in a forest, grove, river, or pond, in order to give it to the departed.

In the country on the rivers Yang-tze and Huai (in China), people prepare an additional tray of food on every fast-day; this custom is the same as above.

After the above ceremony is over the host (i.e. Dânapati) offers tooth-woods and pure water to the guests. The custom of rinsing is the same as explained in chap. v. On taking leave, the invited priests pronounce the words: 'All the meritorious deeds that have been done I gladly approve of.'

Each guest reads a gâthâ (a stanza) separately, but there is no religious ceremony after a meal. The priests can do what they like with the food left over (i.e. U*kkh*ish*t*abho*g*ana); they can either order a boy

---

[1] I have not yet been able to find out this allusion.

to carry it away or give it to the needy who are entitled to eat such food. Or if it be in a year of famine and it be feared that the host is mean, one should ask the host if that which is over may be taken away. There is no rule, however, for a host himself to gather up the remains of the feast. Such is the general rule for receiving offerings on an Upavasatha-day in India.

Sometimes the ceremony differs in one point or other: the host sets up holy images beforehand, and when noontide is at hand all the guests have to sit down and stretch forth their folded hands before these images, and each has to meditate upon the objects of worship. That done, they begin to eat. Sometimes the guests select one priest to go before the image and worship and praise the Buddha in a loud voice, kneeling down and stretching forth his folded hands.

(Note by I-tsing): 'Kneeling' is to put the two knees down to the ground, with both thighs supporting the body. It was wrongly rendered by the 'Mongolian way of kneeling,' in the older translations. But this is done in all the five parts of India; why then should we call it the 'Mongolian way of kneeling?'

The chosen priest (see above) has to speak of nothing but praise of the Buddha's virtues. The host (i.e. Dânapati) offers lights and scatters flowers, with undivided attention, full of respect; he anoints the priests' feet with powdered perfume and burns incense abundantly, which latter is not done by separate individuals[1].

An offering of music, such as the drum and stringed instruments, accompanied by songs, is made if the host likes it. Then the meal begins as each is served; and when it is finished, water from a jar is poured out *in a basin* before each guest. Then the head of the table (i.e. Sthavira) pronounces for the sake of the host a short Dânagâthâ. This latter is an alternative manner for receiving the offerings of food (on a fast-day) in India.

But the Indian way of eating is different from that of China in various points. I wish now to roughly sketch the general mode of taking food according to the Vinaya rules.

---

[1] It is often the case that several men burn incense one after another. On this occasion, I-tsing says, it is not done separately.

Pañ*k*abhoganîyam and Pañ*k*akhâdanîyam are often mentioned in the Vinaya[1]. Bhoganîyam means what is to be swallowed and eaten (i. e. wet and soft food), and Khâdanîyam, what is to be chewed or crunched (i. e. hard and solid food). Pañ*k*a being 'five,' we can translate the former by Chinese Wu-tan-shih[2] (i. e. five kinds of food), which has been hitherto known as the five kinds of proper food[2] in the general sense according to the meaning. The five Bhoganîyas are: 1. rice; 2. a boiled mixture of barley and peas; 3. baked corn-flour; 4. meat; 5. cakes. Pañ*k*akhâdanîyam is to be translated by Wu-chio-shih (i.e. five kinds of chewing food): 1. roots; 2. stalks; 3. leaves; 4. flowers; 5. fruits. If the first group of five (i. e. Pañ*k*abhoganîyas) be eaten, the other group of five is in no wise to be taken by those who have no reason for taking more food, but if the latter five be eaten first, the former five can be taken as one likes.

We may regard milk, cream, &c., as besides the two groups of the five mentioned above; for they have no special name given in the Vinaya, and it is clear that they are not included in the proper food.

Any food made of flour (such as pudding or gruel), *if so hard that* a spoon put in it stands upright without inclining any way, is to be included among cakes and rice. Baked flour mixed with water is also included in one of the five, if a finger-mark can be made on the surface of it.

As to the five countries of India, their boundaries are wide and remote; roughly speaking, *the distance from Central India* to the limit in each direction (lit. east, west, south, and north) is about 400 yoganas, the remote frontier not being counted in this measurement. Although I, myself, did not see all these parts of India, I could nevertheless ascertain anything by careful inquiry.

All food, both for eating and chewing, is excellently prepared in various ways. In the north, wheat-flour is abundant; in the western district, baked flour (rice or barley) is used above all; in Magadha

---

[1] E. g. the Sa*m*yuktavastu, book x (Nanjio's Catal., No. 1121), and Pâtimokkha, Pâ*k*. 37, S. B. E., vol. xiii, p. 40. For Khâdanîya and Bhoganîya, Childers, s. v.

[2] 五噉食 in Chinese, 五正 in the older translation.

(in Central India) wheat-flour is scarce, but rice is plentiful [1]; and the southern frontier and the eastern border-land have similar products to those of Magadha.

Ghee, oil, milk, and cream are found everywhere. Such things as cakes and fruit are so abundant that it is difficult to enumerate them here. Even laymen rarely have the taste of grease or flesh. Most of the countries have the rice which is not glutinous in abundance; millet is rare, and glutinous millet is not found at all. There are sweet melons; sugar-canes and tubers are abundant, but edible mallows are very scarce. Wan-ching (a kind of turnip) grows in sufficient quantities; there are two kinds of this, one with a white seed, the other with a black seed. This has recently become known as Chieh-tze (mustard seed) in China. Oil is extracted from it and used for flavouring purposes; this is done in all countries. In eating leaves of it as a vegetable we find them of the same taste as Wan-ching (a kind of turnip with a white root below the ground). But the root is hard, not like the Chinese turnip. The seed is somewhat larger and can no longer be considered 'mustard seed.' The change in the growth of this plant is considered to be something like the change of an orange-tree into a bramble when brought north of the Yang-tze River [2].

When I was in the Nâlanda monastery, I discussed this point with the Dhyâna master Wu-hing [3], but we were doubtful still and could not exactly distinguish one from the other. None of the people of all the

---

[1] Central India seems to have been suited for rice cultivation from early times. Names of king *S*uddhodana (Pure-rice), who settled in Kapilavastu, and his four brothers, Clear-rice, Strong-rice, White-rice, and Immeasurable-rice, show the importance of this cultivation to the *S*âkyas (see Oldenberg's Buddha, p. 97 note). Hiuen Thsang, at the beginning of book viii (Julien, vol. iii, p. 409), speaks of Magadha as a very fertile country, good for the cultivation of various kinds of rice.

[2] What he means here is this, that Indian mustard seed (Sarshapa) is larger than the Chinese; its taste is like Chinese turnip, but the roots, being hard, are different from the Chinese; and that the difference may be accounted for by the difference of soil, just as an orange-tree becomes a thorn when it is removed from the Kiang-nan (south of the Yang-tze River) to the north of the river.

[3] A Chinese priest whom I-tsing met unexpectedly in India, and whose Sanskrit name was Pra*gñ*âdeva; his biography is found in the second work of

five parts of India eat any kind of onions [1], or raw vegetables, and therefore they do not suffer from indigestion; the stomach and the intestines are healthy, and there is no trouble in their becoming hard and aching.

In the ten islands of the Southern Sea, the entertainment on the fast-day is made on a grander scale. On the first day the host prepares a Pin-lang nut [2], fragrant oil prepared from Fu-tzŭ [3] (mustaka, Cyperus rotundus), and a small quantity of crushed rice placed on a leaf in a plate; these three items being arranged on a large tablet are covered with a white cloth, water is poured out and kept in a golden jar, and the ground in front of this tablet is sprinkled with water. After these have been prepared, the priests are invited. In the forenoon of the last day, the priests are asked to anoint their bodies and wash and bathe. When the horse-hour (midday) of the second day has passed, a holy image is conveyed (from the monastery) on a carriage or on a palanquin, accompanied by a multitude of priests and laymen, playing or striking drums and musical instruments, making offerings of incense and flowers, and taking banners which shine in the sun,—in this manner it is carried to the courtyard of the house. Under a canopy amply spread, the image of gold or bronze, brilliant and beautifully decorated, is anointed with some aromatic paste, and then put in a clean basin. It is bathed by all those present with perfumed water (gandhodaka). After being wiped with a scented cloth, it is carried into the principal hall of the house, where it is received amidst rich offerings of lights and incense, while hymns of praise are sung. Then the priest first in rank (Sthavira) recites the Dânagâthâ for the host to declare the merit *of a religious feast with regard to the future life.* Then the priests are led outside the house to wash their hands and rinse their mouths, and, after this, sugar-water and Pin-lang fruits (i.e. betel-nuts) are offered to them in sufficient quantity; then they withdraw from the house. In the forenoon of the

---

I-tsing, Memoirs of Eminent Priests who visited India during the T'ang dynasty (Nanjio's Catal., No. 1491); Chavannes' translation, § 52, p. 138.

[1] See chap. xxviii below, p. 137; onions forbidden, *K*ull. V, 34, 1.

[2] I.e. betel-nut; it is called Pin-lang, from the Malay Pinang, which is the fruit of Areca Catechu.

[3] Read 付 for 片.

third day, the host, going to the monastery, announces to the priests: 'It is the time.' They, after bathing, come to the festal house. This time too the image is set up, and the ceremony of bathing it is held more briefly. But the offerings of flowers and incense and music are twice as grand as on the previous morning. Numerous offerings are arranged orderly before the image, and on both sides of it five or ten girls stand in array; and also some boys, according to convenience. Every one of them either *carries* an incense-burner, or holds a golden water-jar, or takes a lamp or some beautiful flowers, or a white fly-flapper. People bring and offer all kinds of toilet articles, mirrors, mirror-cases, and the like, before the image of the Buddha. 'For what purpose are you doing this?' I once inquired of them. 'Here is the field, and we sow our seed of merit,' they replied; 'if we do not make offerings now, how can we reap our future rewards?' It may be said reasonably that such is also a good action. Next, one of the priests, on being requested, kneels down before the image, and recites hymns in praise of the Buddha's virtues. After this two other priests, being requested, sitting near the image, read a short Sûtra of a page or a leaf. On such an occasion, they sometimes consecrate idols (lit. bless idols), and mark the eyeballs of them, in order to obtain the best reward of happiness. Now the priests withdraw at pleasure to one side of the room; and, folding up their Kâshâyas (i.e. yellow robes), and binding their two corners at the breasts, they wash their hands: then they sit down to eat [1].

As to the processes such as strewing the ground with cow-dung, examining water, or washing the feet, and as to the manner of taking or serving food, all these particulars are much the same as in India, with this addition, that in the islands of the Southern Sea the priests take the three kinds of pure meat [2] also. They frequently use leaves sewn together

---

[1] (Note by I-tsing): Ka-Cha (Kâshâya) is a Sanskrit word meaning the reddish colour (colour of Kan-da (?), an orchidaceous plant). It is not a Chinese word; what then is the use of choosing for the transliteration the two Chinese words which indicate robes (i.e. 架裟; 衣 being a sign of its being a robe). According to the Buddhist word of the Vinaya text, the three garments are all called *K*îvara.

[2] Three kinds of pure meat: (1) Meat of animals, &c., is pure when it is not

for plates as capacious as half a mat (on which they sit); and rice-cakes made of one or two Shăng[1] (a Shăng = about 2½ qt.) of non-glutinous grains, are prepared in such a plate. Having made similar vessels capable of one or two Shăng of grains, they bring them and offer them before the priests. Then twenty or thirty kinds of food are served to them. This, however, is the case of an entertainment by comparatively poor people. If it be by kings or rich men, bronze-plates, bronze-bowls, and also leafed plates as large as a mat are distributed: and the number of the several kinds of food and drink amounts to a hundred. Kings on such an occasion disregard their own high dignity, and call themselves servants, and help the priests to the food with every sign of respect. The priests have to receive as much food as is given, but never to resist it, however excessive it may be. If they have only food just enough to satisfy, the host would not be pleased; for he only feels satisfied when seeing food served over-abundantly. Four or five Shăng of boiled rice and cakes in two or three plates *are given to each*. The relations and the neighbours of the host help the entertainment, bringing with them several kinds of food, such as rice-cakes, boiled rice, vegetables for soup, &c. Usually the remainder of the food (i. e. U*kkh*ish*t*abho*g*ana) given to one person may satisfy three persons; but in case of a richer entertainment, it could not be eaten up even by ten men. The food remaining over is left to the priests, who order their servants to carry it *to the monastery*.

The ceremony of the Upavasatha-day reception in China differs from that of India. In China the host gathers the food left over, and the guests are not allowed to take it away. The priests may act according to the custom of their time, being self-contented and free from blame; thus the host's intention of gifts is by no means incomplete. But if the host (i.e. Dânapati) has made up his mind not to gather the food remaining, and asks the guests to take it away, one may act as best suits the circumstance.

---

seen that it is being killed for oneself; (2) When it is not heard that it has been killed for oneself; (3) When it is not suspected that it may have been killed for oneself. See Mahâvagga VI, 31, 14, 2, S. B. E., vol. xvii, p. 117.

Kâ*s*yapa says that this is only a Hînayâna rule and is mean and low.

[1] 'Shăng' here represents the Sanskrit prastha = 32 palas.

After the priests have finished eating, and have washed their hands and mouths, the remaining food is removed, the ground is cleansed, and flowers are scattered on it. There is illumination and burning of incense so that the air is perfumed, and whatever is to be given to the priests is ranged before them. Now perfume paste, about the size of a fruit of the Wu-tree (Dryandra-seeds), is given to each of them, and they rub their hands with it in order to make them fragrant and clean. Next, some Pin-lang fruit (betel-nuts) and nutmegs, mixed with cloves and Baros-camphor, are distributed: in eating these they get the mouth fragrant, the food digested, and the phlegm removed. These fragrant medicinal things and the others are given to the priests, after they have been washed with pure water, and wrapped in leaves.

Now the host, approaching the priest first in rank, or standing before the reciter (of the Sûtras), pours water from the beaked mouth of a jar (Ku*nd*i) into a basin, so that water comes out incessantly like a slender stick of copper. The priest mutters the Dânagâthâs, while taking flowers, and receiving with them the flowing water. First, verses from the words of the Buddha are recited, and then those composed by other persons. The number of the verses may be many or few according to the reciter's will, and according to circumstances. Then the priest, calling out the host's name, prays for happiness upon him, and wishes to transfer the happy reward of good actions done at present to those already dead, to the sovereigns, as well as to the snakes (Nâgas) and spirits; and prays, saying, 'May there be good harvests in the country, happy be the people and other creatures; may the noble teaching of the *S*âkya be everlasting.' I have translated these Gâthâs as seen elsewhere[1]. These are the blessing given by the World-honoured himself, who always said the Dakshi*n*âgâthâs[2] after the meal. This (Dakshi*n*â) means a gift offered, while Dakshi*n*îya is one worthy to be honoured with gifts. The Holy One, therefore, commands us that, after the meal, we should recite one or two Dânagâthâs in order to reward the host's hospitality; and if we neglect it, we are against the holy laws, and are not worthy to con-

[1] See the 'Rules of Confession,' by I-tsing (Nanjio's Catal., No. 1506).

[2] For the examples of Benediction, see Mahâparinibbâna-sutta I, 31; Mahâvagga VI, 35, 8; *G*âtaka I, 119.

sume the food offered. The rule of begging the remaining food is sometimes carried out after the feast.

Then gifts are distributed. Sometimes the host provides a 'wishing-tree' (Kalpa-*v*r*i*ksha), and gives it to the priests; or, *makes* golden lotus-flowers, and offers them to the image of the Buddha. Beautiful flowers as high as the knees, and white cloth, are *offered* in profusion on a couch. In the afternoon, sometimes a lecture is given on a short Sûtra. Sometimes the priests withdraw after passing the night. When they depart, they exclaim 'Sâdhu' and also 'Anumata.' Sâdhu means 'good!' and Anumata is translated by the word Sui-hsi (or *thou* 'art approved')[1]. Whenever gifts are made to others or to oneself, one should equally express approval (i. e. Anumata) *of the action*, for, by rejoicing at and praising another's gifts, one can obtain religious merit. The above is the general custom of entertainment on an Upavasatha-day in the islands of the Southern Sea.

There is another custom followed by the middle class of the people. First day, the priests are invited and presented with betel-nuts; second day, the image of the Buddha is bathed in the forenoon, the meal is taken at noontide, and Sûtras are recited in the evening. There is still another custom practised by the poor class of people. First day, the host presents tooth-woods to priests and invites them; on the morrow, he simply prepares a feast. Or sometimes the host goes and salutes priests, and expresses his wish of invitation without giving gifts.

The custom of reception on a fast-day differs also in the Turkish and Mongolian countries such as Tukhâra (i. e. the Tochari Tartars) and Sûli (west of Kashgar, peopled by Mongols or Turks; sometimes spelt 'Suri').

In these countries the host first presents a flower-canopy and makes offerings to the *K*aitya. A great crowd *of priests* surrounds the *K*aitya and selects a precentor to offer a prayer in a full form. That done, they begin to take meals. Rules about the flower-canopy are mentioned in the 'Record of the West[2].'

---

[1] I-tsing here adds a note on the transliteration of Dânapati. He, as usual, condemns the older translators.

[2] We do not know what this book is. It does not mean Hiuen Thsang's books; much less Fâ-hien's travels. It seems to be a book of his own.

Although the ceremonies of an Upavasatha-day in different countries vary so much in the general arrangements as well as in the food, yet the regulation of the Brotherhood, the protection of purity, the mode of taking food with fingers, and all other rules are much the same. There are some members of the Order who practise some of the Dhûtâṅgas (i. e. special regulations of daily life for Bhikshus), such as living on alms and wearing only the three garments (i. e. pai*nd*apâtikâṅga and trai*k*îvarikâṅga)[1]. Such a Bhikshu would not accept any invitation, and does not care for the gifts of any precious things such as gold, any more than for mucus or saliva, but lives retired in a lonely forest. If we turn to the East (China) and see the custom of reception on a *fast-day*, the host sends a note of invitation to the priests; and even on the next day he does not come and ask in person.

When compared with the rules set by the Buddha, this practice seems short of due respect. The laymen ought to be taught the regulations. Coming to a reception one should bring a filter, and the water supplied for the use of priests must be carefully examined. After eating, one should chew a tooth-wood; if any juice be left in the mouth, the religious ceremony of Upavasatha undertaken will not be complete. In such case the guilt of missing a prescribed time will be incurred, though one should pass the whole night in hunger. It is hoped that one will examine the mode of taking food in India, and discuss the Chinese custom by comparison. *The merit of each practice* will naturally be clear if one has more suitable points than the other. The wise must judge for themselves, as I have no time to devote to a full discussion here.

Some time ago, I tried to argue as follows: the World-honoured One, the highest, the Father of great compassion, exercised mercy over the people who are plunged *in the sea of transmigration*, his great exertion being extended over three great kalpas (i. e. long ages). Wishing that people would follow him, he lived for seven dozens of years preaching his doctrine. He thought that as the foundation of preserving the Laws, the regulations on food and clothing were the first and foremost; but he was afraid that any earthly troubles might come of them, and he therefore made strict rules and prohibitions.

---

[1] For the three garments, see Mahâvagga VIII, 13, 4, note, S. B. E., vol. xvii, p. 212. For the Dhûtâṅgas, see p. 56 below, note.

The regulations are the will of the Master, and one should by all means obey and practise them. But on the contrary there are some who carelessly think themselves guiltless, and who do not know that eating causes impurity.

Some observing one single precept on adultery say that they are free from sin, and do not at all care for the study of the Vinaya rules. They do not mind how they swallow, eat, dress, and undress. Simply directing their attention to the Doctrine of Nothingness is regarded by them as the will of the Buddha. Do such men think that all the precepts are not the Buddha's will? Valuing one and disregarding another results from one's own judgement. The followers imitate one another and never look at those books of precepts; they copy only two volumes of the 'Doctrine of Nothingness,' and say that the principle contained in it embraces all the three deposits (i.e. Tripi*t*aka) of scriptures.

But they do not know that every meal, if unlawful, causes the suffering of pouring sweat *in hell;* nor are they aware that every step wrongly taken brings to one misery of living as a rebel.

The original intention of a Bodhisattva is to keep the air-bag (*which has been given to all beings that are floating in the sea of existence*)[1] tight, without leaking. Not overlooking even a small offence of our own, we can also fulfil the declaration that *this life* is the very last. We can reasonably practise both the Mahâ(yâna) and the Hîna(yâna) doctrines in obedience to the instruction of the merciful Honoured One, preventing small offences, and meditating upon the great Doctrine of Nothingness. If affairs have been well administered and our minds tranquillised, what fault is there in us (*in following both doctrines*)?

Some are afraid of misleading others as well as themselves, and follow only one side of the teaching.

Of course the law of 'Nothingness' is not a false doctrine, but the Canon of the Vinaya (moral discipline) must never be neglected. One should preach the morality (*S*ila) every fortnight, and at the same time confess and wash off one's own sins; one should always teach and encourage the followers to worship the Buddha three times every day.

---

[1] Kâ*s*yapa says that the Nirvâ*n*a-sûtra refers to a Râkshasa's asking the Buddha for an air-bag to cross the sea. But we do not find this allusion in the Pâli text.

The teaching of the Buddha is becoming less prevalent in the world from day to day; when I compare what I have witnessed in my younger days with what I see *to-day* in my old age the state is altogether different, and we are bearing witness to this, and it is to be hoped that we shall be more attentive in future.

The necessity of eating and drinking is permanent, but those who are honouring and serving the Buddha should never disregard any points of his noble teaching.

Again I say: the most important are only one or two out of eighty thousand doctrines of the Buddha; one should conform to the worldly path, but inwardly strive to secure true wisdom. Now what is the worldly path? It is obeying prohibitive laws and avoiding any crime. What is the true wisdom? It is to obliterate the distinction between subject and object, to follow the excellent truth, and to free oneself from worldly attachments; to do away with the existing trammels of the chain of causality; further to obtain religious merit by accumulating numerous good works, and finally to realise the excellent meaning of perfect reality.

One should never be ignorant of the Tripi*t*aka, nor be perplexed in the teaching and principles contained in it. Some have committed sins as numerous as the grains of sand of the Ganges, yet they say that they have realised the state of Bodhi (i.e. true wisdom). Bodhi means enlightenment, and in it all the snares of passion are destroyed. The state in which neither birth nor death is found is the true permanence. How can we thoughtlessly say, as some do, while living in the sea of trouble, that we live in the Land of Bliss (Sukhâvatî)?

One who wishes to realise the truth of permanence should observe the moral precepts in purity. One should guard against *a small defect* which results, just as a small escape of air from the life-belt may result, *in loss of life;* and one should prevent a great offence *that makes one's life* useless, just as a needle the eye of which has been broken off becomes useless. First and foremost of all the great offences are those in food and clothing. Final Liberation (Moksha) will not be very far from one who follows the teaching of the Buddha, but transmigration will go on for evermore for one who disregards the noble words. I have thus far mentioned the lawful practices and briefly described the former examples, all resting on noble authorities, but not on opinions of my own. I hope that I do not offend you in my straightforward statements, and that my Record will help towards the solution of any doubts that you may have. If I did not exactly state the good and bad practices (*of India and China*), who would ever know what is good or bad in the two?

CHAPTER X.

NECESSARY FOOD AND CLOTHING.

It may be observed that the earthly body which requires support is only maintained by food and clothing, while the spiritual knowledge that is beyond the bond of births can only be increased by means of the principle of nothingness. If the use of food and clothing be against proper rules, every step will involve some crime; while tranquillisation of the mind without moral regulation will cause more and more perplexity as one goes on meditating.

Therefore those who seek for Final Liberation (Moksha) should use food and clothing according to the noble words of the Buddha, and those who practise the principle of meditation should follow the teaching of former sages in tranquillising their thoughts. Watch over the life here below, which is but a dungeon for the beings that have gone astray, but look eagerly for the shore of Nirvâ*n*a, which is the open gate of enlightenment and quietude. The ship of the Law should be manned ready for the sea of suffering, and the lamp of wisdom should be held up during the long period of darkness. There are express laws in the Vinaya text on the observance and neglect that are evident in the light of the regulations of clothing and the rules of eating and drinking, so that even beginners in the study can judge the nature of an offence.

Each individual must himself be responsible for the results of his own practices, whether good or bad, and there is no need of argument here. But there are some who are, as teachers of the students, grossly offending against the Vinaya rules; there are others who say that the usage of the world, *even if against the Buddha's discipline*, does not involve any guilt. Some understand that the Buddha was born in India, and Indian Bhikshus follow Indian customs, while we ourselves live in China, and, as Chinese monks, we follow Chinese manners. 'How can we,' they argue, 'reject the elegant dress of the Divine Land (China) to receive the peculiar style *of garments* of India?' For the sake of those who adhere to this view I here roughly state my opinion, founded on the authority of the Vinaya.

The regulations of clothing are the most important for the life of a homeless priest (i. e. Pravragyâ), and I should therefore mention here in detail the style of garments, because these cannot be neglected or curtailed. As to the three garments (collectively called '*k*ivara'), the patches are sewn close in the five parts of India, while in China alone they are open and not sewn. I myself have made inquiry as to the custom adopted in the northern countries (beyond India) *and found out that* patches are sewn close, and never open in all the places where the Vinaya of the four divisions (i.e. *K*aturnikâya) is practised.

Suppose that a Bhikshu of the West (i. e. India) has obtained a priestly dress of China; he would probably sew the patches together and then wear it.

The Vinaya texts of all the Nikâyas mention that the patches ought to be sewn and fastened.

There are strict rules about the six Requisites and the thirteen Necessaries fully explained in the Vinaya. The following are the six Requisites of a Bhikshu:—

1. The Saṅghâ*t*î, which is translated by the 'double cloak.'
2. The Uttarâsaṅga, which is translated by the 'upper garment.'
3. The Antarvâsa, which is translated by the 'inner garment.'

The above three are all called *k*îvara. In the countries of the North these priestly cloaks are generally called kâshâya from their reddish colour. This is not, however, a technical term used in the Vinaya.

4. Pâtra, the bowl.
5. Nishîdana, something for sitting or lying on.
6. Parisrâva*n*a, a water-strainer.

A candidate for Ordination should be furnished with a set of the six Requisites[1].

The following are the thirteen Necessaries[2]:—

---

[1] The eight Parishkâras (Requisites) in the Pâli texts are the bowl, the three robes, the girdle, a razor, a needle, and a water-strainer (Abhidhânappadîpikâ, 439; the Ten *G*âtakas, 120).

[2] Cf. Mahâvyutpatti, 272, where the thirteen are enumerated, though not quite the same. See my additional note at the end.

1. Saṅghâṭî, a double cloak.
2. Uttarâsaṅga, an upper garment.
3. Antarvâsa, an inner garment.
4. Nishîdana, a mat for sitting or lying on.
5. (Nivâsana), an under garment.
6. Prati-nivâsana (a second nivâsana).
7. Saṅkakshikâ, a side-covering cloth.
8. Prati-saṅkakshikâ (a second saṅkakshikâ).
9. (Kâya-proñkhana), a towel for wiping the body.
10. (Mukha-proñkhana), a towel for wiping the face.
11. (Kesapratigraha), a piece of cloth used for receiving hair when one shaves.
12. (Kaṇḍupratikkhadana), a piece of cloth for covering itches.
13. (Bheshagaparishkârakîvara)*, a cloth kept *for defraying* the cost of medicine (*in case of necessity*).

It is expressed in a Gâthâ as follows:—

The three garments, the sitting mat (1, 2, 3, 4).
A couple of petticoats and capes (5, 6, 7, 8).
Towels for the body and face, a shaving-cloth (9, 10, 11).
A cloth for itching and a garment for medicament (12, 13).

These thirteen Necessaries are allowed to any priest to possess—this is the established rule, and one should use these according to the Buddha's teaching. These thirteen, therefore, must not be classed with any other properties of luxury, and these items should be catalogued separately, and be marked, and kept clean and safe.

Whatever you obtain of the thirteen you may keep, but do not trouble to possess all of them. All other luxurious dress not mentioned above should be kept distinct from these necessaries, but such things as woollen gear or carpets may be received and used in compliance with the intention of the givers. Some are wont to speak of the three garments and ten necessaries, but this division is not found in the Indian text, the thirteen having been divided into two groups by some translators on their own authority. They specially mention the three garments, and further allow the ten things to be possessed. But what are the ten things? They could never exactly point them out, and thus allowed some cunning commentators to take advantage of this omission, and the character Shih (什), meaning 'ten,' was interpreted by 'miscellaneous' by these commentators, but this cannot be the meaning attributed by the ancient authority in this case.

The cloth for defraying the cost of medicaments allowed to the priest by the Buddha should consist of silk about 20 feet long, or a full piece of it. (One p'i in the text = about 21½ yards in Japan.) A sickness may befall one on a sudden, and a means *of procuring medicine* hastily sought is difficult to obtain.

For this reason *an extra cloth* was ordained to be kept prepared beforehand, and as this is necessary at the time of illness, one should never use it otherwise. In the way leading to religious practice and charity, the chief object is universal salvation. There are three classes of men as regards their ability, and they cannot all be led in one and the same way. The four Refuges[1], the four Actions[2], and the thirteen Dhûtâṅgas[3] were ordained for men of superior faculties.

---

[1] Four Refuges: (1) Pâ*m*sukûlikâṅga; (2) Pai*nd*apâtikâṅga; (3) V*ri*kshamûlikâṅga; (4) Pûtimûtrabhaishagya. For 1, 2, and 3, see note to the thirteen Dhûtâṅgas below; and for 4, see chap. xxix, pp. 138–139.

[2] Four (proper) Actions are given in the Mûlasarvâstivâdaika*s*atakarman, chap. i (I-tsing's translation, No. 1131 in Nanjio's Catalogue): (1) Not returning slander for slander; (2) Not returning anger for anger; (3) Not meeting insult with insult; (4) Not returning blow for blow.

[3] Thirteen Dhûtâṅgas are certain ascetic practices, the observance of which is meritorious in a Buddhist priest. These are sometimes enumerated as 'twelve' Dhûtagu*n*as, see Kasawara's Dharmasaṅgraha LXIII.

Pâli.	Chinese Explanation.	Literal Translation of the Chinese.
1. Pa*m*sukûlikaṅga*m* (Skt. Pâ*m*sukûlika, 11)	糞掃衣	Having the garments made of rags from the dust-heap (pâ*m*su).
2. Te*k*îvarikaṅga*m* (Skt. Trai*k*îvarika, 2)	但衣之人	Becoming a man who wears only (three) garments.
3. Pi*nd*apâtikaṅga*m* (Skt. Pai*nd*apâtika, 1)	常乞食	Begging constantly.
4. Sapadâna*k*ârikaṅga*m* (Deest)	次第乞食	Begging from door to door.

The possession of rooms, the acceptance of gifts, and the thirteen Necessaries are allowed both to the medium and inferior classes of priests. Hence those whose wishes are few are free from faulty indulgence in luxury, and those who require more do not suffer from want. Great is the compassionate Father (the Buddha), who skilfully answers the wants of every kind, who is the good leader among men and devas. He is called the 'Tamer of the Human Steed' (purushadamyasârathi).

The passage relating to a hundred and one possessions (of which the Chinese school of Vinaya, Nan-shan, is wont to speak) is not found in the Vinaya text of the four Nikâyas.

Although there is a certain reference, in some Sûtras, to 'One hundred and one possessions,' yet it is meant for a special occasion. Even in the house of a layman whose possessions are many, the family possessions do not amount to fifty in number; is it likely that the Son of the *S*âkya (i. e. *S*âkyaputra), whose earthly attachments have been shaken

---

5.	Ekâsanikaṅga*m* (Skt. Ekâsanika, 7)	一坐食	Eating at one sitting.
6.	Pattapi*nd*ikaṅga*m* (Deest)	鉢乞食	Begging with a bowl.
7.	Khalupa*kkh*âbhattikaṅga*m* (Skt. Khalupa*sk*âdbhaktika, 3)	不重受食	Not receiving food twice (or afterwards).
8.	Âra*ññ*akaṅga*m* (Skt. Âra*n*yaka, 9)	住阿蘭若	Living in an Ara*n*ya (forest).
9.	Rukkhamûlikaṅga*m* (Skt. V*ri*kshamûlika, 6)	樹下居	Sitting under a tree.
10.	Abbhokâsikaṅga*m* (Skt. Âbhyavakâ*s*ika, 8)	露處住	Residing in an unsheltered place.
11.	Sosânikaṅga*m* (Skt. *S*mâ*s*ânika, 10)	屍林住	Visiting a cemetery.
12.	Yathâsanthatikaṅga*m* (Skt. Yathâsa*m*starika, 5)	隨處坐	Taking any seat that may be provided.
13.	Nesa*gg*ikaṅga*m* (Skt. Naishadyika, 4)	常坐人	Being in a sitting posture (even while sleeping).

I give the Pâli names because the number and order of the thirteen given in the Commentary exactly correspond with the Pâli; see Dhûtaṅga*m*, Childers. The above 4 and 6 are wanting in the Sanskrit, while a new Dhûtagu*n*a called 'Nâmatika,' i. e. 'wearing a felt,' is added, see *K*ullavagga V, 11, 1, note 3, S. B. E., vol. xx; Burnouf, Introduction, p. 306; Dharmasaṅgraha, p. 48, note.

off, should possess more than one hundred things? Whether this is permissible or not can be ascertained by appealing to reason.

As to fine and rough silk, these are allowed by the Buddha. What is the use of laying down rules for a strict prohibition of silk? The prohibition was laid down by some one; though intended for lessening complication, such a rule increases it. The four Nikâyas of the Vinaya of all the five parts of India use (*a silk garment*). Why should we reject the silk that is easy to be obtained, and seek the fine linen that is difficult to be procured? Is not this the greatest hindrance to religion? Such a rule may be classed with the forcible prohibitions that have never been laid down (by the Buddha).

The result is that curious students of the Vinaya increase their self-conceit and cast slight upon others (*who are using silk*). People who are disinterested and less avaricious are much ashamed of such, and say: 'How is it that they regard self-denial as a help to religion?' But if (*the refusal of the use of silk*) comes from the highest motive of pity, because silk is manufactured by injuring life, it is quite reasonable that they should avoid the use of silk to exercise compassion on animate beings. Let it be so; the cloth one wears, and the food one eats, mostly come from an injury to life. The earthworms (*that one may tread on while walking*) are never thought of; why should the silkworm alone be looked after? If one attempts to protect every being, there will be no means of maintaining oneself, and one has to give up life without reason. A proper consideration shows us that such *a practice* is not right.

There are some who do not eat ghee or cream, do not wear leather boots, and do not put on any silk or cotton. All these are the same class of people as are mentioned above.

Now as to killing. If a life be destroyed intentionally, a result of this action (Karma) will be expected; but if not intentionally, no guilt will be incurred, according to the Buddha's words. The three kinds of meat[1] that are pure are ordained as meats that can be eaten without incurring guilt. If the spirit of this rule be disregarded, it will involve some offence though small.

(In eating the three kinds of meat), we have no intention of killing, and therefore we have a cause or reason that makes our eating of flesh

[1] See chap. ix, p. 46, note 2.

guiltless. (Such meat is as pure) as any other thing which we receive as a gift, and therefore we have an example (or instance) which helps us in making our reasoning very clear. When the cause and instance (of our eating flesh) are so clear and faultless, then the doctrine we advocate becomes also clear and firm. Now the three branches of reasoning have been as clearly constructed as above[1], and besides, we have the golden words of the Buddha to the same effect. What then is the use of arguing any further? As a doubtful reading of 'Five Hundred' (for 'Five Days') has been originated by the pen of an author, and a mistaken idea about 'Three Pigs' (for 'Earth-Boar') has also been received as true by the believers[2], (so people are led to confusion if we go on arguing things too much.)

Such deeds as begging personally for cocoons containing silkworms, or witnessing the killing of the insects, are not permissible, even to a layman, much less to those whose hearts aspire to final emancipation. These deeds, when looked at in this light, prove themselves to be quite impermissible. But supposing a donor (i. e. Dânapati) should bring and present (*some such thing as silk cloth*), then a priest should utter the word 'Anumata' (i. e. 'approved'), and accept the gift in order to have a means of supporting his body while he cultivates the virtues; no guilt will be incurred by so doing. The ecclesiastic garments *used* in the five parts of India are stitched and sewn at random, with no regard to the threads of cloth being lengthway or crossway. The period of making (them) does not exceed three or five days. I think that a full piece of silk can be made into one cassock[3] of five lengths, and into another of seven lengths, the *lining lengths* being three fingers wide, the collar, an inch. This collar has three rows of stitching, while the lining pieces are all sewn together. These cassocks are used in performing a ceremony as occasion may demand. And why should we use a good and excellent one?

---

[1] I-tsing is here trying to construct a syllogism according to the Indian logic; my translation of these passages is as literal as possible, though I am obliged to put in some words in brackets.

[2] 五百 for 五日 and 三豕 for 己亥 are used as instances of mistakes in writing or misprints, but I cannot state how these mistakes came about.

[3] 'Kâshâya,' the yellow robe.

Economy is aimed at in using a ragged garment[1]. One may sometimes gather pieces left on dust-heaps, sometimes pick up abandoned rags in the cemetery groves; when one has accumulated them, one stitches them together and uses the cassock made of them to protect the body against the cold and hot weather. There are some, however, who say that in the Vinaya texts the 'thing to lie on' is the same thing as the three garments (i.e. Tri*k*îvara), but when it became evident that, (*among the 'things to lie on'*), one which is made of the silk from wild cocoons was prohibited, a strange idea was introduced, and it was considered that the priestly garments should not be of silk, and the priests became very particular about choosing linen as the material. But they did not know that in the original text *the thing to lie on* was, from the beginning, a mattress.

Kau*s*eya[2] (n.) is the name for silkworms, and the silk which is reared from them is also called by the same name Kau*s*eya[3] (n.); it is a very valuable thing and is prohibited to be used (for a mattress). There are two ways of making the mattress; one way is to sew a piece of cloth so as to make a bag in which wool is put, the other is to weave (cotton) threads (into a mattress), the latter being something like Ch'ü-shu[4] (a kneeling-mat'). The size of a mattress is two cubits wide and four cubits long; it is thick or thin according to the season. Begging for a mattress is forbidden, but if given by others no guilt is incurred (in accepting it), but the (actual) use of it was not allowed (by the Buddha)[5], and strict rules were laid down in detail. All these are the things to lie on, and are not the same thing as the three garments (i.e. Tri*k*îvara).

Again, the 'right livelihood' mentioned in the Vinaya means, above

---

[1] 衲衣; the text has 納衣 by mistake.

[2] This word occurs in Hiuen Thsang. See Julien, Mémoires, liv. ii, 68.

[3] For some reference to Kau*s*eya, see Mahâvagga VIII, 3, 1; Julien's Hiuen Thsang, I, 253; II, 68, 189.

[4] The Chinese is 氍毹. It may be observed that this name is not Chinese, and that this mat was first brought from India. The Chinese is sometimes 氍氀; I cannot yet find the Sanskrit equivalent. Perhaps Ûr*n*a.

[5] It is often the case that a thing is allowed to be possessed, but not allowed to be used. I-tsing may be thinking of a rule to the above effect, though this is not clear.

all, one's eating (lit. mouth and stomach). The tilling of land should be done according to its proper manner (i. e. to till land for oneself is not permissible, but to do so for a Buddhist community, Saṅgha, is allowable), while sowing or planting are not against the teaching (lit. the net of teaching). If food be taken according to the law, no guilt will be incurred, for it is said in the beginning[1], 'by building up one's character one could increase one's own happiness.'

According to the teaching of the Vinaya, when a cornfield is cultivated by the Saṅgha (the Brotherhood or community), a share in the product is to be given to the monastic servants or some other families by whom the actual tilling has been done. Every product should be divided into six parts, and one-sixth should be levied by the Saṅgha; the Saṅgha has to provide the bulls as well as the ground for cultivation, while the Saṅgha is responsible for nothing else. Sometimes the division of the product should be modified according to the seasons.

Most of the monasteries in the West follow the above custom, but there are some who are very avaricious and do not divide the produce, but the priests themselves give out the work to servants, male and female, and see that the farming is properly done.

Those who observe the moral precepts do not eat food given by such persons, for it is thought that such priests themselves plan out the work and support themselves by a 'wrong livelihood;' because in urging on hired servants by force, one is apt to become passionate, the seeds may be broken, and insects be much injured while the soil is tilled. One's daily food does not exceed one Shăng, and who can *endure* hundreds of sins incurred *while striving to get even that?*

Hence an honest man hates the cumbersome work of a farmer, and permanently keeps away from it (lit. rejects it and gallops away for ever) carrying with him a pot and a bowl.

Such a man sits still in a place in a quiet forest and takes pleasure in company with birds and deer; being free from the noisy pursuit of fame and profit he practises with a view to the perfect quietude of Nirvâ*n*a. According to the Vinaya it is allowable for a Bhikshu to try to gain profits on behalf of the Brotherhood (i. e. Saṅgha), but tilling land and injuring life are not permitted in the Buddha's teaching, for there

[1] In what or by whom? The text has 始日.

is nothing so great in injuring insects and hindering proper action as agriculture. In the books written, we have not seen the slightest reference to acres of land (lit. ten acres, but 'ten' here is as much as to say 'some') that might lead one to a sinful and wrong livelihood; but as to the rules on the three garments that may be faultlessly, nay, rightly carried out, how much [1] pen and ink have been wasted by people! Alas! these matters can only be explained to those who are believing, but not be discussed with those who are sceptical. I only fear that those who are handing down the Laws may embrace an obstinate view.

When I for the first time visited Tâmralipti, I saw in a square outside the monastery some of its tenants who, having entered there, divided some vegetables into three portions, and, having presented one of the three to the priests, retired from thence, taking the other portions with them. I could not understand what they did, and asked of the venerable Ta-shăng Tăng (Mahâyâna Pradîpa [2]) what was the motive. He replied: 'The priests in this monastery are mostly observers of the precepts. As cultivation by the priests themselves is prohibited [3] by the great Sage, they suffer their taxable lands to be cultivated by others freely, and partake of only a portion of the products. Thus they live their just life, avoiding worldly affairs, and free from the faults of destroying lives by ploughing and watering fields.

I also observed, that every morning the managing priest (of that monastery) examined water on the side of a well; that, if there was no insect in it, that water was used, and if there was a life in it, it was filtered; that, whenever anything, even a stalk of vegetable, was given (to the priests) by other persons, they made use of it through the assent of the assembly; that no principal office was appointed in that monastery; that when any business happened, it was settled by the assembly; and

---

[1] J. has 還復 instead of 遠脫復, which is the reading of all other texts. The former is, no doubt, correct. 遠 is certainly a mistake for 還; 脫 is a word used for 'left out' in copying; and thus 還脫 might have been a marginal remark by a copyist, showing that here the character 還 was left out; but gradually these two characters might have got into the text. This is the only explanation I can give; otherwise this passage is unintelligible.

[2] See Chavannes, p. 68, § 32.

[3] Pâtimokkha, S.B.E., vol. xiii, p. 33.

that, if any priest decided anything by himself alone, or treated the priests favourably or unfavourably at his own pleasure, without regarding the will of the assembly, he was expelled (from the monastery), being called a Kulapati (i. e. he behaved like a householder).

The following things also came under my notice. When the nuns were going to the priests in the monastery, they proceeded thither after having announced (their purpose to the assembly). The priests, when they had to go to the apartments of the nuns, went there after having made an inquiry. They (the nuns) walked together in a company of two, if it was away from their monastery; but when they had to go to a layman's house for some necessary cause, they went thither in a company of four. I saw that on the four Upavasatha-days of every month a great multitude of priests, all having assembled there late in the afternoon from several monasteries, listened to the reading of the monastic rites, which they obeyed and carried out with increasing reverence.

I also witnessed the following things. One day a minor teacher (i. e. one who is not yet a Sthavira) sent to a tenant's wife two Shăng (prastha) of rice, carried by a boy. This action was considered to be a sort of trick. The case was brought by a person before the assembly. The teacher was summoned, examined, and he and his two accomplices admitted the charge. Though he was free from crime, yet, being ashamed, he withdrew his name (from the assembly), and retired from the monastery for ever. His preceptor sent him his clothing (which was left behind him) by another person. Thus all the priests submitted to their own laws, without ever giving any trouble to the public court. Whenever women entered into the monastery, they never proceeded to the apartments (of the priests), but spoke with them in a corridor for a moment, and then retired. At that time there was a Bhikshu named A-ra-hu-(not 'shi')la-mi-ta-ra (Râhula-mitra)[1] in that monastery. He

---

[1] This Râhula-mitra may be the same as that Râhulaka whose verses are given in the Subhâsitavali of Vallabhadeva (2900), and in the *S*ârṅgadharapaddhati (135, 14). These verses are (see p. 104, Peterson's Subhâshitavali)—

I. Subh. 2900 : Ya*h* kurute parayoshitsaṅga*m*
Vâ*ñkh*ati ya*s*k*a dhana*m* parakîyam ;
Ya*s*k*a sadâ guruv*ri*ddhavimânî
Tasya sukha*m* na paratra na *k*eha.

was then about thirty years old; his conduct was very excellent and his fame was exceedingly great. Every day he read over the Ratnakû*t*a-sûtra [1], which contains 700 verses. He was not only versed in the three collections of the scriptures, but also thoroughly conversant with the secular literature on the four sciences. He was honoured as the head of the priests in the eastern districts of India [2]. Since his ordination he never had spoken with women face to face, except when his mother or sister came to him, whom he saw outside (his room). Once I asked him why he behaved thus, as such is not holy law. He replied: 'I am naturally full of worldly attachment, and without doing thus, I cannot stop its source. Although we are not prohibited (to speak with women) by the Holy One, it may be right (to keep them off), if it is meant to prevent our evil desires.'

The assembly assigned to venerable priests, if very learned, and also to those who thoroughly studied one of the three collections, some of the best rooms (of the monastery) and servants. When such men gave daily lectures, they were freed from the business imposed on the monastics. When they went out, they could ride in sedan-chairs, but not on horseback. Any strange priest who arrived at the monastery, was treated by the assembly with the best of their food for five days, during which he was desired to take rest from his fatigue. But after these days he was treated as a common monastic. If he was a man of good character, the assembly requested him to reside with them, and supplied him with bed-gear as suited to his rank. But if he was not learned, he was regarded as a mere priest; and, if he, on the contrary, was very learned, he was treated as stated above. Then his name was written down on the register of the names of the resident priests. Then he was just the same as the old residents. Whenever a layman came there with a good

---

II. *S*âri*n*ga. 135, 14:

Unnidrakandaladalântaralîyamâna—
Gu*ñg*anmadândhamadhupâ*ñk*itameghakâle;
Svapnespi ya*h* pravasati pravihâya kântâ*m*
Tasmai vishâ*n*arahitâya namo v*ri*shâya.

[1] Two translations of this Sûtra exist in the Chinese Collection, one in A.D. 25–220, the other in A.D. 589–618 (Nanjio's Catal., Nos. 251 and 51).

[2] The text has the 'Eastern Ârya-de*s*a.'

inclination, his motive was thoroughly inquired into, and if it was his intention to become a priest, he was first shaved. Thenceforth his name had no concern with the register of the state; for there was a register-book of the assembly (on which his name was written down). If he afterwards violated the laws and failed in his religious performances, he was expelled from the monastery without sounding the Gha*n*tâ (bell). On account of the priests' mutual confession, their faults were prevented before their growth.

When I have observed all these things, I said to myself with emotion: 'When I was at home, I thought myself to be versed in the Vinaya, and little imagined that one day, coming here, I should prove myself really one ignorant (of the subject). Had I not come to the West, how could I ever have witnessed such correct manners as these!'

Of these above described some are the monastic rites, while others are specially made for the practice of self-denial; and all the rest are found in the Vinaya, and most important to be carried out in this remote period (from the Buddha's time). All these form the ritual of the monastery Bha-ra-ha[1] at Tâmralipti.

The rites of the monastery Nâlanda are still more strict. Consequently the number of the residents is great and exceeds 3,000[2]. The lands in its possession contain more than 200 villages. They have been bestowed (upon the monastery) by kings of many generations. Thus the prosperity of the religion continues ever, owing to nothing but (the fact that) the Vinaya (is being strictly carried out).

I never saw (in India) such customs as are practised (in China), i. e. (in deciding a matter concerning the monastery), the ordinary officials have a special sitting at the court, and all the priests concerned in the matter attend there in a row, shouting and disputing, or cheating and despising one another, just like ordinary people. The priests run about to see off an officer who is leaving and to welcome a new one who is arriving. When the inspection or examination by the new officer does not reach so far as the matters or things of the monastery, the priests visit

[1] Barahat or Varâha?

[2] 3,000 (not 5,000) in chap. xxxii below, p. 153, and 3,500 in I-tsing's Memoirs. See Chavannes, p. 97.

the residence of the officer and ask the (same) favour through the under-officers (so hastily that) they omit inquiring after the officer's health.

Now why do we become homeless? It is because we wish to keep apart from the worldly troubles in order to abandon the dangerous path of the five fears [1], and thereby to arrive at the peaceful terrace of the noble eightfold (path) [2]. Is it right, then, that we should be involved in troubles, and once again be caught in the net (of sin)?

If we behave so, our wish of attaining the perfect calm (Nirvâ*n*a) will never be fulfilled. Nay, it may be said that we are acting entirely against 'liberation' (Moksha), and do not pursue the way to quietude (Nirvâ*n*a). It is only reasonable that we should support our life practising the twelve Dhûtâṅgas [3], and possessing only the thirteen necessary things [4], according to our circumstances. The influence of Karma (action) is to be done away with; the great benefits conferred by our teacher, our Saṅgha, and our parents are to be requited, and the deep compassion that was shown by Devas, Nâgas, or sovereigns is to be repaid. To behave so is indeed to follow the example of the Tamer of the Hûman Steed (i.e. the Buddha), and to pursue rightly the path of Discipline (Vinaya). And I have thus discussed the mode of life of a priest, and also spoken of the present practices of (China and India). May all the virtuous not find my discussion too tedious!

The distinction of the four Nikâyas (schools) is shown by the difference of wearing the Nivâsana (i.e. under-garment). The Mûlasarvâstivâda-nikâya pulls up the skirt on both sides, (draws the ends through the girdle and suspends them over it), whereas the Mahâsaṅghikanikâya takes the right skirt to the left side and presses it tight (under the girdle) so as not to let it loose; the custom of wearing the under-garment of the Mahâsaṅghikanikâya is similar to that of Indian women. The rules (of putting on the under-garment) of the Sthaviranikâya and of the Sammitinikâya are identical with those of the Mahâsaṅghikanikâya,

---

[1] Five fears are (1) failure of livelihood, (2) bad name, (3) death, (4) a birth in the lower form as an animal, &c., (5) worldly influence.

[2] Rhys Davids, Buddhism, pp. 47, 108; Oldenberg, Buddha &c., p. 211.

[3] See above, p. 56, where thirteen Dhûtâṅgas are mentioned.

[4] See above, p. 55.

except that the former (the Sthavira and Sammiti) leave the ends of the skirt outside, while the latter presses it inwardly as mentioned above. The make of the girdle (Kâyabandhana) is also different[1].

The nun's mode of *putting on the* under-garment is the same as that of a Bhikshu of her respective school. But the Chinese Saṅkakshikâ, shoulder-covering robes, nivâsana, drawers, trousers, robe, and shirt, are all made against the original rules. Not only having both sleeves in one and the same garment, the back of which is sewn together, but even the wearing of the garment is not in accordance with the Vinaya rules. All manners of dress in China are *liable* to produce guilt.

If we come to India in Chinese garments, they all laugh at us; we get much ashamed in our hearts, and we tear our garments to be used for miscellaneous purposes, for they are all unlawful. If I do not explain this point, no one will know the fact. Although I wish to speak straightforwardly, yet I fear to see my hearer indignant. Hence I refrain from expressing my humble thought, yet I move about reflecting upon those points.

I wish that the wise may pay serious attention and notice the proper rules of clothing. Further, laymen of India, the officers and people of a higher class have a pair of white soft cloth for their garments, while the poor and lower classes of people have only one piece of linen. It is only the homeless member of the Saṅgha who possesses the three garments and six Requisites[2], and a priest who wishes for more (lit. who indulges in luxury) may use the thirteen Necessaries[2]. In China priests are not allowed to have a garment possessed of two sleeves or having one back, but the fact is that they themselves follow the Chinese customs, and falsely call them Indian. Now I shall roughly describe the people and their dresses in *G*ambudvîpa and all the remote islands. From the Mahâbodhi eastward to Lin-i (i.e. Champa) there are twenty countries extending as far as the southern limits of Kwan Chou (in Annam)[3]. If we proceed to the south-west we come to the sea; and in the north Kasmîra is its limit. There are more than ten countries (islands) in the Southern Sea, added to these the Si*m*hala

---

[1] One text has 不殊 for 不同 (J.); the latter is the better reading.

[2] See p. 55 above.

[3] See p. 12 above.

island (Ceylon). In all these countries people wear two cloths (Skt. kambala). These are of wide linen eight feet long, which has no girdle and is not cut or sewn, but is simply put around the waist to cover the lower part.

Besides India, there are countries of the Pârasas (Persians) and the Tajiks[1] (generally taken as Arabs), who wear shirt and trousers. In the country of the naked people[2] (Nicobar Isles) they have no dress at all; men and women alike are all naked. From Kasmîra to all the Mongolic countries such as Sûli, Tibet[3], and the country of the Turkish tribes, *the customs* resemble one another to a great extent; *the people in these* countries do not wear the covering-cloth (Skt. kambala), but use wool or skin as much as they can, and there is very little karpâsa (i. e. cotton), which we see sometimes worn. As these countries are cold, the people always wear shirt and trousers. Among these countries the Pârasas, the Naked People, the Tibetans[4], and the Turkish tribes have no Buddhist law, but the other countries had and have followed Buddhism; and in the districts where shirts and trousers are used the people are careless about personal cleanliness. Therefore *the people of* the five parts of India are proud of their own purity and excellence. But high refinement, literary elegance, propriety, moderation, *ceremonies of* welcoming and parting, the delicious taste of food, and the richness of benevolence and righteousness are found in China only, and no other country can excel her. The points of difference from the West are: (1) not preserving the purity of food (see chap. iv); (2) not washing after having been to the urinal (see chap. xviii below); (3) not chewing the tooth-woods (see chap. viii). There are some also who do not consider it wrong to wear an unlawful garment; they quote a passage from an abridged teaching (Sa*m*kshiptavinaya) which reads as follows: 'If

---

[1] Chavannes, p. 25. [2] Chavannes, p. 100. [3] Chavannes, pp. 13, 14.

[4] We know very little of the introduction of Buddhism into Tibet. In A. D. 632 the first Buddhist king of Tibet sent an envoy to India to get the Buddhist Scriptures. I-tsing's date is A. D. 671–695, and says that that country had no Buddhism. We know, however, that some of the Pârasas (Persian settlers) had become Buddhists in Hiuen Thsang's time (see Hiuen Thsang under Persia), and Tibet too was Buddhistic in his time.

anything which is considered to be impure in one country is considered pure in another, it can be practised there without incurring any guilt.' But this passage was misunderstood by some translators; the real meaning is not like the above, as I have fully explained elsewhere[1].

As to the things that are used by a Bhikshu of China, nothing but the three garments are in accordance with the rules laid down by the Buddha. When we incur guilt by wearing an unlawful garment we must give it up.

In a warm country like India one may wear only a single piece of linen through all the seasons, but in the snowy hills or cold villages one cannot subsist (without some more clothes) even if one wish to keep to the rules. Besides, to keep our body in health and our work in progress is the Buddha's sincere instruction to us; and self-mortification and toil are the teaching of heretics. Reject our teacher or follow another; which would you do?

The Buddha allowed the use of a garment called 'Li-pa[2],' which can be worn in any cold regions; this is enough to warm one's body, and there is no religious blame in using it. Li-pa in Sanskrit can be translated 'abdomen-covering cloth.' I shall shortly describe here how it is made. Cut a piece of cloth so as to have no back and to have one shoulder bare. No sleeves are to be attached. Only one single piece is used and made just wide enough to put on. The shoulder part (which may be called a short) sleeve of the cloth is not wide and is on the left-hand side; this must not be wide and large. It is tied on the right-hand side so that the wind may not touch the body. A great quantity of cotton-wool is put in so as to make it very thick and warm. Or sometimes it is sewn together on the right-hand side, and ribbons are attached at the highest point of one's side. Such are the original rules for making the cloth[3].

I saw several pieces of this cloth while in the West; the priests from the north (Sûli, &c.) generally bring and wear it. In the place near the

---

[1] The Mûlasarvâstivâdaikasatakarman, chap. x.

[2] Skt., Repha, Lepa, or the like; I have to leave it uncertain at present.

[3] It is not clear what sort of cloth I-tsing means, and my translation must be regarded as tentative. One image of the Buddha has a cloth over his chest, having a very short sleeve on the left-hand side, which may be I-tsing's 'Li-pa' cloth.

Nâlanda monastery we do not see it, for the climate is so hot that people do not need such cloth. The Buddha allowed this for the people of a cold region. (As to the corresponding Chinese cloth) the back and bare shoulder are in accordance with the proper rules, but the right-hand side of the cloth has an additional (piece), thus making it illegal. If one acts against the proper rules, one is guilty of an offence. One may (legally) cover one's abdomen with the 'Li-pa' cloth to protect oneself against severe cold, or one may wear a thick mantle to keep out the frost.

Before the images of the Buddha or other honoured saints it is usual to have one's shoulder bare, and guilt is incurred by covering it. To become homeless means to become free from troubles.

When one lives indoors in winter, one may well use a charcoal fire, and it is not necessary to have the trouble of wearing many clothes. If one needs thick clothing owing to an illness, one may do temporarily what one likes provided that one does not break the rules. The winter in China, however, is very severe, often piercing our bodies, and without warm clothing our life is in danger. This is a great difficulty in religion, but salvation must include the people of such a region.

Have your sleeves square and your shoulder bare that you may be distinguished from laymen, and wear it in the cold winter instead of the 'Li-pa.' Though not exactly in accordance with the proper rules, it is permissible for a time as it is meant to protect our life. As a wheel wants oiling (so our life wants warmth). We ought to be much ashamed (when we live in an unlawful manner). If we can pass the winter without wearing (an illegal garment) it is all the better. Other things, such as robe, trousers, drawers, and shirt, must never be used; (even if you use these things for a time) you must not wear them when winter is over.

Some, again, wear a half shirt, which was never allowed by the Buddha. In fleeing from the busy (world) and pursuing the important (path) we simply look up to, and accord ourselves with, the noble heart (of the Buddha). One may fail oneself (in carrying out the Buddha's precepts), but one must never mislead others by teaching them or setting a bad example.

You may well supplant old practices with new ones; then it may be said that you all, sitting side by side (in the monastery) on the

Shao Shih[1] mount (in China), make yourselves as lofty as (those on) the Vulture Peak (in India), and that you are as if gathering together in the city of Râgagriha and also communicating with all those in the Imperial seat of China.

The Large River (Hwang Ho in China) unites its pure stream with the lake of Mukilinda (in Buddhagayâ). The Slender Willow (Hsi-lew)[2] joins in its splendour with the tree of Bodhi which is, and will be, ever flourishing with its shining glory until after the field of mulberry-trees has changed (into the sea), or the Kalpa stone has been entirely rubbed away[3]. Praise, then, be to (the Buddha)! Let us make an effort (in following his doctrine)! The sunlike Buddha has set, leaving his doctrine behind for the later ages. If we practise his doctrine, it is just as if we were living in the presence of our great teacher, while if we act against his teaching, many faults will appear in us. It is, therefore, said in a Sûtra: 'Let my precepts be well practised, then I, (the teacher), exist all the same in this world[4]'.

Some may say: 'The virtuous men of the former ages did not speak (against Chinese practices); then why should we, men of the later time, alter the rules?' But it is wrong to say so. For we have to follow the Law (Dharma), and not a man. The Buddha has precisely taught us about this point. If your practices as regards food and clothing have no failure when compared with the rules prescribed in the Vinaya-pitaka, then you can keep to them. To practise the rules but not to learn them is difficult. When a pupil does not practise after having learnt the rules, the teacher is not blamable.

---

[1] This is a mountain situated south of Sung mountain in Ho-nan. A famous temple on the Shao Shih was called Shao-lin.

[2] This is the name of an island where the sun and moon set, in the Shan Hai King; but I-tsing here uses it as if it were the name of a tree.

[3] 'The field of mulberry-trees becoming the sea' is a Chinese simile for a long time. A Kalpa is said to be the period during which an angel can rub away a great stone by her wing coming at times.

[4] Probably the Mahâparinirvâna-sûtra is meant here. Cf. Rhys Davids, Buddhism, p. 82: 'After I am dead let the Law and Rules of the Order, which I have taught, be a Teacher to you' (Book of the Great Decease, VI, 1).

Again, I say in verse:

In the life of man, the first and foremost are food and clothing,
To man these two are the fetter and chain
Which bind him to the field of rebirth.
Let the Noble Word be followed,
Rest and freedom will be his.
If selfishness be his guide,
Sin and trouble will drag him along.
Beware, wise man! Retribution is manifest.
When the Eight Airs[1] retired from your body
The Five Fears[2] will no longer threaten you.
Be ever pure as the gem that is pure even in mud;
As clear as the dews on the lotus leaves.
Clothing is enough, if your body is covered.
Food is sufficient, if you do not die of hunger.
Seek the Moksha (Liberation) only and not man or Deva.
Lead your life practising the Dhûtâṅgas[3].
Finish your years by protecting the living creatures.

Reject the empty birth of the Nine Worlds[4]. Aspire to the perfect course of the Ten Stages[5]. In receiving gifts may you behave as the 500 Arhats would have behaved. In giving blessings may you expect to give them to the 3,000 worlds.

CHAPTER XI.

THE MODE OF WEARING GARMENTS.

I NOW describe, according to the Vinaya, the mode of wearing the religious garments, and the use of ribbons.

Take a garment of five cubits long and fold it into three. At the pleated part of the shoulder, at four or five finger-widths from the collar,

---

[1] The five vital airs in Vedântasâra V, and ten airs according to the followers of Kapila.

[2] See above, p. 66. [3] See above, p. 56. [4] See above, p. 3, and p. 4, note 2.

[5] There are ten stages through which a Bodhisattva goes.

a square piece of five finger-widths each way is to be attached; its four sides are stitched into the garment. Make a small hole in the centre of this square piece, and put a ribbon through the hole. The ribbon may be of silk or cotton of the same size as the shirt-ribbon. The length of the ribbon must be only two finger-widths, both ends of which must be tied fast together and its remainder must be cut off. Attach one more ribbon through holes, and draw it out so as to cross the other ribbon; thus we have two ribbons. The inner fastenings come at the pleated part of the garment at the chest. The fastenings of sleeves are like those of a shirt. Such are the rules[1].

I have thus described for you the proper rules about garments, but the important points only. If you wish to be well acquainted with the method, you must wait until we see each other. The skirt of a garment is also plaited with ribbons. One can turn the skirt up as one likes; this was allowed by the Buddha. At both sides of the skirt a ribbon and a fastening should be attached, to be used in pulling up the skirt a little and tying it in front, during the meal (as one sits on a small and low chair). This is an important rule. When one is in the monastery or before the members of the Saṅgha, it is not necessary for one to wear the bands (or ribbons) or to have one's shoulder bare. But on going out of the monastery or on entering the house of a layman, one should wear them; on other occasions one can have them over the shoulders. While executing private business one can have them in any way one likes. When one is before the image of the Buddha one has to put them in order.

Take the right corner of the garment and put it over the left shoulder and let it hang at the back, not letting it stay on the arm. If one wishes to have the bands (ribbons), the entire shoulder is first to be made bare, and take it to the back by the inside fastenings. Let the corner of the garment come again over the shoulder, and the garment itself be round the neck. Both hands come below the garment (which is so put round the neck); the other corner of the garment hangs in front. The image of king A*s*oka has its garment in this way.

The mode of holding an umbrella while walking is very attractive;

[1] The whole description is obscure, and my rendering is tentative only.

one should regularly wear the upper robe according to the teaching. The umbrella is to be woven with bamboo sticks and to be made as thin as a case of bamboo work, but not doubly covered. The size may be two or three feet (in diameter) according as one desires. The centre should be made double so as to put the handle on. The length of the handle should be in proportion to the width of the cover. The cover of bamboo work may be varnished with lacquer. It may be woven of reed instead of bamboo; this resembles a hat of rattan work. If paper be inserted in weaving, it becomes stronger. We do not use such an umbrella in China; yet it is a very important thing to be used. In the sudden pour of rain our garments may be protected from wet, and in the burning heat of summer we can keep ourselves cool. The use of an umbrella[1] is in accordance with the Vinaya rules and beneficial to our bodies; and there is no harm whatever in using it. Considering the matter in these ways we find that the use of an umbrella is very important. But it is not used in China.

The upper corner of a Kâshâya generally hangs over the fore-arm (lit. the 'elephant-nose') in China. Every Indian priest who came to China also followed the Chinese manner. The fine silk of which the Kâshâya is made slips down from the shoulder; thus making the custom of having it over the arm—a custom against the proper rule.

Afterwards when the Tripi*t*aka Teacher of China[2] came (to India) he advocated that the Kâshâya should hang over the (left) shoulder, but there are several elderly teachers who dislike this mode. The common error of keeping to the old accustomed practices exists wherever we go.

As to the three garments (Tri*k*îvara), if you put some short ribbons instead of the long strings (hitherto used), there will be no point that breaks the rules. If you wear a whole piece put round the lower part of your body instead of the common trousers, it will save you the trouble of sewing and stitching. The water-pot, the alms-bowl, and all that you have should be hung over your shoulders. They must be hung so as to just reach the sides of your body, and the front one must not cross with another behind. The rope which is used in hanging things is not long but just enough to put over the shoulder. When the things hang by

---

[1] *K*ullavagga V, 23, 3, note.

[2] By this Hiuen Thsang is meant.

the chest, the breathing is not easy, and it ought not to be so according to the proper rules.

I shall speak of the pot-bag later[1]. Men of Sûli in the North often let the things that hang over the shoulders cross one another; the rules seem to have been modified in that region, but they are not the rules laid down by the Buddha.

If you have some extra clothes, put them over your shoulder, over the robe (which you wear) and the pot (you carry).

When you pay a visit to a temple or at the house of a layman, you have to go to the hall, put down your umbrella, and then begin to untie the things which are to be hanged. On the wall of the hall many ivory hooks are to be prepared, so as to give a visitor a place where he can hang his things. As to other matters, see chapter xxvi, which is devoted to the rules about meeting a friend.

When the Kâshâya is made of a thin silk, it is too fine, and does not stay on the shoulder; and when you bow in worship it often slips down to the ground. If you wish to make it with a stuff that does not so easily slip down, the best is a rough silk or soft white linen.

As to the Chinese Saṅkakshikâ, that is to say, the side-covering cloth, it will be right if you make it one cubit longer. In wearing the Saṅkakshikâ you have to make the right shoulder bare, and only cover the left shoulder.

A Saṅkakshikâ and a skirt only are usually worn while in one's own rooms. When one goes out and worships the image, one should add the other garments. Now I shall briefly describe the mode of putting on the skirt. According to the rules of the skirt adopted by the Mûlasarvâstivâda school, the skirt is a piece of cloth, five cubits long by two cubits wide. The material may be silk or linen according as one can get it.

The Indians make it single, while the Chinese make it double; the length or width is not fixed. Having put it round the (lower part of your) body, pull it up so far as to cover your navel. Now you have to hold with your right hand the upper corner of your skirt at the left-hand side, and pull out (with your left hand) the other end of your skirt which

---

[1] I-tsing forgot this promise.

is inside around your right-hand side. Cover your left side with the left flap of your upper garment, (and your right side with the right flap).

Bring both ends of your skirt right in front with both hands, join them in the middle and make three twists with them.

Then take the three twists round your back; raise them higher, about three fingers, and then push them down inwards about three fingers. Thus the skirt does not slip off even if you have no strings. Now take a waist-band about five cubits long, let the hooked part come right below your navel, and tie round the upper edge of your skirt.

Both ends of the waist-band must come to your back, and cross each other; then they are again to be pulled back to your left and right sides, where you have to press them fast with your arms, while you join and tie both ends (in front) three times. If the waist-band is too long, you have to cut off; if too short, some must be added. Both ends of the waist-band must not be sewed or decked.

The mode of wearing the skirt above described, distinguishes the Sarvâstivâdanikâya from the other schools, and is called 'parima*nd*ala-nivâsa' (-yati)[1], which is in Chinese the 'round-right wearing of a skirt.' The width of the (waist-)band is similar to that of a finger. The shoe-string, socks-tie, &c., may be round or square, both being allowable. Such a thing as a flax-rope is not allowed to be used in the Vinaya texts.

When you sit on a small chair or a block of wood, you have to hold the upper part of your skirt at a point under the flap of your upper garment, and quickly pull up your skirt so as to come under your thighs (on the seat). Both of your knees are to be covered, but your shanks may be bare without fault.

That the whole skirt should cover from one's navel to the point four finger-widths above one's ankle-bones is a rule followed while one is in a layman's house. But when we are in the monastery, it is allowable to have the lower half of one's shanks bare. This rule was laid down by the Buddha himself; and it must not be modified in any way by our will. It is not right to act against the teaching and follow one's selfish

---

[1] Pâtimokkha, p. 59, note (S. B. E., vol. xiii), 'I will put on my undergarment all round me,' i. e. the Sekhiyâ Dhammâ I, 'parima*nd*ala*m* nivâsessâmîti Sikkhâ Kara*n*îyâ,' J. R. A. S., 1876, p. 92.

desire. When the skirt (nivâsa) you wear is long and touches the ground, you are on the one hand spoiling the pure gift from a believing layman; on the other hand you are disobeying the precepts of the Great Teacher.

Who among you would follow my kind remonstrance? May there be among ten thousands of priests a single person who is attentive to my words!

The skirt (nivâsa) worn in India is put crosswise round the lower part of one's body. The white soft cloth of India, used as a skirt, is two cubits wide, or sometimes half the width (i. e. one cubit).

The poor cannot obtain this cloth, (so much as a regular skirt requires). (To save expense) one may join and stitch both edges of the cloth, and open and put one's legs through, it will answer the purpose.

All the rules of wearing the garment are found in the Vinaya texts. I have briefly described only the important points. A minute discussion can only be made when we see one another.

Further, all the garments of a homeless priest must be dyed to Kan-da (i.e. yellow colour)[1]. The dye may be prepared from Ti-huang (Rehmannia glutinosa), yellow powder, or a thorny Nieh-tree (Pterocarpus indicus). These dyes, however, are to be mixed with the colours made of red earth or red stone-powder. One should see that the colour is not too deep or too light.

To save expense, one may use only dates, red earth, red stone-powder, wild pear, or T'u-tzŭ (earth-purple). The cloth may be worn out in dying with these dyes, but not so much as one needs to get another one.

The dye prepared from mulberry bark, and blue and green colours are prohibited. The true purple and dark brown are not adopted in the West.

As to shoes and sandals, there are some rules laid down by the Buddha. Long shoes or sandals with linings are against the rules. Anything that is embroidered or ornamented the Buddha did not allow to be used. It is minutely explained in the 'Rules about Leathers[2].'

---

[1] Kan-da, or Gan-da, seems to be a Sanskrit word, see p. 46, note 1 above.

[2] I-tsing translated this text belonging to the Vinaya; it only exists in the Korean collection. Mahâvagga V is devoted to the rules concerning the foot-clothing, &c.

CHAPTER XII.

RULES CONCERNING THE NUN'S DRESS AND FUNERAL.

THE Chinese dress of the nuns is that of ordinary women, and the existing mode of wearing it is much against the proper rules. According to the Vinaya, there are five garments for a nun (Bhikshu*n*î).

1. Saṅghâ*t*î.
2. Uttarâsaṅga.
3. Antarvâsa.
4. Saṅkakshikâ.
5. A Skirt. (Cf. p. 55 above.)

The style and rules of the first four are the same as those of the elder (male) members of the Saṅgha, but a part of the skirt is different. In Sanskrit a nun's skirt is called 'Kusûlaka,' which is translated by the 'bin-like garment,' for the shape is like a small bin (Kusûla), both ends of it being sewn together; its length is four cubits, while its width is two. It may cover as far up as the navel, and comes down as low as four fingers above the ankles. In wearing, one should put one's legs through, and pull it up past one's navel. Contracting the top of the skirt round the waist, one should tie it at one's back.

The rules and measures of the band or ribbons of a nun are the same as those of a priest. At her chest and sides there must not be any ties or clothes.

But when her breasts become very high and large, be she young or old, some cloth may be used without fault.

It is wrong if she does not observe the rules because she is ashamed (of her being bare-breasted) before men, or if she decorates herself extravagantly, and thereby incurs guilt in every way. At the death of such a guilty person, the sins (that adhere to her) will be as drizzling rain (so many); if she has even one offence out of many, she should make it good at once. When she is out-of-doors or before a priest, or when she is invited to a layman's house to a feast, her Kâshâya must always be round her neck, and cover her body; the shoulder-ribbon of the Kâshâya is not to be untied. During the meal she must not have her chest bare, but with her hands coming out from under (the Kâshâya). Wearing a Sańkakshikâ[1], having one shoulder bare or having a shirt or trousers are prohibited by the Great Sage himself, and these must not be had by the nuns.

In all the countries of the Southern Sea, the nuns have a special garment, which, though not in accordance with the Indian style, is also called Sańkakshikâ. It is two cubits each way. The edges of it are sewn together except a foot at the centre; the corners are (turned back) an inch and stitched fast. In wearing this, one holds it up and puts one's head and shoulders through, having the right shoulder wholly out of it. No waist-band is used. It covers one's sides, breasts, navel, and knees. If one wishes to wear it, one can do so without fault.

The cloth is lined with only two ribbons; it is good enough to cover the shame. But if one does not like to wear it, one should wear a regular Sańkakshikâ, similar to that of a great Bhikshu (male mendicant). While one is in the monastery or in one's own rooms, a Kusûlaka and a Sańkakshikâ will be sufficient.

(Note by I-tsing): In examining the Indian texts I never met with the name of 'shoulder-covering cloth;' the original is Sańkakshikâ, which is sometimes shortened to Ki-chi in Chinese. It is not called a 'skirt,' but translations of this name were hitherto various.

One should reject a garment which is against the rules and wear one which is strictly according to the teaching. A Sańkakshikâ is made of the whole width and a half of a stuff, either silk or linen, four or five cubits in length. It is worn over one's shoulders, just as one wears 'the five-lined' garment. In all places one should sufficiently cover the shame; even in a urinal one must not have one's shoulders bare.

This garment is to be worn in spring and summer, and warmer clothing can be used in autumn and winter if one likes. Begging food with a bowl one can sufficiently support one's body.

If one, though a female, has a powerful mind, she need not engage

---

[1] This seems to be contradictory to what he said before, for at the beginning of this chapter I-tsing mentioned Sańkakshikâ as one of the nun's dresses. Perhaps he meant here a Chinese one, which is different from that of India.

in shuttle and loom, nor do ordinary (household) works; much less does she need to wear many garments, now five, now ten.

There are some who never think of meditation (Dhyâna) or reading, ever hastening onward driven by earthly desires. There are others who make much of ornament and dress, not caring for the precepts (*S*îla). All these persons are liable to an examination by the lay followers. Nuns in India are very different from those of China. They support themselves by begging food, and live a poor and simple life.

Here a question may be asked: 'The benefit and supply to the female members of the Order are very small, and monasteries of many a place have no special supply of food for them. This being the case, there will be no way of living if they do not work for their maintenance; and if they do so, they often act against the Vinaya teaching and disobey the noble will of the Buddha. How should they decide for themselves as to taking one course and rejecting the other? When once one's body is at ease, one's religion prospers. Pray, let us hear your judgement on these points (lit. right or wrong).'

I answer this question as follows: 'One's original intention was to become homeless, with the purpose of attaining the "final liberation" (Moksha). To cut off the injurious roots of the three (poisonous) trees[1], and to dam the vast volume of the four rolling streams[2]; one should accomplish the "Dhûta" practices and avoid the dangerous path of suffering and enjoyment; with one's mind sincere, and with one's desires suppressed, one should pursue the true path of quietness. Religion will prosper by one's observing the precepts (*S*îla) night and day. If one thinks only of having one's body at ease, one is in the wrong. When one is strict in practice and sincere in conduct in accordance with the Vinaya teaching, one is followed and honoured by dragons (nâga), spirits, devas, and men. Why should one, then, be so anxious about one's livelihood and follow the vain labour (of the worldly course).'

The five garments, a pot, and a bowl are enough for the nuns to subsist upon; and a small apartment is sufficient to maintain their lives.

---

[1] I. e. greed, hate, and stupidity; otherwise called 'three poisons.'

[2] I. e. earthly desire, the state of being, erroneous view, and ignorance; otherwise called 'four yokes.'

Personal possessions can be diminished and the troubles of the lay devotees can thus be avoided; they can be pure like a precious stone lying in the mud or a lotus-flower in water, and thus their life, though called a low one, is, in reality, a life of wisdom that is equal to that of an exalted person.

At the time of *their parents'* death, Bhikshus or Bhikshuṇîs do not always use sufficient care in a funeral service or have the same mourning as common people, and yet consider themselves to be dutiful children.

Some prepare a shrine for the dead in their rooms, and make offerings or spread out a coloured cloth to show that they are in mourning. Others keep their hair unshaven, contrary to the usual practice, or carry a mourning-stick or sleep on a straw mat. All these practices are not the Buddha's teaching, and one can well omit them without fault. What one ought to do is as follows:—First purify and decorate one room for the departed or sometimes put up some (small) canopies or curtains temporarily, and offer perfumes and flowers, while reading Sûtras and meditating on the Buddha. One should wish that the departed spirit may be born in a good place. This is what makes one a dutiful child, and how one requites the benefits conferred by the departed while alive.

Three years' mourning or seven days' fasting are not the only ways in which a benevolent person is served after death. (As these practices[1] confer no benefits), the dead may again be tied to the earthly troubles (i. e. reborn as a living creature) and suffer the chain and fetters (of sins). Thus the dead may pass from darkness to darkness, ever ignorant of the three divisions of the chain of causality (twelve Nidânas), and from death to death, never witnessing the ten stages of perfection[2].

According to the Buddha's teaching, when a priest is dead, after one has recognised him to be really dead, on the same day his corpse is sent on a bier to a cremation-place, and is there burnt. While the corpse is burning, all his friends assemble and sit on one side. They sit either on grass bound together, or on elevations of earth, or on

[1] I. e. three years' mourning and seven days' fasting.

[2] The ten stages through which a Bodhisattva goes.

bricks or stones. The 'Sûtra on Impermanence' ('Anitya-sûtra')[1] is recited by a skilled man, as short as a page or a leaf, so that it may not become tiresome.

(Note by I-tsing): I am sending home this Sûtra together with the Record.

Then they all meditate on the impermanency (of all conditions). On returning to their residence they bathe together, in their clothes, in the pond outside the monastery. If there is no pond, they go to a well and wash themselves. They wear old clothes, so that they may not injure new ones. Then they put on dry clothes. On returning to their apartments, they cleanse the floor with powdered cow-dung. All other things remain as usual. There is no custom as to putting on a mourning-dress. They sometimes build a thing like a stûpa for the dead, to contain his *S*arîra (or relics). It is called a 'Kula,' which is like a small stûpa, but without the cupola on it.

But there is some difference between the stûpas of an ordinary man and an exalted person, as is minutely described in the Vinaya text[2].

It is not right for a priest to lay aside the noble teaching of the *S*âkya the Father, and follow the common usage handed down by the duke of Chou, crying and weeping many a month, or wearing a mourning-dress for three years.

There was a priest named Lin-yu (in the Sui dynasty, A.D. 605–618), who never cried or wept according to the Chinese custom or put on a mourning-dress. He thought much of the dead, and for the latter's sake he practised meritorious actions. Many teachers living near the capital followed his example. Some think that he is not filial. But they do not know that his action is in accordance with the Vinaya.

CHAPTER XIII.

CONSECRATED GROUNDS.

THERE are five kinds of consecrated grounds:—

1. Ki-sin-tso, the ground consecrated by an individual's vow of building a monastery on the spot.

---

[1] Nanjio's Catalogue, No. 727. [2] The Sa*m*yuktavastu, chap. xviii.

2. Kung-in-ch'ih, the ground set apart by means of a proclamation by more than two Bhikshus for building a monastery.

3. Ju-niu-wo, the ground where a building, in shape like a cow lying down, stands.

4. Ku-fei-ch'u, a ruin of a temple or other sacred buildings.

5. Ping-fa-tso[1], the ground chosen and consecrated with a sacred rite (Karma) by Bhikshus.

As to the Ki-sin-tso (1), when a monastery is about to be built and the foundation-stone has been laid, a Bhikshu superintending the work should express his intention as follows: 'On this spot of the monastery or of the house let us build a pure kitchen for the Saṅgha.'

As to the Kung-in-ch'ih (2), when the foundation-stone has been laid, if there be three Bhikshus in charge, one should say to the others: 'Venerable sirs, be attentive, we have marked out and selected this place, and on this very spot of the monastery or of the house we shall build a monastic kitchen for the Saṅgha.'

The second and the third Bhikshus should also pronounce the same. The Ju-niu-wo (3) are monasteries, the buildings of which are like a cow lying down, the gates to the apartments being scattered here and there. Such a building, though it has never been consecrated by a rite, is considered pure (sacred). The Ku-fei-ch'u (4) is a place which has long been abandoned by the Saṅgha. If the Saṅgha comes there again, the very spot that had anciently been used becomes pure, but they must not pass a night without performing a rite (Karma). The Ping-fa-tso (5) is the consecrated ground both by rite (Karma) and declaration. This is explained in the Mûlasarvâstivâdanikâyaikasatakarman.

---

[1] All these names are Chinese, and it is difficult to see what are the originals. In Mahâvagga VI, 34, 4–5, a Kappiya-bhûmi of four kinds is allowed to be used: (1) one that becomes 'Kappiya' by means of a proclamation (I-tsing's 1 and 2); (2) an ox-stall (Gonisâdika, cf. I-tsing's 3); (3) a building belonging to laymen; and (4) a duly chosen one (I-tsing's 5). That I-tsing's Ju-niu-wo, a 'building like a lying cow,' represents the original 'Gonisâdika' (ox-stall) is almost certain, but how it has come about to be understood so is difficult to see. In chap. x above (p. 61), I-tsing says that the Saṅgha gives out bulls, and so a Vihâra may have been in possession of an ox-stall in his time as well as in Buddhaghosa's time. S. B. E., vol. xvii, pp. 120, 121.

When one of these five sacred rules has been carried out, the Buddha says, all Bhikshus can obtain the twofold enjoyments in it: (1) Cooking within and storing without; (2) Storing within and cooking without, both being free from guilt.

Rules of consecrating a ground are much the same when we compare *the ceremonies of* the Saṅghas of the four Nikâyas, witness the practices of the present time, and carefully examine the purport of the Vinaya. If the ground be not yet consecrated, drinking, eating, or lodging on the spot involves guilt; if the rite be performed there is no fault in cooking and lodging thereon.

What we call a monastery is a general designation for the place of residence (for the Saṅgha), the whole of which may be regarded as a monastic kitchen. In every apartment, raw and cooked food may be kept. If sleeping in the monastery is not allowed, all the priests then residing must go out and lodge somewhere. There is, then, the fault of not protecting the sleeping-place (against any evils); and moreover the keeping of provisions in the monastery is allowable (according to the Vinaya). The traditional custom of India is to consecrate the whole monastery as a 'kitchen,' but to take a part of it to be used as a kitchen is also allowed by the Buddha. These points are not the same as those which the Vinaya teachers of China profess to teach.

If one sleeps out of the monastery without consecrating the place to protect the purity of one's garments, one is blamable. If the consecration be duly carried out, the one who sleeps there incurs no guilt. The monastic kitchen wants a consecration. Such is the Buddha's privilege to us, and our own inclination must not be regarded. In the lawful spots for protecting the purity of garments there are differences between the places under trees (or in a village), &c.

The protection of a spot is not intended simply to guard against women; as a (female) servant sometimes enters the kitchen, and yet the (consecrated) kitchen is not to be considered a village, (so a place is sacred when consecrated apart from women). When one enters a village, one's carrying the three garments (Tri*k*îvara) does not mean to guard oneself against women. Then the Karmadâna's (subdirector of the monastery) superintending the monastic works with his three garments, especially when a female comes in, is too strict a custom.

CHAPTER XIV.

THE SUMMER-RETREAT OF THE FIVE PARISHADS.

THE first summer-retreat is on the first day of the dark half of the fifth moon, and the second summer-retreat is on the first day of the dark half of the sixth moon; only on these two days should the summer-retreat be entered upon. No other commencement of the summer-retreat between the two is allowed in the text[1]. The first summer-retreat ends in the middle of the eighth moon, while the second ends in the middle of the ninth moon. On the day on which the summer-retreat closes, priests and laymen perform a great ceremony of offerings (Pûgâ). After the middle of the eighth moon, the month is called Kârttika; a meeting is held on the 'Ka-ti' (Kârttika?) in Kiang-nan (in China), that is, at the time when the first summer ends. The sixteenth day of the eighth moon is the day on which the Ka*th*ina robes are spread out[2] (as a present to the Saṅgha), which is an ancient custom.

It is said in the Vinaya (chap. vii, the Vinaya-saṅgraha): 'If there be a proper opportunity (for going out) one should receive *permission* for a day's *absence*.' This passage means that as one has so many opportunities (i.e. invitations or any other business) one should receive permission for so many days' absence, that is to say, for a matter *to be done* in one night, one should receive a day's permission, and thus even to seven days[3], but one can go to different persons only. If there be an occasion (to meet one and the same man) for a second time, the Vinaya ordains that one should apply again and go off. When the period of absence exceeds seven days, say eight days, or even to forty nights, one should receive permission during the ceremony that is going on. But it is not permissible for one to stay out for the half of the summer-retreat; therefore only forty nights are allowed as the maximum. If

---

[1] A school in China used to have three summer-retreats in one year. For the date of the two retreats, see Mahâvagga III, 2, 2. See my note at the end.

[2] Ka*th*ina-âstâra, see Mahâvagga VII, 1, 3, note (pp. 148–150), and Childers, s.v.

[3] Seven days seem to be the maximum allowance, except on urgent necessity, see Mahâvagga III, 5, 5, &c.

there be a sick person[1] or a difficult affair to be attended to, one should go off; in such a case one will not break the summer-retreat though leave of absence is not taken. The five Parishads[2] of the homeless members have to enter upon the retreat; among these a member of the lower class is permitted to be absent in case of necessity, by asking another to apply for permission on his behalf. Before the Varsha (Rainy-season) rooms are assigned to each member; to the elders (i. e. Sthavira) better rooms are given, and thus gradually to the lowest. In the monastery of Nâlanda such rules are practised at present; the great assembly of priests assigns rooms every year. This is what the World-honoured taught us himself, and it is very beneficial. Firstly, it removes one's selfish intention; secondly, the rooms for priests are *properly* protected. It is most reasonable that the homeless priests should act in this way. Thus the monasteries in the south of the Kiang sometimes assign rooms to priests; this has been handed down by the ancient worthies and is still in practice. Is it seemly that one should occupy a temple and regard it as one's own possession, and pass one's life without knowing whether such a practice as this is permissible or not? During former generations this was not carried out. In the whole of China men of later generations have lost sight of the Law. If the assignment of rooms be practised according to the teaching, it would, indeed, prove to be greatly beneficial (to the Saṅgha).

CHAPTER XV.

CONCERNING THE PRAVÂRA*N*A-DAY.

THE day on which the summer-retreat ends and the season (lit. the year) closes should be the Sui-i (lit. 'according to one's wish' or 'indulgence;' Pravâra*n*a), i. e. pointing out the faults of others, as one likes, according to the three points (i. e. what one has seen, what one has heard, and what one has suspected). Then follows confession and

[1] Cf. Mahâvagga III, 6, 1, &c.

[2] Bhikshus, Bhikshu*n*îs, *S*ikshamâ*n*âs, *S*rama*n*eras, and *S*rama*n*erîs are called the five Parishads; to these sometimes Upâsakas and Upâsikâs are added as seven Parishads in all. See Mahâvagga III, 5, 4, and Childers, s. v. Parisâ (f.).

atoning for faults[1]. A former translation of Pravâra*n*a was Ssc-sse, i.e. 'self-indulgence' according to its sense.

On the night of the fourteenth day (the fifteenth day is the last day of the retreat), the assembly should invite a precentor to mount a high seat and recite a Buddhist Sûtra, when lay devotees as well as priests throng together like clouds or mist. They light lamps continually, and offer incense and flowers. The following morning they all go out round villages or towns and worship all the *K*aityas with sincere mind.

They bring storied carriages, images in sedan-chairs, drums, and other music resounding in the sky, banners and canopies hoisted high in regular order (lit. entwined and arranged), flattering and covering the sun; this is called Sa-ma-kin-li (Sâmagrî)[2], which is translated as 'concord' or 'thronging together.' All great Upavasatha-days are like this day. This is what we call in China 'Ceremony of going around a city.' At the beginning of the forenoon (9 to 11 a.m.) they come back to the monastery, at noon they keep the great Upavasatha-ceremony, and in the afternoon all gather together, each taking in his hand a tuft of fresh rushes. Handling it with their hands or treading on it with their feet they do what they like, first Bhikshus, next Bhikshu*n*îs; then the three lower classes of the members. If it be feared that the time should be too long owing to the largeness of the number, the Saṅgha should order several members to go together and receive the Pravâra*n*a-ceremony. When any offence has been pointed out by another, one should confess and atone for it according to the Law.

At this time, either the laymen present gifts, or the Saṅgha itself distributes them, and all sorts of gifts are brought out before the assembly. The five venerable persons (one each from the five Parishads (?)) should then ask the heads of the assembly (i. e. Sthaviras): 'Can these things be given to the members of the Saṅgha and made

---

[1] Cf. Mahâvagga IV, 1, 14, 'Let the senior Bhikshus say: "I invite the Saṅgha to charge me with any offence of which they think me guilty, which they have seen, or heard of, or which they suspect; may you speak to me, sirs, out of pity towards me; if I see (an offence), I will atone for it."' I-tsing seems to be almost translating these words literally.

[2] Childers, s. v. Sâmaggi and Uposatho, where he calls it 'reconciliation uposatha.'

their own possession, or not?' The heads of the assembly reply: 'Yes, they can.' Then all garments, knives, needles, awls, &c., are received and equally distributed. Such is the teaching (of the Buddha). The reason why they present knives and awls on this day is, that they wish the recipients to obtain (sharp) intelligence and keen wisdom. When thus the Pravâra*n*a ends, all go their ways (lit. to east or west). If they have fully kept their residence in the summer there is no need of passing a night there; this is fully explained elsewhere, and I shall not state it here in detail. The idea of the 'confession of sins' is that, declaring one's own offence and speaking of one's past faults, one would desire to alter (i. e. atone for) the past conduct and repair the future, and to carefully condemn oneself with perfect sincerity. Every half month one should make a Poshadha [1], and every morning and evening one should reflect on one's own offences.

(Note by I-tsing): Poshadha [1]; posha means 'nourishing,' dha means 'purifying,' and thus Poshadha means nourishing (or cherishing) *good quality*, and purifying the guilt of breaking precepts. It was formerly transliterated by Pu-sa, which is too short and wrong.

An offence of the first group (i. e. the Pârâ*g*ika offences or sins involving expulsion from the Brotherhood, see Childers, s. v.) cannot be atoned for. As to an offence of the second group (i. e. Sa*n*ghâdi*s*esha [2]

---

[1] Poshadha here is understood to mean confession, though I-tsing's etymology is very curious. This word can only be traced back to the Pâli Uposatho, 'fasting,' and 'fast-day.' Childers observes that the Northern Buddhists, misled by the change of ava to o, and ignorant of the word Upavasatha, *which does not belong to classical Sanskrit*, have rendered Uposatha by Uposhadha, which is, of course, a mere mechanical adaptation, and has no etymology (Burnouf, Lotus, 450; Introduction, 227), and that in Burnouf's Lotus, 636, we have Uposatha, which is merely an adoption of the Pâli word. When the original Upavasatha has been forgotten while using Uposhadha, the 'u' of Uposhadha might easily be dropped and a false etymology be applied to it.

In the Lalita-vistara we have already Poshadha (p. 46), Poshadeya (p. 15), and Poshadhaparig*ri*hîta (adj. 'in which they hold Poshadha'). In the Brâhmanic Sanskrit we have Upavasatha (fasting) in the *S*atapatha Brâhma*n*a I, 1, 1, 7; III, 9, 2, 7; II, 1, 4, 1. This last gives the idea of staying at one's house.

[2] Chavannes has Sa*n*ghâva*s*esha, see Memoirs, p. 167.

offences or sins requiring suspension and penance but not expulsion, see Childers, s.v.), *the offender should, after a penance, be reinstated* in a community of the Bhikshus forming a body of twenty[1], but if the offence be a slight one, it should be confessed and atoned before those who are not one's equals. In Sanskrit, we say 'Âpattipratidesana,' Âpatti meaning sin or offence, pratidesana, confessing before others.

While thus confessing one's own faults and desiring to be purified, one hopes the sins are expiated being confessed one by one. To confess sins all at once is not permitted in the Vinaya. Formerly we used the word San-kuei, but this does not refer to 'confession.' For kshamâ (the Chinese 'San' in 'San-kuei' stands for kshamâ) is the Western word (i. e. Indian) and means 'forbearance,' while kuei (of 'San-kuei') is a Chinese word meaning 'repentance.'

Repentance has no connexion whatever with forbearance. If we strictly follow the Indian text we should say, when we are atoning for an offence: 'I confess my offence with a sincere mind[2].' From this, it is evident that translating kshamâ by 'repentance' has no authority.

People of the West, when they have made a mistake or unintentionally touched another's body, say 'kshamâ,' sometimes stroking the body of the one whom they have offended, or sometimes touching his shoulder; they do this without regard to their position; if both parties be elders (i. e. Sthaviras), they look at each other with their hands hanging down, or if one party be inferior, the inferior one joins the hands and pays due respect to the other. The idea of kshamâ[3] is 'beg your pardon,' 'please do not be angry.' In the Vinaya, the word kshamâ is used when we apologise to others, but Desana (pratidesana) is used when we confess our sins ourselves.

Fearing lest we should mislead men of later ages, I have thus spoken about the errors introduced in the former time. Although we are accustomed to the present practices, yet we must strive to follow the original rules.

Sanskrit, pravâraṇa, is translated by '(Doing) as one wishes;' it also

---

[1] Cf. Pâṭidesaniyâ Dhammâ, Pâtimokkha, p. 56, S. B. E., vol. xiii.

[2] Pâtimokkha, p. 56, 'I have fallen into a blameworthy offence ..., and confess it.'

[3] Kshămaya, i. e. 'ask pardon,' is meant here.

means 'satisfying,' and it again *conveys the sense* of 'pointing out another's offence according to his wish.'

CHAPTER XVI.

ABOUT SPOONS AND CHOP-STICKS.

As to the mode of eating in the West, they use only the right hand, but if one has had an illness or has some other reason, one is permitted to keep a spoon *for use.* We never hear of chop-sticks in the five parts of India; they are not mentioned in the Vinaya of the Four Schools (Nikâyas), and it is only China that has them. Laymen naturally follow the old custom (of using sticks), and priests may or may not use them according to their inclination. Chop-sticks were never allowed nor were they prohibited, thus the matter should be treated according to the 'abridged teaching,' for when the sticks are used, people do not discuss or murmur.

In China they may be used, for if we obstinately reject their use, people may laugh or complain.

They must not be used in India. Such is the idea of the 'abridged teaching' (Sa*m*kshipta-vinaya).

CHAPTER XVII.

PROPER OCCASION FOR SALUTATION.

THE manner of salutation should be in accordance with the rules, otherwise it is just as much as falling down on the flat ground. The Buddha, therefore, says: 'There are two kinds of impurity with which one should not receive salutation nor salute another.'

If it be against the teaching, every bow one makes involves the guilt of negligence. Now what are the two kinds of impurity?

Firstly, the impurity contracted through eating and drinking. Through the eating of anything or even the swallowing of a dose of medicine one is unfit for salutation before one rinses one's mouth and washes one's hands. Even when one has drunk syrup, water, tea, or honey-water, or had ghee or moist sugar, one is equally unfit before one duly purifies oneself.

Secondly, the impurity contracted by having been to the lavatory.

Having been to the lavatory one becomes impure, and a purification of one's body, hands, and mouth is necessary.

So too when one's body or garments have become impure, stained by anything such as saliva, mucus.

The impurity by not using tooth-woods in the morning is included in this.

At the meeting of the priests or on the fast-day, one should only join one's hands while impure. Joining one's hands is paying honour, and therefore one need not do the complete salutation. If one does, one is acting against the teaching. Salutation must not be done in a busy spot or impure place, or on the way. These points are described in the Vinaya texts. Several practices are hindered by a wrong traditional custom or by a different climate, though one wishes strictly to obey the teaching.

As long as there are some who practise as ourselves, and whom we could look at as guilty companions, none of us will take warning against a small offence[1]!

CHAPTER XVIII.

CONCERNING EVACUATION.

I SHALL now describe shortly the rules concerning evacuation. One should put on a bathing-skirt for the lower part of the body, a Saṅkakshikâ[2] robe for the upper part. One should then fill up a jar (lit. 'touched jar') with water for cleansing purposes, go to the lavatory with that jar, and shut the door in order to hide oneself. Fourteen balls of earth are provided and placed on a brick plate, or sometimes on a small board, outside the lavatory (Var*k*as-kuṭî). The size of the brick or board is one cubit long and half a cubit wide. The earth-balls are to be ground into powder and made into two rows, the powder of

---

[1] This is very difficult to translate. A better rendering may be sought out, but I think I have hit the sense of the passage.

[2] The Saṅkakshikâ is a side-covering robe or cloth, which is worn under all other robes. For this word, see Mahâvyutpatti, § 240, and Julien, Hiuen Thsang, vol. ii, liv. i, p. 33, and p. 55, 7 above.

each ball being placed separately. There must be an additional ball placed there. One should take three other balls in the lavatory, and put them aside. Of these three, one is to be used in rubbing the body, another in washing the body. The manner of washing the body is as follows: one should wash the body with the left hand, and again purify with water and with the earth. There is still one ball left, with which one should roughly wash the left hand once. If there be a piece of card (or peg) it is well to bring it in, but when it has been used one should throw it away outside the lavatory. But if an old paper be used, it must be thrown away in the urinal. After the purification has been done, one should put down (i.e. adjust) the clothes, put the water-jar on one side, open the door with the right hand, and come out holding the jar in the right hand. Again embracing the jar with the left arm but closing the left hand, one should shut the door behind him with the right hand, and leave the urinal. One should now come to the place where the earth-balls are kept, and squat down on one side; if one use a mat, one should place it according as the occasion demands. The jar should be placed on the left knee (?), and be pressed down by the left arm. First the seven earth-balls which are near one's body should be used one by one in order to wash the left hand, and then the other seven one by one to wash both hands.

The surface of the brick and wood (board) should be cleanly washed. There is still another ball with which the jar, arms, abdomen, and feet (soles of feet) are to be washed; when all are pure and clean, one may go away according to one's own desire. The water in the jar is not fit to be put in the mouth and to the lips. One should come back to one's room and wash the mouth with water contained in a clean jar. When one has touched the jar after having been to the lavatory, one should again wash the hands and rinse the mouth, and then one is fit to touch any other utensils. Such are the rules concerning the voiding of the bowels. To save trouble a priest always washes himself; but he who has a page can let the latter wash him.

After having been to the lavatory one should in any case wash one's hands with one or two earth-balls, for purity is the foundation of paying honour. True, there are some who consider these points a very small matter, but there are strict prohibitions in the Vinaya.

Before purification one should not sit on a chair belonging to the Saṅgha, or salute the Three Jewels (Triratna). Such is the way in which Shên-tze (Kâyaputra) subdued a heretic[1]. The Buddha therefore laid down the rules for the Bhikshus. If you practise (his precepts), the merit that comes from following the Vinaya rules will attend you. If not, the guilt that is incurred by disobeying his teaching will come upon you. Such rules as above were never introduced into China. Even if they were taught, people would dislike them, and say, 'in the universal void taught by the Mahâyâna, what is pure and what is impure? Your inside is ever full; what is the use, then, of the outward purification?' But they do not know that they are, by so thinking, neglecting the teaching of the Buddha, and doing wrong to his noble mind.

Guilt is incurred in doing honour to, or receiving it from, each other. Gods (devas) and spirits get disgusted with our ways of wearing garments and eating food.

If one does not wash and purify oneself, the people of the five divisions of India will laugh at one; and such a man will be spoken ill of wherever he goes. The men on whom the propagation of religion rests should hand down the teaching (of the Buddha). Since we have gone forth from worldly troubles, rejected our homes and become homeless, we are bound to obey strictly every word of the *S*âkya, the Father. How could we cast a displeased glance at the contents of the Vinaya? Even if you do not believe these points, you had better try what has been directed. After five or six days you may know the faults of not washing yourselves.

In winter you may use warm water; in the other three seasons you may use what you like. But the use of the small vessel (to keep water in) and the cloth (to wipe one's body) is not in accordance with the Vinaya texts. Some keep water in their mouth and go out of the lavatory; this practice is also against the rules of purification.

The dwelling-place of the priests must have its lavatories kept clean. If one cannot do so oneself, persuade others to do so. A shelter is thus offered to priests who come from all quarters, common and exalted alike. It is important that the expense should be small.

---

[1] I cannot state with certainty what this reference is.

Such is the act of purification, and it is not a vain thing.

Prepare a large vessel which can hold a Shih or two, fill it with earth, and put it near the lavatory. For the purpose of keeping water, a priest is allowed to use a basin of earthenware in case he has no water-jar prepared in his own private rooms.

The basin full of water is to be brought in and placed at one corner of the lavatory, and the body is cleansed with his right hand.

In the watery region (Kiang and Hwai in China) the ground is low, and a (china) pot is often used for the privy. One cannot wash at the same place; and a washing-place should be made separately, with water always flowing out.

The temple Fa-fuh in Fen-chou; the Ling-yen[1] on the mount Tai; the Yü-hsên in the city Hsing; the Pa-ta in Yang-chou; in all these temples in China the lavatories were arranged according to the proper rules, except that of the preparation of water and earth. Had a person taught and altered this point, the arrangement might have been exactly like that of Râ*g*agr*i*ha. It is the fault of the former teachers and not the ignorance of the later pupils that is to be blamed. The earth and the water in the jar, which are to be kept at the lavatory, must be safely placed and sufficiently supplied.

The second jar (from which one pours out water) should have a spout attached to it. If one uses a ku*n*d*î*, it is to be made according as I explained before[2].

A copper jar with a wide mouth and a lid is not fit to be used in washing. If you make another mouth at the side of it, guard the top of its cover with tin, and make a hole at the centre of the pointed top. You may use the copper jar in time of need.

So far I have toiled with my pen and used my paper, the result being the minuteness of my description. I hope that there may be some who will listen to my remonstrance and pursue the (proper) course.

The Great Sage entered Nirvâ*n*a in the twin Sâla-trees, and the Arhats also became ashes in the five parts of India.

---

[1] Page 23, note, above. [2] Chap. vi above.

The Law that has been left behind is only beginning to dawn in its shadow and sound[1]. Go and entrust yourselves to those who have abandoned the worldly life; rise and follow the men who have rejected earthly care. The busy and turpid world of darkness you must quit; the quiet and white life of purity you should pursue. Let both the dirt outside and the error inside be wiped away, and the tying above and the binding below be equally cut off. With your body in quiet and with your mind in purity, the four actions[2] of yours will never be troubled, and the three objects[3] of honour should always be friends.

Then you are not an object of mockery among living men; how should you fear the angry look of the prince of Death (Yama)? We should tax our thoughts as to how to benefit the nine worlds of beings, and complete the good cause (for Buddhahood) through three long ages.

If, as I earnestly hope, one man out of a million improve himself (by my words) I shall not be sorry for the difficulty and bitterness which I endured, during the two dozen years of my toil *.

CHAPTER XIX.

RULES OF ORDINATION.

AS to the ceremonies *pertaining to admission* to the priesthood (lit. 'the homelessness') which are performed in the West, there are minute rules for them, all established by the Sage (Buddha), as can be fully seen in the 'One Hundred Karmas'[4]; but I shall briefly cite here some points only[5] concerning them. Any one who has turned his thoughts (to religion) and is desirous of being a priest (lit. 'a homeless') enters the presence of a teacher of his own choice, and relates to him his wish. The teacher, through some means or other, inquires whether there is any impediment in the way; i. e. such as *patricide*, *matricide*, and the like.

---

[1] He means to say that the influence of the Law is yet small.

[2] I. e. going, staying, sitting, and lying.

[3] I. e. the Three Jewels.

[4] I. e. the Mûlasarvâstivâdanikâyaïkasatakarman, Nanjio's Catal., No. 1131.

[5] Chinese 略指方隅; lit. 'briefly point out squares and angles.'

If he finds no such difficulty he allows what was asked, and accepts him (as a candidate for orders). Having accepted him, the teacher leaves him at leisure ten days or a month, and then imparts to him the five precepts[1].

The man who hitherto was not a member of the seven Assemblies (i. e. seven Parishads)[2] is now called an Upâsaka; this is his first step into the Law of the Buddha. Then the teacher, having arranged a Pa*t*a (or a simple cloak), a Saṅkakshikâ, a Nivâsana, a bowl, and a filter (for the candidate), addresses himself to the Saṅgha, and relates that the candidate has a desire to become a priest (homeless). When the Saṅgha has admitted him, the teacher on his behalf asks the Â*k*âryas (to conduct the ceremony). Then the candidate, in a private place, has his hair and beard shaved by a barber (lit. a man who shaves the head), and takes a bath, cold or warm according to the season. The teacher through some means or other examines him as to whether he is not a eunuch, &c., and then puts the Nivâsana (i. e. under-garment) on the candidate. Then the upper cloak is given him, which he receives, touching it with his head. After putting on his priestly cloak, he receives the bowl. He is now called a homeless priest (i. e. Pravra*g*ita). Next, in the presence of the teacher (Upâdhyâya), the Â*k*ârya imparts to him the ten precepts (i. e. ten *S*ikshâpadas), either by reciting or by reading them. After the priest has been instructed in these precepts, he is called *S*rama*n*era.

(Note by I-tsing): *S*rama*n*era is to be interpreted 'one who seeks for rest,' meaning 'one who wishes to enter Nirvâ*n*a, the complete rest.' The former transliteration was 'Sha-mi,' which is too short and wrong in pronunciation, and this name was interpreted as 'resting in compassion,' which has no authority, though the meaning may have.

---

[1] The text has 學處; lit. 'place or object of learning;' the original is *S*ikshâpadam, i. e. sentence of moral training, precept. Padam, meaning either 'place' or 'sentence,' was here translated by 'place.' The five and ten *S*ikshâpadas are identical with the five and ten *S*îlas respectively; the five being the well-known fundamental precepts or commands of the Buddha, i. e. 'Do not kill, steal, tell a lie, commit adultery, nor drink any intoxicating liquor.' Childers, Sikkhâ, s.v., and Sîla*m*.

[2] See p. 86, note 2, above.

The dignity, the ceremonies, the attitude and method and the rites of asking instruction and announcing one's intention are the same for those who proceed to receive full ordination[1] (as well as those who desire the ordination as *S*rama*n*era). But in case of a *S*rama*n*era a transgression of the twelve particulars set forth in the Vinaya texts does not involve guilt; for a *S*ikshamâ*n*â (fem.), however, there are some modifications of the rule. Now what are the twelve particulars?

1. One must distinguish (between legal and illegal) robes (Nissaggiyâ 1-10).
2. One must not sleep without garments.
3. One must not touch fire[2] (probably Pâ*k*ittiyâ 56).
4. One must not eat too much food (Pâ*k*ittiyâ 35, 36, and 34).
5. One must not injure any living things (Pâ*k*ittiyâ 61).
6. One must not throw filth upon the green grass (Pâ*k*ittiyâ 11 and 20).
7. One must not recklessly climb up a high tree (unless in emergency).
8. One must not touch jewels (Pâ*k*ittiyâ 84; Nissaggiyâ 18 and 19).
9. One must not eat food left from a meal (Pâ*k*ittiyâ 38).
10. One must not dig the ground (Pâ*k*ittiyâ 9).
11. One must not refuse offered food.
12. One must not injure growing sprouts.

The two lower classes of members (i. e. *S*rama*n*eras and *S*rama*n*erîs) need not conform to the twelve, but the *S*ikshamâ*n*âs (fem.) incur guilt if they fail to keep the last five particulars (8-12 above). These three lower members also have to observe the summer-retreat (i. e. Varsha).

The six important rules and six minor rules (for women) are given elsewhere[3]. If they are not guilty of breach of any rules they can be

---

[1] I. e. Upasa*m*padâ; Prof. Rhys Davids prefers 'initiation' to 'ordination' as the translation of Upasa*m*padâ, p. 377, Milinda II, S. B. E., vol. xxxvi; for the ceremony of leaving home (Pabba*gg*â) to become a *S*rama*n*era, and the full ordination (Upasa*m*padâ) to become a Bhikshu, see Childers, s.v., and Mahâvagga I, 28-76.

[2] According to Kâ*s*yapa, this is burning fire in an open ground.

[3] The Vinaya-saṅgraha, chap. xii (Nanjio's Catal., No. 1127), gives the six rules and six minor rules for the female members.

a. The six important rules:—

1. A female must not travel alone.

considered as 'acting in accordance with the laws;' in this case they may properly be included among the five assemblies (i. e. Parishads) and partake of the benefits conferred. It is wrong for a teacher not to impart the ten precepts to one who has become a priest (lit. 'left home'), and not to communicate the complete precepts (Mahâsîla, s. v. Sîla, Childers) out of fear that one should transgress them. For in such a case the novice falsely bears the name (of Sramanera which means) 'seeking rest,' and vainly embraces the appellation (of Pravragita, i. e. one) 'who has gone forth from his home.' It is a great loss to one, though some may think that there is some benefit in being a priest even under such conditions. It is said in a Sûtra[1]: 'He who is counted among the number of priests without receiving the ten precepts has a seat only temporarily open for him. How can he hold the seat and make it permanent (lit. long-period)?'

In China the admission to the priesthood is by public registration. After having shaved one's hair, one takes refuge for a time with a teacher; the latter never holds himself responsible for imparting to one a single prohibitive rule, nor does the pupil himself ask to be instructed in the ten moral precepts.

Before he proceeds to full ordination, he is doing wrong in that he acts according to his own wish. On the day on which he receives full ordination he is ordered to go into the Bodhimandala without any

---

2. A female must not cross a river alone.
3. " " touch the body of a man.
4. " " have the same lodging with a man.
5. " " act as a matchmaker.
6. " " conceal a grave offence committed by a nun.

b. The six minor rules:—

1. A female must not take gold or silver which does not belong to her.
2. " " shave the hair in any place but the head.
3. " " dig up an uncultivated ground.
4. " " wilfully cut growing grass or a tree.
5. " " eat food which is not offered.
6. " " eat food which has once been touched.

[1] The Mahâparinirvâna-sûtra is meant here (Nanjio's Catal., No. 113, not 114, see vol. vi, fol. 13[b] of the older edition).

previous knowledge of the proceedings laid down in the Vinaya. How can he conduct himself becomingly at the time of the ceremony? This is not the way to maintain the laws. Such a man is utterly unfit to be made a resident priest. What wonder then if he become an overburdened debtor, notwithstanding his receiving gifts from others. He ought, in accordance with the teaching, to save others as well as himself. Those who go through public registration should previously ask a teacher about it. The teacher must inquire into the difficulties (*that prevent registration*)[1], and if the candidates be free and fit (lit. pure and clean) the teacher should communicate to them the five precepts. Having seen the candidate's head shaved he should invest him with the Pata (i. e. simple cloak), and at the same time communicate to him the ten precepts.

When the novice has become acquainted with all the religious rites and reached the required age[2], if he be desirous of receiving full ordination, the teacher, having seen his pupil's wish and resolve to keep the precepts, arranges for him the six Requisites (p. 54 above), and asks nine other persons[3] (to take part in the ceremony). The ceremony may be held on a small terrace or within a large enclosure or within a natural boundary. In the area, mats belonging to the Saṅgha may be used, or each individual may use his own. Incense and flowers are prepared in an expensive way. Then the candidate is taught to pay respect three times to each priest present, or sometimes to touch the feet of every priest approaching his person. These two are the ceremonies of salutation according to the teaching of the Buddha. After this ceremony, he is instructed to seek to learn the (great) precepts (Mahâsila). That done three times, the Upâdhyâya invests him before the assembly with the garments and the bowl.

Then the candidate has to carry the bowl around and show it successively to every one of the priests there assembled. If it be a proper one, all the assembled priests say: 'A good bowl;' if they do not say this, they incur the fault of transgressing the Law. After this, the bowl is to be accepted by the candidate according to the Law. Then the Âkârya who conducts the ceremony (Karma) imparts to him *the great*

---

[1] These are the Disqualifications for receiving the ordination, Mahâvagga I, 76.

[2] Twenty years of age, according to Kâsyapa; Mahâvagga I, 49, 5.

[3] There should be ten teachers altogether, according to Kâsyapa.

precepts (Mahâsîla) either by reading the text which is held up before him or by muttering them; for both are allowed by the Buddha. One who has received the precepts is called an Upasa*m*panna[1] (i.e. one who has received the Upasa*m*padâ ordination).

(Note by I-tsing): Upasa*m*panna; upa means 'near' and sa*m*panna 'full' or 'complete,' signifying Nirvâ*n*a. In receiving the complete precepts a person is nearer to Nirvâ*n*a. This idea was vaguely expressed by the older interpretation, Yü-tsö (具足 'complete').

As soon as the ceremony is over, one should quickly measure the shadow of the sun (in order to determine the date of ordination)[2] and also write down the name of the season (there are five).

The following is the way of measuring the shadow. Take a piece of wood about a cubit (one hasta) long, like a slender chop-stick, bending it at a point four finger-breadths from the end[3], in the shape of a carpenter's square (∟), make the shorter end of it point upwards without allowing the other (longer) part to be separated from the perpendicular part of the stick. At noon, when one lays the longer part of the stick along the ground, the shadow of the perpendicular part of it falls on the horizontal part of the stick. One measures the falling shadow with four fingers. If the shadow extends just as long as four finger-breadths, the measure is called one Purusha (or Paurusha)[4], and thus the measurement of time goes on by the names of so many Purushas or sometimes one Purusha and a finger-breadth or half a finger-breadth, or simply one finger-breadth and so on (when not measuring quite so much as one Purusha). In this way (*the differences of time*) are to be measured and considered by adding and reducing of fingers.

(Note by I-tsing): Purusha[4] is 'man;' the reason why the shadow

---

[1] See Childers, s.v.

[2] See also Mahâvagga I, 77.

[3] 'Finger-breadth' is in Sanskrit 'aṅgula;' twelve aṅgulas = one vitasti (a span, Chinese 一搩手), the 'finger-breadth,' must not be confused with 'finger-joint' (Aṅguliparvan), which is also a measure. For instance, see '*K*aturaṅgulam,' Sukhâvatîvyûha, Sanskrit text, § 21, p. 43. See above, p. 28, note.

[4] Purusha, as a measure, generally means the length of a man with his arms and fingers extended, and our nearest corresponding measure would be 'a fathom.' But, according to I-tsing, it seems to mean four aṅgulas (four finger-breadths=

that measures four finger-breadths is called 'one man' (Eka-purusha) is that, when the shadow of the perpendicular stick which itself measures four finger-breadths is also four finger-breadths in length on the horizontal stick, a man's shadow falling on the ground is the same length as the real height of that man. When the shadow of the perpendicular stick is eight finger-breadths in length on the horizontal stick, the man's shadow on the ground is just double the person's height. It is so with a man of medium size; it is not necessarily so with all persons[1]. Other measurements are also made by this method.

It must be mentioned (*that the ordination has taken place*) before the meal or after it. When the weather is cloudy, or at night, one must measure the time in a suitable way.

According to the way adopted in China, one calculates the length of the shadow of the sun with a measure which points upwards, or one uses (*an instrument*) on which the divisions of the twelve hours are marked. What are the five seasons? It is difficult to know, unless through direct instruction, the division of the months, as it differs in different countries. *In India* the first is called the winter season, in which there are four months, i.e. from the 16th of the 9th moon to the 15th of the 1st moon. The second is the spring season, in which there are also four months, i.e. from the 16th of the 1st moon to the 15th of the 5th moon. The third is the rainy season, in which there is only one month, i.e. from the 16th of the 5th moon to the 15th of the 6th moon. The

---

one-third vitasti (span)=one-sixth hasta), and thus we must take Purusha or Paurusha, if used technically, to mean four finger-breadths. Does Saptapaurusha in Sukhâvatîvyûha, Sanskrit text, § 21, p. 43, also mean twenty-eight aṅgulas being technically used? Or seven fathoms, as Prof. Max Müller translates? The Chinese translation by Bodhiruki has 'seven feet' for Sapta-paurusha. The fallen flowers are seven fathoms deep, and when one walks on them, they sink down only four inches (aṅgula). The great difference between seven fathoms and four inches makes us think that in Buddhism, or at any rate in a Buddhist school, Paurusha has been used technically for four aṅgulas as I-tsing tells us. See the Land of Bliss, p. 43, S. B. E., vol. xlix.

A detail of this measure is given in Mûlasarvâstivâdaikasatakarman, book i.

[1] I-tsing seems to be wrong. It must be the same with any one.

fourth is the last season so called, which is only one day and night, i.e. the day and night of the 16th of the 6th moon. The fifth is the long season, i.e. from the 17th of the 6th moon to the 15th of the 9th moon.

This is, however, the division of the year in the Vinaya only, as ordained by the Buddha. In this system of division there is evidently a deep meaning.

According to the usages in different districts there are three seasons[1], or four[2] or six seasons[3], which are mentioned elsewhere[4]. All the priests in India and in the islands of the Southern Sea, when they meet one another for the first time, ask: 'Venerable Sir, how many summer-retreats (Varshas) have you passed?' He who has been questioned replies: 'So many.' If they have passed the same number of summer-retreats, one inquires in which season the other was ordained. If it happens to be in the same season as the other, the interlocutor further questions how many days there were left in that season. If the number of the days is still the same, the one asks whether the other was ordained before the meal or after it, on that day. If both were ordained in the same forenoon, then one inquires the length of the shadow; and if this differs, the seniority of the two is determined. But if the shadow be the same, then there is no difference between them. In this case the order of seats is determined by the earliest arrival, or the managing priest (i.e. Karmadâna) suffers them to decide the matter themselves. Those who go to India must ask[5] these points. This is somewhat different from *the custom* in China, where the priests simply mention the date of

[1] The ordinary division of seasons is into three seasons: Winter, Spring, and Summer. Kâsyapa gives the corresponding months in China as follows: Winter, 15th of the 8th moon to 15th of the 12th moon; Spring, 16th of the 12th to 15th of the 4th moon; Summer, 16th of the 4th to 15th of the 8th moon.

[2] The four seasons are given in Hiuen Thsang, Julien, Mémoires, liv. ii, p. 63.

[3] The six seasons are also given by Hiuen Thsang, Julien, Mémoires, liv. ii, p. 62. These are *S*isira*h* (thaw, 1), Vasanta*h* (spring, 2), Grîshma*h* (summer, 3), Varshâ*h* (rain, 4), *S*arat (harvest, 5), Hemanta*h* (winter, 6). See Prof. Max Müller, Rig-veda (2nd edition), vol. iv, p. xxxv. See my note at the end.

[4] By 'elsewhere' he perhaps meant Hiuen Thsang, Si-yu-ki, at any rate Kâsyapa supposes so.

[5] J. has 閑, i.e. 'must get accustomed to these points.'

ordination. But in the Nâlanda monastery the priests often receive the Upasampadâ[1] ordination (i.e. full ordination) in the early morning, on *the first day* of the 'long season' (17th of the 6th moon, see above), when the day has just begun to dawn. They mean to claim seniority among those who are ordained in the same summer. This is the early dawn of the 17th day of the 6th moon of China; (they do so because, otherwise), they cannot get the second summer-retreat[2].

(Note by I-tsing): This division is in accordance with the summer-retreat of India. If we follow the old practice of China, the second summer-retreat would be on the 17th of the 5th moon.

If one receive the ordination when the night of the 16th day of the 6th moon (i.e. a day before the second summer-retreat begins) is about to end, one would be the junior of all ordained in the same summer. (When one is ordained at the dawn of the 17th of the 6th moon, i.e. the commencement of the second varsha), the candidate obtains the second summer-retreat as well, and he therefore need not make gifts to others after the ordination, except to his teachers, to whom something either trifling or extravagant may be given. Some such thing as a girdle or a filter should be brought and offered to the teachers who are present in the place of the ordination (and take part in it), in order to show sincere gratitude (lit. unerring mind, i.e. Amogha). Then the Upâdhyâya giving out the contents of the Prâtimoksha[3] teaches the candidate the character of the offences and how to recite the precepts.

These having been learnt, the candidate begins to read the larger Vinaya-pitaka; he reads it day after day, and is examined every morning, for if he does not keep to it constantly he will lose intellectual

---

[1] See Childers, s.v.; Oldenberg, Buddha, p. 347 seq.

[2] Two summer-retreats are held in one year; the first begins on the 1st day of the dark half of the 5th moon, and ends in the middle of the 8th moon; and the second begins on the 1st day of the dark half of the 6th moon, and ends in the middle of the 9th moon (see chap. xiv). If one receive the ordination on the 17th of the 6th moon, i.e. the beginning of the second summer, one can claim the residence of the second summer-retreat as well as the first. Choosing the early dawn also means getting an earlier ordination.

[3] See the Vinaya text, part i, S. B. E., vol. xiii.

power. When he has read the Vinaya-pitaka, he begins to learn the Sûtras and Sâstras. Such is the way in which a teacher instructs in India. Although it is a long period since the days of the Sage, yet such a custom still exists unimpaired. These two teachers (i. e. Upâdhyâya and Karmâkârya)[1] are likened to parents. Can it be right for a man who has taken unusual pains to be ordained to pay no more attention to the precepts when he has been ordained?

It is surely a pity that such a beginning should have no satisfactory end. There are some who after having desired to be ordained, when they first met their teachers, have never after ordination approached their teachers again; they neither read the book on precepts nor open the Vinaya texts: such men have been vainly admitted into the religious ranks, and will be a loss to themselves and to others also. Persons of this kind cause destruction to the Law.

The following are the grades (lit. Rules of Practice) of Indian priests. After the Upasampadâ ordination, the priest is called Cha-gâ-ra (i. e. Dahara), which is translated by 'small teacher,' and those who have completely passed ten summer-retreats[2] are called Sthavira (elders), which is translated by 'settled position,' for a Sthavira can live by himself without living under a teacher's care. He can also become an Upâdhyâya.

In letters or any communication one puts down Sramanera N. N., Dahara (small) Bhikshu N. N., or Sthavira Bhikshu N. N.; but if one be learned both in the sacred and secular literatures and famed as virtuous, one should call oneself a Bahusruta N. N. One must not call oneself a Saṅgha N. N. (as they do in China), for Saṅgha is the name of the whole assembly of priests. How then can one individual call himself a Saṅgha, which contains four classes of men (priests)? In India there is no such custom as calling oneself a Saṅgha (as in China).

Any one who becomes an Upâdhyâya must be a Sthavira, and must have passed the full ten summer-retreats. The age of a Karmâkârya and private instructor, and of other teachers who are witnesses, is not

---

[1] For these two teachers, see Mahâvagga I, 32, 1, note, pp. 178–9, S. B. E., vol. xiii.

[2] The number of years for Sthavira given here confirms the statement of Childers, s. v. 'thero' (also Hardy's E. Mon. 11, and Burnouf's Intr. Bud. 288).

limited[1]; they must be fully acquainted with the Vinaya, being themselves pure; and must be either in the full or in the half number[2]. It is said in the Vinaya: 'Those are guilty of defiling others who call a man Upâdhyâya who is not really an Upâdhyâya, or Â*k*ârya who is not an Â*k*ârya, or vice versa, and those also who being themselves Upâdhyâyas refuse to be called so.'

When a man has asked one, saying: 'What is your Upâdhyâya's name?' or 'Whose pupil are you?' and also when one has oneself thought it proper to tell the name of one's Upâdhyâya as required by circumstances, one should say: 'Under the present circumstances I tell you the name of my Upâdhyâya; he is N. N. by name.' One should not wonder that the (pronoun) 'I' is used here[3], for the expression of 'I' is not a haughty word in India and in the islands of the Southern Sea. Even to call others 'you' is not disrespectful language.

It is simply meant to distinguish one from another, and these words never convey an idea of haughtiness, quite unlike the custom of China, which considers the use of 'I' and 'you' rude and unconventional. If one still dislikes the use of 'I,' one may use 'now' instead of 'I[4].' These points are in conformity with the teaching of the Buddha, and must be practised by the priests. Do not join the train of people who are blind to black and white (i. e. wrong and right).

Those white-robed (laymen) who come to the residence of a priest, and read chiefly Buddhist scriptures with the intention that they may one day become tonsured and black-robed, are called 'children' (Mâ*n*ava).

---

[1] The text has 無定年幾事, but 幾 cannot very well be construed here. I should amend the reading by placing 歲 instead of that character; these two are very much alike when written in a running hand.

[2] The text has 中邊數滿; lit. 'full in the medium or the extreme number.' Kâ*s*yapa says that 中數滿 is ten in number, and 邊滿數 is five in number, but why they are called the 'medium' and 'extreme' we do not know.

[3] The reader is reminded that in Chinese, courteous language does not like the use of a pronoun of the first person, but use is made of secondary nouns, such as 'servant,' 'slave,' or one's real name.

[4] This substitute is admissible in Chinese, though it is very strange in English.

Those who (coming to a priest) want to learn secular literature only, without having any intention of quitting the world, are called 'students' (Brahma*k*ârin). These two groups of persons (though residing in a monastery) have to subsist at their own expense.

(Note by I-tsing): In the monasteries of India there are many 'students' who are entrusted to the Bhikshus and instructed by them in secular literature.

On one hand the 'students' serve under the priests as pages, on the other the instruction will lead to pious aspirations. It is therefore very good to keep them, inasmuch as both sides are benefitted in this way. It is worth one bowl of gifts gained by the Dhûta, without any trouble. Even if their service only be counted as gain, they are rather useful; let them bring the tooth-woods or serve at the meals, and it is sufficient to supply the present need. It is not a bad way in any case.

These 'students' must not be fed from the permanent property of the Saṅgha, for this is prohibited in the teaching of the Buddha; but if they have done some laborious work for the Saṅgha, they are to be fed by the monastery according to their merit.

Food made for ordinary purposes or presented by the giver to be used by the 'students' can be given to them without wrong-doing.

The Shadow of the Buddha has faded away from the Dragon River, and the Light of his splendour has disappeared from the Vulture Peak; how many Arhats have we who could hand down the Sacred Law?

Thus it is said in a *S*âstra: 'When the Great Lion closed his eyes, all the witnesses also passed away one after another. The world became ever more defiled by passion. One should be on one's own guard without overstepping (the moral discipline).'

All the virtuous should join in protecting the Law. But if you, being remiss and idle, let human inclination work, what would you do with the men and Devas whose guidance is in your charge?

It is said in the Vinaya: 'As long as there is a Karmâ*k*ârya (the holder of Rules) my Law will not be destroyed. If there be no one who holds and supports the Karma (Rules) my Law will come to an end.' It is also said: 'While my precepts exist, I live.' These are not empty sayings, but have a deep meaning, and therefore should be duly respected. Again I express the same in verse:

The shadow of the Great Master has faded away, and the chief magnates of the Law have also passed from us. The heretics stand high as a mountain, and the small hill of benevolence is also being *ruined*.

To preserve the radiance of the sun-like Buddha is indeed the work of the good and wise. If one follow the narrow path, how can one teach the greater way? (The good Law) has been fortunately handed down to the intelligent, who have diligently to promote it.

It is to be hoped that one will transmit and propagate the Law without defiling it, but making it ever more fragrant to remotest ages. What is meant by 'making the Law ever more fragrant?'

It is stirring up the waves in the Ocean of *S*ila (morality). Thus the teaching of the Buddha may not come to an end though it has already been near its end, and the practice of the Law may not be wrong though it has almost suffered misapprehension. We should make our practice agree with the Right Teaching taught in Râ*g*agr*i*ha, and endeavour to arrive at the point of undefiled discipline laid down at the *G*eta Gardens.

CHAPTER XX.

BATHING AT PROPER TIMES.

Now I shall describe the manner of bathing. Bathing in India is different from that in China. The weather is moderate in all seasons, somewhat different from other districts. There are flowers and fruits always, even in the twelfth month. Snow and ice are unknown. There is frost, but slightly. Though it is hot (in certain seasons), yet the heat is not intense; and even in the warmest season people do not suffer from 'prickly heat[1].' When it is very cold, they have not chapped feet, for they wash and bathe frequently, and think much about the purity of the body. In their daily life they do not eat without having first washed.

Water is exceedingly abundant in the pools everywhere. It is considered meritorious to dig ponds[2]. If we go but one yo*g*ana, we see

[1] The so-called 'prickly heat' is a severe form of Lichen tropicus.

[2] Cf. Si-yu-ki, Julien, Mémóires, liv. viii, p. 466, where two brother Brâhmans, according to the command of Mahe*s*vara Deva, build a monastery and dig a pool to gain religious merit.

twenty or thirty bathing-places; and they vary in size, some being one mou (or about 733½ square yards), others five mou. On all sides of a pond Sâla-trees are planted, which grow to the height of about forty or fifty feet. All these pools are fed by rain-water, and are as clear as a pure river. Near every one of the eight *K*aityas[1] there is a pool in which the World-honoured One used to bathe. The water in these pools is very pure, different from that in others.

There are more than ten great pools near the Nâlanda monastery, and there every morning a gha*n*tî is sounded to remind the priests of the bathing-hour. Every one brings a bathing-sheet with him. Sometimes a hundred, sometimes a thousand (priests) leave the monastery together,

---

[1] The eight *K*aityas are—

1. In Lumbinî Garden, Kapilavastu, the Buddha's birthplace. (Cp. Lalita., p. 94.)
2. Under the Bodhi tree near the Naira*ñ*g*anâ river, Magadha, where Buddhahood was obtained.
3. In Vârâ*n*asî (Benares), in the country of the Kâ*s*îs, the place where the Buddha preached his Law for the first time.
4. In *G*eta Garden, *S*râvastî, where the Buddha's great supernatural powers were displayed.
5. In Kânyakub*g*a (Kanoj), where the Buddha descended from the Trayastri*ms*a Heaven.
6. In Râ*g*ag*ri*ha, where a division among the disciples arose and the Buddha taught them accordingly.
7. In Vai*s*âlî, where the Buddha spoke about the length of his life. Reference to this occasion in I-tsing's Introduction, see p. 5, and also in Si-yu-ki, Julien, liv. vii, p. 390.
8. In the great avenue of the Sâla-trees in Ku*s*inagara, where the Buddha entered Nirvâ*n*a. See my note at the end.

The above names are to be found in (1) Jiun Kâ*s*yapa's Commentary; (2) Mûlasarvâstivâdanikâya-vinaya-sa*m*yuktavastu, book xxxviii, translated by I-tsing, A.D. 710 (Nanjio's Catal., No. 1121); (3) Ash*t*a-mahâ-*k*aitya-stotra, composed by king *S*îlâditya (Nanjio's Catal., No. 1071); (4) most clearly, in the 'Sûtra on the Names of the Great *K*aityas' (Nanjio's Catal., No. 898), see Nanjio's note in the Catalogue. Cf. the eight Stûpas, Mahâparinibbâna-sutta VI, 51–62 (pp. 131–135).

and proceed in all directions towards these pools, where all of them take a bath.

The regulation concerning the bathing-sheet is as follows: Take soft cloth five feet long by a foot and a half wide, and put it round the body (over the under-garment). Draw out and *take off* the ordinary under-garment, and let both ends of the bathing-cloth come in front. Then take hold of the upper corner of the left end with the right hand, and by pulling it up towards the waist let it touch the body; join this with the right end of the cloth; and twisting both together, push them in between the waist and the cloth itself. This is the way of putting on a bathing-sheet. The same is the rule for putting on an under-garment at bed-time. When a man is about to come out of the bathing-place, he should shake his body and emerge from the water very slowly lest he should take out some insects adhering to the cloth. The rules concerning the manner of coming up to the bank are laid down in the Vinaya texts[1]. In case of having a bath in the monastery without going to the pond, the bathing-cloth is put on in the same manner, but the water is poured on by another man, and an enclosure is to be made around the spot for bathing.

The World-honoured One taught how to build a bath-room, to construct a brick pond in an open place, and to make a medical bath in order to cure a disease. Sometimes he ordained the whole body to be anointed with oil, sometimes the feet to be rubbed with oil every night, or the head every morning; for such a practice is very good for maintaining clear eyesight and keeping off the cold.

Concerning all these details, we have sacred authority which is too voluminous to be fully stated here. A detailed account is found in the Vinaya texts[2]. Further, bathing should always take place when one is hungry. Two kinds of benefits are derived by having meals after bathing. First, the body is pure and empty, being free from all

---

[1] In the Mûlasarvâstivâdanikâya-sa*m*yuktavastu, book v (Nanjio's Catal., No. 1121), and the Vinaya-saṅgraha, book xii (Nanjio's Catal., No. 1127).

[2] For the construction of a bathing-room enjoined by the Buddha, &c., see the Mûlasarvâstivâdanikâya-sa*m*yuktavastu, book iii (Nanjio's Catal., No. 1121), and also in the *K*aturvarga-vinayapi*t*aka (Nanjio's Catal., No. 1117).

dirt. Second, the food will be well digested, as the bathing makes one free from phlegm or any disease of the internal organs. Bathing after a good meal (lit. much eating) is forbidden in the 'Science of Medicine' (*K*ikitsâ-vidyâ). Therefore we can see that the (*Chinese*) saying: 'Wash hair when hungry, but bathe after food,' does not hold good in every country. When a bathing-sheet only three feet long is worn (*as usual in China*), it cannot preserve decency, being too short. Bathing without any cloth is contrary to the teaching of the Buddha. People ought to use a bathing-garment made of a cloth the length of which measures four times its breadth; then it can cover the body as is seemly. Such a practice is not only in perfect harmony with the noble teaching of the Buddha, but also produces no shame before men and gods. As to the right or wrong of other matters the wise should carefully judge for themselves.

Even in night bathing one should adhere to the proper custom; how much more then should one cover the body before the people's eyes!

CHAPTER XXI.

CONCERNING THE MAT TO SIT ON.

In the five parts of India there is no such custom as using a mat to sit on while worshipping. Nor is there any reference in the rules of the four Nikâyas to the custom of standing and saluting others three times. General rules for doing homage will be found in other chapters (xxv and xxx). In making a mat for sitting or lying on (Nishîdana) a piece of cloth is cut (in two), and the pieces placed one upon the other and stitched together. Patches (or fringe) are attached to the mat. I have no time to give here a minute description of its size[1]. It is used for preserving the mattress belonging to another, when one happens to sleep

[1] Kâsyapa gives a sketch of the mat, and says: 'Its length is the Buddha's two spans, and its width the Buddha's one span and a half. As the Buddha's fingers were twice as long as ours, the length would be about 4 feet 5 inches, and the width 3 feet $3\frac{3}{4}$ inches. One third of the mat is fringed at the bottom. The venerable Udâyi was very tall; a mat of the measurement then prescribed was too short and his feet extended beyond the edge. Accordingly he brought some

thereon. Whenever one uses anything which is another's possession, whether it be new or old, one must spread (one's own mat) over it. But if the thing be one's own, and be old, one need not use (another mat). But one should avoid destroying gifts of the faithful by dirtying them. The sitting-mat is not used when one performs a salutation.

The priests in the Southern Sea *islands* keep a cloth three or five feet long, doubled up like a napkin, and they use it for kneeling on when they perform a salutation. They carry it on the shoulder when walking. Whenever Indian Bhikshus come *to the islands*, they cannot but smile when they see this custom.

CHAPTER XXII.

RULES OF SLEEPING AND RESTING.

As apartments (in a monastery) are not spacious in India, and the residents are numerous. the beds are removed after the occupants have risen. They are put aside in a corner of the room, or removed outside

---

leaves on which to place his feet. The Buddha saw this and lengthened the measurement. So the lengthened portion must always be fringed or patched, representing leaves.' This must have been an important custom among the

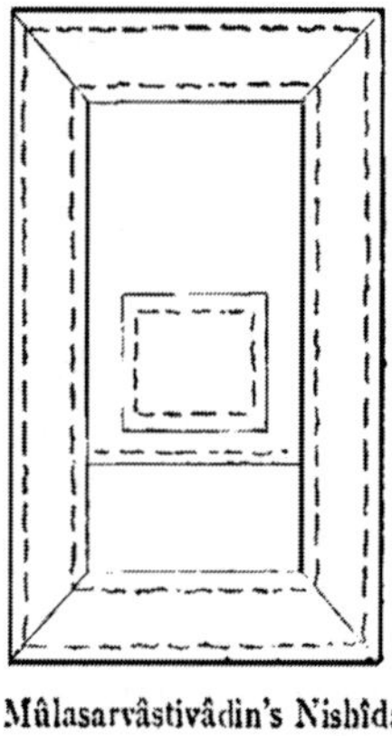

The Mûlasarvâstivâdin's Nishîdana.

Bhikshus, for it was one of the ten theses promulgated by the Vaggian Bhikshus of Vaisâlî that 'a rug or mat need not be of the limited size prescribed if it had no fringe' (see *K*ullavagga XII, 1, 1 (9)). Cf. Pâtimokkha, Pâ*k*ittiyâ 89. See my additional note at the end.

the doors. The width of a bed is two cubits (=3 feet), and its length four cubits (= 6 feet). The mat is made of the same size, and is not heavy. The floor (of an apartment) is cleansed by strewing over it dry cow-dung. Next, chairs, blocks of wood, small mats, &c., are arranged. Then the priests take their seats according to rank, as usual. Necessary utensils are placed on the shelves[1].

There is no such custom as screening one's bed with a cloth (as in China). For, if a man is unfit to sleep in the same apartment with others, he should not do so. And if all are equally qualified, why should one screen oneself from others[2]? In using the bed which is the possession of the Brotherhood (Saṅgha), one should put something between the body and the bed; and it is for this purpose that the mat (Nishîdana) is used. If one does not conform to this rule one is liable to suffer the retribution of the 'black back[3].' We have strict injunctions of the Buddha on this point, and we must be very careful about it.

In the ten islands of the Southern Sea, as well as in the five divisions of India (lit. the West), people do not use wooden pillows to raise the head. It is only China that has this custom.

The pillow-covers are made almost the same way throughout the West. The material is silk or linen; the colour varies according to one's own liking. It is sewed in a square bag one cubit long and a half cubit wide. The pillow is stuffed with any suitable home products, such as wool, hemp-scraps (or waste hemp), the pollen of Typha latifolia (P'u), the catkins of the willow, cotton, reed (Ti), Tecoma grandiflora

---

[1] Concerning the bedsteads, &c., see *K*ullavagga VIII, 1, 4, note.

[2] My translation follows Jiun Kâsyapa's Commentary. Such a novice who has not yet received full ordination is unfit to sleep in the same apartment as those who have received it.

[3] One text has 累 instead of 黑; the latter is decidedly the better reading. In the Mûlasarvâstivâdaikasatakarman we read: 'The Buddha said that Bhikshus must not use the bed-gear belonging to the Brotherhood without putting something on it. He further pointed to a man whose *back was black*, and told Ânanda that that man was a priest under the former Buddha named Kâsyapa, but he fell into Hell on account of his using the bed-gear belonging to the Saṅgha without any proper thing between, and he was born 500 times with *black back*.'

(T'iao), soft leaves, dry moths, the ear-shell (Chüeh-ming, i.e. Haliotis), hemp or beans; it is made high or low, according to the cold or warm season, the object being to get comfort and to rest one's body. There is indeed no fear of its being hard to the touch. But a wooden pillow is rough and hard[1], and it allows the wind to pass below the neck and frequently causes headache. However, usages differ according to the country; I am here simply stating what I heard in a foreign land, and therefore whether one should carry out this or not must be judged by one's own inclination. But warm things keep off cold, and hemp or beans are good for the eyesight, besides very beneficial; thus such things can be used without any mistake. In a cold country, if one expose one's head there often follows a chill (or acute febrile disease). Catarrh in winter months is due to the same cause. If one warm the head at proper times[2] there should not be any trouble or disease. The saying, (in China), 'Head cold and feet warm,' cannot always be relied on.

Sometimes a holy image is placed in the rooms where the priests reside, either in a window or in a niche especially made for it. When they sit at meals, the priests screen the image with a linen curtain. They bathe it every morning, and always offer it incense and flowers. Every day at noon they sincerely make offerings of a portion of whatever food they are going to eat. The case containing the scriptures is placed on one side. At sleeping hour they retire into another room[3]. There is the same custom in the islands of the Southern Sea. The following is the manner in which the priests usually worship in their private rooms. Every monastery has its holy image, which is enshrined in a special temple. The priest must not fail to wash the image after it is constructed during his lifetime. And it is not allowable that the simple offering of food should be made only on a fast day. If these regulations are carried out, then to have the image in the same room is

---

[1] The text has 鞭, 'whip,' but the commentator Kâsyapa happily conjectures that it should be 硬, 'hard;' my translation follows him.

[2] All but the Korean edition have 適一時 instead of 適時; my translation follows the latter.

[3] Or 'they remove the image into a different room.' It is certain, at any rate, that the sleeping-chamber is not the same as the room where the image is.

not wrong. While the Buddha was living, His disciples lived in the same rooms, and an image represents the real person; we can live in the same rooms without any harm. This traditional custom has long been practised in India.

CHAPTER XXIII.

ON THE ADVANTAGE OF PROPER EXERCISE TO HEALTH.

IN India both priests and laymen are generally in the habit of taking walks, going backwards and forwards along a path, at suitable hours, and at their pleasure: they avoid noisy places. Firstly, it cures diseases, and secondly, it helps to digest food. The walking-hours are in the forenoon (before eleven o'clock) and late in the afternoon. They either go away (for a walk) from their monasteries, or stroll quietly along the corridors. If any one neglects this exercise he will suffer from ill-health, and often be troubled by a swelling of the legs, or of the stomach, a pain in the elbows or the shoulders. A phlegmatic complaint likewise is caused by sedentary habits. If any one, on the contrary, adopts this habit of walking he will keep his body well, and thereby improve his religious merit. Therefore there are cloisters (*K*aṅkrama)[1] where the World-honoured used to walk, on the Vulture Peak, under the Bo-tree, in the Deer Park, at Râ*g*ag*ri*ha, and in other holy places. They are about two cubits wide, fourteen or fifteen cubits long, and two cubits high, built with bricks; and on the surface of each are placed fourteen or fifteen figures of an open lotus-flower, made of lime, about two cubits (= three feet)[2] in height, one foot in diameter, and marked (on the surface of each figure) with the footprint of the Sage. At each end of these walks stands a small *K*aitya, equal to a man's height, in which the holy image, i.e. the erect statue of *S*âkyamuni, is sometimes placed. When any one walks towards the right round a temple or a *K*aitya, he does it

---

[1] See Mahâvagga V, 1, 14, note; *K*ullavagga V, 14, 1; Ind. Ant., vol. x, 192.

[2] Read 'two cubits' (chou) for 'two inches' in the text. I-tsing describes the cloisters again in his Memoirs (see my additional note at the end; also Chavannes, p. 96), and gives 'two chou,' i.e. three feet. This is confirmed by Hiuen Thsang (Julien, liv. viii, p. 470); he gives 'three feet.'

for the sake of religious merit; therefore he must perform it with special reverence. But the exercise (I am now speaking of) is for the sake of taking air, and its object is to keep oneself in good health or to cure diseases. Formerly it was termed *Hsing-tao* (or 'walking on a way'); we now term it *Ching-hsing* (or 'perambulating'), both having the same signification. But this suitable practice has long since been discontinued at Tung-ch'uan (i.e. China)! We read in the Sûtras: 'Looking at trees, they walk.' Moreover, we see the very place (where the Buddha used to take a walk) close to the Diamond-seat (i.e. Vagrâsana); only we find there no round (lotus-formed) pedestal (such as they make in China).

CHAPTER XXIV.

WORSHIP NOT MUTUALLY DEPENDENT.

THE rules of salutation are to be practised according to the teaching *of the Buddha*. One who has proceeded to full ordination and whose date of ordination is earlier[1] can claim a salute from the juniors. The Buddha said[2]: 'There are two kinds of men who are worthy of salutation; first, the Tathâgata; second, elder Bhikshus.' This is the golden word of the Buddha; why should we then trouble ourselves to be humble and unassuming? When the junior sees a senior he should quietly show respect and salute with the word 'Vande' (i.e. 'I salute,' but often 'Vandana'); and the senior in accepting the salutation should say 'Ârogya' (n. 'health'), holding his hands right in front. This word implies one's praying that the one addressed may *not* have any *disease* (aroga). If they do not say these words, both parties are faulty. Whether standing or sitting, the ordinary ceremony should not be changed. Those who are worthy of receiving salutation need not salute others *who are inferior to themselves*. Such is the rule among the priests of the five parts of India. It is

[1] Lit. 'the measurement of the shadow is before others.'

[2] Jiun Kâsyapa thinks that this quotation is from the Vinaya-sangraha, book xiii (Nanjio's Catal., No. 1127), where four kinds of those worthy of salutation are enumerated: (1) Tathâgata, to be respected by all; (2) Pravragitas or homeless priests, to be saluted by laymen; (3) Bhikshus who received the Upasampadâ ordination earlier, to be saluted by those who received it later; (4) those who received the Upasampadâ, to be saluted by those who have not yet received it.

unseemly that the junior should expect the senior to stand when the salutation is about to take place. Nor is it right for the senior to be afraid of offending or displeasing the junior while receiving salutation; and from this motive some hastily take hold of the junior and do not allow him to bow; sometimes the junior strenuously seeks to be respected, but is unable to rise to a proper position. Yet they often say: 'If they act otherwise, they are not observing the ceremonies.' Alas! they make little of the noble teaching and give way to personal feeling, and do not conform to the rules of paying respect or receiving honour. One should indeed pay great attention to this point. Who ought to stop this long-prevailing error? (More literally: 'Long is the stream overflowing! Who ought to dam it up?')

CHAPTER XXV.

BEHAVIOUR BETWEEN TEACHER AND PUPIL.

THE instruction of pupils (Saddhivihârika) is an important matter for the prosperity (of religion). If this is neglected, the extinction of religion is sure to follow. We must perform our duties very diligently, and should not (allow ourselves too great license) like a net that allows water to run through it.

It is said in the Vinaya[1]: 'Every morning early *a pupil*, having chewed tooth-wood, should come to his teacher and offer him tooth-wood and put a washing-basin and a towel at the side of his seat. Having thus served him, the pupil should go and worship the holy image and walk round the temple. Then returning to his teacher, he makes a salutation, holding up his cloak, and with clasped hands, touching (the ground with his head) three times, remains kneeling on the ground. Then with bowed head and clasped hands, he inquires of the teacher, saying: "Let my Upâdhyâya be attentive," or: "Let my Â*k*ârya be attentive;" I now make inquiries whether my Upâdhyâya has been well through the night, whether his body (lit. four great elements) has been in perfect health, whether he is active and at ease, whether he digests his food well,

[1] Cf. the Mûlasarvâstivâdanikâya-sa*m*yuktavastu, book xxxv (Nanjio's Catal., No. 1121), and also Mahâvagga I, 25, 6 seq.

whether he is ready for his morning meal.' Inquiries may be short or full according to circumstances. Then the teacher answers these inquiries concerning his own health. Next, the pupil goes to salute his seniors who are in neighbouring apartments. Afterwards he reads a portion of the scripture, and reflects on what he has learnt. He acquires new knowledge day by day, and searches into old subjects month after month, without losing a minute.

Waiting till the time for the simpler meal[1] the pupil should ask to be allowed to partake of a meal, according to his own appetite. What use is there in hurrying to take rice-water before dawn—so hastily that he does not tell even his teacher, nor chew a tooth-wood, nor has he time to inspect water as to insects. He will not even be able to wash and cleanse himself. Is such a man not aware that he transgresses the four points[2] of the Buddha's teaching? All errors proceed from these. I pray that those who are responsible for the preservation of the Law[3] may regulate these points properly.

(Notes by I-tsing): Note 1. Upâdhyâya... Upa='near.' When we pronounce pâ (long), another a is contained in it, and Adhyâya means 'teaching to read.' This term was wrongly transcribed by 'Ho-shang' (和 尙, O-shō and Wa-djō in Japanese). A general name for 'learned men' in the West (India) is Wu-shê[4], but this is not a Buddhistic (or

---

[1] According to the commentator Kâsyapa, the first smaller meal-time is just after sunrise. The simpler meal is breakfast.

[2] The four points of the Buddha's teaching transgressed are (1) eating before sunrise, (2) not telling the teacher of one's going to have a meal, (3) not chewing a tooth-wood, and (4) not inspecting water as to insects (Kâsyapa).

[3] The text has 住 持 之 家; the first two characters are generally translated by 'resident priest.' It is true the term became later an appellation for a 'resident priest,' but by translating so, we do not do justice to the original idea of the term. Originally it was intended for 住 持 三 寶 'preserver or maintainer of the Three Jewels.' At any rate I-tsing uses it here in this sense.

[4] Here four names of the same or different origin are brought together:—

1. Upâdhyâya, a regular name for teacher, used throughout I-tsing's translations and works.

regular) word. In all Sanskrit Sûtras and Vinaya texts the term Upâdhyâya is used, which is translated by 'teacher of personal instruction.' In the northern countries the teacher is generally called Ho-shê; this caused the translators to adopt the erroneous transcription.

Note 2. Â*k*ârya[1] is translated 'teacher of discipline;' it means 'one who teaches pupils rules and ceremonies.' This term was wrongly transcribed 'Â-shao-li' (Â-jari, in Japanese) by the old translators.

Note 3. To tell a teacher of one's own doings, &c., mentioned above, is the custom which is taught in the Ârya-de*s*a; ârya meaning 'noble,' de*s*a 'region,' the Noble Region, a name for the West. It is so called because men of noble character appear there successively, and people all praise the land by that name. It is also called Madhya-de*s*a, i.e. Middle Land, for it is the centre of a hundred myriads of countries. The people are all familiar with this name. The northern tribes (Hu= Mongols or Turks) alone call the Noble Land 'Hindu,' but this is not at all a common name. It is only a vernacular name, and has no special significance. The people of India do not often know this designation, and the most suitable name for India is the 'Noble Land.'

Some say that Indu means the moon, and the Chinese name for India, i.e. Indu, is derived from it; although it may mean this, it is, nevertheless, not the common name. As to the Indian name for the Great Chou (China), i.e. *K*îna, it is only a name and has no special meaning.

Further we ought to note that the whole country comprising the five parts of India is called the 'kingdom of the Brâhmans' (Brahmarâsh*t*ra).

---

2. Ho-shê (和社), used in the North Countries. This may safely be identified with the Kashgarian vernacular of Sanskrit Upâdhyâya, i.e. Hua-hsieh (鶻社).

3. Ho-shang; O-shō or Wa-djō (和尙), a long-used term in China, and said to be derived from the above Kashgarian pronunciation.

4. Wu-shê (烏社), a general name for 'the learned' in India, but not a regular word. This may be also a corruption of Upâdhyâya, and may be the same as the above Kashgarian term.

[1] For the relation of Â*k*ârya to Upâdhyâya, see Mahâvagga I, 32, 1, note, S. B. E., vol. xiii, pp. 178, 179.

Sûli on the north is all called the Mongolian Frontier (or Border). One should not confuse them nor call all of them by one name.

When one has shaved the head, worn a Pa*t*a (simple garment), and received the Upasa*m*padâ ordination after having become 'homeless,' one need not tell one's teachers the five things as is ordained in the Vinaya[1], but must tell everything else; if not, one will be faulty. The five things to be confessed are: (1) the chewing of tooth-wood; (2) drinking water; (3) going to stool; (4) making water; (5) *K*aitya-vandana, or worshipping of a *K*aitya within forty-nine fathoms in the *sacred* boundary. When, for example, the novice is about to eat, he should go near his teacher, and having saluted according to the rule, announce to him as follows: 'Let my Upâdhyâya be attentive; I now announce to you that I wash my hands and utensils, and wish to have a meal.' The teacher should say, 'Be careful.' All other announcements should be made according to this example. The teacher will then tell his pupil what to do, concerning the matter and time of announcement. When there are many things to announce the pupil can do so all at once. After the lapse of five summers from the time that the pupil masters the Vinaya, he is allowed to live apart from his Upâdhyâya. He can then go about among the people and proceed to pursue some other aim. Yet he must put himself under the care *of some teacher* wherever he goes. This will cease after the lapse of ten summers, i.e. *after he is able to understand the Vinaya.* The kind object of the Great Sage is to bring one up to this position. If a priest does not understand the Vinaya, he will have to be under another's care during the whole of his lifetime. If there be no great teacher, he must live under the care of a sub-teacher. In this case the pupil should do all but salutation, for he cannot salute his teacher in the morning, or ask his health, since he must always act in accordance with the Vinaya, with which he is unacquainted; and even if it be necessary to announce any matter, how can he do so *when he himself does not understand the way.* Sometimes he receives from the sub-teacher instruction in the morning and in the evening. Even though the sub-teacher instruct such a pupil, the meaning of the Vinaya text may not be understood as it ought to

[1] In the Mûlasarvâstivâdanikâya-vinaya-sangraha, book xiii.

be. For if he who confesses (i.e. the pupil) cannot rightly indicate his point, how can he who answers (i.e. the teacher) give a proper command. A full confession is, therefore, not to be made. But negligence has long become a habit; pursuing an easy course people do not trouble *to conform to the Law.*

If we practise in accordance with the teaching *of the Buddha*, then the succession of the Law will never be interrupted. If his rules be slighted, what else can there be that is weighty? Thus, it is said in the Vinaya text: 'Rather be a butcher than be a priest who gives others full ordination and leaves them untaught[1].'

The following is also the manner in which a pupil waits on his teacher in India. He goes to his teacher at the first watch and at the last watch in the night. First the teacher bids him sit down comfortably. (Selecting some passages) from the Tripi*t*akas, he gives a lesson in a way that suits circumstances, and does not pass any fact or theory unexplained. He inspects his pupil's moral conduct, and warns him of defects and transgressions. Whenever he finds his pupil faulty, he makes him seek remedies and repent. The pupil rubs the teacher's body, folds his clothes, or sometimes sweeps the apartment and the yard. Then having examined water to see whether insects be in it, he gives it to the teacher[2]. Thus if there be anything to be done, he does all on behalf of his teacher. This is the manner in which one pays respect to one's superior. On the other hand, in case of a pupil's illness, his teacher himself nurses him, supplies all the medicine needed, and pays attention to him as if he were his child.

In the fundamental principles of the Law of the Buddha, teaching and

---

[1] In the Mûlasarvâstivâdanikâya-vinaya-saṅgraha, book xiii, 11 (Nanjio's Catal., No. 1127). The idea is elsewhere expressed, as quoted by Jiun Kâ*s*yapa, as follows: 'Butchers such as a *Ka*n*d*âla will kill many lives but do not destroy the Good Law of the Tathâgata, and therefore may not fall into the three lower existences, i.e. Hell, Brute Creation, and Departed Spirits; but he who initiates others and becomes a teacher, and cannot teach properly, causes destruction to the Good Law, and therefore will certainly fall into Hell.'

This passage is found in the Bhadra*s*îla-sûtra, book iv (Nanjio's Catal., No. 1085).

[2] Cf. Mahâvagga I, 25, 10, 11, 14, and 15.

instruction are regarded as the first and foremost, just as king *K*akravartin very carefully protects and brings up his eldest son; *so carefully is a pupil instructed in the Law.* There is a distinct injunction *of the Buddha's* in the Vinaya; ought we to cast a slight upon this point?

As to *K*aityavandana ('worshipping a *K*aitya') above referred to, when the Great Teacher, the World-honoured, entered into Nirvâ*n*a, and men and gods assembled together, to burn his remains in the fire, people brought there all kinds of perfumes until they made a great pile, which was called *K*iti, meaning 'piling[1].' Derived from this we have afterwards the name of *K*aitya. But there are other explanations of this word: firstly, because it is thought that all the virtues of the World-honoured are deposited together (or collected, *K*it) here; secondly, because it is formed by piling up bricks or earth. The meaning of this word has been thus clearly handed down. Another name for it is Stûpa, the meaning being the same as *K*aitya[2]. A general name adopted by the old translators is T'a (Tō in Japanese)[3], and the special name is Chih-t'i Both are wrong, but both may be used, since people understand by the names what they are, without discussing the meaning of these words. There are two ways of explaining a name in the West (India). Firstly, as a name having a meaning; secondly, as a name having no meaning. The name having a meaning has a reason in the name, and is to be explained according to the meaning of the word. In this case the name and the thing itself are in conformity with each other.

Such names as Shan-ju (i.e. 'well-entered' *into the Mahâyâna*) had a meaning in the beginning, and were given on account of virtuous action, but when people become familiar with the name they do not think of its meaning, and simply call the man by the name Shan-ju because the world calls him so. In this way it has become a name

---

[1] Cf. Mahâparinibbâna VI, 35: Sabbagandhâna*m* *k*itaka*m* 'karitvâ Bhagavato sarîra*m* *k*itaka*m* âropesu*m*. Thus I-tsing's '*K*iti' seems to represent '*K*itakâ,' a funeral pile.

[2] For the difference and relation between *K*aitya and Stûpa, see Prof. Kern's Buddhismus, p. 173 seq., where they are minutely dealt with.

[3] T'a stands for T'a-p'o, 塔婆 (Japanese, Tō-ba). Cf. the Pâli, Thûpa.

having no meaning. Vandana means 'salutation.' When we are about to go out to worship a *K*aitya, and people have asked where we are going, we answer: 'We are going to such and such places to worship *K*aityas.' The meaning of salutation or worship is to respect one's superiors and to remain humble. When one is about to make a salutation or to announce something, one must first adjust the priestly cloak, and gather it up over the left shoulder, pressing the garment (with the right hand) to one's left side, so that it may fit tightly to the body. Now stretching down one's left hand, one should take hold of the left part of the under-garment, while the right hand must follow the grasped part of the skirt and fold (or double) the garment with the lowest part of the skirt so that it well covers the knees; in so doing one should not allow any part of one's body to be seen. Let the back part of the skirt quickly touch the body. Holding up the upper and under-garments one should not allow them to touch the ground. Both heels must be placed together, the neck and back on a level; with the ten fingers flat on the ground one should now *bow* his head. There should be no covering lower down than the knees. Then one should stretch forth one's folded hands and again touch the ground with one's head. Thus should one carefully salute three times. But in an ordinary salutation only once will suffice. There is no such custom as standing up in the middle. Indians think it very strange when they see one *standing up and* making salutation three times. If one fear that there be any dust on the forehead (after the salutation), one should first rub it and again wipe it over. Next, dust on the shins should be wiped off; and with the garments adjusted one should sit down in a corner *of the room*, or stand awhile. *In the latter case*, the honoured one will offer a seat. When one is being censured for some fault, one may stand *all the time* without fail. Such is the traditional custom handed down uninterruptedly from teacher to pupil ever since our Buddha was on earth. It is also found in Sûtras and the Vinaya; it is often said that one approaches the Buddha, touches both his feet, and sits down in a corner *of the room*. But never have we heard of a sitting-mat being used. Having done homage three times, one stands in a corner—such is the Buddha's teaching. There are many seats in the rooms of the honoured elders, and those who come in should sit down according to the proper manner. On sitting down, one's feet touch the ground; but there is no such custom as to sit down at ease[1]. It is *often* said in the Vinaya that one should first make 'Wu-ch'ü-chu-chia'[2]; this is translated by 'squatting,' i.e. having both feet placed on the ground and both knees upright, and the garments tight round the body without letting them down to the ground, and that is an ordinary rule for protecting the garments while speaking of sacred subjects (religious). The same is observed by one who confesses sins before an individual, or by one who does homage to a great assembly, or asks to be forgiven when censured, or salutes the Brotherhood after full ordination.

There is another posture to be adopted while looking on and praising a temple (Gandhakuṭi), i.e. bowing and worshipping with one's folded hands, with both knees resting on the ground. But there is no such custom in any country (but China) as saluting or worshipping while sitting on a couch. Nor do we find such a custom as using a woollen mat (*while worshipping*). Is it reasonable to assume such a *haughty attitude* as the above while wishing to pay respect to others? If one be on a couch or on a mat, one is not paying due respect even in an ordinary social gathering. How much less is this form seemly when worshipping an honoured teacher, or the Great Master! The Indian lecture-halls and dining-rooms are

---

[1] The text has 帖膝, but according to Kâsyapa it ought to be 怗膝 'to rest one's knees (*on the ground*).'

[2] The Chinese 嗢屈竹迦, 'Wu-ch'ü-chu-chia;' Japanese, U-kut-chik-ka. The word in Pâli is Ukkuṭikam-nisîdati; the corresponding word in Sanskrit is given by Childers as Utkaṭuka. The Sanskrit Utkaṭukâsana is translated by 結跏趺坐, 'sitting cross-legged on the hams;' and this posture is quite different from what I-tsing is here mentioning. I-tsing clearly means 'squatting,' but not 'sitting on the hams cross-legged.' His description of this posture quite agrees with that given by Professors Rhys Davids and Oldenberg (*K*ullavagga IV, 4, 10, note): 'This verb does not mean "to sit on the hams" as rendered by Childers. The exact posture, unknown to Europe, is to crouch down on the feet (keeping both toes and heels on the ground) in such a way that the hams do not touch the ground, but come within an inch or two of it. It is regarded in the Piṭakas as a posture of humility.' Another posture of humility is kneeling with the right knee, see Sukhâvatî (L.) § 4 (Dakshiṇagânumaṇḍalam pṛthivyâm pratishṭhâpayati).

never furnished with large couches, but there are only blocks of wood and small chairs, on which people sit while hearing a lecture or having meals. Such is the proper manner.

It has long been customary in China to sit square-kneed. Though one may sit according to the custom of the time being, yet one should distinguish between what is proper and improper.

CHAPTER XXVI.

CONDUCT TOWARDS STRANGERS OR FRIENDS.

In the days when the Great Teacher lived, he himself, being the lord of religion, used to pronounce a welcome whenever a strange Bhikshu arrived. Though the Indian monks have established several rites (for the reception of their friends), yet it is a general rule that whenever any one perceives a person coming (to the monastery), whether he be a stranger or a friend, a disciple or pupil, or an acquaintance, he instantly proceeds to receive him, and pronounce 'Svâgata,' which is translated by 'welcome[1]!' But if he finds the visitor to be a stranger, he proceeds to pronounce another, 'Sushvâgata,' which is translated by 'most welcome[1]!' If one does not pronounce these, then one has deviated from the monastic rite on the one hand, and is guilty according to the Vinaya on the other. This is invariably done without questioning whether the new-comer be a superior or an inferior (to the host). And it is always the case that, *when a person has arrived*, the host takes off the visitor's water-jar and bowl, and hangs them up on pegs on the wall, and bids the new-comer rest, seated comfortably in a private place, if he be a novice; in the front apartment, if he be a venerable guest. If the host be junior to the visitor, he, in honour of his superior, holds the calves of the visitor's legs, then strokes all parts of his body; and if the host be the senior, he strokes his back, but not so far down as his waist and his feet, in order to soothe him. But if they be both equal in age, then no difference is made.

---

[1] Or this may mean, 'the guest then says "Sushvâgata" (in reply) as soon as the "Svâgata" is pronounced,' in this case Sushvâgata would mean 'well-welcomed.'

When (the new-comer) has recovered from his fatigue, having washed his hands and feet, he approaches the place where his superior is, and pays respect to him by prostrating himself once; and, while kneeling, holds his superior's feet. His superior, stretching out his right hand, strokes his inferior's shoulder and back,—but if it is not long since they have separated, he does not stroke him with his hand. Now the teacher inquires after his health, and the pupil answers how he is. Then the latter withdraws on one side, and with due respect sits down. They do not stand as the Chinese do. The general rule in India is to sit on a small block of wood, and all have the feet bare. There is no such custom in the Eastern Hsia (i. e. China), and therefore the ceremony of holding another's feet is not carried out.

It is *often* said in the Sûtras that men and gods came to the Buddha, bowed their heads down to both feet of the Buddha, then withdrew and sat on one side; and this is such a form as I am now describing. Then the host, considering the season of the year, must offer either hot water or some other drink.

Ghee, honey, sugar, or any other eatables and drink, can be offered according to one's desire. Or if it be one of the eight kinds of syrup [1] *allowed by the Buddha*, it must be strained and made clear before one offers it. If it be thick with dregs, it is never allowed *by the Buddha*.

The juice of the stewed apricot is, by nature, thick, and we can reasonably consider it as excluded from *the legal* drinks. It is said in the Vinaya: 'Syrup must be purely strained until its colour becomes like the yellow leaf of the reed.'

Such are the ceremonies of receiving visitors, whether teachers, pupils, disciples, strangers, or friends. It is not right for one to perform Ho-nan (see below) in haste as soon as one reaches *the house of a man*,

---

[1] For the eight kinds of syrup, see Mahâvagga VI, 35, 6, and also the Vinaya-saṅgraha, book viii (Nanjio's Catal., No. 1127), and the Eka*s*atakarman, book v, p. 57 (Nanjio's Catal., No. 1131).

The eight Pânas are, according to I-tsing: mo*k*a, *k*o*k*a, kolaka, a*s*vattha, utpala (or Udumbara), parûsaka, m*ri*dhvikâ, and khar*g*ûra; in Mahâvagga VI, 35, 6: amba, *g*ambu, *k*o*k*a, mo*k*a, madhu, muddikâ, sâluka, and phârusaka. See my additional note at the end.

without regard to one's own garments and cap, either braving cold weather or enduring heat, consequently with the hands and feet benumbed or with sweat all over the body. Such a system of haste is very much against rule.

The teacher is *wrong* if he lets the pupil stand *instead of sitting on one side* while idly talking about anything but religion. Does such a man, indeed, consider the promotion *of the Law* to be of pressing need?

Ho-nan is in Sanskrit Panti (Vande, 'I salute') or Vandana, translated by 'salutation.' As people failed to transcribe the real sound, they called it Ho-nan (Wa-nan or Wa-dan in Japanese), and as one cannot change the accustomed sound, Ho-nan is still used. But if we take the original sound, it ought to be Pan-ti (Vande).

On the road, or in a crowd, such salutation as above mentioned is not proper. But one ought just to stretch forth the folded hands and say with the mouth 'Pan-ti' ('Vande') while bowing down the head. Therefore it is said in a Sûtra: 'Or one only stretches one's folded hands,.... and bows down one's head a little.' Such is *also* the way of doing honour. A man from the South[1] questions one *whom he meets*[2]; he is thus unconsciously conforming to the proper method. Had he only changed the questioning into the word 'Vande' ('I salute'), his action would have been entirely the same as that ordained in the Vinaya.

CHAPTER XXVII.

ON SYMPTOMS OF BODILY ILLNESS.

As I said before (in chap. xxv), one should take a small meal according to one's appetite (or 'considering whether one's own body is light or heavy'), that is to say, according to the condition of the four great elements[3], *of which one's body consists.* If one's appetite

---

[1] Men of the South are, according to the commentator Jiun Kâsyapa, the Vinaya teachers of Kiang-nan (south of the Yang-tsze-kiang), who adhere to the Vinaya of the Ten Readings.

[2] This would probably be an inquiry after one's health.

[3] I.e. earth, water, fire, and air (Mahâbhûta).

be good, an ordinary meal should be taken. If one be indisposed, one should investigate the cause; and when the cause of ill-health has been discovered, one should take rest. When health is recovered one will feel hungry, and should take food first at the next light meal. Day-break is generally called 'the time of phlegm,' when the juice of the night food is still hanging about the chest, being as yet undispersed. Any food taken at this time disagrees.

If, for example, one add fuel when the fire is already flaming, the added fuel will be consumed, but if one put grass over a fire which is not as yet blazing, the grass will remain as it is, and the fire will not even burn.

Lighter meals are allowed by the Buddha in addition to the ordinary meal; be it rice-water or rice itself, food is to be taken according to one's appetite.

If one could subsist on rice-water only, while carrying out the Law, then nothing else should be eaten; but if one want rice-cakes, which will nourish the body, one can have them without fault. Not only is it called a disease when one has a headache and lies in bed, but also the cause of a disease is brought about when eating causes discomfort to one. When sickness has not been cured by medicine, one may eat food at any unprescribed hour if this be the physician's order. 'In such case,' the Buddha said, 'the food is to be given in a private place.' Otherwise food is forbidden at an improper time. The medical science, one of the five sciences (vidyâ) in India, shows that a physician, having inspected the voice and countenance of the diseased, prescribes for the latter according to the eight sections of medical science (see below).

If he does not understand the secret of this *science*, he will, though desirous of acting properly, fall into mistakes. The following are the eight sections of medical science[1]. The first treats of all kinds of sores; the second, of acupuncture for any disease above the neck; the third, of the diseases of the body; the fourth, of demoniac disease; the fifth, of the Agada medicine (i.e. antidote); the sixth, of the diseases of children; the seventh, of the means of lengthening one's life; the eighth, of the

[1] These perfectly agree with the eight divisions of the Âyur-veda, see my additional note at the end.

methods of invigorating the legs and body. 'Sores' (1) are of two kinds, inward and outward. The disease above the neck (2) is all that is on the head *and face;* any disease lower down from the throat is called a 'bodily' disease (3). The 'Demoniac' (4) is the attack of evil spirits, and the 'Agada' (5, but 6 of Âyur-veda) is the medicine for counteracting poisons. By 'Children' (6, but 5 of Âyur-veda) is meant from the embryo stage until after a boy's sixteenth year; 'lengthening life' (7) is to maintain the body so as to live long, while 'invigorating the legs *and body*' (8) means to keep the body and limbs strong and healthy. These eight arts formerly existed in eight books, but lately a man epitomized them and made them into one bundle. All physicians in the five parts of India practise according *to this book,* and any physician who is well versed in it never fails to live by the official pay. Therefore Indians greatly honour physicians and much esteem merchants, for they do not injure life, and they give relief to others as well as benefit themselves. I made a successful study in medical science, but as it is not my proper vocation I have finally given it up.

Further we must notice that the medical herbs in India are not the same as those of China (Eastern Hsia); those which exist in one country are not found in the other, and the materials used cannot be treated in the same way. For instance, the ginseng (Aralia quinquefolia), the Chinese fungus (Pachyma Cocos), the Tang-kuei (Aralia cordata), the Yüan-chih (Polygala sibirica), the tubers of aconite (Aconitum Fischeri), the Fu-tsze (Aconitum variegatum), the Ma-huang (Corchorus capsularis), the Hsi-hsin (Asarum Sieboldii), and such like are the best herbs in the Divine Land (i.e. China), and are never found in the West (i.e. India). Harîtaka (yellow myrobalan) is abundant in India; in North (India) there is sometimes the Yü-chin-hsiang[1] (Kuṅkuma), and the A-wei[2] (assafoetida)

---

[1] 鬱金香, 'Yü-chin-hsiang' (Jap. Golden Turmeric, species of Curcuma), is not yet identified (Giles) from a Chinese source. Kâsyapa, quoting a book on medicine, says that this plant grows in Syria (Ta-ch'in), and blossoms between the second and third months, shaped like safflower, and that the flowers are picked between the fourth and fifth months. This is Sanskrit Kuṅkuma, 'saffron.'

[2] A-wei grows in Persia, eight or nine feet high, the bark is blue-yellow.

is abundant in the western limit of India. The Baroos camphor is found a little in the islands of the Southern Sea, and all the three kinds[1] of cardamoms are found in Dvâra(-vatî)[2]; two kinds[3] of cloves grow in Pulo Condore. Only the herbs above mentioned are used in India in the same way (as in China); all other herbs are not worth gathering.

Generally speaking, a disease which has befallen the body arises from too much eating, but it is sometimes brought about by much labour, or by eating again before the former food has been digested[4]; when illness is thus caused it results in the cholera morbus, in consequence of which one will suffer from a sense of sickness for several consecutive nights, and the swollen belly will continue more than ten days. In such case, those who are rich can buy the costly pill prepared from kidneys, or the valuable glue that comes from Ta-ch'in (Syria), but those who are poor *can do nothing*, and pass away with the morning dews. What can one do when an illness has got the upper hand? Every effort will be in vain, even if the physician of Lu come in the morning and prescribe pills and powder, or if Pien Chi'ao visit in the evening and offer a medical decoction or plaster. Cauterised with fire or with a puncture applied, *one's body* is treated just as wood or stone; except by the shaking of the legs and moving of the head, the sick differs not from a corpse.

Such *results* are indeed due to one's ignorance of the cause of disease, and the want of understanding how to remedy (lit. to moderate and protect). It may be said that people hope for recovery without ground, just like some who, wishing to stop a stream, do not dam it at its

---

The leaf comes out in the third month, and is like the rat-ear. It has no flower or fruit (Kâsyapa).

[1] The three kinds are, according to the commentator, (1) the 'grass' cardamoms, which are abundant in the Ling-nan (i.e. south of the Plum Range=Kwang-tung and Kwang-hsi), (2) the 'white' cardamoms, found in the country of Ka-ko-ra (?), also called the 'many bones,' and (3) the 'flesh' cardamoms growing in the Sû-li country (W. of Kashgar), and is called Ka-kû-lok, this is not found in China.

[2] See p. 10 above.

[3] Two kinds of cloves are Ting-tzŭ-hsiang and Mo-ting-hsiang (Kâsyapa).

[4] Lit. 'having the morning meal before the night meal is digested, and the midday meal before the morning food is passed.'

source; or like those who, being desirous to cut down a forest, do not fell the trees at their roots, but allow the current or the sprouts to increase more and more.

Those who have been learning the Sûtras and *S*âstras will ever grieve, simply gazing at the Tripi*t*aka, *being unable to pursue the study any further*, and those who have been practising the tranquillising of thoughts (i.e. Dhyâna) will long be sighing, thinking of the eight *regions* of meditation (i.e. the four dhyânas and four arûpadhâtus). Those who seek to advance to the 'Master of Classics' (Ming-ching) will have to cut off the bridles at the Gate of the Golden Horse [1], and those who are competing for the 'Advanced Scholar' (Chin-shih) will finally cease to move toward the Court of the Stone Gutter [2]. Is it not a sad thing that *sickness* prevents the pursuit of one's duty and vocation? It is not indeed a small matter for one to lose one's glory and favour, and I therefore describe the above, which the reader will not, I hope, object to as a lengthy repetition. I desire that an established disease may be cured without expending much medicine, and that a fresh disease may be prevented, thus not necessitating a physician;—then a healthy condition of body (lit. the four elements) and the absence of any disease may be expected. Is it not beneficial if people can benefit others as well as themselves *by the study of medicine?*

But the swallowing of a poison, or death and birth, is often due to one's former action (i.e. Karma); *still* it does not follow that a man should hesitate to avoid or further a circumstance *that leads to or averts a disease* in the present life.

CHAPTER XXVIII.

RULES ON GIVING MEDICINE.

EVERY living creature is subject either to the peaceful working or failure of the Four Great Elements (i.e. Mahâbhûta). The eight seasons

[1] Chinese, Chin-ma-men; it is the Imperial palace for scholars, the Han-lin. So called from a bronze horse placed there by Wu-ti, of the Han dynasty.

[2] Chinese, Shih-ch'ü-shu, the Imperial library and office of compilation; this is said to have been originally built by Hsiao-ho, minister of the founder of the Han dynasty, to keep the books spared in the Ch'in dynasty.

coming one after another, the development and change *of the bodily condition* are ceaseless. Whenever a disease has befallen one, rest and care must at once be taken.

Therefore the World-honoured (i.e. Lokagyesh*th*a = the Buddha) himself preached a Sûtra on the Art of Medicine[1], in which he said: 'Failure of health (lit. moderation) of the Four Great Elements is as follows:—

1. The Chü-lu, i.e. making the body slothful and heavy, owing to an increase of the element earth.
2. The Hsieh-po, i.e. having very much eye-mucus or mouth-water, owing to an accumulation of the element water.
3. The Pi-to, i.e. having head and chest very feverish, owing to the overpowering heat caused by the element fire.
4. The P'o-to, i.e. violent rush of breath, owing to the moving influence of the element air[2].'

---

[1] This Sûtra has not yet been translated into Chinese (Kâ*s*yapa).

[2]

(CHINESE.)	(JAPANESE.)	(SANSKRIT.)
1. Chü-lu	Go-ro	Gulma (or may be Guru, or Gaurava).
2. Hsieh-po	Shō-ha	*S*leshman (=Kapha). Cf. Pâli Semho.
3. Pi-to	Hit-ta	Pitta.
4. P'o-to	Ba-ta	Vâta.

Of these Chü-lu (1) only is difficult to be restored. Gulma is a 'diseased swelling of the abdomen' or 'chronic enlargement of the spleen' in medicine. Though this can well be represented by Chü-lu, the phonetical probability is rather in favour of Guru or its derivation. We must, however, wait for a confirmation from a Sanskrit or Pâli source.

As to the latter three (2, 3, 4) we have no difficulty in restoring them, for these represent what is called 'Tri-dosha,' a 'disturbance of the three humours of the body,' i.e. phlegm (Kapha or *S*leshman), bile (Pitta), and wind (Vâta). Buddhaghosa seems to mean these three (or four) 'doshas' by saying 'Semhâdi-dos'-ussanna-kâyâ' in his explanation of the words 'Abhisannakâyâ' (*K*ullavagga V, 14, 1); 'Semha' of course representing '*S*leshman.' By Vâta, 'wind,' is meant a 'disease caused by wind,' e.g. 'Udaravâtâbâdha,' i.e. a 'disease caused by wind in the stomach' (Mahâvagga VI, 14, 1). The above points are pretty well confirmed by Su*s*ruta Dhanvantari's pupil (who may be the man whom I-tsing mentions as the epitomiser of the eight divisions of the Âyur-veda, p. 128). In his work on Medicine, I, 1, Su*s*ruta says: *S*ârîrâs tv annapânamûlâ vâtapittakapha*so*n*i*tasannipâtavaishamya-

These are what we call in China, (1) the sinking heaviness, (2) the phlegmatic disease, (3) the yellow fever, (4) the rising breath or air (dizziness, asthma, or cold). But if we discuss sickness according to the common custom, there are only three kinds (instead of four), i.e. disease caused by the air (Vâta), fever (Pitta), and phlegmatic disease (Kapha), and the 'sinking heaviness' (1) is similar to the 'phlegmatic' in its condition, and accordingly the disease of the element earth is not distinguished from that of the element water. To find out the cause of illness one should examine oneself in the morning. If one feel any disturbance in the four elements on inspection, then the abstaining from eating is first to be observed. Even in great thirst one must not take any syrup or water, for this is the strictest prohibition in this *science*. This abstinence is to be continued, sometimes a day or two, sometimes four or five days, until the disease has been quite cured. There will be no failure *in recovery*. If one feel that there is food remaining in the stomach, one should press or stroke *the belly* at the navel, drink as much hot water as one can, and put the finger inside the throat to cause vomiting; drinking and ejecting, one should continue the same till the remnant of food is exhausted.

Or there is no harm if one drink cold water, and hot water mixed with dry ginger is also an excellent thing. During the day, at least, *on which the treatment is adopted*, the patient must abstain from eating, and food should be taken for the first time the following morning. If this be difficult, some other measure must be taken under the circumstances. In case of violent fever, the application of cooling by means of water is prohibited; in case of the 'sinking heaviness' (1) and 'shivering cold' the best remedy is to remain near the fire, but in hot and damp places lying south of the River (Yan-tsze) and the Range (Plum) the above rule is not to be applied, and when a fever arises in these regions,

---

nimittâ*h*, 'Bodily diseases have their origin in (irregularity of) food and drink, their apparent causes being the derangement of *the humours*, i.e. air, bile, phlegm, blood, or of all these combined.'

Here 'so*n*ita-sannipâta' may stand for I-tsing's 'Chü-lu' (1); both seem to refer to one and the same disease, though the names differ from one another. For annapânamûlâ*h*, compare p. 129, line 6, above.

cooling by water is efficacious. When suffering from a 'Fêng-chi[1],' the best remedy is to anoint the wounded and painful spot with oil, and to warm it with a heated bed-sheet. If one anoint the same with warm oil good also results. Sometimes we find that for some ten days phlegm fills the gullet, water coming incessantly out of the mouth and nose, and the accumulated breath, being enclosed in the air-pipe, causes acute pain to the throat; in such a case speaking is difficult, on account of want of voice, and all food is tasteless.

Fasting is an effective cure, without any trouble of cauterising the head or rubbing the throat. This is in accordance with the general rule of the science of medicine[2], i. e. healing a disease without using a decoction or any medicine.

The reason is that when the stomach is empty violent fever abates, when the juice of food is absorbed a phlegmatic disease is cured, and when the internal organs are at rest and bad breath dispersed, a severe cold will naturally be over. There will be no failure in a cure if this method be adhered to.

There is, indeed, no trouble in feeling the pulse; what use is it, then, to inquire one's fate of a diviner?

Each man is himself the king of physicians, and any one can be *G*îvaka[3]. T'an-lan[4], the Master of the Law, used to cure disease by moderating the temperature—a thing a hermit alone can do. Hui-ssŭ[5], the Dhyâna-master, destroyed an evil sickness (by meditation) while sitting in a room—a thing common knowledge can never attain to. If it be necessary to consult some famous physician in Lo-yang, the eastern capital, then the poor and needy are (on the ground of expense) cut off from the ford *of life;* and when it is a case of gathering the best herbs

---

[1] Fêng-chi, lit. 'wind-pressure,' is not very clear. The commentator supposes that it is lock-jaw. I think it represents 'Vâta-âbâdha,' rheumatism (Childers).

[2] In these chapters, the Vidyâ, not the Vinaya, is I-tsing's guide; he knew something of medicine, as he himself says, p. 128 above.

[3] A famous physician in the Buddha's time. See Mahâvagga VIII, 1, 4 seq.

[4] T'an-lan is a patriarch of the Sukhâvatî school. Died A.D. 542.

[5] Hui-ssŭ (E-shi) is the third patriarch of the Tien-thai sect. Died A.D. 577. See Nanjio's Catal., Appendix iii. 10, or 續高僧傳二十一.

from the western field, the parentless and helpless will lose their way. But the fasting we are now speaking of is simple and admirable, for it can be practised equally by poor and rich. Is it not important?

Food should be abstained from in all other diseases, such as a sudden appearance of a carbuncle or a smaller boil; a sudden rush of blood causing fever; a violent pain in the hands and feet; any injury to the body caused by heavenly phenomena (such as lightning), climate, or sword and arrow; a wound inflicted by falling down; an acute febrile disease or cholera morbus; the half-day diarrhoea, a headache, heart-disease, eye-disease, or toothache. A pill called 'San-têng' (lit. the equal mixture of the three) is also good for curing several sicknesses and not difficult to obtain. Take the bark of Harîtaka (or kî)[1], dry ginger, and sugar, and prepare the three in equal quantities; grind the former two and mix them with the sugar by means of some drops of water, and then prepare them in pills. About ten pills for one dose, every morning, is the limit, and no dieting is required. In case of diarrhoea, about two or three doses are sufficient for recovery. The benefit derived from this pill is very great, as it can relieve a patient from giddiness, cold, and indigestion; and that is why I mention it here. If there be no sugar, jelly or honey will suffice. If one bite a piece of Harîtaka every day and swallow its juice, one's whole life will be free from disease. These points which form the science of medicine were handed down from *S*akra Devendra, as one of the five sciences of India, which is followed throughout the five parts of that country. In it, the most important rule is fasting. The old translators taught that if *a disease* be not cured by abstaining from food for seven days, one should then seek help from Avalokite*s*vara. Most of the Chinese were not accustomed *to such a practice*, and considered it as a separate religious fast, thus never attempting to study or practise it *as a science*. This *error* is due to want of knowledge concerning the science of medicine on the part of the *old* translators. In case of *sickness brought about* by swallowing a 'red stone' (Tan-shih), a chronic illness or the swelling of the stomach, one may also adopt the above-mentioned method.

(Note by I-tsing): I fear that there may be some who swallow a 'red

---

[1] I.e. yellow myrobalan, Mahâvagga VI, 6, 1.

stone[1]' (Tan-shih); it is not a good thing to take, though it suppresses hunger. The Fei-tan (the 'flying red stone[2]') is never found in any country *but China.* The swallowing of a stone is practised only in the Divine Land (i.e. China), but a crystal or an adularia (lit. 'white stone') sometimes produces fire; if swallowed, one's body is 'burnt and cracked.' People of these days do not distinguish this, and those who die of this fault are innumerable. Thus one should be deeply aware *of its danger.*

Poisons such as that of snake-bites are not to be cured by the above-mentioned method. While abstaining from food, walking and working are to be strictly avoided.

He who is taking a long journey can walk without any harm through fasting; but when *the disease for which he is fasting* is cured, he must take a rest, and eat newly-boiled rice and drink a quantity of well-boiled lentil-water mixed with some spice. If one feel chilly the last-named water is to be drunk with some pepper, ginger, or the Piper longum (Pippalî)[3]. If one feel cold, Kashgarian onions (Palâ*nd*u) or wild mustard must be applied.

It is said in the *S*âstra on medical treatment[4]: 'Anything of acrid or hot flavour removes a cold, with the exception of dry ginger.' But if mixed with other things it is also good. One should moderate and rest the body during as many days as one has been abstaining from food. Drinking cold water is to be avoided; other dieting is to be carried out according to medical advice. If one drink rice-water it is to be feared that the phlegm will be increased. In case of being troubled by cold, eating will not hurt one; for a fever, the medical decoction is that prepared by well boiling a bitter ginseng (the root of Aralia quinquefolia).

Tea is also good. It is more than twenty years since I left my native country, and this alone *as well as the ginseng decoction* was the medicament to my body, and I had hardly any serious disease.

---

[1] 'Red stone' is identified with the 'Red sand' (Tan-sha), i.e. cinnabar or red sulphuret of mercury, by the commentator Kâ*s*yapa.

[2] The 'Flying Cinnabar,' if swallowed, enables a man to fly (Kâ*s*yapa).

[3] These three pungent substances make 'teka*t*ula gruel,' Mahâvagga VI, 17, 1. For Pippalî, see Mahâvagga VI, 6, 1, note 6.

[4] Not identified.

There are in China more than four hundred kinds of herbs, stones, stalks, and roots, most of which are excellent and rare in colour and taste, and very fragrant in their smell; thereby we can cure any disease and control the temper. In the healing arts of acupuncture and cautery and the skill of feeling the pulse China has never been superseded by any country of *Gam*budvîpa (India); the medicament for prolonging life is only found in China. Our hills are connected with the Himâlaya, and our mountains are a continuation of the Gandhamâdana [1]; all sorts of things strange and precious are found there in abundance. From the character of men and the quality of things, China is called the 'Divine Land.' Is there any one, in the five parts of India, who does not admire China? All within the four seas respectfully receive *the command*. They (Indians) say that Mañgusrî [2] is at present living in that country (China). When they hear that one is a priest of the Deva-putra, all pay great honour and respect, wherever one goes. Deva means 'heaven' and putra 'son;' the priest of the Deva-putra is more fully 'One who has come from the place where dwells the Son of Heaven of *K*îna (China) [3]. We

---

[1] This mountain range, Gandhamâdana, is generally translated by 'Fragrant mountain,' sometimes more fully, 'Hsiang-tsui,' i.e. 'Fragrant intoxicating mountain.' It is the region of the Anavatapta lake, from which the four rivers, *S*itâ, Gaṅgâ, Sindhu, and Vakshu (Oxus) derive their source. This lake is perhaps the Manasarowar lake (lat. 31° N., long. 81° 3), and Hiuen Thsang's identification with the lake Sirikol (lat. 38° 20 N.) on the plateau of Pamir may be altogether wrong (see Eitel's Handbook, s. v. Anavatapta). So we should take the Gandhamâdana as the high plateau north of the Himâlaya, on which the lake Anavatapta lies. I-tsing mentions this mountain again in chap. xxxiv, p. 169.

[2] The Indians seem to have had some impression of Mañgusrî's dwelling in China in I-tsing's time. We meet with this statement again in chap. xxxiv, p. 169.

[3] The reader is reminded that the Chinese Emperor is still called the 'Son of Heaven,' an old term used by Confucius or his direct disciples (B.C. 551-479). Deva-putra is a literal translation of 'Son of Heaven' (Tien-tze).

The name, *K*îna, which I-tsing is using, is taken from Sanskrit, and probably is the same as *K*îna of Indian literature. But how long this name had been used in India or from which name of China it had been taken is uncertain. It was once supposed to have been taken from the Ch'in dynasty (B.C. 222), forming a landmark in Indian chronology, but this supposition was given up

see that the herbs and stones are indeed excellent and of rare quality, but the tending and protection of the body, and the inspection of the causes of disease are very much neglected. Therefore I have here described the general methods *of medical treatment* in order to meet the wants of the time. When fasting does not hurt at all, one should begin medical treatment according to the proper method. The medical decoction prepared from the bitter ginseng specially serves to remove a fever. Ghee, oil, honey, or syrups relieve one from cold. In the country of Lâ*t*a[1] in W. India, those who are taken ill abstain from food, sometimes half a month, sometimes a full month. They never eat until the illness *from which they are suffering* is entirely cured. In Central India the longest period of fasting is a week, whereas in the islands of the Southern Sea two or three days is the limit. This is due to the differences of territory, custom, and the constitution of the body.

I do not know whether or no fasting for curing a disease should be practised in China. But if abstaining from food for a week prove to be fatal, it is because disease does not remain in the body, for while a disease is in the body, fasting even for more days does not cause death. I witnessed some time ago a man who abstained from food for thirty days and recovered again. Why then should we doubt the efficacy of long fasting?

Nor is it good to force a sick person when attacked by a violent fever to drink hot rice-water or to take food, simply noticing that he is ill but not inspecting the cause of his illness. Nay, it is a dangerous thing!

There may be a case of recovery by such treatment, yet it is not after all worth teaching people to follow. Such is strictly prohibited in the science of medicine. Further, in China, people of the present time eat fish and vegetables mostly uncooked; no Indians do this. All vegetables are to be well cooked and to be eaten after mixing with the assafoetida, clarified butter, oil, or any spice.

People (in India) do not eat any kind of onions. I was tempted and ate them sometimes, but they cause pain while taking a religious fast

---

by several scholars. Nothing is certain but that *K*îna was used as denoting the Chinese in Hiuen Thsang's and I-tsing's time.

[1] In the B*ri*hat-sa*m*hitâ LXIX, 11, Mâlava, Bharoach, Surat (Surâsh*t*ra), Lâ*t*a, and Sindhu are mentioned in one group; compare p. 9, note 1, above.

and injure the *belly*, besides spoiling the eyesight and increasing disease, and causing the body to become more and more weak. This is why Indians do not eat them. Let the wise be attentive to my statement, and practise what is useful while giving up what is objectionable; for if one do not act according to what a physician has prescribed there is no fault on the part of the latter.

If practised accordingly, *the method above mentioned* will bring ease to the body, and perfection to religious work, thus completing benefits both to others and to oneself. If the method be rejected, *the result* will be a feeble body and narrow knowledge, and the success of others as well as of oneself will be altogether destroyed.

CHAPTER XXIX.

HURTFUL MEDICAL TREATMENT MUST NOT BE PRACTISED.

THERE are some places where a low custom has long been prevalent, i. e. whenever a sickness arises people use the urine and feces as medicaments, sometimes the dung of pigs or cats, which is put on a plate or kept in a jar. People call it the 'Dragon Decoction,' which, though beautifully named, is the worst of impure filth. Even in eating onions which are allowed (by the Buddha), one keeps oneself in a separate room of one's own accord, and purifies oneself by washing and bathing for seven days before one comes among the Brotherhood. While one's body is as yet impure one never enters an assembly, one is not fit to walk round a Stûpa (tope), and must not salute or worship.

As *onions* have a foul smell and are impure they are not permitted to be eaten except in case of illness[1]. The healing by a 'putrid rejected substance'—one of the four Refuges[2] of a Bhikshu—consists in the using of a putrid and old thing which has been thrown away; the object being to economise things to such an extent that only enough is left for

---

[1] So *K*ullavagga V, 34, 1 and 2 (S. B. E., vol. xx, p. 154).

[2] The four Refuges by which a Bhikshu has to live are explained in the *K*atur-varga-vinaya, chap. xxxv (Nanjio's Catal., No. 1117); these are the four Nissâyas* of Mahâvagga I, 30, 4, (1) Pi*nd*iyâlopabhogana*m*; (2) Pa*m*sukûla*k*ivara*m*; (3) Rukkhamûlasenâsana*m*; (4) Pûtimuttabhesa*gg*a*m*. Cf. p. 56, note 1, above, and see below.

bare subsistence. A valuable *medicine* is, of course, open to any, and it is never wrong to take it.

Sanskrit words for 'putrid-rejected-medicine' are Pûti-mukta (or -mukti)-bhaisha*g*ya [1] which are to be translated by the words 'putrid or old-rejected-medicine.'

Feces and urine are permitted to be used as medicine in the Vinaya, but these are the dung of a calf and urine of a cow [2]. In India, those who have been condemned as lowest criminals have their body besmeared with dung and are forcibly driven out to a wilderness, being excluded from the society of men. Those who carry off feces and clear away filth have to distinguish themselves by striking sticks [3] while going about; when one has by mistake touched any of them, one thoroughly washes oneself and one's garments.

Our Great Master was in the habit of avoiding, first of all, people's murmurs and slander while managing affairs according to circumstances. Would He then allow the use of such foul things as filth assuredly in opposition to the wish of the people of His time? The reasons why He would not do so are fully explained in the Vinaya. It is, indeed,

---

[1] There is much controversy about the meaning of these words among the Chinese interpreters. Some would have Pûti-mûtra-bhaisha*g*ya, i.e. 'having urine as medicine;' this is no doubt correct. I-tsing and others, on the other hand, would have Pûti-mukta-bhaisha*g*ya, and hold that it means the old medicine which was once used and thrown away, and that it is not the same as urine or feces. I fancy that as the original Pâli words, 'Pûti-mutta-bhesa*gg*a' (Mahâvagga I, 30, 4), may stand for either 'Pûti-mûtra-bhaisha*g*ya' or 'Pûti-mukta-bhaisha*g*ya,' thus a difference of opinion may have arisen. Pûti-mutta*m* means 'decomposing urine' (of a cow, Mahâvagga VI, 14, 7), which is also mentioned below. Cf. the translation of Mahâvagga I, 30, 4, 'The religious life has decomposing urine as medicine for its resource.' The Vinaya text, part i, S.B.E., vol. xiii.

[2] So Buddhaghosa in Mahâvagga VI, 14, 7: Mutta-harîtakan ti gomutta paribhâvita*m* harîtaka*m*.

[3] This statement is confirmed by Fâ-hien. He says in chap. xvi of his narrative: '*Kand*âla is the name for those who are held to be wicked men, and live apart from others. When they enter the gate of a city or a market-place, they strike a piece of wood to make themselves known, so that men know and avoid them, and do not come into contact with them.' Legge's Travels of Fâ-hien, p. 43.

mean to give others *as medicine* such *a foul substance as urine or feces.* One should not let people follow such a practice and make it a constant custom. If this be heard of by foreigners, the transforming influence of our country will be lessened. And again, why shall we not use all those fragrant herbs that exist in abundance? *Foul substances* are what we dislike, how can we bear to give them away? And as an antidote for snake-bites we have the 'stones' of sulphur, flowers of sulphur, and gamboge, and it is not very difficult to keep a piece by one. When infected by fever or malaria we have the decoctions of liquorice root, *hêng-shan*[1], and bitter ginseng, which are not very difficult to keep prepared. Cold can always be removed by taking some ginger, pepper, and the fruit of Piper longum. Solid and dry sugar can satiate hunger and thirst when eaten. If there be nothing laid by to meet the cost of medicine, want of money is certain at the time of need. Are we free from fault if we disregard the teaching and do not practise it as we ought? People use money lavishly and neglect to provide for imminent need; if I did not notify them, who would understand the points clearly? Alas! People would not take good medicine, and, seeking the least expense, would use the 'Dragon Decoction.' Though their motive may be to get some benefits from such medicine, yet they are not aware of their grave offence to the noble teaching. Some followers of the Ârya-sammiti school speak of the Pûti-mukta-bhaisha*g*ya (as being the foul substance), but of course it is a different school from ours, and we have nothing to do with it. Though the Vinaya-dvâvi*m*s*ati-prasannârtha-*s*âstra (Nanjio's Catal., No. 1139) has also a certain reference *to such medicine*, this book is not what is studied in the Âryasarvâstivâda school.

CHAPTER XXX.

ON TURNING TO THE RIGHT IN WORSHIP.

'WALKING round towards the right' is in Sanskrit Pradakshi*n*a. The prefix Pra has many meanings; and now, as forming a part of this word, it expresses 'proceeding round.' Dakshi*n*a means 'right,' and signifies generally any matter respectable and convenient. They (Indians)

[1] Lit. 'constant mountain;' it is a kind of wild tea, according to Kâ*s*yapa.

call, consequently, the right hand Dakshi*n*a, implying that to follow the right is respectable and convenient. It is therefore suitable to the ceremony of walking round. Dakshi*n*â (as a feminine noun) also means 'gift,' in which case it differs (in signification) from what is mentioned above, as I explained before (see chap. ix, p. 48). Throughout the five divisions of India, they all call the east 'front' and the south 'right,' though one cannot say the right and left in the same manner (i.e. one cannot say left for north).

We should read in the Sûtras the phrase: 'walking round towards the right three times[1],' but it is wrong, if one translates it simply by 'walking round the Buddha's side.' This phrase in the Sûtras: 'three times walking round towards the right,' is a full description of the walking; and there is another curtailed one: 'a hundred thousand times walking round,' without saying 'towards the right.'

What is walking towards the right or towards the left, however, would seem a little difficult to determine. Is it the walking round towards the right, if a man proceeds towards his own right-hand side? Or is it to step out towards his left-hand side? Once I heard an explanation of a learned man in China, that the 'walking round towards the right' means to have one's right hand inside the circle (he makes)[2], and that the 'walking round towards the left' means to have one's left

---

[1] E.g. Mahâparinibbâna, chap. vi, 46: padakkhi*n*a*m* katvâ.

[2] This is no doubt a right explanation according to the Indian custom, but I-tsing speaks against it.

Kâ*s*yapa gives an illustration as follows:—

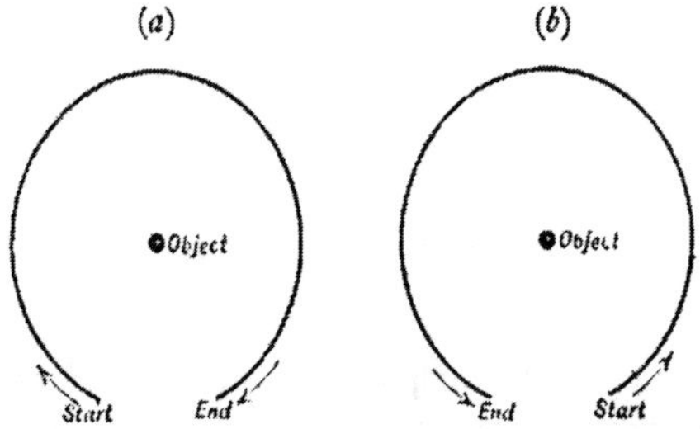

(*a*) Pradakshi*n*a*m* k*ri*, i.e. 'turn one's right hand towards an object.'

(*b*) Prasavya*m* k*ri*, i.e. 'turn one's left hand towards an object.'

hand inside that circle; and that, in fact, therefore, when one walks round towards one's left-hand side, the 'walking round towards the right' has been accomplished. This is merely that learned man's opinion, which is not at all proper. This has made the ignorant puzzled at the proper mode, and misled even some eminent persons who obsequiously agreed to it. Now, how should we settle the matter, inferring by principles alone? It is simply to rely on the Sanskrit texts, and to give up individual inclinations. To proceed towards the right-hand side (i. e. not turning towards the right) is the walking round towards the right [1], and to proceed towards the left-hand side is the walking round towards the left. This is the rule *set forth* by the Buddha, which is beyond our dispute.

Next (we shall treat of) 'the time' and 'improper time.' In the Sûtra which treats of 'the time [2],' there are different bearings with regard to times suitable to several circumstances. But, in the Vinaya books of the four schools (Nikâya), it is unanimously affirmed that the noon (lit. horse-hour, i. e. twelve o'clock) is the proper time (for the meal). If the shadow (of a dial) has passed as little even as a single thread, it is said to be an improper time (for the meal). If a person who guards himself against the fault (of missing the time) wants to get the exact cardinal points, he has to calculate the north star at night, and at once to observe (the quarter of) the south pole (i. e. 'south star') [3]; and, (doing this), he

---

[1] According to I-tsing, Pradakshi*n*am means 'walking towards one's own right, i. e. turning one's left hand towards an object.' Kâ*s*yapa again shows this as follows:—Pradakshi*n*am k*ri*, according to I-tsing.

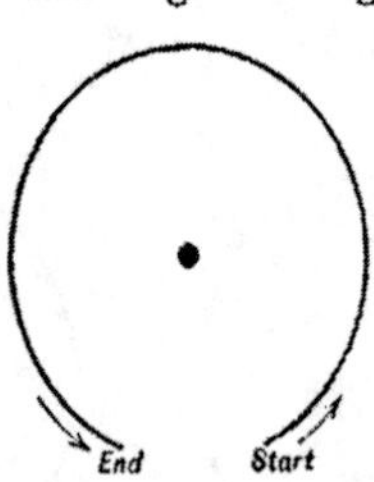

[2] The Sûtra on proper and improper time (Nanjio's Catal., No. 750).

[3] Each observation of time requires to see: (1) the direction of the meridian (which is obtained by observing the pole-star); (2) the time when a more southern (and therefore more quickly moving) star goes through the meridian.

is enabled to determine the exact line[1] (of the south and the north). Again he has to form a small earthen elevation at a suitable place. This mound is to be made round, of one foot diameter, and five inches high, at the centre part of which a slender stick is to be fixed. Or, on a stone stand, a nail is to be fixed, as slender as a bamboo chop-stick, and its height should be four fingers' width long. At the exact moment of the horse-hour (noon) a mark is to be drawn along the shadow (of the stick, fallen on the stand). If the shadow has passed the mark, one should not eat. In India such (dials) are made almost everywhere, which are called Velâ*k*akras, i. e. time-wheels. The way of measuring the shadow is to observe the shadow of the stick, when it is shortest: this is exact midday. But in the *G*a*m*budvîpa, the length of the shadows differs, owing to different situation of places. In the province of Lo[2], for instance, there falls no shadow; but the case is different in other places. Again, for instance, in the *S*rîbhoga country, we see the shadow of the dial-plate neither become long nor short, in the middle of the 8th month (i. e. about the time of the autumnal equinox). At midday no shadow falls from a man who stands on that day. The case is the same in the middle of spring (i. e. about the time of the vernal equinox)[3].

---

[1] 禺中 in Chinese, which is the hour in which the sun is in the position 巳, Ssŭ (Serpent or Virgo), and our 9-11 a. m. The point of the compass corresponding to this is SSE. ¾ E.

[2] The province of Lo is probably Central India. Lo was the capital of China and the centre of 'all under heaven' (洛, 天下之中), and I-tsing may have once for all used it as meaning Central India, though very strange.

[3] If I-tsing's 'middle of the 8th month' and 'middle of spring (2nd month)' were exactly the autumnal and vernal equinoxes respectively, it would have been easy to settle where *S*rîbhoga was. In the old Japanese calendar, which is practically the same as that of China, the 'middle of the 8th month' or 'middle of spring' does not mean the 15th day of the 8th and 2nd months respectively, but simply the day on which the day and night are of equal length. But we are ignorant whether it was so in China in I-tsing's time or not; we are not safe in taking them as exact equinox days. Besides, I-tsing may be writing according to a calendar then current in Sumatra or India. All we can say with certainty is that the equinoxes fall on a day either before or after the 15th of the 2nd and

The sun passes just above the head twice in a year. When the sun travels in the south, the shadow (of a man) falls northwards, and becomes as long as two or three feet, and when the sun is in the north, the shadow is the same at the south side (of a man). In China the shadow in the northern part differs in length from that in the southern part; the doors in the north country are always made to face the sun. When it is midday in the eastern sea coast of China (Hai-tung) it is not yet so in Kwan-hsi (i.e. the region on the west of Shen-si in China). Thus since there are natural differences, one cannot insist on one case being universal. Therefore it is said in the Vinaya: 'the hour is determined according to midday in respective places.' As every priest is desirous to act according to the holy laws, and as eating is necessary every day, so he must be careful in measuring the shadow in order to eat at the fixed time. If he fails (even) in this, how can he carry out other precepts? Eminent men therefore, who preach and carry out the laws, and who are not surprised at the minute and complicated rules, should take a dial with them even when travelling by sea, much more so, when they are on the land. The following is a saying in India: 'He who observes the water *as to insects* and the time *as to midday* is called a Vinaya-teacher.'

Besides, clepsydrae are much used in great monasteries in India. These together with some boys who watch them are gifts from kings of many generations, for the purpose of announcing hours to the monastics. Water is filled in a copper vessel, in which a copper bowl floats. This bowl is thin and delicate, and holds two Shăng (prasthas) of water (about two pints). In its bottom a hole is pierced as small as a pin-hole, through which the water springs up; this hole is to be made larger or smaller

---

8th months, according to the Chinese calendar. According to I-tsing, the 8th month is Kârttika, in which the autumnal equinox generally falls. See my additional note to p. 85 at the end.

Now as to the position of *S*rîbhoga. If the present Palembang were *S*rîbhoga in I-tsing's time, the 'middle of the 8th month' would be six days after the autumnal equinox in Sumatra. But, on the other hand, if the 'middle of the 8th month' were exactly the equinox day in autumn, then *S*rîbhoga must be sought somewhere on the Equator or some 2·5 degrees north of Palembang. Professor Lamp of Kiel Observatory kindly helped me in these points.

according to the time of the year. This must be well set, measuring (the length of) hours.

Commencing from the morning, at the first immersion of the bowl, one stroke of a drum is announced, and at the second immersion, two strokes; at the third immersion, three strokes. But, at the fourth immersion, besides four strokes of a drum, two blasts of a conch-shell, and one more beat of a drum are added. This is called the first hour, that is when the sun is at the east (between the zenith and the horizon). When the second turn of four immersions of the bowl is done, four strokes (of a drum) are sounded as before, and a conch-shell is also blown, which is followed by two more strokes (of a drum). This is called the second hour, that is the exact (beginning of the) horse-hour, (i. e. noon). If the last two strokes are already sounded, priests do not eat, and if any one is found eating, he is to be expelled according to the monastic rites. There are also two hours in the afternoon which are announced in the same way as in the forenoon. There are four hours at night which are similar to those of day. Thus division of one day and one night together makes eight hours. When the first hour at night ends, the sub-director (Karmadâna) announces it to all, by striking the drum in a loft of the monastery. This is the regulation of the clepsydra in the Nâlanda monastery. At sunset and at dawn, a drum is beaten ('one round') at the outside of the gate. These unimportant affairs are done by the servants ('pure men')[1] and porters. After sunset till the dawn, the priests never have the service of striking the Gha*nt*â, nor is it the business of those servants ('pure men') but of the Karmadâna. There is a difference of four and five (strokes of the Gha*nt*â), which is fully mentioned elsewhere[2].

The regulation of the clepsydra is somewhat different in the monasteries of Mahâbodhi and Ku*s*inagara, where a bowl is immersed sixteen times between morn and midday.

In the country of Pulo Condore of the Southern Sea, a large copper vessel (or pot) filled up with water is used. In its bottom a hole is

---

[1] Those who clean things, see below, p. 154.

[2] Kâ*s*yapa suggests that this quotation may be the Vinaya-saṅgraha, book xi (Nanjio's Catal., No. 1127), but nothing more is found in that text.

opened through which the water is let out. Every time when the vessel becomes empty, a drum is beaten once, and when four strokes are made, it is midday. The same process is made till sunset. There are also eight hours at night as at day-time, so that it makes sixteen hours altogether. This clepsydra is also a gift from the king of that country.

Owing to the use of those clepsydrae, even in thick clouds and in a dark day, there is no mistake whatever about the horse-hour (i. e. noon), and even when rainy nights continue, there is no fear of missing the watches. It is desirable to set such ones (in monasteries in China), asking for the royal help, as it is a very necessary matter among the Brotherhood.

In order to set a clepsydra, one has first to calculate (the lengths of) the day and night, and then to divide them into hours. There may be eight immersions of the bowl from morn to midday. If it happens that the immersions are less than eight (when it is midday), the hole of the bowl is to be opened a little wider. To set it right, however, requires a good mechanician. When the day or night becomes gradually shorter, half a ladle (of water) is to be added, and when the day or night grows gradually longer, half a ladle is to be let off.

But as its object is an announcement *of time,* it may be reasonable and also allowable for the Karmadâna to use a small bowl (for the same purpose) in his own apartment.

Though there are five watches (at night) in China, and four hours in India, there are only three hours, according to the teaching of the Tamer[1], i. e. one night is divided into three parts[2]. The first and the third are occupied by remembrance, mutterings (of prayers), and meditation; and during the middle hour, priests sleep, *binding their thoughts* (or, with attention). Those who deviate from this, are guilty of violating the law, except in the case of disease, and if they carry it on with reverence, they are, after all, doing good to themselves as well as to others.

---

[1] One of the epithets of the Buddha; the full Sanskrit is Purusha-damya-sârathi, i. e. 'the tamer of the human steed.'

[2] According to this, night and day make six hours.

CHAPTER XXXI.

RULES OF DECORUM IN CLEANSING THE SACRED OBJECT OF WORSHIP.

THERE is no more reverent worship than that of the Three Honourable Ones (Three Jewels), and there is no higher road (cause) to perfect understanding than *meditation* on the Four Noble Truths. But the meaning of the Truths is so profound that it is a matter beyond the comprehension of vulgar minds, while the Ablution of the Holy Image is practicable for all. Though the Great Teacher has entered Nirvâ*n*a, yet his image exists, and we should worship it with zeal as though in his very presence. Those who constantly offer incense and flowers to it are enabled to purify their thoughts, and also those who perpetually bathe his image are enabled to overcome their sins that involve them in darkness[1]. Those who devote themselves to this work will receive invisible[2] (Avig*ñ*apta) rewards, and those who advise others to perform it are doing good to themselves as well as to others by the visible[2] (Vig*ñ*apta) action. Therefore it is desired that those who wish *to accumulate* religious merit should set their minds on performing these deeds.

In Indian monasteries, when the monastics are going to bathe the image in the forenoon, the priest in charge (Karmadâna) strikes a Gha*nt*â (a gong) *for an announcement*. After stretching a jewelled canopy over the court of the monastery, and ranging perfumed water-jars in rows at the side of the temple, an image either of gold, silver, copper, or stone is put in a basin of the same material, while a band of girls plays music

---

[1] Lit. 'action caused by sloth,' i. e. 昏沈之業; Sanskrit, Styânakarma, Styâna being a technical term used in the Buddhist metaphysics. I-tsing uses it here in a wider sense.

[2] Chinese, 無表, i. e. 'invisible;' 有作, i. e. 'visible.' 表 and 作 are both translations of the Sanskrit word 'Vig*ñ*apta,' the former being adopted by the new translators, the latter by the old (i. e. before Hiuen Thsang).

there. The image having been anointed with scent, water with perfume is poured over it.

(Note by I-tsing): Sanskrit, 'Karma-dâna,' Karma being 'action,' dâna, 'giving,' i. e. 'One who gives others various actions.' This term was hitherto translated by 'Wei-na[1],' which is not right; Wei is

---

[1] Wei-na (維那) is in Sanskrit 'Karma-dâna;' the sense of Karma-dâna is represented by the first word, 'Wei,' i. e. 'arranging' or 'laying down direction' (維 for 綱維), while the latter 'na' is added to show that the original word had the sound 'na' at the end.

An analogous case is to be found in Shan-ting (禪定), Sanskrit, 'Dhyâna.' 'Shan' represents 'Dhyâ,' showing that the original had this sound at the beginning, while 'ting' is a translation of the word 'Dhyâna,' i. e. 'meditation.' There are many such words, and they belong to the Sinico-Sanskrit class of Buddhist words (梵漢並存).

Karma-dâna is a priest whose duty it is to announce the commencement of any service or ceremony, &c., by striking a bell, and to superintend the preparation of food. I-tsing in his Memoirs of Chinese Travellers in India (Nanjio's Catal., No. 1491, vol. i) says: 'One who builds a monastery is called the "owner of the monastery, i. e. Vihârasvâmin." The keeper, the warder of the gate, and he who announces the affairs of the Saṅgha are called Vihârapâlas, in Chinese, the "protectors of the house." But one who sounds the Gha*n*/*t*â (gong) and superintends food is called Karma-dâna, which is in Chinese the "giver of actions" (i. e. manager). The word, Wei-na, is insufficient' (Chavannes, Memoirs, p. 89). In Hiuen Thsang's texts we meet once with the term, Wei-na (Julien's Vie de Hiouen Thsang, vol. i, p. 143; Beal's Life of Hiuen Thsang, book iii, p. 106), and the Wei-na sounds the gong when Hiuen Thsang is received at the Nâlanda Vihâra. Wei-na was correctly commented there by Julien as 'le Karmadâna—le sous-directeur.' Julien's note probably rests on I-tsing's explanation. Beal, however, took Wei-na as pure Sanskrit, and a far-fetched explanation of the words was made; he says (book iii, p. 106, note):

'In the original, Wei-na, i. e. Vena, the early riser. He is the sub-director of the convent. Vena, in the sense of the rising sun, or the early riser, is found in the *Ri*g-veda, vide Wallis, Cosmology of the *Ri*g-veda, p. 35. But Vena has also the sense of the "knower," and hence the Chinese rendering "Chi-sse," "he who knows things, or business." He is, according to Julien, also called Karmadâna,

Chinese, meaning 'systematising' or 'arranging,' while 'na' is Sanskrit; and 'Karmadâ' is represented in the Chinese 'wei.'

The scent is prepared as follows: take any perfume-tree, such as sandal-wood or aloes-wood, and grind it with water on a flat stone until it becomes muddy, then anoint the image with it and next wash it with water.

After having been washed, it is wiped with a clean white cloth; then it is set up in the temple, where all sorts of beautiful flowers are furnished. This is the ceremony performed by the resident members under the management of the priest in charge (Karmadâna).

In individual apartments also of a monastery, priests bathe an image every day so carefully that no ceremony is omitted. Now as to the flowers, any sort, either from trees or from plants, may be used as offering. Fragrant flowers blossom continually in all seasons, and there are many people who sell them in the streets. In China, for instance, during summer and autumn, pinks and lotus-flowers flourish here and there; in spring the 'golden thorns,' peaches, and apricots blossom everywhere. The althea, pomegranate, red cherry, and plum flower one after another in season.

The garden hollyhock, the fragrant grass in the forest and such like must be picked, brought in, and arranged, ready to be offered. They ought not to be left in the orchards to be simply looked at from afar.

---

which appears to be allied to the Chinese *Hing* (Karma). The Pâli equivalent is Bhattuddesako.'

To Beal, the sound 'Wei-na' seems to have been only a guide in finding out the original. The Chinese rendering, 'Chi-sse,' i. e. 'he who knows things,' does not well support Beal's conjecture, because 'Chi-sse' is a common name for an officer in charge.

This term Karma-dâna similarly puzzled some of the Chinese priests. The commentator, Jiun Kâsyapa, mentions that some have taken Wei-na as pure Sanskrit, and explained it by 'keeping the Order (Vinayin?),' or 'pleasing the Saṅgha' (Venya?).

It is difficult to admit any explanation but I-tsing's, i. e. Wei-na stands for Karma-dâna, which is practically the same as those of Julien and the commentator Kâsyapa. Besides, Vena is very un-Buddhistic to range with Vihârapâla or Vihârasvâmin.

But sometimes in the winter one may not be able to procure flowers at all; in this case one may make artificial flowers by cutting silks and anointing them with good scents, and may offer these before the image of the Buddha. This is a very good way.

Copper images, whether large or small, are to be brightened by rubbing them with fine ashes or brick-powder, and pouring pure water over them, until they become perfectly clear and beautiful like a mirror. A large image must be washed in the middle and the end of a month by the whole assembly of priests, and a small one every day, if possible, by individual priests. By so doing, one may gain great merit at small expenditure.

If one take up with two fingers the water with which an image has been washed, and drop it on the head, it is called the 'water of good omen' by which one may wish for good luck. One should not smell the flowers that have been offered to an image, nor should one trample on them even when taken off, but put them aside in a clean place. It should never happen that a priest should neglect to wash the holy image during his whole life, and *he is to be blamed* if he do not even care to offer those beautiful flowers which are to be found everywhere in the fields. He must not be inactive and remiss, resting and simply looking at the gardens and pond, avoiding the trouble of *picking flowers and bathing images*, nor should he lazily finish his worship by simply opening the hall and doing general homage. If such be the case, the successive line of teacher and pupil will be broken, and the method of worship will not be according to authority.

The priests and the laymen in India make *K*aityas or images with earth, or impress the Buddha's image on silk or paper, and worship it with offerings wherever they go. Sometimes they build Stûpas of the Buddha by making a pile and surrounding it with bricks. They sometimes form these Stûpas in lonely fields, and leave them to fall in ruins. Any one may thus employ himself in making the objects for worship. Again, when the people make images and *K*aityas which consist of gold, silver, copper, iron, earth, lacquer, bricks, and stone, or when they heap up the snowy sand (lit. sand-snow), they put in the images or *K*aityas two kinds of *S*arîras. 1. The relics of the Great Teacher. 2. The Gâthâ of the Chain of Causation.

The Gâthâ is as follows:—

> [1] 'All things (Dharmas) arise from a cause.
> The Tathâgata has explained the cause.
> This cause of things has been finally destroyed;
> Such is the teaching of the Great *S*rama*n*a (the Buddha).'

If we put these two in the images or *K*aityas, the blessings derived from them are abundant. This is the reason why the Sûtras [2] praise in parables the merit of making images or *K*aityas as unspeakable. Even if a man make an image as small as a grain of barley, or a *K*aitya the size of a small jujube, placing on it a round figure, or a staff like a small pin, a special cause for good birth is obtained thereby, and will be as limitless as the seven seas, and good rewards will last as long as the coming four births. The detailed account of this matter is found in the separate Sûtras [3].

Teachers and others should always be attentive to this point. The washing of the holy image is a meritorious deed which leads to a

---

[1] Kâ*s*yapa gives the original as follows:—

> 'Ye dharmâ hetuprabhavâsteshâ*m* hetu*m* tathâgata uvâ*k*a I
> Teshâ*m* *k*a yo nirodha eva*m*vâdî mahâ*s*rama*n*a*h* II'

This famous stanza is given in Burnouf's Lotus, p. 522, and is identical with our verse here. The Pâli version is given in Mahâvagga I, 23, 5 and 10; and it is called 'Dhammapariyâya':—

> 'Ye dhammâ hetuppabhavâ tesa*m* hetu*m* tathâgato âha
> Tesa*ñ* *k*a yo nirodho eva*m*vâdî mahâsama*n*o.'

Professors Oldenberg and Rhys Davids translate as follows:—

'Of all objects which proceed from a cause, the Tathâgata has explained the cause, and he has explained their cessation also; this is the Doctrine of the Great Sama*n*a.'

The translators add that this stanza doubtless alludes to the formula of the twelve Nidânas, which explains the origination and cessation of what are called here 'Dhamma hetuppabhava.' See Mahâvagga I, 23, 5, S. B. E., vol. xiii. Instances of this stanza being buried or carved on the stone in the Stûpa are seen in Burnouf's note (Lotus, p. 522).

[2] See below.

[3] The Sûtras which recommend the making of the images, &c., are numerous, and Kâ*s*yapa gives six of them (e.g. Nanjio, No. 523).

meeting with the Buddha in every birth, and the offering of incense and flowers is a cause of riches and joy in every life to come. Do it yourself, and teach others to do the same, then you will gain immeasurable blessings.

In the eighth day of the fourth month [1], I saw somewhere in China several priests or laymen bringing out an image to the roadside; they washed the image properly, but did not know how to rub it, and left it to be dried by the wind and sun, without regard to the proper rules.

CHAPTER XXXII [2].

THE CEREMONY OF CHANTING.

THE custom of worshipping the Buddha by repeating his names has been known in the Divine Land (China) as it has been handed down (and practised) from olden times, but the custom of praising the Buddha by reciting his virtues has not been in practice. (The latter is more important than the former), because, in fact, to hear his names only does not help us to realise the superiority of his wisdom; whilst in reciting his virtues in descriptive hymns, we may understand how great his virtues are. In the West (India) priests perform the worship of a *K*aitya [3] and the ordinary service late in the afternoon or at the evening twilight. All the assembled priests come out of the gate of their monastery, and walk three times round a Stûpa, offering incense and flowers. They all kneel down, and one of them who sings well begins to chant hymns describing the virtues of the Great Teacher with a melodious, pure, and sonorous voice, and continues to sing ten or twenty *s*lokas. They in succession return to the place in the monastery where they usually assemble.

---

[1] This day is kept up as the Buddha's birthday. The custom of bathing the Buddha still exists in Japan.

[2] A French translation by M. Fujishima, a Japanese priest, will be found in the Journal Asiatique (Nov.–Dec.), 1888, p. 416.

[3] The text has '*K*aitya-vandana,' *K*aitya being the name of the sacred buildings containing relics of the Buddha or saints. For I-tsing's explanation of this word, see chap. xxv, p. 121 (there, *k*it = adj.), and for the names of the eight *K*aityas of the Buddha, see chap. xx, p. 108.

When all of them have sat down, a Sûtra-reciter, mounting the Lion-seat (Si*m*hâsana), reads a short Sûtra. The Lion-seat of well-proportioned dimensions is placed near the head priest. Among the scriptures which are to be read on such an occasion the 'Service in three parts[1]' is often used. This is a selection by the venerable A*s*vaghosha. The first part containing ten *s*lokas consists of a hymn in praise of the three 'Honourable Ones[2]' (Triratna). The second part is a selection from some scriptures consisting of the Buddha's words. After the hymn, and after reading the words of the Buddha, there is an additional hymn, as the third part of the service, of more than ten *s*lokas, being prayers that express the wish to bring one's good merit to maturity.

These three sections follow one another consecutively, from which its name—the Three-part Service—is derived. When this is ended, all the assembled priests exclaim 'Subhâshita!' that is, 'well-spoken,' from su = well, and bhâshita = spoken[3]. By such words the scriptures are extolled as excellent. They sometimes exclaim 'Sâdhu[4]!' signifying 'well done!' instead of the other.

After the Sûtra-reciter has descended, the head priest rising bows to the Lion-seat. That done, he salutes the seats of the saints[5], and then

---

[1] Lit. the 'thrice-opened service.'

[2] The 'Three Honourable Ones' are not Amitâbha, Avalokite*s*vara, and Mahâsthâma, as M. Fujishima supposed (p. 417, Journal Asiatique, Nov.–Dec. 1888). See my note below, p. 160.

[3] All the etymologies except those in notes are I-tsing's.

[4] J. has Sâdhu; the other editions have P'o-tu, which would make the original Badu, or Bade as in Fujishima's translation; but I do not see how Bade could mean 'bien.' In favour of the reading 'Sâdhu,' moreover, we have several points: (1) It is explained by 'Well!' or 'Well done!' a usual exclamation in India. (2) I-tsing uses again and again the same characters and interpretation in his other translations, e. g. see the translation of the Mûlasarvâstivâdaika*s*ata-karman (Nanjio's Catal., No. 1131). (3) 婆 'Ba' or 'P'o' for 娑 'Sa' or 'Sha,' or vice versa, is one of the most numerous misprints in Chinese Buddhist texts, e. g. P'o-lo-tu-lo stands for Sanskrit *S*alâtura, the native place of Pâ*n*ini; P'o is evidently a misprint for Sa. See Julien, Hiuen Thsang, tom. i, 165; ii, 125; ii, 312. Quoted by Weber, p. 218, History of Sanskrit Literature (Trübner).

[5] Kâ*s*yapa says that the word 'saints' here means Bodhisattvas and Arhats.

he returns to his own. Now the priest second in rank rising salutes them in the same manner as the first, and afterwards bows to the head priest.

When he has returned to his own seat, the priest third in rank performs the same ceremonies, and in the same manner do all the priests successively. But if a great crowd be present, after three or five persons have performed the above ceremony, the remaining priests salute the assembly at one and the same time, after which they retire at pleasure. The above is a description of the rites practised by the priests in Tâmralipti[1] in the Eastern Âryade*s*a (E. India).

In the Nâlanda monastery the number of priests is immense, and exceeds three thousand[2]; it is difficult to assemble so many together in one place. There are eight halls and three hundred apartments in this monastery. The worship can only take place separately, as most convenient to each member. Thus, it is customary to send out, every day, one precentor to go round from place to place chanting hymns, being preceded by monastic lay servants and children carrying with them incense and flowers[3]. He goes from one hall to another, and in each

---

[1] An ancient kingdom and city (now Tamluk, at the mouth of the Hooghly), a centre of trade with India and China in I-tsing's time.

[2] J. has 3,000, but all the other texts 5,000; the former is a right reading, for I-tsing, in chap. x, p. 65, gives the number of priests in Nâlanda as 'more than 3,000,' and in his Memoirs, as '3,500.' See Chavannes' translation, p. 97.

[3] (*a*) 'To send out one precentor' is in Chinese 差一能唱導師, lit. 'To send out one teacher who takes the lead in chanting.' This is a priest.

(*b*) 'Monastic lay servants,' lit. 'pure men.' It is pretty certain that they are not, as Julien thought, priests. Hiuen Thsang on one occasion sends out a 'pure man' to pull down and trample under foot a document which was put up by a heretic; when the 'pure man' was asked who he was, he answered, 'I am the servant of Mahâyânadeva' (Beal, Life of Hiuen Thsang, book iv, p. 161). A 'pure man' is attending at a meal (Fâ-hien, chap. iii). In I-tsing's Record we have many similar instances. A 'pure man' carries a chair and utensils when a priest goes to a reception (chap. ix, p. 36); he carries away the remnant of the food eaten by a priest (chap. ix, p. 47); he cultivates the field for the church

he chants the service, every time three or five *s*lokas in a high tone, and the sound is heard all around. At twilight he finishes this duty. This precentor generally is presented by the monastery with some special gift (Pû*g*â). In addition there are some who, sitting alone, facing the shrine (Gandhaku*t*î), praise the Buddha in their heart. There are others who, going to the temple, (in a small party) kneel side by side with their bodies upright, and, putting their hands on the ground, touch it with their heads, and thus perform the Threefold Salutation. These are the ceremonies of worship adopted in the West (i. e. in India)[1]. Old and

---

(chap. x, p. 61); the time-drum is beaten by him, but he is not allowed to strike the gong announcing the beginning of a service (chap. xxx, p. 145). And when a priest is very learned (bahu*s*ruta) or has finished the study of one Pi*t*aka, the Saṅgha gives him the best rooms and servants (lit. 'pure men to serve him') (chap. x, p. 64). He may be a professed Upâsaka, but he is not a priest in any case. The 'pure man' is probably 'purifying man.' In Japan, the monastic gardener is often called by this name. It does not signify 'Brâhmans,' as Julien supposed (Mém., liv. ii, p. 78), in any case; and 'Vimala,' suggested by Legge (Fâ-hien, chap. iv, p. 18, note), is very doubtful. Perhaps Pâli 'Ârâmiko' (*K*ull. p. 282).

(*c*) The word 'children,' for which we have the author's own explanation (chap. xix, p. 105): 'Those Upâsakas who come to the abode of a Bhikshu chiefly in order to learn the Sacred Books, and intending to shave their hair and wear a black robe, are called "children"' (i. e. 'mâ*n*ava').

Now the question is whether the latter two, i. e. the 'pure men' and 'children,' who carry incense and flowers, take part in chanting. We can answer this question in the negative or in the affirmative. Probably not. 'One who takes the lead in chanting' does not imply that that person is taking the lead in chanting in this service, for the name may be used technically. I explain this, because, from Fujishima's translation, it appears as if a priest is conducting a procession of priests. All I-tsing mentions is one priest, 'pure men,' and 'children,' and no other priests go with them.

[1] The 'West' in I-tsing never means Western India, but India in general. Taking the 'West' as Western India, as M. Fujishima does, is a blunder that would not arise, had one carefully compared all the names of India used in the text. In this case, at any rate, it cannot mean Western India, for the Nâlanda monastery is in Central India, seven miles north of ancient Râ*g*agri*h*a (Cunningham, Anc. Geogr., vol. i, p. 467).

infirm priests are allowed to use small mats whilst worshipping. Though, (in China), the hymns in praise of the Buddha have long existed, yet the manner of using them for a practical purpose is somewhat different from that adopted in India[1] (lit. 'Brahma-râsh*t*ra'). The words which begin with 'Praise be to the signs of the Buddha,' and are used when worshipping the Buddha (in China), should be intoned in a long monotonous note, and the rule is to proceed thus for ten or twenty *s*lokas at one time. Further, Gâthâs such as the one beginning with 'O Tathâgata!' are really hymns in praise of the Buddha[2].

It is true that, when the note is much lengthened, it is difficult to understand the meaning of the hymn sung. A delightful thing it is, however, to hear a skilful person recite 'The Hymn in one hundred and fifty verses[3],' 'that in four hundred verses,' or any other song of praise at night, when the assembled priests remain very quiet on a fasting night (such as the night of an Uposatha). In India numerous hymns of praise to be sung at worship have been most carefully handed down, for every talented man of letters has praised in verse whatever person he deemed most worthy of worship. Such a man was the venerable Mât*ri*ke*t*a, who, by his great literary talent and virtues, excelled all learned men of his age. The following story is told of him. While the Buddha was living, He was once, while instructing his followers, wandering in a wood among the people. A nightingale in the wood, seeing the Buddha, majestic as a gold mountain, adorned by his perfect

---

[1] The text has Fan=Brahman for 'Brahma-râsh*t*ra,' meaning India in general; he says in chap. xxv, p. 118, that the whole territory of the five divisions of India is called the 'Brahman kingdom;' not simply 'Central India,' as M. Fujishima makes it out.

[2] What I-tsing wishes to make clear is this: that the praising of the Buddha exists both in China and India, but the Indians chant in a long sing-song fashion, while the Chinese read the text or Gâthâ in the ordinary way. He would have the text or Gâthâ chanted in China.

[3] The hymns in 150 verses and in 400 verses are those of Mât*ri*ke*t*a; the 150 verses were translated into Chinese by I-tsing while he was staying in the Nâlanda monastery (A. D. 675–685), and revised by him afterwards (A. D. 708). It is called 'Sârdha*s*ataka-Buddhapra*s*a*m*sâgâthâ.' For the translation, see Nanjio's Catal., No. 1456. The 400 verses were not translated into Chinese.

signs, began to utter its melodious notes, as if it sang in praise of him. The Buddha, looking back to his disciples, said: 'The bird, transported with joy at sight of me, unconsciously utters its melodious notes. On account of this good deed, after my Departure (Nirvâ*n*a) this bird shall be born in human form, and named Mât*rik*e*t*a[1]; and he shall praise my virtues with true appreciation.' Previously, as a follower of another religion, when born as man, Mât*rik*e*t*a had been an ascetic, and had worshipped Mahe*s*varadeva. When a worshipper of this deity, he had composed hymns in his praise. But on becoming acquainted with the fact that his birth[2] had been foretold, he became a convert to Buddhism, robed in colour, and free from worldly cares. He mostly engaged himself in praising and glorifying the Buddha, repented of his past sins, and was desirous henceforward of following the Buddha's good example, regretting that he could not see the Great Teacher himself, but his image only. In fulfilment of the above prediction (Vyâkara*n*a), he wrote hymns in praise of the Buddha's virtues to the greatest extent of his literary powers.

He composed first a hymn consisting of four hundred *s*lokas, and afterwards another of one hundred and fifty[3]. He treats generally of the Six Pâramitâs, and expounds all the excellent qualities of the Buddha, the World-honoured One. These charming compositions are equal in beauty to the heavenly flowers, and the high principles which they contain rival in dignity the lofty peaks of a mountain. Consequently in India all who compose hymns imitate his style, considering him the father of literature. Even men like the Bodhisattvas Asaṅga and Vasubandhu admired him greatly.

Throughout India every one who becomes a monk is taught Mât*rik*e*t*a's two hymns as soon as he can recite the five and ten precepts (*S*îla).

This course is adopted by both the Mahâyâna and Hînayâna schools. There are six reasons for this. Firstly, these hymns enable us to know the Buddha's great and profound virtues. Secondly, they show us how to compose verses. Thirdly, they ensure purity of language[4]. Fourthly,

---

[1] I-tsing notes 'Mât*ri*=mother, *K*e*t*a=lad or child.'

[2] Lit. 'his name had been foretold.'

[3] See above, p. 156, note 3.

[4] Lit. 'they cause the organ of speech or tongue to become pure.'

the chest is expanded in singing them. Fifthly, by reciting them nervousness in an assembly is overcome. Sixthly, by their use life is prolonged, free from disease. After one is able to recite them, one proceeds to learn other Sûtras. But these beautiful literary productions have not as yet been brought to China[1]. There are many who have written commentaries on them, nor are the imitations[2] of them few. Bodhisattva *G*ina himself composed such an imitation. He added one verse before each of the one hundred and fifty verses, so that they became altogether three hundred verses, called the 'Mixed' hymns (probably Sa*m*yukta-pra*s*a*m*sâ). A celebrated priest of the Deer Park, *S*âkyadeva[3] by name, again added one verse to each of *G*ina's, and consequently they amounted to four hundred and fifty verses (*s*lokas), called the 'Doubly Mixed' hymns.

All those who compose religious poems take these for their patterns. Bodhisattva Nâgâr*g*una wrote an epistle in verse which is called the Suh*ri*llekha[4], meaning 'Letter to an intimate friend;' it was dedicated

---

[1] I-tsing sent home a translation of the 150 verses, together with our Record, as he says towards the end of this chapter.

[2] This imitation may be 'Samasyâ-verse,' as M. Fujishima supposed; the text has 和, which is the 'imitation of a rhyme' in China.

[3] It may be *S*akradeva, as M. Fujishima restored, but more likely *S*âkyadeva, as transcribed by I-tsing, who is very strict in Sanskrit words generally. It is not likely that he would use the same characters for both *S*âkya and *S*akra, as the old translators did. See 'India, what can it teach us?' note on 'Renaissance,' p. 303. Kâ*s*yapa also gives *S*âkyadeva in his Commentary.

[4] This is a famous little poem of Nâgâr*g*una. We have a Tibetan translation, as well as three Chinese translations. The date of the Tibetan seems to be uncertain, while the dates of the Chinese are quite certain; the first translation in A.D. 431 by Gu*n*avarman (Nanjio's Catal., No. 1464), the second in A.D. 434 by Saṅghavarman (No. 1440), and the third in A.D. 673 by I-tsing himself, when he first arrived at Tâmralipti, in India (No. 1441; here Nanjio gives the date A.D. 700–712, for the date of I-tsing's journey was not yet ascertained in his time).

An English translation of the Tibetan, with some discussions, was published in the Journal of the Pâli Text Society, 1886, pp. 1–31, by Dr. Wenzel, who has also brought out a German translation. Another English version, with the Chinese text, by Mr. S. Beal (1892, Luzac & Co.). The Tibetan contains 123 verses,

to his old Dânapati, named *G*i-in-ta-ka (*G*etaka)[1], a king in a great country in Southern India, who was styled So-to-pho-hân-na (Sadvâhana[1], or *S*âtavâhana). The beauty of the writing is striking, and his

---

and the Chinese 153; the number in Tibetan may probably represent that of the Sanskrit *s*lokas.

[1] The addressee of Nâgâr*g*una's epistle, king So-to-pho-hân-na, whose private name was *G*i-in-ta-ka, is not as yet identified with certainty. Information about him may be summed up as follows:—

(1) Chinese source. Hiuen Thsang speaks of him as a king of Southern Kosala, and gives a legend concerning Nâgâr*g*una and the king. The king's name is, according to him, Sadvâha; the corresponding Chinese words being 'In-ching,' which mean the 'leader of the good' (Julien, Mémoires, liv. x, p. 95). I-tsing, in his translation of the Suh*ri*llekha, says: 'This is a poem written by Nâgâr*g*una as a letter to his intimate friend, the king of Shêng-shih (乘 士 國).' Shêng-shih means 'riding on the scholars' or 'borne by the scholars;' this may be Sadvâhana, used here as the name of his country. Cf. I-tsing's translation of *G*îmûta-vâhana, i. e. Shêng-yun, or 'borne by the cloud' (乘 雲). See below. It is true there is another reading for Shêng-shih, namely Shêng-tu (乘 土), and Beal supposed it to be Sindhu, but his supposition is untenable when we see that I-tsing used a different transliteration for Sindhu (above, p. 9). Moreover, Shêng is never used for transliteration so far as I know; Julien, too, does not seem to have met with an instance of this character being used in transcribing a Sanskrit word, for he does not give the phonetic value of it in his 'method.' But as we do not find a king called 'Sadvâhana' in India, we have at present to leave it unconfirmed.

(2) Tibetan source. According to Târanâtha (see Geschichte des Buddhismus, übersetzt von Schiefner, pp. 2, 71, 303, and 304), the king's name was Udayana (or Utrayana), and he was also called Ântivâhana, which Schiefner doubtfully identifies with the Greek name Antiochos, but there is another reading for this, i. e. *S*ântivâhana. Further, Udayana was (l. c., p. 303) called *G*etaka when, as a boy, he was met by Nâgâr*g*una. See Prof. Max Müller's letter, Journal of Pâli Text Society, 1883, p. 75.

With the help of the above information we can restore So-to-pho-hân-na to Sadvâhana, and *G*i-in-ta-ka to *G*etaka. For some more discussions, see Max Müller's letter above referred to, Dr. Wenzel's Suh*ri*llekha (Journal of Pâli Text Society, 1886), Nanjio's note (his Catal., No. 1464), and Mr. Beal's Suh*ri*llekha

exhortations as to the right way are earnest. His kindness excels that of kinship, and the purport of the epistle is indeed manifold. We should, he writes, respect and believe the Three Honourable Ones[1] (i. e. Triratna,

---

(1892, Luzac & Co.). I may add here that Beal tried to restore *G*i-in-ta-ka to Sindhuka and to make him a Pahlava king, but unfortunately I-tsing again uses a different transliteration for Sindhuka (see his Eka*s*atakarman, Nanjio's Catal., No. 1131; J., book vii, p. 65).

As the restoration of the name is still uncertain, it is fair to point out here that So-to-pho-hân-na (Japanese, Sha-ta-ba-kan-na) is nearer to *S*âtavâhana than to Sadvâhana. Further, a conjecture may be formed that it was originally *S*âtavâhana and corrupted into something like Sadavâhana or Sadvâhana, just as *S*âtakar*n*i is in Pâli Sadakâ*n*i, and the Chinese, not knowing the original, gave a fanciful etymology to the name and interpreted it as the 'leader of the good.' How did the Tibetan come to mention *S*ântivâhana or Ântivâhana? We know from Wilson's Works (vol. iii, p. 181, as quoted by Prof. Max Müller) that *S*âtavâhana is a synonym of *S*âlivâhana, the enemy of Vikramâditya. The *S*aka era which begins in A. D. 78 is also called the *S*âlivâhana era; see Max Müller, 'India, &c.,' 1883, p. 300. *S*âlivâhana may have been read *S*ântivâhana, the l being misread as nt, and afterwards the *S*â also being read Â, the name may have become Ântivâhana. It is very curious to find so many names for one and the same person. We must wait for some corroboration from an Indian source. Cf. Ind. Ant., 1873, 106.

[1] Chinese, 三尊, i. e. the 'Three Honourable Ones.' I-tsing uses this term as identical with the 'Three Precious Ones,' i. e. Triratna. In his Record it occurs seven times, and, except in two cases, it is doubtful what he means. Here, in our case, the term must mean the Triratna and nothing else, for he is giving a general summary of the Suh*ri*llekha, and we see that in the beginning of the book in question, the Three Jewels, i. e. the Buddha, Dharma, and Saṅgha, are mentioned; and further, in chap. xxxv, p. 188, the context shows us that the term means Triratna. M. Fujishima took it as meaning Amitâbha, Avalokite*s*vara, and Mahâsthâma (Journal Asiatique, Nov. 1888, p. 417), as quoted by Prof. Cowell (S. B. E., vol. xlix, p. ix). But whether these three holy beings had formed a triad and occupied the foremost place at the time of Nâgâr*g*una or A*s*vaghosha is doubtful. Amitâbha and Avalokite*s*vara appear in the Suh*ri*llekha, but not Mahâsthâma. Fâ-hien, in his Record, once uses the term, 'Three Honourable Ones.' Prof. Legge rightly treated it as identical with the 'Three Precious Ones' (Fâ-hien, p. 116, note); so did Beal in his Suh*ri*llekha (p. 9).

Tibetan Suh*ri*llekha, verse 4), and support our fathers and mothers (verse 9). We should keep the precepts (*S*îla, verse 11), and avoid committing sinful deeds (verses 10–12).

We should not associate with men until we know their character. We must regard wealth and beauty as the foulest of things[1] (verses 25, &c.). We should regulate well our home affairs, and always remember that the world is impermanent. He treats fully of the conditions of Pretas (departed spirits) and of the brute creation (Tiryagyoni), likewise of those of the gods, men, and the hell spirits. Even though fire should be burning above our head, he further writes, we ought to waste no time in putting it out, but should keep in view perpetually our Final Liberation (Moksha), reflecting on the truths of the 'Chain of Causality' (twelve Nidânas[2], verses 109–112).

Since I wrote the above I found a most satisfactory passage, confirming my statements, in I-tsing's translation of the Eka*s*atakarman of the Mûlasarvâstivâda-nikâya (Nanjio's Catal., No. 1131; J., p. 38). It is as follows:—

(1) 歸依佛陀兩足中尊.
(2) 歸依達磨離欲中尊.
(3) 歸依僧伽諸衆中尊.

(1) I take refuge with the Buddha as the most *honourable* of the Bi-ped.

(2) I take refuge with the Dharma as the most *honourable* among all things that refer to the freedom from desire.

(3) I take refuge with the Saṅgha as the most *honourable* of all assemblies.

The same idea is found in Dîpava*m*sa XI, 35; there king A*s*oka says:

Buddho dakkhi*n*eyyân' aggo, Dhammo aggo virâgina*m* ı
Sa*m*gho *k*a pu*ññ*akkhettaggo, tî*n*i aggâ sadevake ıı

'The Buddha is the best among those who are worthy of presents, the Dhamma is the best of all things which refer to the extinction of the passions, and the Sa*m*gha is the best field of merit; these are the three best objects in the world of men and devas.'

[1] Lit. 'We should practise the *meditation of impurity* with regard to all the wealth and beauty.'

[2] For the twelve Nidânas, see Prof. Oldenberg's Buddha, chap. ii, p. 223 seq.; for the eight Paths, pp. 128, 211; for the four Truths, p. 209; for this last also Prof. Rhys Davids' Buddhism, p. 106 seq.

He advises us to practise the threefold wisdom[1] (three Pra*gñ*âs), that we may clearly understand the 'noble eightfold path' (eight Ârya-mârgas), and teaches us the 'four truths' (four Âryasatyas) to realise the twofold attainment of perfection[2]. Like Avalokite*s*vara, we should not make any distinction between friends and enemies (cf. verse 120). We shall then live hereafter in the Sukhâvatî[3] for ever, through the power of the Buddha Amitâyus (or Amitâbha, verse 121), whereby one can also exercise the superior power of salvation over the world.

In India students learn this epistle in verse early in the course of instruction, but the most devout make it their special object of study throughout their lives. As, in China, the Sûtras about Avalokite*s*vara (chapter 24 in Saddharmapu*nd*arika)[4] and the Last Admonition of the Buddha (abridged Mahâparinirvâ*n*a-sûtra)[5] are recited by young priests, as the 'Composition of the One Thousand (Chinese) Characters' (Ch'ien-tʒŭ-wên)[6] and the 'Book of Filial Piety' (Hsiao King)[7] are learnt by lay-students, just so the work above referred to is studied (in India) with great earnestness, and is regarded as standard literature. There is another work of a similar character called '*G*âtakamâlâ[8].' *G*âtaka means

---

[1] Wisdom obtained (1) from study (*S*ruta), (2) by thought (*K*i*m*tâ), (3) by meditation (Bhâvanâ), see Kasawara Dharma-sangraha, cx, p. 28; the note from the Chinese list given in p. 63 ought to have been placed under cxiv, three *G*ñânas. See also Childers, s.v. Pa*ññ*â.

[2] Kâ*s*yapa says that twofold attainment of perfection is the attainment of the great wisdom and the great compassion that a Buddha possesses.

[3] I. e. The Land of Bliss; see Max Müller on this (Introd. Sukhâvatî-vyûha, S. B. E., vol. xlix, pp. v–xii).

[4] I. e. Samantamukha-parivarta Avalokite*s*vara-vikurva*n*a nirde*s*a; Kern, chap. 24, but chap. 25 of the common Chinese text of Kumâra*g*îva. Also Nanjio's Catal., No. 137. This is still widely read in the East.

[5] Nanjio's Catal., No. 122; referred to, p. 6, note 1, above.

[6] A Chinese school-book written by Chou Hsing-ssŭ, about A.D. 504.

[7] Another common book of instruction, translated by Prof. Legge, S. B. E., vol. iii.

[8] The Sanskrit text of Ârya *S*ûra's *G*âtakamâlâ was published by Prof. Kern in the Harvard Oriental Series, vol. i, edited by Prof. Lanman, 1891.

We have a translation in the Chinese Tripi*t*aka, though it does not much agree

'previous births,' and mâlâ 'garland;' the idea being that the stories of the difficult deeds accomplished in the former lives of the Bodhisattva (afterwards the Buddha) are strung (or collected) together in one place. If it were to be translated (into Chinese) it would amount to more than ten rolls[1]. The object of composing the Birth-stories in verse is to teach the doctrine of universal salvation in a beautiful style, agreeable to the popular mind and attractive to readers. Once king *S*îlâditya[2], who was exceedingly fond of literature, commanded, saying: 'Ye who are fond of poetry, bring and show me some pieces of your own to-morrow morning.' When he had collected them, they amounted to five hundred bundles[3], and, on being examined, it was found that most of them were *G*âtakamâlâs. From this fact one judges that *G*âtakamâlâ is the most beautiful (favourite) theme for laudatory poems. There are more than ten islands in the Southern Sea; here both priests and laymen recite the *G*âtakamâlâ, as also the verses above mentioned[4]; but the former has not yet been translated into Chinese[5]. King *S*îlâditya versified the story of the Bodhisattva *G*îmûtavâhana[6] (Ch. 'Cloud-borne'), who

---

with the original. See Nanjio's Catal., No. 1312; it was translated into Chinese A.D. 960–1127.

[1] Prof. Kern's edition has 1,340 verses and contains thirty-four *G*âtakas, while the Chinese has four volumes containing only fourteen *G*âtakas (Nanjio's Catal., No. 1312). A comparison of this text with the Pâli and Chinese texts will be very important. It has since been translated by Mr. Speyer, 1895.

[2] King *S*îlâditya of Kanoj died towards the end (A.D. 655, not 650) of the Yung Hui period (A.D. 650–655). See Beal, Life of Hiuen Thsang, p. 156; Julien, Vie, iv, p. 215; and Max Müller, 'India, what can it teach us?' p. 286.

[3] 夾 means 'folded between boards.' We know well that Sanskrit MSS. were kept in this way. Not *s*lokas, as M. Fujishima makes it out.

[4] I. e. 150 verses, 400 verses, and Suh*ri*llekha.

[5] Since then, it was translated in A.D. 960–1127 (Nanjio's Catal., No. 1312). As the date of Ârya *S*ûra is not yet settled, I may add here that one of his works was translated into Chinese A.D. 434, and we cannot place him later than this.

[6] This is, no doubt, the Buddhist play Nâgânandam; it was edited in Calcutta in 1864 by Chandra Ghosha, and in Bombay, 1893, by Govind Brahme and Para*ñ*gape. A translation appeared in 1872 (Trübner) by Mr. Boyd, with a preface

surrendered himself in place of a Nâga. This version was set to music (lit. string and pipe). He had it performed by a band accompanied by dancing and acting, and thus popularised it in his time. Mahâsattva *K*andra (lit. 'Moon-official,' probably *K*andradâsa), a learned man in Eastern India, composed a poetical song about the prince Vi*s*vântara (Chinese, Pi-yu-an-ta-ra)[1], hitherto known as Sudâna, and people all sing and dance[2] to it throughout the five countries of India.

---

by Prof. Cowell. Though, in the prologue, this play, like the Ratnâvalî, is assigned to *S*rî Harshadeva (= *S*îlâditya), Prof. Cowell would ascribe it to Dhâvaka for several reasons. He also advocates an early date for it. Now we know that the play cannot be later than I-tsing's stay abroad (A. D. 671–695), and that *S*îlâditya died about A. D. 655 (see p. 163, note 2). Prof. Weber has discussed the subject in Literarisches Centralblatt, 8 Juni, 1872, No. xxiii, p. 614. Mr. S. Beal's correspondence about these passages in the Academy, Sept. 29, 1883, No. 595, pp. 217, 218, is simply a blunder; he makes out that *S*îlâditya was accustomed himself to take the part of *G*îmûtavâhana on the stage—this is utterly impossible. The story of *G*îmûtavâhana is told in the Kathâ-sarit-sâgara I, 175. For the discussion about this play, see M. S. Lévi, Le Théatre Indien, 1890, pp. 190–195, 319, 320.

[1] This is, of course, a song about the Vi*s*vântara-(= Vi*s*va*m*tara, Kern)-*g*âtaka, being the Buddha's last birth but one. This *G*âtaka is found in Kern's *G*âtakamâlâ (9th) and Morris' *K*ariyâpi*t*aka (9th). See Childers, s. v. Vessantara. This seems to be the most famous among Buddhists, for it is heard from the mouths of all the Buddhist travellers in India: (1) Fâ-hien refers to Sudâna (= Vessantara) in his travels (Legge's, ch. xxxviii, p. 106); (2) Sung-yun tells us that he and his companions could not refrain from tears when they were shown the picture of the sufferings of this prince, in the White Elephant Temple near Varusha (Beal, Catena, p. 4); Hiuen Thsang speaks of him (Julien, Mémoires, liv. ii, p. 122). See Mr. R. L. Mitra's Nepalese Buddhist Literature, p. 50, and Hardy's Manual of Buddhism, pp. 116–124.

In the French translation of M. Fujishima, these passages were entirely misunderstood; see Journal Asiatique, Nov. 1888, p. 425. He seems to have taken Pi-yu as Avadâna*s*ataka, and An-ta-ra as Ândhra, instead of Pi-yu-an-ta-ra as Vi*s*vântara, which is my restoration. I do not know how Pi-yu in our text could mean Avadâna, much less Avadâna*s*ataka. It is true Julien gives in his

[2] For this note, see next page.

A*s*vaghosha also wrote some poetical songs and the Sûtrâlankâra*s*âstra[3]. He also composed the Buddha*k*aritakâvya (or 'Verses on the Buddha's career'). This extensive work, if translated, would consist of more than ten volumes[4]. It relates the Tathâgata's chief doctrines and works during his life, from the period when he was still in the royal palace till

---

Hiuen Thsang (Index, p. 494, last volume) 'Pi-yu,' 'les Avadâna;' but one must never confound this Pi-yu with the Pi-yu of our text, for the former is a translation of Avadâna, meaning 'example' or 'parable,' while the latter is simply a transliteration, which cannot mean anything unless restored to the Sanskrit original. Pi-yu-an-ta-ra can represent nothing but Vi*s*vântara, a prince who was also called Sudâna, according to Chinese writers. See Köppen, Religion des Buddhas, i, 325, note. Sudâna does not occur in the Sanskrit text of the Vi*s*vântara-*g*âtaka as an epithet of the king. Prof. Kern also wrote to me to the same effect, see the additional note at the end. For 'yu' read 'shu' (輸 as J. has it).

[2] The text has 無 for 舞 J.; I follow the latter.

[3] This work was translated into Chinese by Kumâra*g*îva about A.D. 405 (see Nanjio's Catal., No. 1182). M. Fujishima gives Ala*m*kâralika-*s*âstra (Ala*m*kâra*t*îkâ?), but perhaps he means 'Sûtrâlankâra-*s*âstra of A*s*vaghosha.' Alankâra*t*îkâ is Asangha's work (Nanjio's Catal., No. 1190).

[4] This important work was published by Prof. Cowell in the Anecdota Oxoniensia, and translated by him in the S. B. E., vol. xlix. We have Tibetan and Chinese translations of this 'Mahâkâvya,' both in twenty-eight chapters. The Chinese version of Sanghavarman, A.D. 414–421, has been translated by Beal in the S. B. E., vol. xix; the Chinese is in five volumes and about 2,310 verses, according to Beal's division, while Prof. Cowell's Sanskrit text has about 1,368 *s*lokas (though the latter part is by a later hand). I-tsing says that it would amount to more than ten volumes. He generally means 300 *s*lokas by one volume; if so in this case, the Buddha*k*aritakâvya I-tsing mentions may have contained 300 × 10 = 3,000 *S*lokas. I-tsing does not seem to have remembered the then existing translation of Sanghavarman. A minute comparison of the Sanskrit with the Chinese original will throw light on several doubtful points in both texts, and at the same time we may see how far Beal's translation is justifiable. His version has already served to verify numerous ingenious corrections proposed by some scholars; see especially Kielhorn's 'Zur A*s*vaghosha's Buddha*k*arita' (Aus den Nachrichten der K. Gesellschaft der Wissenschaften zu Göttingen, Philologisch-histor. Klasse, 1894, No. 3); the last part referring to Beal's translation.

his last hour under the avenue of Sâla-trees:—thus all the events are told in a poem.

It is widely read or sung throughout the five divisions of India, and the countries of the Southern Sea. He clothes manifold meanings and ideas in a few words, which rejoice the heart of the reader so that he never feels tired from reading the poem. Besides, it should be counted as meritorious for one to read this book, inasmuch as it contains the noble doctrines given in a concise form. I am sending to you the 'Hymn in one hundred and fifty *s*lokas[1]' and the 'Epistle of Nâgârguna' (Suh*ri*llekha), both translated for special objects, trusting that those who like praise-songs will often practise and recite them.

CHAPTER XXXIII.

AN UNLAWFUL SALUTATION.

THERE are distinct rules concerning salutation. It is right to perform the devotional exercise six times day and night, strenuously moving hands and feet, or to reside quietly in one room, only performing the duty of collecting alms, carrying out the Dhûtâṅgas[2], and practising the principle of self-contentment. And it is proper to wear only three garments (Tri-*k*îvara), and not to possess any luxurious things; one should ever direct one's thought to Final Liberation (lit. 'non-birth') by fleeing from the enticements of the world. It is not right to observe the same rules and ceremonies of the Order in various ways. Nor is it seemly for one wearing the mendicant robe to salute common laymen in such places as a market. Go and examine the Vinaya texts; such observances are forbidden in them. The Buddha said: 'There are only two groups which you ought to salute. First, the Three Jewels; second, the Elder Bhikshus[3].' There are some who bring the image of the Buddha to the highway in order to get money from people, thus defiling the holy objects of worship by dust and dirt. There are others who bend their

[1] The 150 verses of Mât*r*ike*t*a; see above, and Nanjio's Catal., No. 1456.

[2] See Childers, s. v. The thirteen Dhûtâṅgas are certain ascetic practices, the observance of which is meritorious in a Buddhist priest. See also above, p. 56.

[3] See above, p. 115, note 2.

body, wound their face, cut their joints, or injure their skin, wishing to gain a livelihood by thus falsely displaying (signs of mortification) as if for a good purpose. Such customs do not exist in India. Do not let men be misled by such practices any more!

CHAPTER XXXIV.

THE METHOD OF LEARNING IN THE WEST.

ONE single utterance of the Great Sage (the Buddha) comprises all (the languages throughout) the 'three thousand' worlds. This is taught in (the words ending with) the seven case- and nine personal-terminations[1], according to the ability of those who tread the 'five paths[2],' and provides a means of salvation. There is a store of doctrine appealing to thought only, and the King of heaven (Devânâm-indra) protects this scripture of inexpressible ideas. When, however, the doctrine is expressed in words, and interpreted (e.g. in Chinese), the people of China can understand (the meanings contained in) the letters of the original sound[3]. Expression in words causes a man to develop his intellect according to his various circumstances and mental faculties. It leads a man from perplexity into conformity with truth, and secures him perfect quietude (i.e. Nirvâ*n*a).

The highest truth (Paramârtha-satya) is far beyond the reach of word or speech, but a concealed truth (Sa*m*v*ri*ti-satya) may be explained by words or phrases.

---

[1] The seven cases are grammatically termed 'Sup' (=case-ending). Native grammarians count only seven cases, and the vocative case is included in the nominative. The nine terminations are grammatically called 'tiṅ,' which means all the personal terminations in the conjugation of a verb. M. Fujishima translates it by 'declensions,' which must be a mistake.

[2] The five Gatis: gods, men, the brute creation, the departed spirits, and hells.

[3] This passage is by no means easy. 'Letters of the original sound' is as much as to say 'the Sanskrit language.' Kasawara translated by 'the root-sound characters,' but with a query; Fujishima by 'les lettres qui produisent des sons,' but he leaves out 'China,' which is in the text. My rendering follows the commentator Kâ*s*yapa's interpretation.

(Note by I-tsing[1]): Paramârtha-satya, the 'highest truth,' and Sa*m*v*ri*ti-satya, the 'secondary or concealed truth.' The latter is interpreted by the old translators as the 'worldly truth,' but this does not fully express the meaning of the original. The meaning is that the ordinary matters conceal the real state, e.g. as to anything, such as a pitcher, there is earth only in reality, but people think that it is a pitcher from erroneous predication. In case of sound, all musical notes are but sound, yet people wrongly attribute the idea of a song to it. The subjective intellect alone is at work, and there is no distinct object. But ignorance (Avidyâ) covers the intellect, and there follows illusory production of various forms of an object. Such being the case, one does not know what one's own intellect is, and thinks that an object exists outside the mind. For instance, one may think that there is a snake[2], while there is only a rope before one. Thus the idea of snake being erroneously attributed to the rope, the true intellect ceases to shine. The reality or true state thus covered (by a *mistaken attribution*) is termed sa*m*v*ri*ti, 'covering.' The Chinese characters, Fuh-tsŏ[3], a compound expressing the idea of the Sanskrit, Sa*m*v*ri*ti, must be treated as a Karmadhâraya (Descriptive)[4]. These two truths may be termed 'Chên-ti' and 'Fuh-ti[5].'

But the old translators have seldom told us the rules of the Sanskrit language. Those who lately introduced the Sûtras to our notice spoke only of the first seven cases. This is not because of ignorance (*of grammar*), but they have kept silence thinking it useless (*to teach the eighth*), (i.e. the vocative)[6]. I trust that now a thorough study of Sanskrit grammar may clear up many difficulties we encounter whilst engaged in translation. In this hope, I shall, in the following paragraphs, briefly explain some points as an introduction to grammar.

---

[1] This note is left out in M. Fujishima's translation. As all the notes are I-tsing's own, I have paid equal attention to them and added them to the text throughout.

[2] Snake and pitcher are very common examples in Indian philosophy.

[3] 覆俗, 'covered'=common.

[4] He is here applying Sanskrit grammar to the Chinese compounds.

[5] 眞諦, 覆諦, 'Real truth' and 'covered truth.'

[6] Page 174 below.

(Note by I-tsing): Even in the island of Pulo Condore[1] (in the south) and in the country of Sûli (in the north)[2], people praise the Sanskrit Sûtras, how much more then should people of the Divine Land (China), as well as the Celestial Store House (India). teach the real rules of the language! Thus the people of India said in praise (*of China*): 'The wise Mañgusrî is at present in Ping Chou[3], where the people are greatly blessed by his presence. We ought therefore to respect and admire that country, &c.' The whole of their account[4] is too long to be produced.

Grammatical science is called, in Sanskrit, *S*abdavidyâ, one of the five Vidyâs[5]; *S*abda meaning 'voice,' and Vidyâ 'science.' The name for the general secular literature in India is Vyâkara*n*a[6], of which there

---

[1] See p. 10 seq. above. [2] Page 49 above.

[3] It is curious to see that Mañgusrî Kumârabhûta, who is often invoked at the beginning of the Mahâyâna books, is in some way or other connected with China. A tradition that he was then present in China seems to have been prevalent in India. I-tsing twice alludes to him; first, in chap. xxviii, p. 136, he says that people say Mañgusrî is living in China; and again, here, he says that Mañgusrî is at present in Ping Chou (a district in Chi-li, now called Chêng-ten Fu, in China). Pragña, an Indian priest who came to China A. D. 782, is said to have started on hearing that Mañgusrî was then in the East. This is that Pragña who was translating the Mahâyânabuddhi Sha*t*pâramitâ-sûtra (No. 1004), together with King-ching (Adam), the Nestorian missionary and the builder of the famous monument of the Christian mission in China *. Whether Pragña found Mañgusrî in China or not we do not hear. Mañgusrî seems to have been a stranger in India. We have some allusion to this in Burnouf's Lotus, p. 502, App. iii: 'Il est étranger au Népâl, car il vient de Sirsha, ou plus exactement de Çîrcha, "la tête," lieu que le Svayambhû Purâ*n*a et le Commentaire Newari du traité en vingt-cinq stances (Pañ*k*avi*m*satika) comme une montagne de Mahâtchin, sans aucun doute Mahâtchîna, "le pays des grands Tchînas."'

[4] I-tsing seems to be quoting these passages from a book.

[5] The five Vidyâs are (1) *S*abdavidyâ, 'grammar and lexicography,' (2) *S*ilpasthânavidyâ, 'arts,' (3) *K*ikitsâvidyâ, 'medicine,' (4) Hetuvidyâ, 'logic,' and (5) Adhyâtmavidyâ, 'science of the universal soul' or philosophy.

[6] Vyâkara*n*a is really 'grammar.' On the technical meaning of Vyâkara*n*a in Buddhist literature, see Burnouf, Introduction, p. 54. In Hiuen Thsang it is said: 'The books of the Brahmans are called Vyâkara*n*a; they are extensive and are in 1,000,000 *s*lokas,' see Julien, Vie, liv. iii. p. 165.

are about five works, similar to the Five Classics[1] of the Divine Land (China).

I. The Si-t'an-chang (Siddha-composition)[2] for Beginners.

This is also called Siddhirastu[3], signifying 'Be there success' (Ch. lit.

---

[1] Shih-king, Shu-king, Yi-king, Ch'un-ch'iu, and Li Ki, see S. B. E., vols. iii, xvi, xxvii, xxviii, and also Legge's separate edition, She-king, the Book of Poetry (Trübner).

[2] Translators of Chinese texts are wont to translate 'Si-t'an-chang' by 'Siddha-vastu,' and I wondered if I could find an authority for this rendering. Although I have examined many a Chinese text bearing on grammar, yet I have never met a passage showing us that we are justified in translating 'Si-t'an-chang' by 'Siddha-vastu.' Hiuen Thsang gives a book of twelve 'sections' as an elementary book (Julien, Mémoires, liv. ii, p. 73); Fan-i-min-i-chi, book xiv, 17 a, partly quoted by Julien in his note, does not help us much. In the corresponding passage of Hiuen Thsang, the English translator, Mr. Beal, calls the book of twelve 'sections' Siddha-vastu in his note, and erroneously thinks that I-tsing's Si-ti-ra-su-tu is a mistake for Si-ta-va-su-tu. 'Si-ta-va-su-tu,' on the other hand, may be a corruption of Si-ti-ra-su-tu (Siddhir-astu, a common Maṅgala, see the beginning of Hitopadeśa, and Prof. Max Müller, the Kâśikâ, p. 10). We have the following four names:—

(1) 'Si-t'an-chang,' 'the Siddha-composition.' Fujishima, Beal, and even Julien translated it by 'Siddha-vastu.'

(2) 'Twelve Chang' (Hiuen Thsang, liv. ii, p. 73), which may be 'twelve syllabic sections' or 'a syllabary in twelve sections,' probably representing an Akshara book.

(3) 'Siddhir-astu.' This, being at the beginning of the book, may later have become its name.

Of these, 2 must be different from 3, for 3 is in eighteen sections, while 2 is in twelve. But both 2 and 3 are also called Si-t'an-chang, which seems to be a name common to such elementary books. In this Prof. Kielhorn recognises the Mâtṛkâ-viveka (Ind. Ant., xii, 226), and Prof. Bühler, a Siddha-table (on the Brahma alphabet).

[3] The commentator Kâśyapa may help us as to this book. He says: 'This book was lost in China, and the teaching of it can no longer be obtained there; fortunately, in Japan, however, the study of this book is still kept up, but owing to the difficulty and minuteness the learning is a hard task.' He gives Siddhir-astu in Devanâgarî, and adds that Siddham, as a masculine, means 'that which accom-

'complete be good luck!') for so named is the first section of this small (book of) learning.

There are forty-nine letters (of the alphabet)[1] which are combined with one another and arranged in eighteen sections; the total number of syllables is more than 10,000, or more than 300 *s*lokas Generally speaking, each *s*loka contains four feet (pâdas), each foot consisting of eight syllables; each *s*loka has therefore thirty-two syllables.

---

plishes,' and Siddhi, as a feminine, means 'that which is accomplished.' If this had been studied in Japan, we might still have the book in existence. We have a book called 'The Eighteen Sections of the Siddha' in the Bodleian Library collection (Jap. 16), but the composition by a Japanese only dates A. D. 1566. We have another much earlier book called 'Siddha-pi*t*aka' or 'Siddha-kosha,' a work of Annen, whose preface is dated A. D. 880. One part (vol. viii) of this book is devoted to the eighteen sections of the Siddha; it begins with 'O*m* nama*h* Sarva*gñ*âya, Siddhâm' (sic), and its contents are as follows:—

I. The Siddhâm (i. e. vowels), sixteen. All the fourteen vowels with a*m*, a*h*. Ziogon's MS., a copy of which may be seen in the Anecdota Oxoniensia (Aryan Series, vol. i, pt. iii), calls these fourteen (or sixteen) vowels 'Siddhăm.'

II. The body characters (i. e. consonants), thirty-five.

III. The produced characters (i. e. syllables). Here, under this head, come the eighteen sections: (1) Kakha section, (2) Kyakhya section, and so on, till (18) Kkakkhi section.

The eighteen sections contain some 10,000 (6,613 according to my counting) characters, though the book itself says that there are 16,550 characters. These particulars all pretty well agree with I-tsing's statement, i. e. forty-nine letters of the alphabet excepting a*m* and a*h*, eighteen sections, 10,000 or more syllables, 300 or more *s*lokas (this word is often used in counting the number of syllables only). Still it is not safe to conclude anything from these points. I-tsing may be referring to the *S*iva-sûtra. Siddham, more often Siddhâm, in the latest and mistaken sense, means 'alphabet.' In earlier books it is used to denote vowels only; in the copy of the Hôriuji MSS. the first fourteen (vowels) are called 'Siddham,' according to Ziogon's marginal note, though originally it may have been meant for an auspicious invocation. For Siddham, see Max Müller's note, Sukhâvatî-vyûha, Introd., vii, S. B. E., vol. xlix.

[1] After this comes the long extract found in the Siddha-ko*s*a (Jap. 15). I shall give it in my preface.

Again there are long and short *s*lokas; of these it is impossible here to give a minute account.

Children learn this book when they are six years old, and finish it in six months. This is said to have been originally taught by Mahe*s*vara-deva (*S*iva).

II. The Sûtra.

The Sûtra is the foundation of all grammatical science. This name can be translated by 'short aphorism[1],' and signifies that important principles are expounded in an abridged form. It contains 1,000 *s*lokas[2], and is the work of Pâ*n*ini, a very learned scholar of old, who is said to have been inspired and assisted by Mahe*s*vara-deva, and endowed with three eyes; this is generally believed by the Indians of to-day. Children begin to learn the Sûtra when they are eight years old, and can repeat it in eight months' time.

III. The Book on Dhâtu[3].

This consists of 1,000 *s*lokas, and treats particularly of grammatical roots. It is as useful as the above Sûtra.

IV. The Book on the Three Khilas.

Khila means 'waste land,' so called because this (*part of grammar*) may be likened to the way in which a farmer prepares his fields for corn. It may be called a book on the three pieces of waste land. (1) Ash*t*adhâtu[4] consists of 1,000 *s*lokas; (2) Wen-ch'a (Ma*nd*a or

---

[1] More literally, 'What is short in expression and clear in meaning.'

[2] Cf. the published text of Pâ*n*ini (Böhtlingk), which has about 956 *s*lokas.

This Sûtra is what Hiuen Thsang called Pâ*n*ini's Word-book in 1,000 *s*lokas, see Julien, Mémoires, liv. ii, p. 126; in the Life of Hiuen Thsang this book is also mentioned as 'Short Sûtra in 1,000 *s*lokas,' see Julien, Vie, liv. iii, p. 165, 'Il y a un livre, en mille *s*lokas, qui est l'abrégé dû Vyâkara*n*am.'

[3] Cf. Dhâtupâ*th*a, the 'Book on Verbal Roots.' M. Fujishima gives Dhâtuvastu, which is simply imaginary. Ind. Ant., xii, p. 226, note.

[4] The Ash*t*adhâtu, Ma*nd*a, and U*n*âdi are all mentioned in Hiuen Thsang. In Julien's Vie, liv. iii, p. 166, he translates: 'Il existe un Traité des huit limites (terminations) en huit cents *s*lokas.' This refers to the Ash*t*adhâtu of I-tsing. Cf. Loka-dhâtu, Dharma-dhâtu in Chinese. Eight hundred *s*lokas in Hiuen Thsang.

Mu*nd*a[1]) also consists of 1,000 *s*lokas; (3) U*n*âdi[2] too consists of 1,000 *s*lokas.

1. Ash*t*adhâtu. This treats of the seven cases (Sup) and ten Las (ल)[3], and eighteen finals (Tiṅ, 2 × 9 personal terminations).

a. The seven cases[4]. Every noun has seven cases, and every case has three numbers, i.e. singular (Ekava*k*ana), dual (Dviva*k*ana), and plural (Bahuva*k*ana); so every noun has twenty-one forms altogether. Take the word 'man,' for instance. If one man is meant it is 'Purusha*h*,' two men, 'Purushau,' and three (or more) men, 'Purushâ*h*.' These forms of a noun are also distinguished as the heavy and light (probably 'accented and unaccented'), or as pronounced by the open and closed breathings[5] (perhaps 'nouns with an open vowel or those with a closed vowel'). Besides the seven cases there is the eighth,—the

---

[1] Wen-ch'a perhaps represents Sanskrit Ma*n*d*a*, Mu*n*d*a*, Manta, or such like; this is, of course, the Men-tse-kia of Hiuen Thsang, which Julien restores to Sanskrit Ma*n*d*aka as 'nom d'une classe de mots dans Pâ*n*ini' (Vie, liv. iii, p. 166). But it is not used so in Pâ*n*ini, and what is the Ma*n*d*aka or Mu*n*d*aka or Mantaka is not yet certain. In Hiuen Thsang it is said that this book treats of suffixes, though from Julien's rendering this point is not so clear as the original Chinese. 3,000 *s*lokas in Hiuen Thsang. See 'India, what can it teach us?' 1883, p. 344. Can it be Ma*n*d*ûkî *s*ikshâ?

[2] The U*n*âdi-sûtra is said to be 2,500 *s*lokas in Hiuen Thsang against I-tsing's 1,000 *s*lokas.

[3] This refers to Pâ*n*ini's abbreviations La*t* (=present), Laṅ (=imperfect), Li*t* (=perfect), Liṅ, Lu*t*, Luṅ, L*ri*t, L*ri*ṅ, Le*t*, and Lo*t* (for the remaining tenses).

[4] Kâ*s*yapa adds the names of the seven (or eight) cases as follows:—

1. Nom.	N*ri*de*s*a for Nirde*s*a.	5. Abl.	Apâdatti*h* (?).
2. Acc.	Upade*s*a*n*a.	6. Gen.	Svâmibhâvâdi*h* (?).
3. Inst.	Kart*ri*kara*n*a.	7. Loc.	Sa*m*nidhânâdi (?).
4. Dat.	Sa*m*pradadika for -dattika.	8. Voc.	Âmantra*n*a.

See additional note at the end.

[5] These sentences are translated literally, but it is not quite clear what sort of nouns he means. Anyhow the sentences refer to a noun, for I-tsing is writing these under the head of 'the seven cases of a noun' (*a*). The translation by M. Fujishima, 'Dans la conjugation, il y a une double voix (Âtmanepada et Parasmaipada),' is quite inadmissible.

vocative case (Âmantrita), which makes up the eight cases. As the first case has three numbers, so have the remaining ones, the forms of which, being too numerous to be mentioned, are omitted here. A *noun* is called Subanta [1], having (3 × 8) twenty-four (inflected) forms.

β. The ten Las (ल) [2]. There are ten signs with L (*for the verbal tenses*); in conjugating (lit. expressing) a verb, the distinctions of the three times, i.e. past, present, and future, are expressed.

γ. The eighteen finals (Tiṅ). These are the forms of the first, second, and the third person [3] (*of the three numbers of a verb*), showing the differences *of the worthy and unworthy, or this and that* [4]. Thus every verb (*in one tense*) has eighteen different forms which are called Tiṅanta [5].

2. Wen-ch'a (Ma*nd*a or Mu*nd*a) treats of the formation of words by means of combining (a root and a suffix or suffixes). For instance, one of many names for 'tree' in Sanskrit is V*ri*ksha [6]. Thus a name for a thing or a matter is formed by joining (the syllables) together, according to the rules of the Sûtra, which consist of more than twenty verses [7].

3. The U*n*âdi [8]. This is nearly the same as the above (Ma*nd*a), with the exception that what is fully explained in the one is only mentioned briefly in the other, and vice versa.

---

[1] Subanta, i.e. 'that which has "sup" at the end,' 'sup' being the case-ending. See the beginning of this chapter, p. 167, note 1.

[2] See above, p. 173, note 3.

[3] Lit. Uttama, Madhyama, and Prathama.

[4] We should expect here 'Âtmanepada and Parasmaipada.' 'This and that' may be a vague way of expressing the grammatical terms 'Âtmane' and 'Parasmai,' for Chinese has no grammatical terms for these. Still, 'worthy and unworthy' is very strange.

[5] Tiṅanta, 'that which has "Tiṅ" at the end;' 'Tiṅ' being the personal terminations of a verb.

[6] V*ri*ksha is an U*n*âdi word formed from Vra*sk* with affix sa and kit (U*n*âdi, 3, 66).

[7] M. Fujishima translates: 'Le Ma*nd*a (?) est un ensemble de mots. C'est ainsi que l'arbre est l'agglomération d'un nombre plus ou moins grand de fibre et de canaux (le nom de l'arbre en Skt. est V*ri*ksha)' (Journal Asiatique, Nov. 1888, p. 429). I do not think that M. Fujishima understood I-tsing's meaning; he put in brackets that important instance 'V*ri*ksha,' which I-tsing gave in the text. 'On forme ce qu'on appelle un Ma*nd*a,' moreover, is not in the text.

[8] The U*n*âdi is a class of primary suffixes beginning with u.

Boys begin to learn the book on the three Khilas (or 'three pieces of waste land') when they are ten years old, and understand them thoroughly after three years' diligent study.

V. The V*ri*tti-sûtra[1] (Kâ*s*ikâv*ri*tti).

This is a commentary on the foregoing Sûtra (i.e. Pâ*n*ini's Sûtra). There were many commentaries composed in former times, and this is the best of them.

It cites the text of the Sûtra, and explains minutely its manifold meaning, consisting altogether of 18,000 *s*lokas. It exposes the laws of the universe[2], and the regulations of gods and men. Boys of fifteen *begin to study this commentary*, and understand it after five years.

If men of China go to India for study, they have first of all to learn this (*grammatical*) work, then other subjects; if not, their labour will be thrown away. All these books should be learnt by heart. But this, as a rule, applies only to men of high talent, while for those of medium or little ability a different measure (method) must be taken according to their wishes. They should study hard day and night, without letting a moment pass for idle repose. They should be like the Father K'ung (i.e. Confucius), by whose hard study the leather binding of his Yi-king[3] was three times worn away; or imitate Sui-shih[4], who used to read

---

[1] For the Kâ*s*ikâ, see Max Müller's notices in the Academy, Sept. 25 and Oct. 2, 1880; the Indian Antiquary, Dec. 1880; 'India, what can it teach us?' 1883, p. 339.

[2] The 'Laws of all that is within the universe' seems curious as said of a commentary on grammar, and this is not the case with the Kâ*s*ikâ. This sentence can be taken to mean 'the rules of all that is in the Sûtra,' as M. Fujishima does, but not very well. My rendering agrees with that of Kâ*s*yapa and of Kasawara.

[3] According to the Chinese biographer, Ssŭ-ma Ch'ien, while Confucius was reading the Yi-king, i.e. the Book of Divination, the leather binding of this book was worn away three times. See S. B. E., vol. xvi, Introd. i, p. 1.

[4] J. has 歲精 for 歲釋 This seems to refer to the story of Tung Yü of the Wei dynasty, who used to say to his pupils: 'Read a book a hundred times, then you will understand it by yourself.' But I-tsing has Sui-shih instead of Tung Yü. Was Sui-shih another name for him?

a book a hundred times. The hairs of a bull are counted by thousands, but a unicorn has only one horn[1]. The labour or merit of learning the above works is equal to that of proceeding to (the grade of) the Master of Classics ('Ming-king')[2].

This V*ri*tti-sûtra is a work of the learned *G*ayâditya[3]. He was a man of great ability; his literary power was very striking. He understood things which he had heard once, not requiring to be taught twice. He revered the Three Honourable Ones (i.e. Triratna), and constantly performed the meritorious actions. It is now nearly thirty years since his death[4] (A.D. 661–662). After having studied this commentary, students begin to learn composition in prose and verse, and devote themselves to logic (Hetuvidyâ) and metaphysic (Abhi-

---

[1] That is to say, 'Few are clever.'

[2] I follow J., which reads 上明經.

[3] *G*ayâditya, joint author with Vâmana of the Kâ*s*ikâv*ri*tti. The text of the Kâ*s*ikâ was published by Pa*nd*it Bâla*s*âstrî, Professor of Hindu Law in the Benares Sanskrit College (1876, 1878). Bâla*s*âstrî has assigned 1, 2, 5, and 6 to *G*ayâditya, and the rest to Vâmana. The MS. of the Kâ*s*ikâ, discovered by Prof. Bühler in Kashmir (Report, p. 72), assigns the first four to *G*ayâditya, and the last four to Vâmana. For further discussions, see Max Müller's 'India, what can it teach us?' p. 341; Kielhorn's Kâtyâyana and Patañgali. p. 12, note. Cf. Peterson's Second Report, p. 28; Bhandarkar, Second Report, p. 58.

[4] *G*ayâditya's death falls in A.D. 661–662, for the date of I-tsing's composition must be between the 11th month of A.D. 691 and the 5th month of A.D. 692. I-tsing sent this Record through the Venerable Ta-ts'in on the 15th day of the 5th month in the 3rd year of the T'ien-shou period, i.e. A.D. 692. His composition must be earlier than this, but must be later than (the 11th month of) A.D. 691, for he says in chap. xxviii that he spent more than twenty years since his departure from home in (the 11th month of) A.D. 671. Moreover he says, towards the end of the present chapter (xxxiv), that he passed four years in Bhoga, after he came there from India; this statement perfectly agrees with the above dates. Four years before A.D. 691–692 would be A.D. 688–689, and we know that he was in Bhoga in the 6th month of A.D. 689. Further, see my preface. The time of *G*ayâditya's death, A.D. 660, fixed by Prof. Max Müller ('India, &c.,' p. 346), is near enough. M. Fujishima mentions A.D. 650–670, which is the widest limit one can put down (Journal Asiatique, Nov. 1888, p. 430).

dharmakosha). In learning the Nyâya-dvâra-târaka-sâstra[1], they rightly draw inferences (Anumâna); and by studying the Gâtakamâlâ[2] their powers of comprehension increase. Thus instructed by their teachers and instructing others[3] they pass two or three years, generally in the Nâlanda monastery in Central India, or in the country of Valabhî (Walâ) in Western India. These two places are like Chin-ma, Shih-ch'ü, Lung-mên, and Ch'ue-li[4] in China, and there eminent and accomplished men assemble in crowds, discuss possible and impossible doctrines, and after having been assured of the excellence of their opinions by wise men, become far famed for their wisdom. To try the sharpness of their wit (lit. 'sharp point of the sword'), they proceed to the king's court to lay down before it the sharp weapon (of their abilities); there they present their schemes and show their (*political*) talent, seeking to be appointed in the practical government. When they are present in the House of Debate, they raise their seat[5] and seek to prove their wonderful cleverness.

---

[1] This is an Introduction to Logic, composed by Nâgârguna, and translated into Chinese by I-tsing, A. D. 711. See Nanjio's Catal., Nos. 1223, 1224.

[2] See chap. xxxii, p. 162 above, note 8. It was translated by J. S. Speyer.

[3] 函丈傳授, a technical expression for the 'transmission from teacher to pupils.' Lit. 'instructing, with a space of ten feet between the two.'

[4] These are the seats of learning in China.

(1) Chin-ma (金馬門, lit. 'Metal Horse Gate') is the Han-lin or Imperial Academy, so called from a bronze horse placed there by 武帝, Wu-ti, emperor of the Han dynasty (B. C. 142–87).

(2) Shih-ch'ü (石渠) is the library and the place where the Literati employed by Imperial order assemble.

(3) Ch'ue-li (闕里) is in Ch'ü-fu (曲阜), the native place of Confucius, and therefore a centre of the literati. It is in Shan-tung.

(4) Lung-mên (龍門, lit. 'Dragon Gate') is the native place of Ssŭ-ma Ch'ien, the great historiographer, and also the place where Tsze Hsia, a disciple of Confucius, dwelt (in Ho-nan).

[5] 重席, lit. 'to multiply or double the seats,' is not very clear. Kâsyapa says that it was an Indian custom that when a disputant had been beaten, his seat had to be given up to the victorious opponent, who took it, and added it to his own. I-tsing uses this term also in his Memoirs of the Eminent Priests. See Chavannes, p. 127 (cf. note 3).

When they are refuting heretic doctrines all their opponents become tongue-tied and acknowledge themselves undone. Then the sound of their fame makes the five mountains (of India) vibrate, and their renown flows, as it were, over the four borders. They receive grants of land, and are advanced to a high rank; *their famous names are*, as a reward, *written* in white on their lofty gates[1]. After this they can follow whatever occupation they like.

VI. The *K*ûr*n*i.

Next, there is a commentary on the V*ri*tti-sûtra entitled *K*ûr*ni*, containing 24,000 *s*lokas.

It is a work of the learned Patañ*g*ali. This, again, cites the former Sûtras (Pâ*n*ini), explaining the obscure points (lit. 'piercing the skin') and analysing the principles contained in it, and it illustrates the latter commentary (V*ri*tti), clearing up many difficulties (lit. 'removing and breaking the hair and beard of corn')[2].

Advanced scholars learn this in three years. The labour or merit is similar to that of learning the Ch'un-ch'iu and the Yi-king in China.

VII. The Bhart*ri*hari-*s*âstra.

Next, there is the Bhart*ri*hari-*s*âstra. This is the commentary on the foregoing *K*ûr*ni*, and is the work of a great scholar Bhart*ri*hari. It contains 25,000 *s*lokas, and fully treats of the *principles* of human life as well as of grammatical science, and also relates the reasons of the rise and decline of many families. The author was intimately acquainted

---

[1] The Chinese is 賞素高門, and by no means clear. My rendering is only tentative. M. Fujishima translates: 'Alors ceux dont la réputation a été ainsi consacrée reçoivent du roi quelque domaine et ils sont pourvus de plus d'un titre qui leur donne accès à la cour, ou bien le prince leur accorde une certaine récompense; après quoi ces hommes d'élite emploient leur temps à leur volonté' (pp. 431–432).

[2] Here we see that I-tsing is bringing in the meaning of *K*ûr*n*i. *K*ûr*n*i means 'grinding,' and is used as the name of Patañ*g*ali's commentary. This, no doubt, refers to Patañ*g*ali's important work, Mahâbhâshya, and, as Prof. Max Müller points out, Patañ*g*ali is called *K*ûr*n*ikr*i*t, or *K*ûr*n*ikâra, the author of *K*ûr*n*i. See 'India, what can it teach us?' 1883, p. 347. For Mahâbhâshya, see Weber's History, pp. 219–226, and Kielhorn's note, Indian Antiquary, March, 1886, p. 80.

with the doctrine of 'sole knowledge' (Vidyâmâtra), and has skilfully discussed about the Hetu and Udâhara*n*a [1] (the cause and example of logic). This scholar was very famous throughout the five parts of India, and his excellences were known everywhere (lit. 'to the eight quarters'). He believed deeply in the Three Jewels (i.e. Ratnatraya), and diligently meditated on the 'twofold nothingness' (*S*ûnya) [2]. Having desired *to embrace* the excellent Law he became a homeless priest, but overcome by worldly desires he returned again to the laity. In the same manner he became seven times a priest, and seven times returned to the laity. Unless one believes well in the truth of cause and effect, one cannot act strenuously like him [3]. He wrote the following verses, full of self-reproach:

Through the enticement of the world I returned to the laity.
Being free from secular pleasures again I wear the priestly cloak.
How do these two impulses
Play with me as if a child?

He was a contemporary of Dharmapâla [4]. Once when a priest in the monastery, being harassed by worldly desires, he was disposed to return

---

[1] No texts have 'Hetu-vidyâ' here, which is given in M. Fujishima's translation, J. A., 1888, p. 432.

[2] The 'twofold nothingness,' 'both Âtman and Dharma are but an empty show.'

[3] I-tsing seems to admire Bhart*ri*hari's conduct.

[4] All editions but one have 'Dharmapâla,' while one edition has 諸法師, i.e. 'several teachers of the Law,' which seems to be a misprint; for one would not say, 'he was a contemporary of several teachers of the Law,' without having previously mentioned the teachers. I-tsing has never mentioned any 'teachers of the Law' before. Among the grammarians mentioned above by I-tsing (i.e. Pâ*n*ini, *G*ayâditya, and Patañ*g*ali), *G*ayâditya was alone put down as a Buddhist, but not as a priest, and therefore not a 'teacher of the Law.' Thus from the context we are forced to adopt another reading. The Japanese edition, as the result of a collation from many texts, has 'Dharmapâla,' and rejects the solitary reading, 'several teachers of the Law.' There is no doubt whatever as to the correctness of the reading 'Dharmapâla.' M. Fujishima unfortunately had a bad text, and translated it vaguely. After I wrote the above, I found that Kâsyapa's text had 'Dharmapâla, a teacher of the *S*âstra;' this again confirms our reading 'Dharmapâla,' and admits of no more doubt.

to the laity. He remained, however, firm, and asked a student to get a carriage outside the monastery. On being asked the cause, he replied: 'It is the place where one performs meritorious actions, and it is designed for the dwelling of those who keep the moral precepts (*S*îla). Now passion already predominates within me, and I am incapable of adhering to the excellent Law. Such a man as myself should not intrude into an assembly of priests come here from every quarter.'

Then he returned to the position of a lay devotee (Upâsaka), and wearing a white garment continued to exalt and promote the true religion, being still in the monastery. It is forty years since his death (A.D. 651–652)[1].

VIII. The Vâkya-discourse.

In addition there is the Vâkya-discourse (Vâkyapadîya)[2]. This contains 700 *s*lokas, and its commentary portion has 7,000 (*s*lokas). This is also Bhart*ri*hari's work, a treatise on the Inference supported by *the authority* of the sacred teaching, and on Inductive arguments.

IX. The Pei-na.

Next there is Pei-na (probably Sanskrit 'Be*d*a' or 'Ve*d*a')[3]. It contains 3,000 *s*lokas, and its commentary portion is in 14,000 (*s*lokas). The *s*loka portion was composed by Bhart*ri*hari, while the commentary portion is attributed to Dharmapâla, teacher of the *S*âstra. This book fathoms the deep secrets of heaven and earth, and treats of the philosophy of man (lit. 'the essential beauty of the human principles'). A person who has studied so far as this (*book*), is said to have mastered grammatical science, and may be compared to one who has learnt the Nine Classics and all the other authors of China. All the above-mentioned books are studied by both priests and laymen; if not, they cannot gain the fame of the well-informed (lit. 'much heard,' Bahu*s*ruta, or 'Knowing much of the *S*ruti').

---

[1] See note 4, p. 176 above.

[2] Edited by Pa*nd*it Manavalli, Benares, 1884–1887. Ind. Ant., xii, 226.

[3] A work of this name, i.e. Be*d*a-v*ri*tti, is found in Mr. S. K. Bhandarkar's Catalogue of the MSS. in the Deccan College, Bombay, 1888, p. 146, No. 381; Aufrecht's Catalogus Catalogorum, p. 198, under *G*anmâmbhodhi. This was pointed out by Prof. Bühler; see notes at the end.

The priests learn besides all the Vinaya works, and investigate the Sûtras and *S*âstras as well. They oppose the heretics as they would drive beasts (deer) in the middle of a plain, and explain away disputations as boiling water melts frost. In this manner they become famous throughout *G*ambudvîpa (India), receive respect above gods and men, and serving under the Buddha and promoting His doctrine, they lead all the people (to Nirvâ*n*a). Of such persons in every generation only one or two appear. They are to be likened to the sun and moon, or are to be regarded as dragon and elephant [1]. Such were Nâgâr*g*una, Deva, A*s*vaghosha [2] of an early age; Vasubandhu, Asaṅga, Saṅgabhadra, Bhavaviveka in the middle ages; and *G*ina, Dharmapâla, Dharmakîrti, *S*îlabhadra, Si*m*ha*k*andra, Sthiramati*, Gu*n*amati, Pra*gñ*âgupta (not 'Matipâla'), Gu*n*aprabha, *G*inaprabha (or 'Paramaprabha') of late years [3].

None of these great teachers was lacking in any of those kinds of qualities (virtues) above mentioned, secular or sacred. The men free from covetousness, and practising self-content, lived matchless lives. Men of such character have scarcely been found among the heretics or other people.

(Note by I-tsing): Their lives are fully described in the 'Biography of the Ten Virtuous Men (or Bhadantas) of India [4]' (*G*ina—*G*inaprabha).

---

[1] Kâ*s*yapa says that it is not 'Dragon *and* Elephant,' but it is 'Dragon-Elephant,' for the best kind of elephant is called dragon (=Nâga). He seems to be right; so in Pâli, 'ete nâgâ mahâpa*ññ*â' (Samantapâsâdikâ, p. 313).

[2] I-tsing thus gives Nâgâr*g*una first, then Deva and A*s*vaghosha. This order was changed in the French translation of M. Fujishima (Journal Asiatique, Nov.–Dec. 1888, p. 434), as quoted by Prof. Cowell in his Buddha*k*arita (Preface, p. v, Aryan Series, Anecdota Oxoniensia). I-tsing does not place A*s*vaghosha first and before Nâgâr*g*una. As a patriarch of the Northern Buddhism, however, A*s*vaghosha has an earlier place than the rest, for he is the twelfth patriarch, while Nâgâr*g*una and Deva occupy the fourteenth and fifteenth respectively.

[3] The text has 遠='remote' (1), 中='middle' (2), and 近='recent' (3). M. Fujishima has (1) 'dans les temps anciens,' (2) 'dans les temps modernes,' and (3) '*parmi nos contemporains.*' Prof. Wassilief has expressed a doubt about the accuracy of M. Fujishima's rendering in the Zapiski of the Petersburg Archaeological Society, iv, 32. I have no objection to his translation (2), but '*parmi nos contemporains*' (3) is somewhat misleading.

[4] I am trying to find out what this book is, though not yet successful.

Dharmakîrti made a further improvement in Logic (after *G*ina); Gu*n*aprabha popularised for a second time *the study* of the Vinaya-pi*t*aka; Gu*n*amati devoted himself to the school of the Dhyâna (i.e. meditation), and Pra*g*ñâgupta (not Matipâla) fully expounded the true doctrine by refuting all antagonistic views. As invaluable gems display their beautiful colours in the vast and unfathomable ocean where whales alone can live; and as medical herbs present their excellent qualities on the Fragrant Peaks (Gandhamâdana) of immeasurable height, so all kinds of worthy men are found among those who adhere to the Buddha-dharma, which is wide and comprehensive. These men could compose a work on the spot, whatever subject was required. What need then was there for them of fourteen steps[1]? Such men could commit to memory the contents even of two volumes[2], having heard them only once. What, then, was the need to them of reading a book a hundred times (as Sui-shih did, see above, p. 175)?

(Note by I-tsing): A heretic composed 600 *s*lokas, with which he disputed with Dharmapâla[3]; the latter understood and remembered his opponent's verses, hearing them only once before the assembly.

The Brâhmans are regarded throughout the five parts of India as the most honourable (caste). They do not, when they meet in a place, associate with the other three castes, and the mixed classes of the people have still less intercourse with them. The scriptures they revere are the four Vedas, containing about 100,000 verses; 'Veda' hitherto was wrongly transcribed by the Chinese characters 'Wei-t'o;' the meaning of the word is 'clear understanding' or 'knowledge.' The Vedas have been handed down from mouth to mouth, not transcribed on paper or leaves. In every generation there exist some intelligent Brâhmans who can recite the 100,000 verses. In India there are two traditional

---

[1] This probably refers to the story that T'so-chi was commanded by his brother Wên Ti (of Wei) to compose a Chinese poem in seven steps; he did so. The Indian teachers are able to compose verses at once, not wanting an interval of seven steps. But why 'fourteen'?

[2] 'Two volumes;' probably the 600 *s*lokas of the heretic were in two volumes. I-tsing generally means by 'one volume' 300 *s*lokas.

[3] The story is fully told in Hiuen Thsang, Mémoires, v, 288–290.

ways by which one can attain to great intellectual power. Firstly, by repeatedly committing to memory the intellect is developed[1]; secondly, the alphabet fixes one's ideas. By this way, after a practice of ten days or a month, a student feels his thoughts rise like a fountain, and can commit to memory whatever he has once heard [not requiring to be told twice]. This is far from being a myth, for I myself have met such men.

In Eastern India there lived a great man (Mahâsattva) named *K*andra[2] (lit. 'Moon-official,' it may be '*K*andradâsa'), being *like* a Bodhisattva, endowed with great talent. This man was still alive when I, I-tsing, visited that country. One day a person asked him: 'Which is the more injurious, temptation or poison?' He at once answered: 'There is indeed a great difference between the two; poison is injurious only when it is swallowed, whilst the other destroys (burns) one's intellect when only contemplated.'

Kâsyapa-mâtaṅga and Dharmaraksha[3] preached good tidings in the eastern capital Lo (Honan-fu); the fame of Paramârtha[4] reached even to the Southern Ocean (i.e. Nanking), and the venerable Kumâra*g*îva[5] supplied a virtuous pattern to the foreign land (China). Afterwards

---

[1] J. has 覆審生智, which my translation follows. But the other editions have 生覆審智, of which it is difficult to make sense. M. Fujishima tried to translate it from the latter reading, but not very well. J. is decidedly better.

[2] 名日月官 in all editions; if we follow this, it ought to be, 'He was named the Sun-moon' (something like Sûrya*k*andra or Sûryasoma). But as we had before a man called 'Moon-official,' a native of Eastern India, and styled Mahâsattva, we have reason to think that this reading is a misprint for 名曰月官, i.e. 'He was named Moon-official,' and to take this as the same man with 'Moon-official' of chap. xxxii, p. 164. Kâsyapa actually says that a Korean text has 曰 for 日, and therefore the name is 'Moon-official,' but not 'Sun-moon-official.'

[3] These two were the first Indian Buddhists in China; they came to China in A.D. 67, and translated several Sûtras. Nanjio's App. ii, 1 and 2.

[4] Paramârtha came to China A.D. 548, and translated thirty-one works.

[5] Kumâra*g*îva came to China about A.D. 401, and translated fifty Sanskrit books into Chinese. Nanjio's App. ii, 59, 104–105.

the Bhadanta Hiuen Thsang followed out his professorial career in his own country. In this way, both in the past and present, have teachers spread far and wide the light of Buddhism (or 'the Sun of the Buddha').

To those who learn the doctrines of 'existence' and 'non-existence' the Tripi*t*aka itself will be their Master, while for those who practise the Dhyâna (meditation) and Pra*gñ*â (wisdom) the seven Bodhi-aṅgas[1] will be a guide.

The following are the (most distinguished) teachers who now live in the West. *G*ñâna*k*andra, a master of the Law, lives in the monastery Tila*dh*a (in Magadha)[2]; in the Nâlanda monastery, Ratnasi*m*ha; in Eastern India, Divâkaramitra[3]; and in the southernmost district, Tathâgatagarbha. In *S*rîbho*g*a[4] of the Southern Sea resides *S*âkyakîrti, who travelled all through the five countries of India in order to learn, and is at present in *S*rîbho*g*a (in Sumatra).

All these men are equally renowned for their brilliant character, equal to the ancients, and anxious to follow in the steps of the Sages. When they have understood the arguments of Hetuvidyâ (logic), they aspire to be like *G*ina (the great reformer of logic); while tasting the doctrine of Yogâ*k*ârya they zealously search into the theory of Asaṅga.

When they discourse on the 'non-existence' they cleverly imitate Nâgâr*g*una; whilst when treating of the 'existence' they thoroughly fathom the teaching of Saṅghabhadra. I, I-tsing, used to converse with these teachers so intimately that I was able to receive invaluable instruction personally from them (lit. 'I came closely to their seats and desks and received and enjoyed their admirable words').

---

[1] The seven constituents of Bodhi, i. e. recollection, investigation, energy, joy, calmness, contemplation, and equanimity. See Childers, s. v. bo*gg*h*a*ṅgo; Burnouf, Lotus, 796; Kasawara, Dharma-sa*m*graha, § 49; Mahâvyutpatti, § 39.

[2] Tila*dh*a monastery is Tila*dh*aka of Hiuen Thsang (Julien, Mémoires, viii, 440, and Vie, iv, 211). I-tsing mentions this monastery as two yo*g*anas distant from Nâlanda in his Memoirs (see Chavannes, p. 146, note). Modern Tillâra, W. of Nâlanda. Cf. Cunningham, Ancient Geography of India, i, 456.

[3] A Divâkaramitra is referred to as a Buddhist Bhadanta in the Harsha*k*arita, the Kashmir edition, pp. 488 and 497. M. Fujishima gives *S*akramitra by mistake. See Julien, Méthode pour Déchiffrer les Noms Sanscrits, p. 70.

[4] For *S*rîbho*g*a, see my note, pp. 143–144.

I have always been very glad that I had the opportunity of acquiring knowledge from them personally which I should otherwise never have possessed, and that I could refresh my memory of past study by comparing old *notes* with new ones.

It is my only desire to receive the light handed down from time to time, and my satisfaction is in the fact that I have learned the Law [in the morning], and my wish is to dispel my hundred doubts rising as dust, and (if my wish be fulfilled in the morning) I shall not regret dying at eventide[1].

While still gathering a few gems left behind on the Vulture Peak, I picked up some very choice ones; when searching for jewels deposited in the Dragon River (Nâganadî=*A*giravatî), I have obtained some excellent ones. Through the unseen help of the Three Jewels and by the far-reaching influence of the royal favour, I was enabled at last to turn the course of my travel eastward, sailed from Tâmralipti[2], and arrived at *S*rîbhoga[3].

Here I have remained over four years, and, employing my time in various ways, have not yet determined to leave this place for my native country.

CHAPTER XXXV.

THE RULE AS TO HAIR.

THROUGHOUT the five divisions of India no one with unshaven head (lit. 'with long hair') may take all the final vows (lit. 'may receive the complete precepts'), nor is there any precedent for this in the Vinaya, nor did such a custom ever exist of old. For if a priest conform to the same habits as a layman, he cannot abstain from faults. If one cannot carry out the precepts, it is useless to vow to observe them.

Therefore if a man's mind be set on the priesthood, he should demand to be shaved, wear the coloured cloak, purify his thoughts, and make the

---

[1] Cf. Confucius's saying, 朝聞道夕死可矣, in the Lun-yü.—Legge, Analects, p. 168 (Clarendon Press, 1893).

[2] An ancient trading-port in E. India, near the mouth of the Hooghly.

[3] See above, pp. 143–144, note 3.

'Final Liberation' his aim. He should observe the five, and then the ten precepts, without fail. He who vowed to observe all the precepts with a perfect mind should practise them in accordance with the Vinaya texts.

After having learnt the Yogâ*k*ârya-*s*âstra (No. 1170), he ought to study thoroughly Asaṅga's eight *S*âstras.

(Note by I-tsing): The eight *S*âstras are—

1. Vidyâmâtra-vi*m*s*a*ti(-gâthâ)-*s*âstra or Vidyâmâtrasiddhi (by Vasubandhu) (Nanjio's Catalogue of Chinese Tripi*t*aka, No. 1240).
2. Vidyâmâtrasiddhi-trida*s*a-*s*âstra-kârikâ (by Vasubandhu) (Nanjio's Catal., No. 1215).
3. Mahâyânasamparigraha-*s*âstramûla (by Asaṅga) (Nanjio's Catal., Nos. 1183, 1184, 1247).
4. Abhidharma(-saṅgîti)-*s*âstra (by Asaṅga) (Nanjio's Catal., No. 1199; Commentary by Sthitamati, No. 1178).
5. Madhyântavibhâga-*s*âstra (by Vasubandhu) (Nanjio's Catal., Nos. 1244, 1248).
6. Nidâna-*s*âstra (Nos. 1227, 1314 by Ullaṅgha, No. 1211 by *S*uddhamati).
7. Sûtrâlaṅkâra-*t*ikâ (by Asaṅga, No. 1190).
8. Karmasiddha-*s*âstra (by Vasubandhu, Nos. 1221, 1222).

Although there are some works by Vasubandhu among the above-mentioned *S*âstras, yet the success (*in the Yoga system*) is assigned to Asaṅga (*and thus the books of Vasubandhu are included among Asaṅga's*).

When a priest wishes to distinguish himself in the study of Logic he should thoroughly understand *G*ina's eight *S*âstras.

(Note by I-tsing): These are—

1. The *S*âstra on the meditation on the Three Worlds (not found).
2. Sarvalaksha*n*adhyâna-*s*âstra (kârikâ) (by *G*ina) (Nanjio's Catal., No. 1229).
3. The *S*âstra on the meditation on the object (by *G*ina). Probably Âlambanapratyayadhyâna-*s*âstra (Nanjio's Catal., No. 1173).
4. The *S*âstra on the Gate of the Cause (Hetudvâra) (not found).
5. The *S*âstra on the gate of the resembling cause (not found).
6. The Nyâyadvâra(târaka)-*s*âstra (by Nâgâr*g*una) (Nanjio's Catal., Nos. 1223, 1224).

7. Pragñapti-hetu-sangraha(?)-sâstra (by Gina) (Nanjio, No. 1228).
8. The Sâstra on the grouped inferences (not found).

While studying the Abhidharma (metaphysics) he must read through the six Pâdas [1], and while learning the Âgamas [2] he must entirely investigate the *principles of the* four Classes (Nikâya). When these have all been mastered, the priest will be able successfully to combat heretics and disputants, and by expounding the truths of the religion to save all. He teaches others with such zeal that he is unconscious of fatigue. He exercises his mind in contemplating the 'Two-fold Nothingness.' He calms his heart by means of the 'eight Noble Paths,' attentively engages himself in the 'four Meditations,' and strictly observes the rules of the 'seven groups' (Skandhas) [3].

Those who pass their life in this manner are of high rank.

There are those who, though they cannot act as the above, but must remain at home, yet are not bound much by home affairs. They live

---

[1] These are six different treatises on Metaphysics, which all belong to the Sarvâstivâda School, Nos. 1276, 1277, 1281, 1282, 1296, and 1317.

[2] These are the Âgamas (a division of the Tripitaka):—

(1) Dîrghâgama (30 Sûtras, cf. Dîghanikâya, 34 suttas).
(2) Madhyamâgama (222 Sûtras, cf. Maggimanik., 152 suttas).
(3) Samyuktâgama (Samyuttanikâya, 7760 suttantas).
(4) Ekottarâgama (Anguttaranikâya, 9557 suttantas).

There are five 'Nikâyas' in Pâli, the fifth being Khuddakanikâya (15 sections).

[3] The seven Skandhas contain certain priestly offences:—

(1) Pârâgika offence is that which involves expulsion.
(2) Sanghâdisesha offences are thirteen in number, and require suspension and penance, but do not involve expulsion.
(3) Sthûlâtyaya is a grave offence (Thullakkaya).
(4) Prâyaskittika offences are ninety-two in number, and require confession and absolution (Pâkittiya).
(5) Naisargika are thirty in number. They are the Prâyaskittika sins, accompanied with forfeiture (Nissaggiya).
(6) Dushkrita, 'sinful acts' (Dukkata).
(7) Durbhâshita, 'evil speaking' (Dubbhâsita).

See Âpattikhandho, Childers' Pâli Dictionary, Kullavagga IX, 3, 3.

uprightly and are desirous to quit *worldly cares*. If they are asked for anything, they offer it to the deserving.

They wear very simple dress, only desiring decency. They hold firmly the eight precepts, and remain diligent throughout their lives.

(Note by I-tsing): The eight precepts are—(1) not killing, (2) not stealing, (3) not committing adultery, (4) not telling a lie, (5) not drinking an intoxicating beverage, (6) neither taking pleasure in music, nor wearing garlands and anointing with perfumes, (7) not using a high and wide couch, and (8) not taking food at forbidden hours.

They trust in, and respect the Three Honourable Ones (i.e. the Three Jewels), and devoting themselves to the attainment of Nirvâ*n*a (or aiming at Nirvâ*n*a) they concentrate their thoughts on it.

These are the persons next in order (*to the high classes*).

There are those who, remaining within the confines (*of worldly affairs*), support their wives and bring up their children. They honour those superior to themselves most respectfully, and have mercy on those that are lower than themselves.

They receive and keep the five precepts, and always observe the four fasting-days (Upavasatha).

(Note by I-tsing): The four fasting-days are—

(*a*) In the dark half of the moon (the moonless half, Kâlapaksha), the 8th and 14th (in Pâli, also 'A*tth*amî' and '*K*âtuddasî'), or the 10th and 15th.

(*b*) In the bright half of the moon (the moonlit half, *S*ukrapaksha), the 8th and 15th (in Pâli, also 'A*tth*amî' and 'Pañ*k*adasî').

On these days one should receive the eight precepts, and *the rite* is called the 'Holy Practice.' If one receive only the eighth precept without the other seven ('not eating except at a prescribed time' is the eighth precept, see above), one's merit (lit. 'cause of happiness') is very small. The purpose of the eighth precept is to prevent the other seven precepts' being transgressed, but not to keep one's stomach hungry in vain.

They behave toward others with sympathy, and carefully restrain themselves. They pursue some faultless occupation, and pay tribute to the authorities. Such are also regarded as good men.

(Note by I-tsing): By faultless occupation is meant trading, because it does not injure life. It is customary at present in India to regard traders as more honourable than farmers; this is because agriculture injures the life of many insects. In cultivating silkworms or in slaughtering animals one contracts a great cause of suffering.

Many millions of lives will be injured during the whole year. If accustomed to such practice for a long time, though without considering it faulty, one will suffer the retribution in numberless ways in future births. He who does not follow such occupation is called the 'faultless.'

But there are graceless people who, spending their lives in an aimless manner, do not know the three Refuges (i. e. Refuge to the Buddha, the Dharma and the Priesthood), and do not observe a single precept during the whole of their lives; how can these men who do not understand that Nirvâ*n*a is a state of perfect tranquillity be aware that their future births will revolve like a wheel?

Under this misapprehension they commit sin after sin. Such persons form the lowest class.

CHAPTER XXXVI.

THE ARRANGEMENT OF AFFAIRS AFTER DEATH.

THERE is a full description in the Vinaya of the manner of arranging the affairs of a deceased Bhikshu. I shall here briefly cite the most important points. First of all an inquiry should be made as to whether there are any debts, whether the deceased has left a will, and also if any one nursed him while ill. *If there be such*, the property must be distributed in accordance with the law. Any property remaining must be suitably divided.

This is a verse from the Udâna (a division of the Tripi*t*aka)[1]:

'Lands, houses, shops, bed-gear,
Copper, iron, leather, razors, jars,

---

[1] See Max Müller, Dhammapada, S. B. E., vol. x, p. ix, and Childers, s. v. Tipi*t*aka*m*. About twenty lines beginning with this Udâna are found agreeing verbatim in the Vinaya-saṅgraha (Nanjio's Catal., No. 1127), vol. vii, chap. xxix, p. 38, in the Japanese edition (Bodl. Jap. 65).

Clothes, rods, cattle, drink, food,
Medicine, couches, the three kinds of
Precious things, gold, silver, &c.,
Various things made or unmade;
These should be classed as divisible
or indivisible, according to their character.
This is what was ordained by the World-honoured Buddha.'

The following is the specification:—Lands, houses, shops, bed-gear, woollen seats, and iron or copper implements are not distributable. Among those last named, however, large or small iron bowls, small copper bowls, door-keys, needles, gimlets, razors, knives, iron ladles, braziers, axes, chisels, &c., together with their bags; earthen utensils, i.e. bowls, smaller bowls, ku*nd*ikas (pitchers) for drinking and for cleansing water, oil-pots and water-basins are distributable; the rest are not. Wooden and bamboo implements, leather bedding, shaving things; male and female servants; liquor, food, corn; lands and houses, are all to be made the property of the priests assembling from every quarter. Among these, things which are movable are to be kept in storehouses, and to be used by the assembly. Lands, houses, village-gardens, buildings, which are immovable, become also the property of the assembly. If there remain clothes or anything wearable, whether cloaks, bathing-shirts, dyed or undyed, or waterproofs, pots, slippers, or shoes, they are to be distributed on the spot to the priests then assembled. A garment which has one pair of sleeves cannot be divided, but a white garment which is made double may be divided as one likes.

Long rods are to be used as banner-staffs before the *G*âmbûnada-var*n*a image *of the Buddha*. Slender ones are to be given to the Bhikshus, to be used as metal staffs.

(Note by I-tsing): The origin of the image called '*G*âmbûnadavar*n*a' is mentioned in the Vinaya. When the Buddha was not among the assembly, the members of the order were not very reverential; this circumstance caused the rich Anâthapi*nd*ada to ask the Buddha, saying, 'I wish to make a *G*âmbûnadavar*n*a (golden coloured) image of thee, to put in front of the Assembly.' The Great Master allowed him to make this image.

The metal staff is in Sanskrit 'Khakkhara[1],' representing the sound (*produced by the staff, when carried in walking*). The old translator translated it by 'metal staff,' for the sound is produced by metal; you can call it 'staff-metal' if you like. As I myself saw, the staff used in the West (India) has an iron circle fixed on the top of it; the diameter of the circle is two or three inches, and at its centre there stands a tube-like metal butt four or five aṅgulas in length. The stick itself is made of wood, either rough or smooth, its length reaching to a man's eyebrows. About two inches down *from the top circle* there is fastened an iron chain, the rings of which are either round or elliptic, and are made by bending a wire and joining its ends in another ring, each being made as large as you can put your thumb through. Six or eight of these chains are fastened through the top circle. These chains are of iron or copper. The object of (using) such a staff is to keep off cows or dogs while collecting alms in *the village*. It is not necessary to think of carrying it so as to tire one's arms. Moreover, some *foolishly* make the staff all of iron, and place on the top four iron circles. It is very heavy and difficult for an ordinary person to carry about. This is not in accordance with the original rules.

Quadrupeds, elephants, horses, mules, asses for riding, are to be offered to the Royal Household. Bulls and sheep should not be distributed, but belong to the whole assembly. Such goods as helmets, coats of arms, &c., are also to be sent to the Royal Household. Miscellaneous weapons, after having been made into needles, gimlets, knives, or heads for metal staffs, are distributed among the priests then assembled. If not sufficient for all the priests, the elders alone may take them.

Things such as nets are made into network for windows. Paints of good quality, such as yellow, vermillion, azure, blue, green, are sent to the temple to be used for colouring images and the ornaments around.

White and red earth and inferior blue substances are distributed to the assembled priests. The wine if it is nearly sour is to be buried in the ground, and when it has turned into vinegar the priests may use it.

---

[1] This name seems to have been used as meaning a staff carried by Buddhists, though not a proper Sanskrit word. See Mahâvyutpatti, 268; H. Th. ii, 509. Cf. 'Kattara-da*n*d*a,' Mahâvagga V, 6, 2; *K*ullavagga VIII, 6, 3, and *G*âtaka i, 9.

But if it remain sweet it must be thrown away, but it must not be sold. For the Buddha has said: 'Ye Bhikshus, who have been ordained by me, must not give wine to others, nor take it yourselves. Do not put wine into your mouths, even so little as a drop fallen from the point of a reed.' If one eat corn-flour mixed with wine, or soup made from the dregs of wine, one is guilty. One must not be doubtful on this point, for there is a prohibitive rule about this in the Vinaya. I know that the monastery of the Holy Rock[1] (in China) uses water for mixing corn-flour. The former residents of this monastery had sense enough to avoid using wine for this purpose, thereby incurring no guilt.

Medical substances are to be kept in a consecrated (lit. 'pure') store, to be supplied to sick persons when needed. Precious stones, gems, and the like are divided into two portions, one being devoted to pious objects (Dhammika), the other to the priests' own use (Saṅghika). The former portion is spent in copying the scriptures and in building or decorating the 'Lion Seat.' The other portion is distributed to the priests who are present. Things such as chairs inlaid with jewels are to be sold, and (the receipts) are to be given to those present.

Wooden chairs are to be made common property[2]. But the scriptures and their commentaries should not be parted with, but be kept in a library to be read by the members of the Order[2]. Non-Buddhistic books are to be sold, and (the money acquired) should be distributed among the priests then resident. If deeds and contracts are payable at once, (the money is) to be realised and to be immediately distributed; if they are not payable at once, the deeds should be kept in the treasury, and when they fall due, (the money) should be devoted to the use of the Assembly[2]. Gold, silver, wrought or unwrought goods, shells (cowrie, Kapardaka), and coins, are divided into three portions, for the Buddha, for Religion (Dharma), and for the priesthood (Saṅgha). The portion for the Buddha is spent in repairing the temple, stûpas that contain holy hair or nails, and other ruins.

The portion belonging to Religion is used for copying the scriptures and building or decorating the 'Lion Seat.' Another portion belonging to the Assembly is distributed to the resident priests.

---

[1] 靈巖, 'Ling-yen,' above, p. 23, note 1.

[2] Of the *K*atuddisasaṅgha.

The six Requisites[1] of a priest are to be given to the sick nurse. The fragmentary articles remaining are to be suitably divided.

A full account of this subject is found in the larger Vinaya.

CHAPTER XXXVII.

THE USE OF THE COMMON PROPERTY OF THE SAṄGHA.

In all the Indian monasteries the clothing of a Bhikshu is supplied out (of the common funds) of the resident priests. The produce of the farms and gardens, and the profits arising from trees and fruits, are distributed annually in shares to cover the cost of clothing. Here is a question. Seeing that the rice or any other food in possession of the deceased becomes the property of the church, how can an individual priest obtain his share from what has become church property? We reply thus: the giver presents villages or fields in order to maintain the priests in residence. Is it reasonable then that he who gives food should wish the recipient to live without clothing? Further, if we examine the actual management (of daily affairs), a householder gives clothing to one who serves him. Why should the head of the community refuse a similar gift? Therefore it is lawful to supply clothing as well as food.

Such is the general opinion of the priests of India, though the Vinaya rules are sometimes silent, sometimes explicit on this point. The Indian monasteries possess special allotments of land, from the produce of which the clothing of the priests is to be supplied. The same is the case in *some of* the Chinese temples. By virtue of the original intention of the giver of the field, any one (living) in the monastery, be he priest or layman, can obtain gifts from the same source. But no one will be at fault if he do not partake of the food. A gift to the church, whether a field, or house, or some insignificant thing, is understood to be given for the clothing and food of the priests. There is no doubt whatever on this point. If the original intention of the benefactor was unreservedly charitable, then the benefits of the gift can be considered as conferred upon all, though presented to the church only.

---

[1] See chap. x, p. 54 above.

Thus the church can make use of the benefaction as it likes, without any fault, as long as it carries out the original intention of the giver.

But in China, an individual generally cannot get clothing from the church property, and is thus obliged to provide for this necessity, thereby neglecting his proper function. Not that one who obtains his food and clothing should live without any bodily or mental labour, but it is a fact that one can be much freer, if one lives in the monastery engaged simply in meditation and worship, without needing to take thought about procuring clothes and food.

With nothing but the three garments (made of rags) from a Pâ*m*su (dust-heap), begging food from house to house, living under the trees in an Ara*n*ya (forest), one may lead the holy life of an ascetic[1]. Inward meditation and knowledge increase in proportion as one's aim is firmly fixed on reaching the Path to Final Liberation (Moksha). Love and compassion being shown outwardly, one's mind is directed to the Ford of Salvation. A life ended in this way is the highest. The priestly garments must be supplied out of the common property of the resident priests, and anything such as bed-clothes, &c., must be equally distributed, but not be given to an individual only; thus church property should be guarded by them more carefully than their own possessions. If there be several contributions, the church should give away *in charity* the greater and keep the smaller. This is in accordance with the noble teaching of the Buddha, for he expressly said: 'If you use things properly, there will not be any fault found in you. You will be able to maintain yourselves sufficiently, and be free from the trouble and cost of arduously seeking a *livelihood*.'

It is unseemly for a monastery to have great wealth, granaries full of rotten corn, many servants, male and female, money and treasures hoarded in the treasury, without using any of these things, while all the members are suffering from poverty. The wise should always act according to the proper judgement of what is right or wrong.

There are some monasteries which do not supply food for the residents, but divide everything among them, and make them provide their

---

[1] Such a life of the old Buddhists still existed in I-tsing's time, see p. 50 above. The life is in accordance with the Dhûtâṅgas, see p. 56, note, above.

own food, and such monasteries do not admit a stranger to reside there. Thus those who come from any quarter are induced by these monasteries themselves to lead an unlawful life (or, 'the authorities of such a house would be responsible for the unlawful manner of life of all the priests coming in contact with them'). Evil retribution would inevitably overtake those who cause such an unlawful practice, and no one but they themselves would suffer future consequences.

CHAPTER XXXVIII.

THE BURNING OF THE BODY IS UNLAWFUL.

FOR the Buddhist mendicants there is but one method of study to pursue. Those who are but beginners in the study are intent on becoming brave and bright, while ignorant of their Sacred Books. They follow in the steps of those who considered the burning of fingers as a devout deed, and the destroying of their body by fire as a blessed action. They follow their own inclination, thinking in their heart such actions to be right. True, there are some references to such deeds in the Sûtras, but they are meant for laymen, for it is right for them to offer, not only any treasures in their possession, but even their own life, when needed. Therefore it is often said in the Sûtra: 'If a person incline his heart to the Law,' &c., and thus it does not refer to the mendicants themselves. Why? The homeless mendicants should strictly confine themselves to the rules of the Vinaya. If they are not guilty of transgressing them, they are acting in conformity with the Sûtra. If there be any transgression of the precepts, their obedience is at fault.

As priests, they should not even destroy one stalk of grass, though the temple be covered with it. They should not steal even a grain of rice, though they be starving in a lonely field. But it is right for a layman, such as he who is known by the name of 'Lovely-to-see-for-All-Beings[1],' to offer food by roasting his own arm. The Bodhisattva

[1] In Sanskrit, Sarvasattvapriyadarsana, who is constantly addressed as 'young man of good family.' The story of burning his body, &c., is told in Saddharmapundarîka XXII, in which Prof. Kern recognises a Buddhist version of the myth of the phoenix, see S. B. E., vol. xxi, p. 378 seq.

gave away his male and female offspring*, but a mendicant need not look for a male and female in order to give away. The Mahâsattva offered his own eyes and body*, but a Bhikshu need not do so. Hsien Yü (*Ri*shi-nandita?)[1] surrendered his life, but this is not a precedent to be followed by a Vinaya student. King Maitrîbala sacrificed himself, but the mendicant ought not to follow his example. I hear of late that the youths (of China or India, probably the former) bravely devoting themselves to the practice of the Law, consider the burning of the body a means of attaining Buddhahood, and abandon their lives one after another.

This should not be. Why? It is difficult to obtain the state of human life after a long period of transmigration. Though born in a human form a thousand times, one may yet not have wisdom, nor hear the seven Bodhyaṅgas[2], nor meet the Three Honourable Ones (Ratnatraya). Now we are lodged in an excellent place, and have embraced an admirable teaching. It is but vain to give up our insignificant body after having studied but a few *s*lokas of the Sûtra. How can we think much of such a worthless offer, so soon after we have begun to meditate on 'impermanence?'

We ought strictly to observe the precepts, requiting the four kinds of benefits[3] conferred upon us, and engage ourselves in meditation in order to save the three classes of beings[4]. We must feel how great a danger lies even in a small fault, just as if one were holding an air-tight bag (in) swimming across a bottomless sea. We must be strictly on our guard while practising to gain wisdom, just as in putting the spurs into a running horse on thin ice.

Thus conducting ourselves and helped by good friends, our mind will be stable till the last moment of our life. With resolutions rightly formed, we should look forward to meeting the coming Buddha Maitreya. If

---

[1] According to Kâ*s*yapa this was an epithet of Maitrîbala, whose *G*âtaka is found in the *G*âtakamâlâ (8th). See Kern's edition, p. 41.

[2] See Childers, s. v. Bog*gh*aṅgo.

[3] The benefits conferred by the Buddha (1), king (2), parents (3), and benefactors (4).

[4] The world of passion (Kâmaloka); that of form (Rûpaloka); that without form (Arûpaloka), i.e. Tribhava.

we wish to gain the 'lesser fruition' (of the Hînayâna), we may proceed to pursue it through the eight grades of sanctification [1]. But if we learn to follow the course of the 'greater fruition' (of the Mahâyâna), we must try to accomplish our work through the three Asaṅkhya Kalpas.

I have never heard any reason why we should rashly give up our life. The guilt of suicide is next to the breach of the prohibitions in the first class [2]. If we carefully examine the Vinaya texts, we never see any passage allowing suicide.

We learn from the Buddha's own words the important method of controlling our sensations. What use is it to burn our body in destroying our passions? The Buddha did not allow even castration, but on the other hand he himself encouraged the releasing of fishes in a pond. The Buddha's word forbids us to transgress a weighty precept and follow our own will. We are disregarding his noble teaching if we take refuge in such a practice as burning our bodies. But we are not discussing concerning those who wish to follow the practice of a Bodhisattva without receiving the Vinaya rules at all, and to sacrifice themselves for the good of others.

CHAPTER XXXIX.

THE BYSTANDERS BECOME GUILTY.

AN action such as burning the body is regarded usually as the mode of showing inward sincerity. Two or three intimate friends combine and make an agreement among themselves to instigate the young students to destroy their lives. Those who first perish in this way are guilty of the Sthûla-offence [3], and those who later follow their example are liable to the Pârâgika-offence [4], for they wish to obtain a reward whilst disobeying the law (prohibiting suicide), and firmly adhere to their ill-formed resolution, seeking death by transgressing the precepts. Such men have never studied the Buddha's doctrine. If fellow-students encourage this practice they incur the guilt (that cannot be atoned for),

---

[1] See Childers, Ariyapuggalo.

[2] The first are the Pârâgika-offences, see Childers, s. v.

[3] The grave offences, see Childers, s. v. Thûlo; p. 187 above.

[4] The first and worst group of offences, see Childers, s. v.

just as when the eye of a needle is knocked off (it can never be restored). Those who say to one: 'Oh, why do you not throw yourself into the fire?' commit the sin (which cannot be undone), just as a broken stone cannot be united. One has to be careful of this point. The proverb says: 'It is better to requite the favours of others than to destroy one's own life, and it is better to build up character than to defame one's name.' It was the Bodhisattva's work of salvation to offer his body to a hungry tiger[1]. It is not seemly for a *S*rama*n*a to cut the flesh from his body in order to give it away instead of a living pigeon[1]. It is not in our power to imitate a Bodhisattva. I have roughly stated what is right or wrong according to the Tripi*t*aka. The wise should be fully aware of what is the proper practice to follow.

In the River Ganges many men drown themselves every day. On the hill of Buddhagayâ too there are not unfrequently cases of suicide. Some starve themselves and eat nothing. Others climb up trees and throw themselves down.

The World-honoured One judged these misled men to be heretics. Some intentionally destroy their manhood and become eunuchs.

These actions are entirely out of harmony with the Vinaya Canon. Even those who consider such practices to be wrong are afraid of sinning if they prevent such actions. But if one destroy life in such a way, the great object of one's existence is lost.

That is why the Buddha prohibited it. The superior priests and wise teachers never acted in any such harmful way as the above-mentioned. I will now state in the following chapter the traditions handed down by the virtuous men of old.

CHAPTER XL.

SUCH ACTIONS WERE NOT PRACTISED BY THE VIRTUOUS OF OLD.

NOW as to my teachers, my Upâdhyâya (i.e. teacher in reading) was the venerable Shan-yü[2] (a Chinese priest), and my Karmâ*k*ârya (i.e. teacher in discipline) was Hui-hsi[3], Master of Dhyâna (i.e. meditation). After the seventh year of my age I had the opportunity of

---

[1] See notes at the end. [2] 善遇. [3] 慧習. J. has 慧智.

waiting on them. Both of them were teachers of great virtue who lived in the monastery Shên-t'ung, built (A.D. 396) by the Dhyâna-master, (Sêng-) Lang, a sage of the Chin-yü Valley of T'ai Shan. Shan-yü was a native of Teh Chou, and Hui-hsi, of Pei Chou[1]. Both thought that the solitary forest life, though good for one's self, had little power to benefit others, and came to P'ing-lin, where, according to rule, they took up their abode in the temple of 'Earth-Cave' (T'u-k'u), overlooking the clear stream named 'Stooping Tiger[2].' The temple is situated about forty Chinese miles west of the capital of Ch'i Chou (in Shan-tung).

They were in the habit of preparing an unlimited store of food, by which means they could freely supply the people or make offerings to the Buddhas. Whatever gifts they received, they gave away freely and willingly. It may be said of them that their Four Vows (Pra*n*idhâna)[3] were limitless as heaven and earth, and the salvation they preached to the people by the Four Elements of Popularity (Saṅgraha-vastu[4]) was very liberal, and those who were saved by them were innumerable as the sand or dust. They dutifully built temples wherein to live, and did many meritorious deeds. Now I shall briefly state the seven virtues of my Upâdhyâya, Shan-yü.

1. The Wide Learning of my Teacher.

Besides his deep insight into the Tripi*t*aka, he was well read in very many authors. He was equally learned in both Confucianism and Buddhism, and skilled in all the six arts of the Confucian school. He was well versed in the Sciences of Astronomy, Geography, and Mathematics, the Arts of Divination, and the Knowledge of the Calendar; thus he could explore the secret of anything, had he cared to do so. How vast in him was the Ocean of Wisdom, with its ever-flowing tide! How brilliant was his garden of literature, with its ever-blooming flowers!

---

[1] 俗緣在於德貝二州矣, lit. 'The worldly connexions of these priests were respectively in the provinces Teh and Pei,' which is another way of saying 'they were born there.' Other editions except J. have an unintelligible reading here. Teh Chou is Chi-nan in Shan-tung.

[2] 俯虎淸澗, but J. has 枕 for 虎. [3] 四弘誓願.

[4] See Childers, Saṅgaho: Mahâvyutp., § 31.

The works of his own production, the pronouncing dictionary of the Tripi*t*aka, and several word-books have been handed down to later generations. He used to say, 'There is no character *in* Chinese which I do not know' (more lit. 'It is not a character, if I do not know it').

2. The Immense Ability of my Teacher.

My teacher was skilled in writing according to the styles of the 'Seal Character,' Chuan and Chou[1], and also the styles of Chung and Chang[2]. He had a good ear for the musical notes of string- and wind-instruments, as in the case of Tzŭ Ch'i[3], who could tell whether *the lute of Yü Po-ya* expressed a peak or a stream. He could use the axe as skilfully as the artisan Shih removes a (little bit of) mud like a (fly's) wing[4]. Thus it may be said of him that a wise man is not a mere utensil[5] (as we should say, 'he is not a one-stringed instrument').

3. My Teacher's Intelligence.

When my teacher was studying the Sûtra of the Great Decease (Mahâparinirvâ*n*a-sûtra), he read it through in one day. When he re-read the same for the first time he finished the whole in four months, carefully testing the hidden doctrine contained in it, and earnestly searching

---

[1] (1) 篆, Chuan, the 'seal' character, is said to have existed in two styles, the greater and the smaller. The 'greater seal' is said to have been invented about B.C. 800 by Shih-chou, a minister of the Chou dynasty, while the 'smaller seal' style is assigned to Li-ssŭ, the notorious minister of the first Ch'in emperor (B.C. 221–210). In this 'smaller seal' style is written the first Chinese dictionary, 說文, 'Shuo-wên,' published A.D. 100. See p. 203, note 4, below.

(2) 籀, Chou, the 'seal' character, named after the inventor, is identical with the 'greater seal,' above-mentioned.

[2] (1) 鍾繇 of Wei (A.D. 220–260), who wrote the 'Official Servant's' style well.

(2) 張 is 張芝, who was skilled in the running hand.

[3] 鍾子期 (a connoisseur of music), name of a musical woodcutter in the story of 俞伯牙, a lute-player who never played after the former's death.

[4] Shih once removed a little bit of mud on the top of the nose with his axe without causing any injury, see *K*wang-tze XXIV, iii, ii, 6, S.B.E., vol. xl, p. 101.

[5] Cf. the Analects, book ii, p. 150, 君子不器.

for its deep meaning. In educating a little boy he was in the habit of beginning with half a character; one cannot imagine his having occasion to grasp his sword (on account of anger with his pupil). He would instruct a man of great ability as if he were filling a perfect vessel, and the instructed would have the benefit of being beautified by precious gems. Some time ago, when people had become destitute of principle during the last period of the Sui dynasty (A.D. 589-617), my teacher removed to the town of Yang[1] in consequence of the disturbance. Many priests agreed, when they saw him there, that he was but a fool, as he was plain and rustic in personal appearance. They compelled the new-comer to read the Sûtra of the Great Decease, and ordered two under-teachers to see it done sentence by sentence. His tone was grave and sorrowful as he raised his voice in reading. From sunrise till afternoon all the three cases of the Sûtra were read through. There was no one amongst those present who did not praise and congratulate him, and they bade him rest, greatly commending his wonderful powers. People know this incident full well, and this is not merely my own eulogy.

4. The Liberality of my Teacher.

Here is an instance of his bargaining. Whatever price one demands, that he gives. Be the article dear or cheap, he does not mind, and never beats down the price. If some balance be due to him and the debtor bring the sum, he will not receive it at all. Men of his time considered him a man of unsurpassed generosity.

5. The Loving-kindness of my Teacher.

With him honesty had a greater weight than riches. He followed the practice of a Bodhisattva; when one begged from him, he never refused. His constant wish was to give away three small coins every day. Once during a cold winter month there came a travelling priest named Tao-an, who had walked a long way, braving a heavy snow-storm, and his feet were bitterly frozen. He was obliged to stay in the village for a few days; his swollen feet were wounded and covered with sores. The villagers conveyed him in a carriage to the monastery

[1] Yang-chou, in the province of Kiang-su.

where my teacher dwelt. As soon as the latter came out to the gate and saw the poor man's feet, without regard to himself he bound up the sores with his own garment. The garment was one newly-made and worn that day for the first time. The bystanders would have hindered him, saying that he had better get an old garment so that he should not stain the new one. In reply he said: 'When rendering help in a case of bitter suffering, what time have we to make use of anything but what is at hand.' All those who saw or heard of this action praised him much. Although such a deed is not in itself very difficult to accomplish, nevertheless its like is not often practised.

6. My Teacher's Devotion to Work.

My teacher read through all the eight classes of the Pra*g*ñâpâramitâ-sûtra a hundred times, and read the same again and again when he afterwards perused the whole of the Tripi*t*aka.

As regards the practice of the meritorious deeds necessary for entrance into the Pure Land (Sukhâvatî), he used to exert himself day and night, purifying the ground where the images of the Buddhas were kept, and where the priests abode. He was rarely seen idle during his life. He generally walked bare-footed, fearing lest he should injure any insects. Training his thought and directing his heart, as he did, he was hardly ever seen inactive and remiss. The stands of incense dusted and cleaned by him were beautiful, like the lotus-flowers of Sukhâvatî that unfolded for the sake of the nine classes of the saved beings [1]. The sight of the hall of the Sûtras, decked and adorned by him, was something like the sky above the Vulture Peak, showering down the Four Flowers.

One could not but praise his religious merit when one saw his work in the sanctuary. He was personally never conscious of getting tired; he expected the end of his life to be the end of his work. His leisure from reading he devoted to the worship of the Buddha Amitâyus (= Amitâbha). The four signs of dignity were never wanting in him. The sun's shadow never fell upon him idle (i.e. 'he never wasted a minute of time marked by the sun's course'). The smallest grains of sand,

---

[1] See my Amitâyur-dhyâna-sûtra, iii, S. B. E., vol. xlix, p. 188 seq.

when accumulated, would fill up heaven and earth. The deeds which make up salvation are of various kinds.

7. His Fore-knowledge of the Decrees of Heaven[1].

One year before his death, he collected all his own writings and other books in his possession, and heaping them up into a great pile, he tore them up and made them into mortar to be used (as material) for the two statues of the Vagra[2], which were then in preparation. His pupils came forward and remonstrated with him, saying: 'Our Honoured Master, if it be necessary to use papers, let us use blank papers instead.' The Master replied: 'I have long been entirely taken up with this literature, by which I have been led astray. Ought I to-day to allow it to mislead others? If I do, it is as bad as causing one to swallow a deadly poison or leading one into a dangerous path. That would never do. A priest may lose sight of his proper function if he attain too great success in secular work. The permission to do both is given by the Buddha to men of superior talent only, but *indulgence* in any but one's proper avocation will lead to great error. What one does not wish to have oneself, must not be given to others[3].' On hearing this, the pupils retired, saying: 'It is well.' But the important books, such as Shuo-wên[4] and other lexicons, were given to the pupils. He then taught them, saying: 'When you have done a rough study of the Chinese classics

---

[1] 知命. I-tsing borrowed this term from Confucius's saying (Analects, book ii, 4). That is to say, 'he knew the time of his death beforehand.'

[2] 金剛兩軀. The 'Diamond' may mean the 'Diamond-Hero,' i. e. Vagrapâ*n*i, a name of Indra as a guardian god of Buddhism. But the use of the character 'Diamond' in Buddhistic Chinese is not strictly confined to its literal sense, and it may mean here some images of the Buddha.

[3] Analects, book xii, 2, Confucius's saying: 'not to do to others as you would not wish done to yourself.'

[4] 說文. The famous dictionary compiled A. D. 100 by 許愼, Hsü Shên, and containing about 10,000 characters, analysed with a view to prove the 'hieroglyphic' origin of the Chinese language. See p. 200, note 1, above.

and history, and acquired a vague knowledge of the characters, you should turn your attention to the Excellent Buddhist Canon. You must not let this snare prove too great an attraction.' Previous to his death he told his pupils that he was certainly going to leave this world after three days; that he should die while holding a broom [1], and his remains were to be left in the marshy wilderness. Early in the morning on the third day he walked by the clear stream, and sitting down quietly under a white willow-tree which stood desolate, near to the green waving reeds, he passed away holding a broom in his hand. One of his pupils, the Dhyâna-master, Hui-li by name, went to see his teacher there early that very morning. But what is it? The latter is silent. The pupil drew near and touched the master's body with his hands. He felt warmth still proceeding from the master's head, but the hands and feet were already cold. Then weeping, he called together all the distant friends. When all had assembled, the priests grieved and wept so much that the sad scene might be compared with the red river [2] pouring out its stream of blood on the earth; his lay-followers also sobbed and cried, so that the confused crowd might be compared to the gems on the precious mountain broken to pieces. Sad it is that the tree of Bodhi should wither so soon; it is also piteous that the vessel of the Law should sink so suddenly. He was buried in the west garden of his monastery. He was sixty-three years of age. What he left behind him after his death consisted of only three garments, a pair of slippers and shoes, and the bed-clothes which he was using.

When my teacher died, I was twelve years old. The great elephant (i.e. 'great teacher') having departed, I was destitute of my refuge.

Laying aside my study of secular literature, I devoted myself to the Sacred (Buddhist) Canon. In my fourteenth year I was admitted to the Order, and it was in my eighteenth year that I formed the intention of travelling to India, which was not, however, realised till my thirty-seventh year. On my departure, I went to my late master's tomb to

---

[1] Perhaps as a sign of his not forgetting the sweeping of the sanctuary until death.

[2] Lit. 'the golden river.'

worship, and to take leave. At that time, seared foliage of the trees around had already grown so as to half embrace the tomb, and wild grasses filled the graveyard. Though the spirit world is hidden from us, nevertheless I paid him all honour just as if he had been present[1]. While turning round and glancing in every direction, I related my intention of travelling. I invoked his spiritual aid, and expressed my wish to requite the great benefits conferred on me by that benign personage (lit. 'face').

The Dhyâna-master, Hui-hsi, my second teacher, exclusively devoted himself to the study of the Vinaya. His mind was clear and calm. He never neglected the devotional exercises which were to be performed, six times day and night. He was never tired of teaching from morning till night the four classes of the devotees[2] (Bhikshu, -*n*î, Upâsaka, and Upâsikâ). It may be said of him that even in time of confusion he is quite free from alarm, nay, that he is more peaceful and quiet; and no one, be he priest or layman, has ever found him partial.

The Saddharmapu*nd*arîka was his favourite book; he read it once a day for more than sixty years; thus the perusal amounted to twenty thousand times. Although he happened to live during the troublous times of the last period of the Sui dynasty (A.D. 589–617), and to wander here and there guided by fate alone, yet he never relinquished[3] his determined idea (of reading). He possessed the six organs of sense in perfection, and the four elements[4] of a healthy body. He never had any illness during the sixty years of his life. Whenever he began to recite the Sûtras near the stream, there appeared an auspicious bird which came and alighted in a corner of the hall. While he was reciting, the bird also cried as if it were influenced by his voice, and as if listening to him. He was ever good in disposition, and well acquainted with musical

---

[1] 如在之敬, see Analects, book iii, 12. [2] 四輩.

[3] J. reads 癈, i.e. 'incurable disease,' while the other texts read 廢, 'to abandon,' which I follow.

[4] 四大, four great constituents of the body: earth, water, fire, and air.

notes[1]. He was especially skilled in writing the running hand, and also the 'clerk's style.' He was never weary of guiding and instructing. Although he did not care much for the study of secular books, yet he was naturally gifted and well versed in them. Both his Gâthâ on the six Pâramitâs and the words of prayer composed by him were written on the lamp-stands of the Temple of the Earth-cave[2]. Afterwards when he was engaged in copying the Saddharmapu*nd*arîka (the 'Lotus of the Good Law') he compared the styles of the famous handwritings (of old), and *chose* the best of all [3] (in copying). Breathing out the impure air, and keeping scents in his mouth, he was in the habit of purifying himself by washing and bathing. Suddenly there once appeared miraculously on this Sûtra a relic of the Buddha. When the copy of the Sûtra was finished, the title on each scroll was impressed in golden letters, which were beautiful by the side of the silver hooks of the scroll[4]. He deposited them in the jewelled cases, which, being in themselves bright, added to the brilliancy of the gemmed rollers. The then ruling emperor came to T'ai Shan, and hearing the news, asked the owner to present the copy to the imperial household, to be used in worship.

These two teachers of mine, Shan-yü and Hui-hsi, were the successors of the former sage, (Sêng-) Lang the Dhyâna-master.

Lang the Dhyâna-master was born in the time of the two dynasties of Ch'in[5], and was celebrated beyond all the five classes of people. He received offerings from all quarters; he in person visited the gate of every almsgiver. He taught men according to circumstance and ability. His deeds were suited to the needs of the devotees. The exercise, however, of his personal influence was far above the worldly affairs. The

---

[1] 則感鵰雞就聽善緣情體音律. This is a very strange sentence. My translation follows the explanatory marks of the separate Japanese edition.

[2] T'u-k'u, see p. 199 above.

[3] 極銓名手盡其上施. My translation follows Kâsyapa.

[4] A splendid specimen of the MS. of the Chinese Saddharmapu*nd*arîka can be seen in the library of the Indian Institute, Oxford.

[5] The former Ch'in, A.D. 350–394, and the latter Ch'in, A.D. 384–417.

temple of Shên-t'ung[1] (i.e. 'Miraculous Power') was named thus after him. His religious character was beyond our understanding. Full information is given in his separate biography (Liang-kao-sêng-ch'uan).

At that time the rulers respected Buddhism, and people were devotional (about A.D. 350–417).

When they were intending to build this temple, on entering the forest they heard a tiger roaring near the northern stream of T'ai Shan. On emerging from it they again heard a horse neighing[2] in the southern valley of the mountain. The water in the Heavenly Well[3], though constantly drawn, never decreased, and the grains in the Celestial Granary[3], though perpetually taken out, did not diminish in quantity. The man himself has long disappeared, but the influence left behind him is not yet lost. These two teachers of mine, and another resident priest, the venerable Dhyâna-master, Ming-teh, were well versed in the Vinaya doctrine and fully acquainted with the purport of the Sûtras. As instructors of the disciples they severely prohibited the practice of such things as burning one's fingers or destroying one's body by fire[4], which were never taught by the Buddha. I myself received instruction from these teachers in person, and did not get my information from a hearsay statement. You should also carefully examine the above points of the sages of old, and give your attention to the teaching of the ancients.

From the time that the white horse[5] was unbridled till the dark elephant was saddled[6], Kâsyapamâtaṅga and Dharmaraksha[5], illumining the world by their rays (of wisdom), became as it were the sun and moon of the Divine Land (China), and K'ang-sêng-hui and Fâ-hien[6], by

---

[1] 神通寺, built A.D. 396, above, p. 199; Liang-kao-sêng-ch'uan, book v.

[2] I-tsing perhaps has in his mind the story told of Asvaghosha, the author of the Buddhakarita, that he miraculously made horses neigh before a king.

[3] These were perhaps made in memory of Sêng-Lang the Sage.

[4] I-tsing comes back here to the subject of this chapter.

[5] These two priests came to China A.D. 67, the first translators of Buddhist texts, which are said to have been brought loaded on a white horse. The White Horse monastery was built at Lo-yang. One work of translation is ascribed to Kâsyapamâtaṅga, and five to Dharmaraksha. Nanjio's Catal., App. ii, 1–2.

[6] K'ang-sêng-hui, an Indian of Tibetan origin, who came to China A.D. 241,

virtue of their example, became the ford and bridge to the Celestial Treasure House (India). Tao-an and Hui-yen[1] were stooping like tigers on the south of the rivers Yang-tze and Han; Hsiu and Li[2] were flying high like falcons on the north of the rivers Hwang and Chi.

Successors in the Order were found regularly and continuously; thus the wave of wisdom has been perpetuated uncorrupted. Devout laymen praised and appreciated the unceasing fragrance of the Law. We have never heard that any of those teachers allowed the practice of burning one's fingers.

Nor have we ever seen the burning of one's body permitted by them. The mirror of the Law is before our eyes, and the wise should carefully learn therefrom.

The Dhyâna-master, Hui-hsi, used, in the stillness of the evening, to sympathise with me in my boyhood, and comforted me with many a kind word. Sometimes his talk was about the (frailty of) yellow leaves (i.e. about impermanence), so that he might divert me from my intense longing for my mother.

Sometimes he spoke to me telling me of the habit of young crows[3], and urging that I should strive to repay the great love with which I had been brought up. Sometimes he said: 'You must arduously strive to promote the prosperity of the Three Jewels, so that they may not cease

---

and translated two works. Fâ-hien is a well-known Chinese traveller in India, A.D. 399–414; translated four works and wrote the account of his own journey. I-tsing here probably refers to Fâ-hien's travel by saying 'the dark elephant was saddled.' Kâsyapa has no explanation. Nanjio's Catal., App. ii, 21, 45.

[1] Tao-an died A.D. 389. He first proposed to use the common surname Shih=*S*âkya, and was followed everywhere. Hui-yen, who submitted himself to the Eastern Tsin, A.D. 317–419, was the founder of the White Lotus Society. The Pure Land School was first preached by him. He sent his disciples to Udyâna to get Sanskrit texts, A.D. 408.

[2] 惠休 and 法厲, i.e. Hui-hsiu and Fâ-li. Both lived in the time of the Sui dynasty (A.D. 589–618), Hui-hsiu being a teacher of the Mahâyâna-sa*m*parigraha School. For Fâ-li, see next page.

[3] I.e. 'filial piety.' In China crows are said to return to their parents as much food as they receive while young.

to exist; nor should you indulge in the study of secular literature to such an extent as to render your life useless.' Even when I had reached the age of ten years, I could only listen to his instruction; I was not yet able to fathom his meaning. Every morning at the fifth watch I went to his room to ask what to do. Each time the master showed his affection by patting me with his hand as lovingly as a kind mother fondles her child. Whenever he had any nice food, he used to give me the most delicate portion. If I asked him for anything, I was never disappointed. My Upâdhyâya, Shan-yü, was a strict father to me, while the Dhyâna-master, Hui-hsi, was a tender mother. Thus our relations were almost as perfect as though we had been kinsmen.

When I reached the age of Ordination, Hui-hsi became my Upâdhyâya. Once after I had sworn to the Precepts, when he was taking the air on a fine night, suddenly as he was burning incense, my master, overcome by emotion, thus instructed me: 'It is long since the Great Sage attained Nirvâ*n*a, and now his teaching is becoming misinterpreted. Many are those who wish to bow to the Precepts, yet few are they who observe them. You must abstain with firm resolve from the important things prohibited, and not transgress the first group (meaning the Pârâ*g*ika-offences). If you are guilty of any of the other transgressions, it is I who will suffer in hell on account of you. Besides, you ought not to do such hurtful things as to burn your fingers or destroy your body with fire.' On the same day that the Holy Precepts had been graciously imparted to me, I was thus instructed and happily favoured with his pity.

Since that time I have made such a strenuous effort that whenever I found myself liable to fail, I feared greatly that I had already committed an offence, however small it might be. I devoted myself to the study of the Vinaya for five years.

I could fathom the depth of the comments composed by Fâ-li[1], the Vinaya teacher, and explain accurately the principles treated by another Vinaya teacher, Tao-hsüan[2], in his works. As soon as I had become

---

[1] 法厲 died A.D. 635. A teacher of the Nirvâ*n*a School, and author of the commentary of the *K*aturvarga-vinaya. See p. 208, note 2.

[2] 道宣 died A.D. 667. The founder of the Vinaya School, author of some eight works. See Nanjio's Catal., App. iii. 21.

acquainted with the Vinaya rules (lit. 'observance and transgression'), my teacher ordered me to deliver one lecture on this subject.

While I was attending his lecture on the Greater Sûtra[1], I went round begging food, having only one meal, and sat up all night, without lying down.

The forest monastery where we lived was very distant from the village, but I never neglected this practice. Whenever I think of the kind instruction of my great teacher my tears overflow.—I do not know whence they come.

We see that, when a Bodhisattva wishes in pity to save those who are suffering, he is willing to throw himself even into the blazing flame of a great fire, and, when a philanthropist thinks of looking after a child of poverty he watches even the narrow entrance of a small house. This is no mistake. I received all instruction personally from him, and I did not learn from him by hearsay. One day he graciously said to me: 'At present I do not lack those who wait on me, and you should no longer remain with me, for it hinders your study.' Then I departed from him, with a metal staff in my hand, for Eastern Wei, where I devoted myself to the study of the Abhidharma(-saṅgîti) and the Samparigrahasâstra (Nanjio's Catal., iii, Nos. 1178, 1199; 1183, 1184, 1247). From thence I went to the Western Capital (Si-an Fu), carrying a satchel on my back, and there I studied diligently the Kosa and the Vidyâmâtrasiddhi (Nanjio's Catal., iii, Nos. 1267, 1269; 1197, 1210, 1238, 1239, 1240). On my departure for India I returned from this capital to my native place[2]. I sought advice from my great teacher Hui-hsi, saying: 'Venerable Sir, I am intending to take a long journey; for, if I witness that with which I have hitherto not been acquainted, there must accrue to me great advantage. But you are already advanced in age, so that I cannot carry out my intention without consulting you.' My teacher thus answered me: 'This is a great opportunity for you which will not occur twice. (I assure you) I am much delighted to hear of your

[1] A separate Japanese edition takes this sentence quite differently. It seems inadmissible to take 大經 as 'generally.'

[2] His home was in Fang-yang, now Chao-chou (涿) in Chi-li.

intention so wisely formed (lit. "I am aroused by your righteous reasons"). Why should I indulge any longer my personal affection?

'If I live long enough (to see you return), it will be my joy to witness you transmitting the Light. Go without hesitation; do not look back upon things left behind. I certainly approve of your pilgrimage to the holy places. Moreover it is a most important duty to strive for the prosperity of Religion. Rest clear from doubt.'

Thus not only was my intention graciously approved, but now I had his command, which I could not in any case disobey.

At last I embarked from the coast of Kwang-chou (Canton), in the eleventh month in the second year of the Hsien Hêng period (A. D. 671), and sailed for the Southern Sea. Thus I could journey from country to country, and so could go to India for pilgrimage. On the eighth day in the second month in the fourth year of the Hsien Hêng period (A. D. 673), I arrived at Tâmralipti[1], which is a port on the coast of Eastern India. In the fifth month I resumed my journey westwards, (while) finding companions here and there. Then I went to the Nâlanda monastery and to the Diamond Seat, and thus at last visited all the holy places. Then I retraced the course of my journey and arrived at *S*rîbho*g*a[1].

It may be said of him that he was a great, good, and wise teacher, who perfected the Brahma*k*arya (religious studentship), and mastered the true teaching of the Purushadamya-sârathi (Tamer of the human steed, i. e. the Buddha). Nor do we err in speaking thus. In fact he became the typical man of the period, satisfying the needs of the world and guiding the life of mankind.

I was brought up and instructed by him personally until I reached manhood. Coming across this raft in the ocean of existence I advanced one day's voyage (nearer to the shore). I was fortunate enough to discover the Ford of Life in association with these two teachers. Good actions or charity, however insignificant, are generally praised in songs and music by the people. How much more then should such great wisdom and benevolence as that of my teachers be eulogised in poem or composition!

My poem is as follows:—

'My loving father and mother! You protected me in the past ages.

---

[1] Cf. chap. xxxiv, towards the end, p. 185.

You brought and entrusted me in my boyhood to the care of these intelligent teachers. You did this, suppressing your love and grief, while I was still a helpless child. Whilst taking lessons, I practised from time to time what I had learnt. I rooted my character in the soil of good admonitions and rules. The two teachers[1] were to me as sun and moon giving light. Their virtues may be compared to those of the Yin and Yang (i.e. "the positive and negative principles that pervade nature"). The point of my sword of wisdom was sharpened by them. And by them also my body of the Law was nourished. They were never tired in their personal instruction. Sometimes they taught me throughout the whole night, taking no sleep; sometimes for the whole day, without any food. The most gifted man looks often as if he is possessed of no special talent, and yet such a man's wisdom is too deep to be gauged by us. Such men were my teachers.

'Light disappeared from the Mount T'ai (his two teachers left T'ai Shan, see the beginning of this chapter). Virtue was hidden in the riverside of Ch'i (the two teachers came to Ch'i, and settled there; one died in Ch'i). The sea of wisdom was in them vast, and stretched far. The grove of meditation flourished luxuriantly. Their styles of composition were very elegant; their power of mental abstraction very wonderful. "Grind, but you cannot reduce the mass. Dye, but you cannot make it black[2]." On the eve of his departure from this world, my teacher (Shan-yü) showed a strange sign. A curious example was manifested when the bird listened to a man's reading[3]. While I was still young, one (Shan-yü) passed away[4], leaving the other (Hui-hsi) behind. Whatever meritorious deeds I may have accomplished, I offer as masses for the deceased. To one I would repay after his death the benefits conferred on me during his lifetime. To the other may I be able to requite his kindness in his lifetime, though I be far separated from him. May we meet each other some day in order that we may prolong our happiness.

'May I receive their instruction at each successive birth, in order to secure Final Liberation. I hope that my charity may increase to a mountain-height by the practice of righteousness.

---

[1] Shan-yü and Hui-hsi. [2] 論語. [3] P. 205 above. [4] P. 204 above.

'Deep as the depth of a lake be my pure and calm meditation. Let me look for the first meeting under the Tree of the Dragon Flower[1], when I hear the deep rippling voice of the Buddha Maitreya. Passing through the four modes of birth[2], I would desire to perfect my mind, and thus fulfil the three long Kalpas (ages) required for Buddhahood.'

Fearing lest my readers should think my statement about the literary power of my teacher groundless, I shall give a specimen of his style. Once on the fifteenth day of the second month (this day was kept up as the day of Nirvâ*n*a)[3], priests and laymen crowded to the South Hill—where (Sêng-) Lang the Dhyâna-master resided (T'ai Shan). They visited the strange objects of the 'Heavenly Well[4]' and 'Celestial Granary[4],' and worshipped at the holy niche and the sacred temple. There they performed a grand ceremony of worship and almsgiving. About this time all the literary men in the dominion of the king of Ch'i assembled there, each having oceans of writings and mountains of literature at his command. They were all vying for distinction[5], and boasting of their excellent character[6].

It was proposed that they should compose a poem celebrating the statue of the deceased Lang and his temple, and they unanimously put my teacher Hui-hsi forward to compose the same. He accepted the offer without hesitation.

---

[1] Tree of the dragon-flower, meaning a Nâga-tree. There is a belief that the coming Buddha Maitreya will be born in Ketumati and gain Buddhahood under a Nâga-tree, after the manner of *S*âkyamuni, who gained Buddhahood under the Bodhi-tree.

[2] Four modes of birth, i. e. (1) birth from the womb, (2) from eggs, (3) from moisture, (4) miraculous birth. See p. 3 note, above.

[3] In Buddhaghosa's Samanta-pâsâdikâ it is said: 'Visâkhâ-pu*nn*amadivase pa*kk*ûsasamaye parinibbute Bhavagati.' The corresponding passage of the Chinese translation of Buddhaghosa's introduction has: 'The Buddha having entered Nirvâ*n*a early in the morning of the 15th day of the 2nd month.' See Oldenberg, Vinaya-pi*t*akam, iii, p. 283; and my additional note to p. 14, at the end.

[4] See p. 207, note 3, above.

[5] Lit. 'like an awl in a sack.'

[6] Lit. 'having a precious stone in a box.'

It seemed just as if the flowing stream had stirred up its waves and helped him while he was writing on the walls. He did not stop for a moment, but continued writing with fluent pen. He finished without delay the composition, which needed no addition or correction.

His poem was as follows:—

'In great brightness shone the Sage of old.
Far and wide as the ocean was his excellent counsel spread.
A lonely valley was his resort, and here was his residence.
Good fortune smiled upon him to no purpose.
Vast and desolate are the mountains and rivers through eternity.
Men and generations pass away with the passing ages.
Spiritual knowledge alone can fathom the problem of non-existence.
What else do we see but the picture of the old Sage left behind?'

Having seen this poem of my teacher, the whole assembly of literary men were of one mind in greatly admiring it. Some deposited their pens on a branch of a pine-tree, whilst others threw their inkpots down the side of a rock. They said: 'Si Shih[1] (name of a woman whose beauty was regarded as ideal) has shown her face; how can Mu Mo[2] (name of an ugly woman who served the Yellow Emperor) make her appearance?' There were many clever men present, but none was able to compete with the rhymes. The rest of my teacher's works are separately collected.

I, I-tsing, respectfully send greeting to all the venerable friends of the Great Chou[3], with whom I used to hold light conversation (Vâhya-kathâ) or discuss the sacred Law (Dharma-kathâ), with some of whom I made acquaintance when I was young, while others became bosom friends in

---

[1] 西施. [2] 嫫母.

[3] 大周, 'Great Chou,' meaning 'China,' for the reign of the usurper queen (A. D. 690–704) was called 'Chou' (not 'Chou,' A. D. 951–960). The supposition that the occasional notes in I-tsing's texts are by a later hand, because the notes use the words 'Chou-yuen,' 周言, i. e. the 'language of Chou,' must be given up at once when we see that I-tsing himself uses the name 'Chou' for 'China.' Compare p. 7 note, above; and also Chavannes, Memoirs of I-tsing, p. 203, note to p. 36.

middle age; the more gifted of these became spiritual teachers, but many insignificant men were among them. In the forty chapters of the present work I have treated only of important matters, and what I have recorded is customary at the present time among the teachers and pupils of India. My record rests distinctly on the words of the Buddha, and is not evolved from my own mind. Our life passes swiftly like a rapid river. We cannot prognosticate in the morning what will happen in the evening. Thus fearing lest I may not be able to see you and state these things to you in person, I send the record and present it to you before my return. Whenever you have time to spare, pray study the matter recorded in the book, and thus you may approach my heart. All that I state is in accordance with the Âryamûlasarvâstivâdanikâya (School) and no other.

Again I address you in rhyme as follows:—

'The good doctrine of our master have I respectfully recorded.
Oh, that great and gracious counsel!
All rests on the noble teaching of the Buddha;
I cannot say that my humble intellect has sought it out.
I may not have any chance of a personal meeting with you.
Thus I send on my record to you beforehand.
I shall be happy if you find this work worth keeping.
Let it even accompany you in your carriage.
Let the word of a humble man even such as myself be accepted.
Following in the footprints of sages of a hundred past generations,
I sow the beautiful seed for thousands of years to come.
My real hope and wish is to represent the Vulture Peak[1] in the Small Rooms[2] of my friends, and to build a second Râ*g*ag*ri*ha City in the Divine Land of China.'

---

[1] G*ri*dhrakû*t*a near Râ*g*ag*ri*ha, now called *S*ailagiri.

[2] Name of a peak of the mountain Sung in Honan where many of his friends lived. I-tsing perhaps uses this name in both senses.

Names of the Books which are referred to in I-tsing's Works, but not found in the India Office Collection.

---

1. 西方記. The 'Record of the West,' i. e. India.
Si-fang-chi. See p. 49, note 2, above, and folio 25[b], vol. i, Nan-hai-ki-kwei-nei-fa-*k*whan (sic), No. 1492 (India Office copy).

2. 西方十德傳. The 'Lives of the Ten Virtuous Men of the West.'
Si-fang-shih-teh-ch'uan. See p. 181 above, and folio 11[b], vol. iv, of Nan-hai-ki-kwei-nei-fa-*k*whan (sic), No. 1492 (India Office copy).

3. 中方錄. The 'Record of the Madhyade*s*a.'
Chung-fang-lu. See Chavannes, Memoirs of the Eminent Priests who visited India during the T'ang Dynasty, by I-tsing, p. 88; and folio 18[a], vol. i, of Ta-than-si-yu-kin-fa-kao-san-*k*whan (sic), No. 1491 (India Office copy).

All the above seem to have been I-tsing's own works. They may be found in some of the Buddhist libraries of China, Korea, or Japan.

ADDITIONAL NOTES.

To the **Map.** Transfer **Lâ*t*a** to the Gulf of Cambay, according to the note to p. 9 below.

Page 2, note 2. **Lieh-tze** says in his work, bk. i, p. 4 a, 'The pure and light air rose and became heaven, while the turpid and heavy (air) descended and became earth.' Compare Faber's Licius, p. 4.

P. 2, n. 5. The **Sâṅkhya Philosophy** is dualism (Prak*ri*ti and Purusha). 'One' may be a misprint for 'two,' though all the existing texts read 'one' here.

P. 3, n. 3. For the eighteen **Buddha-dharma**, see Hardy's Manual of Buddhism, p. 381.

P. 6, n. 1. The Sûtra of the **Buddha's Last Instruction** can only be the Mahâparinirvâ*n*a-sûtra. In the Pâli text, VI, 5, we read: 'It may be, O Bhikshus, that there may be doubt or misgiving in the mind of some Bhikshu as to the Buddha or the Truth or the Saṅgha or the Path or the Way (Buddhe vâ Dhamme vâ Saṅghe vâ Magge va Pa*t*ipadâya vâ). Inquire, Bhikshus, freely, &c.' The Buddha repeated this three times, but all were silent. Thereupon Ânanda (not Aniruddha as in Chinese) said: 'Verily I believe that in the whole assembly no one has any doubt as to the Buddha, &c.' See S. B. E., vol. xi, p. 113. I-tsing mentions two recensions of this Sûtra, belonging to the Mahâyâna and Hînayâna. The latter being in Java was probably the Pâli text. He saw the Mahâyâna text and examined it, but only obtained a copy of one chapter of it. Chavannes, Memoirs, p. 61.

P. 9, n. 1. **Lâ*t*a** is mentioned in the B*ri*hat-sa*m*hitâ LXIX, 11, together with Sindhu, Surâsh*t*ra (Surat), Bharoach, and Mâlva (J. R. A. S., vol. vii, p. 94). I-tsing says that it is in W. India, and mentions it often with Sindhu. A Chinese, Hiuen-chao, in going to Lâ*t*a, passed Va-ka-la (supposed to be Valkh), Kapi*s*a, and Sindhu, and then reached there (Chavannes, pp. 23-26). Prof. Bühler informs me that Lâ*t*a is Central Gujerat, the district between the Mahî and Kîm rivers, and its chief city is Broach (Bharuka*kkh*a).

P. 14, n. 1. The **Sudar*s*ana-vibhâshâ Vinaya,** a commentary to the Vinaya, was a bare translation of Buddhaghosa's Samantapâsâdikâ from the southern Buddhist books. The introductory portion agrees with the Pâli text, indeed, word for word, verses in Pâli being also represented in verse in Chinese. It, of course, contains some verses of the Dîpava*m*sa, which are quoted by

Buddhaghosa. I am trying to translate the historical portion of this work. It is interesting to see that a work of Buddhaghosa, who went to Ceylon A. D. 430, and thence to Burma A. D. 450, was translated into Chinese A. D. 489, and that the name of the author should never have been known in China.

P. 22, n. 2. **Pu-ra**, in full Pu-ra-bha-da-ra (the original uncertain). 'The shoes are those in which cotton or some things of that kind are added to leather and stitched together; the middle part is higher (than the other)' (the Sudar*s*ana-vibhâshâ, vol. xvii, p. 13 a). They seem to be something like 'shoes with thick lining' (Mahâvagga V, 13, 13); 'I allow the use of the Ga*n*a*m*ga*n*ûpâhana*m*' (Upânah).

P. 27, l. 25. The 'touched' water jar seems to represent the Pâli **Â*k*amana-kumbhî**, a 'water-pot used for rinsing purposes,' Mahâvagga I, 25, 19.

P. 29, n. 4. **Kalandaka** or Kalantaka is no doubt 'squirrel,' but not a bird. The Chinese translation of Samantapâsâdikâ, commenting on this word in the Suttavibhaṅga, Pârâ*g*. I, 5, 1, 'Vesâliyâ avidûre Kalandaka-gâmo nâma hoti,' names it a 'forest-rat.' Compare Rhys Davids, Mahâparin.-sutta III, 57 (p. 56); Burnouf, Introd., 456. The story is differently told in Hiuen Thsang, Mémoires, liv. ix, p. 29.

P. 54, n. 2. **The Thirteen Necessaries**:—

MAHÂVYUTPATTI, 272.	I-TSING.	MAHÂVAGGA VIII, 20, 2.	
1. Saṅghâtî	1.	1. Saṅgâtî	Ti*k*îvara
2. Uttarâsaṅga	2.	2. Uttarâsaṅga	
3. Antarvâsa	3.	3. Antaravâsaka	
4. Saṅkakshikâ	7.	. . . .	Saṅka*kkh*ika [1]. (*K*ullav. X, 17, 2, and Bhikkhunîpâ*k*it. 96.)
5. Pratisaṅkakshikâ	8.		
6. Nivâsana	5.	. . . .	Nivâsana. (Mahâvag. I, 25, 9, &c.)
7. Pratinivâsana	6.	. . . .	Pa*t*inivâsana [2]. (Mahâvag. I, 25, 9; *K*ullav. VIII, 11, 3.)
8. Ke*s*apratigraha*n*a	11.		
9. Snâtra*s*â*t*aka	Deest	. . . .	Udakasâ*t*ika. (Mahâvag. VIII, 15, 7.)
10. Nishîdana	4.	5. Nisîdana	
11. Ka*nd*upratikkhadana	12.	7. Ka*nd*upa*t*i*kkh*âdi [3]	

[1] Davids-Oldenberg: vest. The old Comment.: Saṅka*kkh*ikan nâma adhakkhakam ubhanâbhi tassa pa*t*i*kkh*âdanatthâya (Vinaya-pi*t*aka IV, p. 345).

[2] A 'second undergarment' in Chinese. The 'house dress'? (Davids-Oldenberg).

[3] Mahâvagga VIII, 17, 1; Pâ*t*imokkha, Pâ*k*ittiya 90. It is four spans by two spans, sometimes called Va*n*abandhana*k*ola, Mahâv. VI, 14, 5.

MAHÂVYUTPATTI, 272.	I-TSING.	MAHÂVAGGA VIII, 20, 2.
12. Varshasâtîkîvara	Deest	4. Vassikasâtika[1]
13. Parishkârakîvara	13. Bheshaga-parishkâra-kîvara	9. Parikkhâra-kolaka[2]
	9. Kâya-proñkhana	
	10. Mukha-proñkhana	8. Mukhapuñkhana-kolaka
		6. Pakkattharana[3]

P. 71, n. 4. Compare the **words of Mahâkâsyapa** in Buddhaghosa's Samantapâsâdikâ (p. 283): 'Yâva dhammavinayo titthati tâva anatîtasatthukam eva pâvakanam hoti, vuttam h' etam Bhagavatâ: yo vo mayâ Ânanda dhammo ka vinayo ka desito paññatto so vo mam' Akkayena satthâ 'ti.'

P. 85, n. 1. As the **Kârttika** month begins in the middle of the Chinese eighth month, which is generally the day of autumnal equinox, we can compare the months as follows:—

FIVE SEASONS (in the Vinaya)[5].	CHINESE (from 16th till 15th day).	INDIAN.		SIX SEASONS[4].
Winter	9–10 months	Mârgasîrshah	Nov.–Jan.	*Sisirah* (Thaw).
	10–11 "	Paushah		
	11–12 "	Mâghah	Jan.–March	Vasantah (Spring).
	12–1 "	Phâlgunah		
Spring	1–2 "	*Kaitrah*	March–May	Grîshmah (Summer).
	2–3 "	Vaisâkhah		
	3–4 "	*Gyaishthah*	May–July	Varshah (Rain).
	4–5 "	Âshâdhah		
Rainy Season[6]	5–6 "	*Srâvanah*	July–Sept.	*Sarat* (Harvest).
Last Season[7]	the 16th of the 6th month			
Long Season	6–7 months	Bhâdrapadah		
	7–8 "	Âsvinah	Sept.–Nov.	Hemantah (Winter).
	8–9 "	Kârttikah[8]		

P. 86. **Pravârana** is the closing ceremony of the Varsha residence, lasting only

[1] The 'robes for the rainy season.'

[2] Mahâvagga VIII, 20, 1. This is a piece of cloth requisite (for making water-strainers or bags), but it seems to take the place of 'bheshaga-parishkâra-kîvara' of I-tsing.

[3] The bed-covering or cushion to sit on.

[4] Prof. Max Müller, Veda-samhitâ IV, p. xxxv.

[5] See above, pp. 101, 102.

[6] The earlier period of the Varsha. So also in Mahâvagga III, 2, 2: 'The earlier time for entering upon the Vassa is the day after the Âsâlha full moon.'

[7] The later period of the Varsha. Mahâvagga: 'The later period (for entering upon the Vassa) is a month after the Âsâlha full moon.' For the connection of the double period with that of the Brâhmanas and Sûtras, see S. B. E., vol. xiii, p. 300, note.

[8] The ceremony of the Kathina-âstâra is on the 16th of the 8th moon. Further, see Mahâvagga VII, 1, 3, note.

one day. It is also an occasion for giving presents to the priests. See Mahâvagga IV. Pâli, pavâra*n*â (f.).

P. 95, l. 16. '**Two dozen years**' is 'two Chi' in Chinese. Chi generally means twelve; if so here, it will be twenty-four years. We have only twenty years from 671 till 692, when he sent the Record. Chi is also used for ten, and so here; and it is 'two decades,' or 'two rounds.' Compare p. 4, l. 18; he uses 'eight decades' (Chi) for the Buddha's age, who is said to have lived eighty-one years.

P. 100, n. 3. Compare the Eka*s*atakarman (No. 1131), bk. i, fol. 9 (Bodl. Library), where the way of measuring the shadow is explained at length.

P. 102, nn. 1, 3. The three seasons are otherwise enumerated: 1. Hemanta (winter); 2. Grîshma (summer); 3. Varsha (rain).

P. 108, n. 1. Compare the eight Stûpas in Mahâparinib.-sutta (towards the end), and Csoma, Asiatic Researches, vol. xx, pp. 296, 315.

P. 110, n. 1. Kâ*s*yapa's measure of **Nishidana** agrees with that of the Pâ*t*imokkha VII, Pâ*k*ittiyâ 89. He takes **Sugata-vidatthi** as the 'Buddha's span,' as in Dickson's translation (J. R. A. S., vol. viii, p. 118). James d'Alwis, the 'Accepted Span' (J. A. S., Ceylon, 1874); compare S. B. E., vol. xiii, p. 8, note 2; p. 54, note 3.

P. 114, n. 1. I-tsing's description of the *K*a**ṅkrama** of Nâlanda, where the Buddha used to take walks (Chavannes, Memoirs, p. 96):—'Au centre est un petit "*K*aitya." De l'est de l'autel à l'angle de la salle, il y a l'emplacement d'un *promenoir* de Fo (Buddha); il est fait de rangées de briques; il est large d'environ deux *coudées*, long de quatorze ou quinze et élevé de plus de deux. Sur le promenoir on a façonné, avec de la chaux qu'on a laissée blanche, des représentations de fleur de lotus; elles sont hautes d'environ deux coudées et larges de plus d'un pied; il y en a quatorze ou quinze; elles marquent les traces des pieds de Fo (Buddha).'

P. 125, n. 1. The **eight kinds of Syrup** (**pâna**):—

I-tsing's explanation given in the Eka*s*atakarman, bk. vi.	The Pâli in Mahâvagga, bk. vi, 35, 6.
1. *K*o*k*apâna. 'The *K*o*k*a is sour like Prunus mume (plums), and in form like the pods of Gleditchia sinensis, Lam. The *K*o*k*a plant (or tree) is also called "Tan-da-lî" (Ta*nd*ulîya? or perhaps for Kadalî; so Buddhaghosa: *K*o*k*apânan ti a*tth*ika-kadali-phalehi katapâna*m*). The pericarp is one or two finger-breadths in width, and three or four inches in length. Indians eat it regularly (perpetually).'	3. *K*o*k*apâna. The plantain syrup (Buddhaghosa and Profs. Oldenberg and Rhys Davids). *K*o*k*a may also be cocoa-nut or cinnamon, according to Böhtlingk and Roth, s. v.

I-tsing's explanation given in the Ekasata-karman, bk. vi.

2. Mo*k*apâna.

'The Mo*k*a is proper banana (or plantain; Chinese, Pa-chiao); when we put a little pepper on the fruit and press it hard with the fingers, it changes itself into fluid.'

3. Ku-la-ka-pâna (Kolaka, 'black pepper'?).

'The fruit is like the sour date (i. e. wild spinous date, a variety of Zizyphus vulgaris, Lam.).'

4. A*s*vatthapâna.

'This is the Bodhi-tree; the syrup is prepared from the fruit of the Bodhi-tree.'

5. Udumbarapâna.

'Its fruit is like Li (Prunus communis, Huds.; a plum).'

(Phonetically it can also stand for Utpala, 'lily;' we have in Pâli Sâlûka, 'water-lily,' but I-tsing says the 'fruit,' not the 'root.')

6. Parûsakapâna.

'Its fruit is like Ying-yü (Vitis labrusca, L., a kind of wild grape-vine).'

7. M*ri*dhvikâpâna.

'This is the syrup prepared from the grapes.'

8. Khar*g*ûrapâna.

'It is like a small date in its shape. It tastes bitter but somewhat sweet. It comes mostly from Persia, but grows also in the Madhyade*s*a (India), but that which grows in India tastes somewhat differently. The tree grows wild (independently), and resembles

The Pâli in Mahâvagga, bk. vi, 35, 6.

4. Mo*k*apâna.

Mo*k*a-pânan ti ana*tth*ikehi kadaliphalehi kata-pâna*m* (Buddhaghosa). This is also the plantain-tree, but there seems to be some difference between Mo*k*a and *K*o*k*a with regard to seed (A*tth*ika).

(1). Ambapâna (mango).

1, 2, 5, 7 of the Pâli have no corresponding names in I-tsing's list.

(2). *G*ambupâna (rose-apple).

(5). Madhupâna (honey).

8. Phârusakapâna.

This is the Grewia Asiatica of Linnaeus. See Böhtlingk-Roth, s. v. Parûsaka (Oldenberg and Rhys Davids).

6. Muddikâpâna.

The grape-juice.

(7). Sâlûkapâna (root of the water-lily).

I-tsing's explanation given in the Ekasata-karman, bk. vi.	The Pâli in Mahâvagga, bk. vi, 35, 6.
Tsung-lü (Trachycarpus excelsa, Thbg., a species of palm). It bears fruit abundantly. When it was brought to P'an-yü (Kwang-tung) people called it "Persian date" (compare 11,623 Giles). It tastes much like a dried persimmon (Diospyros kaki, L. F., or date plum, often called "China fig").' (Khargûra is the wild date-palm tree, Phoenix sylvestris.)	

I-tsing further explains the five fruits allowed by the Buddha in the Ekasata-karman (Nanjio's Catal., No. 1131), bk. v, p. 69, of the Japanese edition:—

(1) Harîtaka.
(2) Vibhîtaka.
(3) Âmalaka.
(4) Marika.
(5) Pippalî (not Pippala, as in Mahâvagga VI, 6, 1).

These five agree perfectly with those given in Mahâvagga VI, 6, 1.

P. 127, n. 1. **The eight sections of Medicine** which I-tsing describes are no doubt the **eight divisions of the Âyur-veda.** He mentions an epitomiser of these divisions, who seems to have been a famous physician and contemporary of I-tsing (or just before I-tsing). This epitomiser may be **Susruta,** who calls himself a disciple of Dhanvantari, one of the Nine Gems in the Court of Vikramâditya.

Prof. Wilson says in his Works, vol. iii, p. 274:—

'The **Âyur-veda,** which originally consisted of one hundred sections, of a thousand stanzas each, was adapted to the limited faculties and life of man, by its distribution into eight subdivisions, the enumeration of which conveys to us an accurate idea of the subject of the Ars Medendi amongst the Hindus. The **eight divisions** are as follows:—

I. ***Sâlya*** (I-tsing's (1) cure of sores).

The art of extracting extraneous substances, grass, earth, bone, &c., accidentally introduced into the human body, and by analogy, the cure of all phlegmonoid tumours and abscesses. *S*alya means a dart or arrow.

II. ***Sâlâkya*** (I-tsing's (2) art of acupuncture).

The treatment of external organic affections or diseases of the eyes, ears, nose, &c. It is derived from *S*alâkâ, "a thin and sharp instrument," and is borrowed from the generic name of the slender probes and needles used in operation on the parts affected.

The above two divisions constitute the surgery of modern schools.

III. **Kâya-*k*ikitsâ** (I-tsing's (3) treatment of the diseases of the body).

The application of the Ars Medendi (*K*ikitsâ) to the body in general (Kâya). It forms what we mean by the science of medicine.

IV. **Bhûta-vidyâ** (I-tsing's (4) treatment of demoniac disease).

The restoration of the faculties from a disorganised state induced by demoniacal possession. The art vanished before the diffusion of knowledge, but it formed a very important branch of medical practice through all the schools, Greek, Arabic, or European.

V. **Kaumâra-bh*ri*tya** (I-tsing's (6) treatment of the diseases of children).

The care of infancy, comprehending not only the management of children from their birth, but the treatment of irregular lactic secretion, and puerperal disorders in mothers and nurses.

VI. **Agada** (I-tsing's (5) Agada medicine).

The administration of antidotes — a subject which, as far as it rests upon scientific principles, is blended with our medicine and surgery.

VII. **Râsâyana** (I-tsing's (7) application of the means of lengthening one's life).

Chemistry, or more correctly alchemy, as the chief end of the chemical combinations it describes, and which are mostly metallurgic, is the discovery of the universal medicine—the elixir that was to render health permanent, and life perpetual.

VIII. **Vâ*g*îkara*n*a** (I-tsing's (8) methods of invigorating the legs and body).

Promotion of the increase of the human race—an illusory research, which, as well as the preceding, is not without its parallel in ancient and modern times.'

Prof. Wilson further remarks:—'We have, therefore, included in these branches all the real and fanciful pursuits of physicians of every time and place. **Su*s*ruta**, however, confines his own work to the classes ***S*âlya** and ***S*âlâkya** or surgery; although, by an arrangement not uncommon with our own writers, he introduces occasionally the treatment of general diseases and the management of women and children when discussing those topics to which they bear relation.' (See Wilson's Works, vol. iii, p. 276.)

P. 164, n. 1. **Vi*s*va*m*tara-sudâna.** Prof. H. Kern wrote to me in answer to my inquiry about the name:—'I have not met with **Sudâna** as a name or surname of Vi*s*va*m*tara, neither in Sanskrit nor in Pâli sources. Even the word as an appellative, a Bahuvrîhi compound, though explainable, is unknown to me. H. K.'

P. 169, n. 3. As the statement that a **Nestorian Missionary** was translating a Buddhist Sûtra will probably surprise my readers, I think it best to give a full account of the fact from a Buddhist book. It is indeed curious to find the name of **MESSIAH** in a Buddhist work, though the name comes in quite accidentally. The book is called 'The New Catalogue of the Buddhist Books compiled in the Chêng Yüan Period' (A.D. 785-804), in the new Japanese edition of the Chinese Buddhist Books (Bodleian Library, Jap. 65 DD, 結 六, p. 73; this book is not in Nanjio's Catalogue).

The seventeenth volume (p. 73) gives the story, which runs as follows:—'Pra*gñ*a, a *S*rama*n*a of Kapi*s*a in N. India, came to China viâ Central India, Si*m*hala (Ceylon), and the Southern Sea (Sumatra, Java, &c.), for he heard that Ma*ñg*u*s*rî was in China. He arrived at Canton (Kwang-tung). In the third year of the Chien Chung period (A.D. 782) he came to the Upper Province (North). In the second year of the Chêng Yüan period (A.D. 786) he met a relation of his, who came to China before him.

'*He translated*, together with King-ching, a priest from Persia named Adam, who was in the monastery of Tâ-ch'in (Syria), the Sha*t*pâramitâ-sûtra from a Mongolian text. They finished seven volumes. But at that time Pra*gñ*a was not acquainted with the Mongolian language, nor did he understand the language of T'ang (Chinese). King-ching (Adam) did not know the Brahma language (Sanskrit), nor was he versed in the teaching of the *S*âkya (Buddha). Though they pretended to be translating the text, yet they could not, in reality, obtain a half of its precious (meanings). They were seeking vainglory privately, and wrongly trying their luck. Some people presented a memorial (to the Imperial Court) accusing them of this fact; the will of the accusers was done. The Emperor (Tê-tsung), who was intelligent, wise, and accomplished, who revered the Canon of the *S*âkya (Buddha), examined what they had translated, and found that the principles contained in it were obscure and the wording was rough.

'[1]Moreover, the Sa*ṅ*ghârâma of the *S*âkya and the monastery of Tâ-ch'in (Syria) differ much in their customs, and their religious practices are entirely opposed to each other. King-ching (Adam) ought to hand down the teaching of **MESSIAH (Mi-shi-ho)**[2], and the *S*âkyaputriya-*S*rama*n*as should propagate the Sûtras of the Buddha. It is to be wished that the boundaries of the doctrines may be made distinct, and the followers may not intermingle. The right must remain away from the wrong, just as the rivers Ching and Wei flow separately.' For Adam and his famous monument, see Dr. Legge's Christianity in China in the Seventh and Eighth Centuries (Clarendon Press).

P. 173, n. 4. I meant to give here Kâ*s*yapa's Devanâgarî for all these names, and his explanations of their meanings, but I omit them for the present, hoping to get a better MS. of the commentary in time. As to the style of the Devanâgarî characters, Prof. Bühler thinks that they are very bad corruptions of a model in

---

[1] Hereafter the sentences seem to be a part of the imperial edict.

[2] 彌尸訶 in Chinese.

rather ancient Siddha-mât*ri*kâ script, somewhat similar to that of the Horiuzi palm-leaves (see Anecdota Oxoniensia, Aryan Series, vol. i, pt. 3), but perhaps 100–150 years later (A. D. 700–750; the original palm-leaves date A. D. 609); and that the copyist had no notion of what he wrote.

The names of the cases in Pâ*n*ini are:—

1. Nom. Prathamâ (the first).
2. Acc. Karman, Dvitiyâ.
3. Inst. Kara*n*a, Tritîyâ.
4. Dat. Sampradâna, *K*aturthî.
5. Abl. Apâdâna, Pa*ñk*amî.
6. Gen. Shash*th*î (the sixth).
7. Loc. Adhikara*n*a, Saptamî.
8. Voc. (a nom.) Âmantrita.

The case-relations in Ka*kk*âyana's Grammar (Senart, Ka*nd*o VI):—

2. Kamma*m* (or by some, Upayoga).
3. Kara*n*a*m*.
4. Sampadâna*m*.
5. Apâdâna*m* (or by some, Nissakka).
6. Sâmî.
7. Okâso or Avakâso (or by some, Bhummo).

P. 180, n. 3. That the **Pei-na** of I-tsing would probably be a grammatical work called **Be*d*â** was pointed out to me by Professor G. Bühler. I add here his note to me, dated October 9, 1895:—

'There is a title in Sanskrit which would correspond to your "Pe-na," "Pe-*n*a," or "Pi-*d*a," and that is **Be*d*â**. A work of this name, Be*d*â-v*ri*tti (बेडावृत्ति), is mentioned in Mr. S. K. Bhandarkar's Catalogue of the MSS. in the Deccan College, Bombay, 1888, p. 146, No. 381, and in Aufrecht's Catalogus Catalogorum, p. 198, under *G*anmâmbhodhi (meaning "the ocean of birth," and the commentary is appropriately called Be*d*â-v*ri*tti, i. e. "the boat-commentary," to cross the ocean).

'Now **Be*d*â** is the same as Ve*d*â, and means "a boat" (see BW. sub voce), or as much as Naukâ, which again is a very common title for Sanskrit works, as you may see from the Catalogus Catalogorum. I think this is the Sanskrit equivalent of the mysterious Pe-na or Pe-*d*a. But, of course, I do not know what Bhart*ri*hari's "boat" was. I-tsing's description of it is very vague—as vague as most of his descriptions, which make me doubt that he ever read the works he mentions. G. B.'

P. 181, l. 12. Sthiramati and Sthitamati. There seems to be a certain confusion between the two names on the part of Chinese translators. In Hiuen Thsang, Sthiramati is Kien-hui and Sthitamati An-hui. I-tsing here has An-hui, but it seems to be meant for Sthiramati (so also Kasawara and Fujishima). Sthiramati and Gu*n*amati are often (if not always) mentioned together. Both were in Nâlanda (Mémoires, liv. ix, p. 46); a monastery in Valabhî was inhabited by the two (Mémoires, liv. xi, p. 164). In a Valabhî grant published by Prof. Bühler (Ind. Ant., 1877, p. 91), the grantee is the monastery *S*rî Bappapâda (l. c., 1878, p. 80), built by Â*k*ârya Bhadanta Sthiramati; and Prof. Bühler thinks that it must be the same monastery as that mentioned by Hiuen Thsang. The Life of Buddha, by Ratnadharmarâ*g*a (compiled 1734, a translation by

Schiefner, 1848), mentions Sthiramati as Asaṅga's pupil, and Gu*n*amati as that of Vasubandhu. This again makes the two contemporaries. In our Record also the two are put together (if our restoration be correct). So far all is in harmony. In the Chinese Pi*t*aka, Kiuen-hui's work was translated as early as A.D. 397-439 (No. 1243). As the two names have a somewhat similar meaning and sound, there seems to have arisen a confusion, and it is advisable to take I-tsing's An-hui as Sthiramati, as it appears with Gu*n*amati in this as in the other accounts. But it is also possible that Sthitamati was a contemporary of these two. Compare Târanâtha's Buddhismus, p. 160.

P. 196, ll. 1 and 3. The would-be Bodhisattva who gave away his son and daughter is Vi*s*vântara (Vessantara, known as Sudâna in Chinese). See Kern's *G*âtakamâlâ IX; Hardy's Manual of Buddhism, p. 120; *K*ariyapi*t*aka, No. 9. The story of giving away the eyes, &c., is told in the *S*ibi-*g*âtaka (Kern, l. c., p. 9); Fausböll, *G*âtaka, vol. iv, No. 499, p. 402.

P. 198, ll. 7-9. For 'one who offered his body to a hungry tiger,' see the Vyâghrî-*g*âtaka (Kern, *G*âtakamâlâ, p. 2), and in the Chinese translation (No. 1312), vol. i, p. 3 a. For 'one who saved a living pigeon,' see the *S*ibi-*g*âtaka, p. 6 a, in the Chinese text (l. c.); the Sanskrit text is quite different from the Chinese.

CORRIGENDA.

Page 5, line 17. Read 'Prince Mâra' for 'Prince of Mâra.'

P. 7, l. 16. Read 'tâ-chung-pu' for 'tâ-sêng-pu.'

P. 9, l. 13. For 'Tu-fan' read 'T'u-fan'; this aspiration seems to be important, as the original is a derivative of 'T'ub' with 'P'od,' both meaning 'be able.' Mongol., 'T'übet' (so pronounced); Marco Polo, 'Thebeth'; Chinese, 'T'u-po-t'o,' 'T'u-p'o,' or 'T'u-fan.' Giles gives 'Turfan' for 'T'u-fan' (see his Dictionary, No. 3383), but here it is Tibet, because I-tsing often mentions in his Memoirs the Chinese princess who married Sroṅ-tsan-gam-po, king of Tibet in his time, and calls her 'T'u-fan-kung-chu,' Chavannes, Memoirs, p. 50 (§§ 18, 19); the Chinese, vol. i, p. 9 b.

P. 17, l. 16. Read 'Kukku*t*a' for 'Kuku*t*a.'

P. 35, note 1. Omit 'weekly.'

P. 91, l. 26. Read '-ku*t*î' for '-kutî.'

P. 118, l. 7. Read 'A-shê-li' for 'Â-shao-li.'

P. 165, l. 7 from bottom. Read 'Dharmaraksha' for 'Saṅghavarman.'

P. 180, l. 18. Read 'Be*d*â or Ve*d*â' for 'Be*a*a or Ve*d*a.'

INDEX.

Words in italics are Chinese. All the Chinese transcriptions from Sanskrit or Pâli are also distinguished in the same way.

THE END.